Recommended Reference Books for Small and Medium-sized Libraries and Media Centers

American Reference Books Annual
Advisory Board

RECOMMENDED REFERENCE BOOKS

for Small and Medium-sized Libraries and Media Centers

Volume 26

2006 Edition

Shannon Graff Hysell, Associate Editor

LIBRARIES
U N L I M I T E D
Member of the Greenwood Publishing Group

Westport, Connecticut • London

LIBRARIES UNLIMITED
A Member of the Greenwood Publishing Group, Inc.
88 Post Road West
Westport, CT 06881
1-800-225-5800
www.lu.com

Library of Congress Cataloging-in-Publication Data

Main entry under title:

Recommended reference books for small and medium-
    sized libraries and media centers.

    "Selected from the 2006 edition of American
reference books annual."
    Includes index.
    I. Reference books--Bibliography. 2. Reference
services (Library)--Handbooks, manuals, etc.
3. Instructional materials centers--Handbooks,
manuals, etc. I. Hysell, Shannon Graff
II. American reference books annual.
Z1035.1.R435   011'.02   81-12394
ISBN 1-59158-380-2
ISSN 0277-5948

Contents

Introduction

Recommended Reference Books for Small and Medium-sized Libraries and Media Centers (RRB), now in its twenty-sixth volume, is designed to assist smaller libraries in the systematic selection of suitable reference materials for their collections. It aids in the evaluation process by choosing substantial titles in all subject areas. The increase in the publication of reference sources and availability of reference databases in the United States and Canada, in combination with the decrease in library budgets, makes this guide an invaluable tool.

Following the pattern established in 1981 with the first volume, RRB consists of book reviews chosen from the current edition of *American Reference Books Annual*. This nationally acclaimed work provides reviews of reference books, CD-ROMs, and Internet sites published in the United States and Canada within a single year, along with English-language titles from other countries. ARBA has reviewed more than 61,500 titles since its inception in 1970. Because it provides comprehensive coverage of reference sources, not just selected or recommended titles, many are of interest only to large academic and public libraries. Thus, RRB has been developed as an abridged version of ARBA, with selected reviews of resources suitable for smaller libraries.

Titles reviewed in RRB include dictionaries, encyclopedias, indexes, directories, bibliographies, guides, atlases, gazetteers, and other types of ready-reference tools. General encyclopedias that are updated annually, yearbooks, almanacs, indexing and abstracting services, directories, and other annuals are included on a selective basis. These works are systematically reviewed so that all important annuals are critically examined every few years. Excluded from RRB are regional guides in the areas of biological sciences and travel guides. All titles in this volume are coded with letters that provide worthwhile guidance for selection. These indicate that a given work is a recommended purchase for smaller college libraries (C), public libraries (P), or school media centers (S).

The current volume of RRB contains 522 unabridged reviews selected from the 1,554 entries in ARBA 2006. These have been written by more than 200 subject specialists throughout the United States and Canada. Although all titles in RRB are recommended acquisitions, critical comments have not been deleted, because even recommended works may be weak in one respect or another. In many cases reviews evaluate and compare a work in relation to other titles of a similar nature. All reviews provide complete ordering and bibliographic information. The subject index organization is based upon the *Library of Congress Subject Headings*. References to reviews published in periodicals (see page xxi for journals cited) during the year of coverage are appended to the reviews. All reviews are signed.

The present volume contains 37 chapters. There are four major subdivisions: "General Reference Works," "Social Sciences," "Humanities," and "Science and Technology." "General Reference Works," arranged alphabetically, is subdivided by form: bibliography, biography, handbooks and yearbooks, and so on. The remaining three parts are subdivided into alphabetically arranged chapters. Most chapters are subdivided in a way that reflects the arrangement strategy of the entire volume: a section on general works and then a topical breakdown. The latter is further subdivided, based on the amount of material available on a given topic.

RRB has been favorably reviewed in such journals as *Booklist*, *School Library Media Quarterly*, *Journal of Academic Librarianship*, and *Library Talk*. The editors continue to strive to make RRB the most valuable acquisition tool a small library can have.

In closing, the editors at Libraries Unlimited would like to express their gratitude to the contributors whose reviews appear in this volume. We would also like to thank the members of the Advisory Board, whose ideas and input have been invaluable to the quality of ARBA, ARBAonline, and RRB.

Contributors

Gordon J. Aamot, Head, Foster Business Library, Univ. of Washington, Seattle.

Stephen H. Aby, Education Bibliographer, Bierce Library, Univ. of Akron, Ohio.

Anthony J. Adam, Reference Librarian, Prairie View A & M Univ., Coleman Library, Tex.

Michael Adams, Reference Librarian, City Univ. of New York Graduate Center.

Jim Agee, Asst. Director and Technical Services Manager—Acquisitions/Serials, James A. Michener Library, Univ. of Northern Colorado, Greeley.

Frank J. Anderson, Librarian Emeritus, Sandor Teszler Library, Wofford College, Spartanburg, S.C.

Robert T. Anderson, Professor, Religious Studies, Michigan State Univ., East Lansing.

Charles R. Andrews, Dean of Library Services, Hofstra Univ., Hempstead, N.Y.

Helene Androski, Reference Librarian, Univ. of Wisconsin—Madison.

Susan B. Ardis, Acting Head of Science Libraries Div., Univ. of Texas, Austin.

Alan Asher, Art/Music Librarian, Univ. of Northern Iowa, Cedar Falls.

Susan C. Awe, Asst. Director, Univ. of New Mexico, Albuquerque.

Christopher Baker, Professor of English, Armstrong Atlantic State Univ., Savannah, Ga.

Thomas E. Baker, Assoc. Professor, Department of Criminal Justice, Univ. of Scranton, Pa.

Neil Barron, Author.

Mark T. Bay, Electronic Resources, Serials, and Government Documents Librarian, Hagan Memorial Library, Cumberland College, Williamsburg, Ky.

Leslie M. Behm, Reference Librarian, Michigan State Univ. Libraries, East Lansing.

Sandra E. Belanger, Reference Librarian, San Jose State Univ. Library, Calif.

Carol Willsey Bell, Head, Local History and Genealogy Dept., Warren-Trumbull County Public Library, Warren, Ohio.

Laura J. Bender, Science Librarian, Univ. of Arizona, Tucson.

Elaine Lasda Bergman, Librarian, Health Care Association of New York State, Rensselaer.

John B. Beston, Professor of English, Santa Fe, N.Mex.

Barbara M. Bibel, Reference Librarian, Science/Business/Sociology Dept., Main Library, Oakland Public Library, Calif.

Adrienne Antink Bien, Medical Group Management Association, Lakewood, Colo.

Daniel K. Blewett, Reference Librarian, College of DuPage Library, College of DuPage, Glen Ellyn, Ill.

Polly D. Boruff-Jones, Assoc. Librarian, Indiana Univ.—Purdue Univ. Indianapolis.

Georgia Briscoe, Assoc. Director and Head of Technical Services, Law Library, Univ. of Colorado, Boulder.

Simon J. Bronner, Distinguished Professor of Folklore and American Studies, Capitol College, Pennsylvania State Univ., Middletown.

Janet Dagenais Brown, Assoc. Professor and Education and Social Sciences Librarian, Wichita State Univ., Kans.

Patrick J. Brunet, Library Manager, Western Wisconsin Technical College, La Crosse.

John R. Burch Jr., Director of Library Services, Cambellsville Univ., Ky.

Frederic F. Burchsted, Reference Librarian, Widener Library, Harvard Univ., Cambridge, Mass.

Joanna M. Burkhardt, Head Librarian, College of Continuing Education Library, Univ. of Rhode Island, Providence.

Hans E. Bynagle, Library Director and Professor of Philosophy, Whitworth College, Spokane, Wash.

Diane M. Calabrese, Freelance Writer and Contributor, Silver Springs, Md.

Diana Caneer, Library Assistant, McCracken County Public Library, Paducah, Ky.

Danielle Marie Carlock, Reference and Instruction Librarian, Arizona State Univ. at the Polytechnic campus, Mesa.

E. Wayne Carp, Professor of History, Pacific Lutheran Univ., Tacoma, Wash.

G. A. Cevasco, Assoc. Professor of English, St. John's Univ., Jamaica, N.Y.

Bert Chapman, Government Publications Coordinator, Purdue Univ., West Lafayette, Ind.

Boyd Childress, Reference Librarian, Ralph B. Draughon Library, Auburn Univ., Ala.

Hui Hua Chua, U.S. Documents Librarian, Michigan State Univ. Libraries, East Lansing.

Holly Dunn Coats, Asst. Librarian, Florida Atlantic Univ., Jupiter, Fla.

Donald E. Collins, Assoc. Professor, History Dept., East Carolina Univ., Greenville, N.C.

Paul Gerard Connors, Research Analyst, Michigan Legislative Service Bureau, Lansing, Mich.

Barbara Conroy, Career Connections, Santa Fe, N.Mex.

Rosanne M. Cordell, Head of Reference Services, Franklin D. Schurz Library, Indiana Univ., South Bend.

Kay O. Cornelius, (formerly) Teacher and Magnet School Lead Teacher, Huntsville City Schools, Ala.

Paul B. Cors, Catalog Librarian, Univ. of Wyoming, Laramie.

Gregory A. Crawford, Head of Public Services, Penn State Harrisburg, Middletown, Pa.

Mark J. Crawford, Consulting Exploration Geologist/Writer/Editor, Madison, Wis.

Alice Crosetto, Librarian, Univ. of Toledo, Ohio.

Cynthia Crosser, Social Sciences and Humanities Reference, Fogler Library, Univ. of Maine, Orono.

Gregory Curtis, Director, Northern Maine Technical College, Presque Isle.

Joseph W. Dauben, Professor of History and History of Science, City Univ. of New York.

Melvin Davis, Asst. Professor, Interlibrary Loan Librarian, Middle Tennessee Univ., Murfreesboro.

Barbara Delzell, Librarian, St. Gregorys Univ., Shawnee, Okla.

R. K. Dickson, Asst. Professor of Fine Arts, Wilson College, Chambersburg, Pa.

Scott R. DiMarco, Director of Library Services and Information Resources, Mansfield Univ., Mansfield, Pa.

Margaret F. Dominy, Information Services Librarian, Drexel Univ., Philadelphia.

G. Kim Dority, G. K. Dority & Associates, Castle Rock, Colo.

John A. Drobnicki, Professor and Head of Reference Services, City Univ. of New York—York College, Jamaica.

Lucy Duhon, Serials Librarian, Univ. of Toledo, Ohio.

David J. Duncan, Reference Librarian, Humanities, Wichita State Univ., Ablah Library, Kans.

Joe P. Dunn, Charles A. Dana Professor of History and Politics, Converse College, Spartanburg, S.C.

Bradford Lee Eden, Head of Cataloging, Univ. of Nevada at Las Vegas.

Marianne B. Eimer, Interlibrary Loan/Reference Librarian, SUNY College at Fredonia, N.Y.

Mark Emmons, Librarian and Assoc. Professor, Univ. of New Mexico, Albuquerque.

Lorraine Evans, Instruction and Reference Librarian, Auraria Library, Denver, Colo.

Benet Steven Exton, St. Gregorys Univ. Library, Shawnee, Okla.

Elaine Ezell, Library Media Specialist, Bowling Green Jr. High School, Ohio.

Ignacio J. Ferrer-Vinent, Science Reference/Instruction Librarian, Auraria Library—Univ. of Colorado at Denver.

Judith J. Field, Senior Lecturer, Program for Library and Information Science, Wayne State Univ., Detroit.

Jerry D. Flack, Professor Emeritus, Retired.

Holly A Flynn, Mathematics Librarian, Michigan State Univ., East Lansing.

James H. Flynn Jr., (formerly) Operations Research Analyst, Dept. of Defense, Vienna, Va.

Michael A. Foley, Honors Director, Marywood College, Scranton, Pa.

David K. Frasier, Asst. Librarian, Reference Dept., Indiana Univ., Bloomington.

Susan J. Freiband, Assoc. Professor, Graduate School of Librarianship, Univ. of Puerto Rico, San Juan.

David O. Friedrichs, Professor, Univ. of Scranton, Pa.

Jeanne D. Galvin, Chief of Reference, Kingsborough Community College, City University of New York, Brooklyn, N.Y.

Zev Garber, Professor and Chair, Jewish Studies, Los Angeles Valley College, Calif.

Susan J. Gardner, Collection Development Coordinator—Leavey Library, Univ. of Southern California, Los Angeles.

Denise A. Garofalo, Director for Telecommunications, Mid-Hudson Library System, Poughkeepsie, N.Y.

Carol Anne Germain, Networked Resources Education Librarian, Univ. at Albany, N.Y.

John T. Gillespie, College Professor and Writer, New York.

Lois Gilmer, Library Director, Univ. of West Florida, Fort Walton Beach.

Caroline L. Gilson, Coordinator, Prevo Science Library, DePauw Univ., Greencastle, Ind.

Edward L. González, Science Librarian/Assoc. Librarian, IUPUI University Library, Indianapolis, Ind.

Larissa Anne Gordon, Librarian, Wilmington College, Dover, Del.

Rachael Green, Reference Librarian, Noel Memorial Library, Louisiana State Univ., Shreveport.

Laurel Grotzinger, Professor, Univ. Libraries, Western Michigan Univ., Kalamazoo.

Kara JoLynn Gust, Asst. Instruction Librarian, Michigan State Univ., East Lansing.

Linda W. Hacker, Reference Librarian, SUNY Brockport, Brockport, N.Y.

Michael W. Handis, Assoc. Librarian for Technical Services and Collection Management, CUNY Graduate Center, New York.

Ralph Hartsock, Senior Music Catalog Librarian, Univ. of North Texas, Denton.

Karen D. Harvey, Assoc. Dean for Academic Affairs, Univ. College, Univ. of Denver, Colo.

Maris L. Hayashi, Asst. University Librarian, Florida Atlantic Univ., Boca Raton.

David Henige, African Studies Bibliographer, Memorial Library, Univ. of Wisconsin, Madison.

Christina L. Hennessey, Systems Librarian, Loyola Marymount Univ., Los Angeles, Calif.

Mark Y. Herring, Dean of Library Services, Winthrop Univ., Dacus Library, Rock Hill, S.C.

Joseph P. Hester, SRO-Learning, Claremont, N.C.

Ladyjane Hickey, Head of Cataloging and Business, Management and Marketing Bibliographer, Newton Gresham Library, Sam Houston State Univ., Huntsville, Tex.

Susan Tower Hollis, Assoc. Dean and Center Director, Central New York Center of the State Univ. of New York.

Sara Anne Hook, Professor of Informatics and Assoc. Dean for Academic Affairs and Undergraduate Studies, UP School of Informatics, Indiana Univ., Purdue Univ., Indianapolis.

Mihoko Hosoi, Public Services Librarian, Cornell Univ., Ithaca, N.Y.

Jonathan F. Husband, Program Chair of the Library/Reader Services Librarian, Henry Whittemore Library, Framingham State College, Mass.

Shannon Graff Hysell, Staff, Libraries Unlimited.

David Isaacson, Asst. Head of Reference and Humanities Librarian, Waldo Library, Western Michigan Univ., Kalamazoo.

Richard D. Johnson, Director of Libraries Emeritus, James M. Milne Library, State Univ. College, Oneonta, N.Y.

Melissa M. Johnson, Evening Reference—Instruction Librarian, Lynn Univ., Boca Raton, Fla.

Danielle Andrea Kane, Science Librarian, UCSC, Santa Cruz, Calif.

Thomas A. Karel, Assoc. Director for Public Services, Shadek-Fackenthal Library, Franklin and Marshall College, Lancaster, Pa.

John Laurence Kelland, Reference Bibliographer for Life Sciences, Univ. of Rhode Island Library, Kingston.

Jane Kessler, Reference Librarian, Unive. at Albany, N.Y.

Christine E. King, Education Librarian, Purdue Univ., West Lafayette, Ind.

Njoki W. Kinyatti, Assoc. Professor and Head of Collection Development, York College of the City University of New York, Jamaica.

Lori D. Kranz, Freelance Editor, Chambersburg, Pa.

Betsy J. Kraus, Librarian, Lovelace Respiratory Research Institute, National Environmental Respiratory Center, Albuquerque, N.Mex.

Marlene M. Kuhl, Library Manager, Baltimore County Public Library, Reisterstown Branch, Md.

George Thomas Kurian, President, Encyclopedia Society, Baldwin Place, N.Y.

Keith Kyker, Educational Media Specialist, Okaloosa School District, Crestview, Fla.

Robert V. Labaree, Reference/Public Services Librarian, Von KleinSmid Library, Univ. of Southern California, Los Angeles.

Sharon Ladenson, Social Sciences Bibliographer and Reference Librarian, Michigan State Univ. Libraries, East Lansing.

Peter Larsen, Physical Sciences and Engineering Librarian, Univ. of Rhode Island Libraries, Kingston.

Jim Latchney, Cataloging and Reference Librarian, Michigan State Univ., East Lansing.

Rob Laurich, Head of Reference & Collection Development, The City College of New York.

Martha Lawler, Assoc. Librarian, Louisiana State Univ., Shreveport.

Bernadette A. Lear, Asst. Librarian, Penn State Harrisburg, Middletown, Pa.

Charles Leck, Professor of Biological Sciences, Rutgers Univ., New Brunswick, N.J.

John A. Lent, Drexel Hill, Pa.

Michael Levine-Clark, Reference Librarian, Univ. of Denver, Colo.

Tze-chung Li, Professor and Dean Emeritus, Dominican Univ.

Charlotte Lindgren, Professor Emerita of English, Emerson College, Boston, Mass.

Robert M. Lindsey, Reference/Instruction Librarian, Pittsburg State Univ., Pittsburg, Kans.

Megan W. Lowe, Reference/Instruction Librarian, University Library, Univ. of Louisiana at Monroe.

John Maxymuk, Reference Librarian, Paul Robeson Library, Rutgers Univ., Camden, N.J.

John J. McCormick, Reference Librarian, Lamson Library, Plymouth State Univ., Plymouth, N.H.

Shelly McCoy, Head, Digital User Services Department, Univ. of Delaware Library, Newark.

Glenn S. McGuigan, Reference Librarian, Penn State Abington, Abington, Pa.

Peter Zachary McKay, Business Librarian, Univ. of Florida Libraries, Gainesville.

Lillian R. Mesner, Arbor City Indexing, Nebraska City, Nebr.

Michael G. Messina, Assoc. Professor, Dept. of Forest Science, Texas A & M Univ., College Station.

G. Douglas Meyers, Chair, Dept. of English, Univ. of Texas, El Paso.

Robert Michaelson, Head Librarian, Seeley G. Mudd Library for Science and Engineering, Northwestern Univ., Evanston, Ill.

Ken Middleton, User Services Librarian, Middle Tennessee State Univ., Murfreesboro.

Seiko Mieczkowski, Cocoa Beach, Fla.

Bill Miller, Director of Libraries, Florida Atlantic Univ., Boca Raton.

James Mitchell Miller, Univ. of South Carolina, Columbia.

Terri Tickle Miller, Slavic Bibliographer, Michigan State Univ. Libraries, East Lansing.

Wendy Miller, Reference Librarian, Lexington Public Library, Ky.

Jim Millhorn, Head of Acquisitions, Northern Illinois Univ. Libraries, DeKalb.

Paul A. Mogren, Head of Reference, Marriott Library, Univ. of Utah, Salt Lake City.

K. Mulliner, Asst. to the Director of Libraries, Ohio Univ. Library, Athens.

Paul M. Murphy III, Director of Marketing, PMX Medical, Denver, Colo.

Valentine K. Muyumba, Monographic Cataloging Librarian, Indiana State Univ., Terre Haute.

Madeleine Nash, Asst. Professor and Reader Services Librarian, Kingsborough Community College, CUNY, Brooklyn, N.Y.

Charles Neuringer, Professor of Psychology and Theatre and Film, Univ. of Kansas, Lawrence.

Shawn W. Nicholson, State Documents and Social Sciences Librarian, Michigan State Univ., East Lansing.

Marshall E. Nunn, Professor, Dept. of History, Glendale Community College, Calif.

Herbert W. Ockerman, Professor, Ohio State Univ., Columbus.

James W. Oliver, Chemistry Librarian, Michigan State Univ., East Lansing.

Lawrence Olszewski, Director, OCLC Library and Information Center, Dublin, Ohio.

John Howard Oxley, Faculty, American Intercontinental Univ., Atlanta, Ga.

Mark Padnos, Coordinator of Public Services, Bronx Community College, N.Y.

Robert Palmieri, Professor Emeritus, School of Music, Kent State Univ., Ohio.

J. Carlyle Parker, Librarian and Univ. Archivist Emeritus, Library, California State Univ., Turlock.

Lesley A. Paul, Reference Librarian, Herkimer County Community College, Herkimer, N.Y.

Stefanie S. Pearlman, Asst. Professor of Law Library and Reference Librarian, Schmid Law Library, Univ. of Nebraska, Lincoln.

Julia Perez, Biological Sciences Librarian, Michigan State Univ. Libraries, East Lansing.

Christina K. Pikas, Technical Librarian, Johns Hopkins Univ., Applied Physics Laboratory, Laurel, Md.

Jack Ray, Asst. Director, Loyola/Notre Dame Library, Baltimore, Md.

Patrick J. Reakes, Journalism/Mass Communications Librarian, Univ. of Florida, Gainesville.

Nancy P. Reed, Information Services Manager, Paducah Public Library, Ky.

Allen Reichert, Electronic Access Librarian, Courtright Memorial Library, Otterbein College, Westerville, Ohio.

James C. Roberts, Asst. Professor of Sociology and Criminal Justice, Univ. of Scranton, Pa.

John B. Romeiser, Professor of French and Dept. Head, Univ. of Tennessee, Knoxville.

Jill Rooker, Assoc. Professor and Program Coordinator, Instructional Media, Univ. of Central Oklahoma, Edmond.

Patricia Rothermich, Reference/Business Librarian, Courtright Memorial Library, Otterbein College, Westerville, Ohio.

Michele Russo, Acting Director, Franklin D. Schurz Library, Indiana Univ., South Bend.

Seth Ryan, LLC, Aurora, Colo.

Nadine Salmons, Technical Services Librarian, Fort Carson's Grant Library, Colo.

Manuel Frank Santos, Jones International Univ, Broomfield, Colo.

John Schlinke, Access Services Librarian, Roger Williams Univ., Bristol, R.I.

Diane Schmidt, Asst. Biology Librarian, Univ. of Illinois, Urbana.

Willa Schmidt, (retired) Reference Librarian, Univ. of Wisconsin, Madison.

Ralph Lee Scott, Assoc. Professor, East Carolina Univ. Library, Greenville, N.C.

Colleen Seale, Humanities and Social Sciences Services, George A. Smathers Libraries, Univ. of Florida, Gainesville.

Stephen J. Shaw, Reference/Bibliographic Instruction Librarian, Prairie View A&M Univ., Tex.

Susan Shultz, Reference and Instruction Librarian, DePaul Univ., Chicago, Ill.

Leena Siegelbaum, Bibliographer of Eastern European Law, Harvard Univ., Cambridge, Mass.

Mary Ellen Snodgrass, Freelance Writer, Charlotte, N.C.

Lisa Kay Speer, Special Collections Librarian, Southeast Missouri State Univ., Cape Girardeau.

Kay M. Stebbins, Coordinator Librarian, Louisiana State Univ., Shreveport.

Martha E. Stone, Coordinator for Reference Services, Treadwell Library, Massachusetts General Hospital, Boston.

John W. Storey, Professor of History, Lamar Univ., Beaumont, Tex.

William C. Struning, Professor, Seton Hall Univ., South Orange, N.J.

Timothy E. Sullivan, Asst. Professor of Economics, Towson State Univ., Md.

Philip G. Swan, Head Librarian, Hunter College, School of Social Work Library, New York.

Marit S. Taylor, Reference Librarian, Auraria Libraries, Univ. of Colorado, Denver.

Polly J. Thistlethwaite, Assoc. Librarian for Public Services, CUNY Graduate Center, New York.

Susan E. Thomas, Head of Collection Development/Assoc. Librarian, Indiana Univ. South Bend.

Mary Ann Thompson, Asst. Professor of Nursing, Saint Joseph College, West Hartford, Conn.

Linda D. Tietjen, Senior Instructor, Instruction and Reference Services, Auraria Library, Denver, Colo.

Vincent P. Tinerella, Asst. Professor/Reference Librarian, Northern Illinois Univ., DeKalb.

Bradley P. Tolppanen, History Bibliographer and Head of Circulation Services, Eastern Illinois Univ., Charleston.

Elizabeth Kay Tompkins, Asst. Professor, Kingsborough Community College—CUNY, Brooklyn, N.Y.

Gregory M. Toth, Reference Librarian, State Univ. of New York, Brockport.

Diane J. Turner, Science/Engineering Liaison, Auraria Library, Univ. of Colorado, Denver.

Robert L. Turner Jr., Librarian and Assoc. Professor, Radford Univ., Va.

Chris Tuthill, Interlibrary Loan/Scanning Services Librarian, Univ. of Maine, Orono.

Nancy L. Van Atta, Dayton, Ohio.

Leanne M. VandeCreek, Social Sciences Reference Librarian, Northern Illinois Univ., DeKalb.

Graham R. Walden, Professor, University Libraries, Ohio State Univ., Columbus.

J. E. Weaver, Dept. of Economics, Drake Univ., Des Moines, Iowa.

Kathleen Weessies, Maps/GIS Librarian, Michigan State Univ., East Lansing.

Karen T. Wei, Head, Asian Library, Univ. of Illinois, Urbana.

Deborah Jackson Weiss, Graduate Student, Simmons College Graduate School of Library and Information Science, Boston, Mass.

Marilyn Domas White, Assoc. Professor, College of Information Studies, Univ. of Maryland, College Park.

Robert L. Wick, Professor Emeritus, Auraria Library, Univ. of Colorado, Denver.

Agnes H. Widder, Humanities Bibliographer, Michigan State Univ., East Lansing.

Mark A. Wilson, Professor of Geology, College of Wooster, Ohio.

Terrie L. Wilson, Art Librarian, Michigan State Univ., East Lansing.

Julienne L. Wood, Head, Research Services, Noel Memorial Library, Louisiana State Univ. in Shreveport.

Neal Wyatt, Collection Management Librarian, Chesterfield County Public Library, Va.

Hope Yelich, Reference Librarian, Earl Gregg Swem Library, College of William and Mary, Williamsburg, Va.

Henry E. York, Head, Collection Management, Cleveland State Univ., Ohio.

Courtney L. Young, Reference Librarian, Beaver Campus Library, Penn State Beaver, Monaca.

L. Zgusta, Professor of Linguistics and the Classics and Member of the Center for Advanced Study, Univ. of Illinois, Urbana.

Anita Zutis, Adjunct Librarian, Queensborough Community College, Bayside, N.Y.

Journals Cited

FORM OF CITATION	JOURNAL TITLE
AG	*Against the Grain*
BL	*Booklist*
BR	*Book Report*
Choice	*Choice*
JAL	*Journal of Academic Librarianship*
LJ	*Library Journal*
LMC	*Library Media Connection*
RUSQ	*Reference & User Services Quarterly*
SLJ	*School Library Journal*
TL	*Teacher Librarian*
VOYA	*Voice of Youth Advocates*

Part I
GENERAL REFERENCE WORKS

1 General Reference Works

ACRONYMS AND ABBREVIATIONS

C, P, S

1. **Acronym Finder. http://www.acronymfinder.com/.** [Website]. Free. Date reviewed: Jan 06.

The *Acronym Finder* is a useful, free site that provides users with the definitions of 3,00,000 acronyms —both those well known and some that are not. The search mechanism is simple. The user puts in the acronym in the right-hand search box and selects whether they would like to search for the exact acronym or the acronym that begins with the specified letters in the left-hand box. The site limits search results to 300 acronyms. If the site comes up with too many hits, the user can then sort the results by most common, slang, organizations and schools, or by field (e.g., information technology, science and medicine). Each acronym links to Amazon.com for titles that may be of interest to the user. Hence, the downside of this site: Because it is a free site it is heavily sponsored by advertisers. The user will have to sort through the many advertisements that continually pop up while waiting for their results. Several new features have recently been added to this Website. Search results are now view their search results according to "rank," which are distinguished by commonness, popularity, or relevance. Also, the site now features "categories" with each search result; therefore, if one searches for ERP they will find that there are 7 under the category of Information Technology, 17 under Military and Government, and 11 under Science and Medicine. This site will be useful for librarians working the reference desk.—**Shannon Graff Hysell**

C, P, S

2. **The American Heritage Abbreviations Dictionary.** 3d ed. New York, Houghton Mifflin, 2005. 294p. $6.95. ISBN 0-618-62123-7.

This 3d edition of *The American Heritage Abbreviations Dictionary* provides users with over 20,000 popular abbreviations commonly found in business, correspondence, and the Internet—1,000 more than what was found in the last edition (see ARBA 2004, entry 1). With the new popularity of text messaging and chat rooms, many of the new entries will help users translate these abbreviations. Some of the new abbreviations added to this 3d edition are: BFF (best friend forever), D2D (dusk to dawn), LDR (long-distance relationship), romcom (romantic comedy), and URAQT (you are a cutie). Along with these fun abbreviations are abbreviations for science terms, foreign terms, and business and financial terms.

This work continues to be a handy, inexpensive guide to have for the ready-reference shelf as well as home offices. It is not as comprehensive (or as bulky) as the Gale Group's large, four-volume *Acronyms, Initialisms, & Abbreviations Dictionary* (34th ed.; see ARBA 2005, entry 1) but is useful just the same.—**Shannon Graff Hysell**

ALMANACS

C, P, S
3.   **Chambers Book of Facts 2006.** New York, Houghton Mifflin, 2005. 992p. index. $22.00. ISBN 0-550-10137-3.

Library reference shelves are home to a variety of almanacs. *Chambers Book of Facts* is one that will fit in well among the others. As the title indicates, this work focuses on facts not text. Thus, it contains a plethora of charts, tables, and brief entries about a myriad of subjects.

Divided into 13 sections, many reference questions will be quickly answered by using this useful and up-to-date book. The sections are "Space"; "Earth"; "Climate and Environment"; "Time"; "Natural History"; "Human Life"; "History"; "Social Structure"; "Communication"; "Science, Engineering and Measurement"; "Arts and Culture"; "Sport and Games"; and "Thought and Belief." The charts and statistical information are current as of 2005. Also, due to its slightly British slant, some information not normally found in other such works is easily accessible, such as the counties of the United Kingdom, UK road distances, and the poets laureate of England and the United Kingdom.

Although the table of contents will get the user to the appropriate section of the book, it is generally faster to use the index, especially if searching for an event or the name of an individual. The index, although in excess of a hundred pages, is not complete, however. For example, the index includes Mohs' hardness scale as a phrase, but it is not included under the term hardness. Many individuals needing to find such information may not know the official name of the scale and, therefore, will not find the scale listed.

Since *Chambers Book of Facts* is inexpensive and covers material not found in other almanacs, such as a listing of world heritage sites, military ranks of various countries, and the ranks of aristocracy, it will be a worthwhile additional purchase to supplement and complement standard almanacs such as the *World Almanac and Book of Facts* (2005 ed.; see ARBA 2005, entry 4). In addition, the hardcover binding will see it through many years of use before it will need to be replaced.—**Gregory A. Crawford**

C, P, S
4.   **Chase's Calendar of Events 2006.** 49th ed. New York, McGraw-Hill, 2006. 751p. illus. index. $64.95pa. (w/CD-ROM). ISBN 0-07-146110-8.

This is the 49th edition of this useful reference work, which provides a day-by-day listing of 12,000 holidays, events, special days, weeks and months. Entries cover astronomical phenomena, religious observances, civic holidays, federal proclamations, festivals, anniversaries, and birthdays. A "Spotlight" section at the front of the volume is included to help users easily find significant anniversaries and events for the year. The day-by-day listing is followed by a section with ready-reference information, mostly relating to calendars, such as perpetual calendars for the years 1753-2100. Entries are indexed by name/title and location, as well as by categories. There appear to be some inconsistencies in the categories. Alcoholism is included as a category but diabetes is not. To find all diabetes-related events, users must look under the more comprehensive category of "Health and Welfare."

This edition comes with a CD-ROM, which can be browsed by name or date. Users can also search by name, date, description, attendance, state, or categories and print the results. There is very brief rollover help for all major interface elements, as well as a more in-depth help file. A search for diabetes-related events returned all seven events listed in the print version under the category "Health and Welfare." However, browsing by name revealed an inconsistency in treatment of titles with the print index. For example, American Diabetes Month is listed under Diabetes Month, American in the print index, but in the CD-ROM browse feature it is listed under American Diabetes Month. A consistent approach would be more helpful.—**Jane Kessler**

C, P, S

5.   Christianson, Stephen G. Messina, Lynn M., ed. **The International Book of Days.** Bronx, N.Y., H. W. Wilson, 2004. 889p. illus. maps. index. $140.00. ISBN 0-8242-0975-3.

Imagine a combination of the *Chronicles of the World* and *Chase's Calendar of Events* might look like and you will have an idea of this newest entry into the field of chronologies combined with religious and secular holiday celebrations. This new title, a companion volume to the author's *The American Book of Days* (4th ed.; see ARBA 2004, entry 4), covers significant international events for every day of the year. The criteria for inclusion is broad: "to provide readers with information on historical events of military, scientific, ethnic, political, and cultural significance from around the world."

The 1,500 entries run from 100 to 200 words and cover events, holidays, and people from 125 countries. They are organized by month and day. There are two to eight entries for each day. Each month's section begins with an essay on its length, weather, the origin and history of its name, and the gem or birthstone associated with it. Random entries for each day follow. They are not arranged by topic or year, nor are they alphabetic. The featured event is in bold type but the year of its occurrence is part of the explanatory text. This requires more effort for those seeking events for a specific year or century. The potentially useful introductory "List of Days and Events" neglects to list dates.

On the positive side, even the briefest entries manage to capture the essence of what makes each event notable and provides added value through the accompanying text. For example, the entry for the first recorded lunar eclipse (March 19, 721 B.C.E.) discusses ancient astronomical history and beliefs and compares them to modern scientific findings. It also gives an explanation of an eclipse and describes the three types. Political and military events are succinctly explained and key issues, the impact, and resolution are all incorporated in the text. Biographical entries give the person's vital statistics and brief background, and go on to illustrate why he or she is important. Events and people important in American history have brief entries and the user is directed to *The American Book of Days* for a more extensive article. These cross-references are hit or miss in relation to the cited title. Some important people do not appear in the review title. Among them are Rosa Parks, Marian Anderson, and Shirley Chisholm. All of them do appear in the referenced title. *See* references at the end of entries are puzzling. They direct the reader to "related articles in this volume" but do not give article titles, dates, or even page numbers. The user must go to the index to access them. In addition to the 35-page index there are 6 appendixes. Three deal with the history of the calendar, the concept of an era, and the names of the days of the week, respectively. The other three are texts of important international document, such as the Charter of the United Nations.

All in all this title is a mixed bag. Well-written, informative essays are offset by technical problems. Given the plethora of chronologies, such as the DK Chronicles series, and quick access via the Internet to "what happened on this day" sites (http://www.historychannel.com, http://memory.loc.gov, www.historycentral.com), some of which include links to primary sources and provide references, one wonders if the content alone will be enough to give this latest volume staying power. [R: SLJ, Aug 05, p. 73]—**Marlene M. Kuhl**

C, P, S

6.   *The New York Times* **Almanac 2005.** John W. Wright, ed., with Editors and Reporters of *The Times*. New York, Penguin Books, 2005. 996p. index. $11.95pa. ISBN 0-14-303427-8. ISSN 1523-7079.

The New York Times Almanac is divided into seven sections, including the year in review, the United States, the world, science and technology, awards and prizes, and sports. Because of its arrangement, users may find it easier to locate information than in its best-known and more popularly written peer, *The World Almanac and Book of Facts* (2005 ed.; see ARBA 2005, entry 4). Whereas *The World Almanac* includes thumbnail black-and-white illustrations throughout, such as for biographies of all U.S. presidents, and selected color illustrations of news events, *The New York Times Almanac* does not. *The New York Times Almanac* provides, for example, the winners at the Cannes Film Festival and all the winners of the Bollingen Prize for Poetry, as well as very detailed information about Nobel and Pulitzer Prize winners. *The World Almanac* omits Cannes and includes only the current year's Bollingen winner, under the category of "Miscellaneous Book Awards"; however, it provides a complete list the Miss America winners. Both almanacs contain news stories signed by their authors; the major *New York Times Almanac* stories are written by that newspaper's staff reporters. There is a selective index and color inset of world maps in *The New York Times Almanac*, but the CIA's *The World Factbook* (see entry 32), which is available in print and freely available at http://www.cia.gov/cia/publications/factbook/, is one of the most reliable almanac sources of all types of information about countries worldwide. Because of the reliability of its authorship, not to mention its modest price, as well as the sheer enjoyment gained by browsing through it, *The New York Times Almanac* would be a very worthwhile addition to any library.—**Martha E. Stone**

BIBLIOGRAPHY

National and Trade Bibliography

P

7. **The Complete Directory of Large Print Books & Serials 2005.** New Providence, N.J., R. R. Bowker, 2005. 2112p. index. $290.00/set. ISBN 0-8352-4675-2. ISSN 0000-1120.

The size of this directory attests to the demand for large print titles. It was initially published in 1970 as *Large Type Books in Print*, and earlier reviews indicated how slight the volume was (see ARBA 93, entry 30, and ARBA 89, entry 15). It is clear that an increased sensitivity to the needs of the visually impaired, along with the graying of the population, has spurred the growth of large print and the need for this type of directory. The physical organization of the work remains essentially unchanged since the publication of previous editions. It is divided into nine index sections starting with the title index and concluding with a newspapers and periodicals index. The title index includes full bibliographic data, and those employing the subject indexes are required to refer to the former for ordering purposes. The 2005 edition provides bibliographic information on more than 22,000 titles, with about 1,800 of those being new to the work. A small minority of the titles indicate the font size of the work, and R. R. Bowker explains in the foreword that they furnish such information only if it is provided by the publisher. In future editions R. R. Bowker should be more aggressive in requiring publishers of large print titles to furnish this vital information. The work is printed in 12-point font, which will allow the targeted audience easy access to the information. All in all, this unique source should be a standard work for all libraries and institutions that deal with the visually impaired.—**Jim Millhorn**

BIOGRAPHY

International

C, P, S

8. **Newsmakers 2005 Cumulation: The People Behind Today's Headlines.** Farmington Hills, Mich., Gale, 2006. 690p. illus. index. $199.00. ISBN 0-7876-8082-6. ISSN 0899-0417.

Newsmakers provides short biographies with portraits and lists of additional sources for persons (and some musical groups) prominent in the media. Biographies of living persons are followed by obituaries of people featured in previous volumes. A rough categorization of the 2005 volume shows biographies from the realms of acting, writing, sports, U.S. government, fashion, science/medicine/technology, music, filmmaking, foreign government, photography, media, education, and others. The 2005 volume includes cumulative nationality, occupation, subject, and names indexes. *Newsmakers* appears quarterly and in this annual cumulation. It is also available on diskette/magnetic tape and online.

Newsmakers is similar in coverage to *Current Biography* (CB; see ARBA 2005, entry 21), although the annual CB has more entries than *Newsmakers*. Unlike CB, *Newsmakers* has often quite lengthy bibliographies, discographies, and filmographies of a subject's work. The "Sources" section is often considerably larger than those in CB and often includes a list of online sources. Even where the "Sources" sections are of similar size, *Newsmakers* and CB often cite different sources. Any library with an interest in current figures should have both *Newsmakers* and CB.—**Frederic F. Burchsted**

C, P

9.   **Who: A Directory of Prominent People.** Kay Gill, ed. Detroit, Omnigraphics, 2005. 556p. index. $58.00pa. ISBN 0-7808-0703-0.

For those who need to reach LL Cool Jay or Chris Evert, or want to know what team Yao Ming plays for, or who manages the Ansel Adams estate the 2005 *Who: A Directory of Prominent People* (formerly titled *Names in the News*), will certainly help. Omnigraphics, guided by an advisory board of Florida librarians, constructed this directory of more than 7,000 "high-profile" individuals, which includes musicians, astronauts, politicians, writers, athletes (listed by sport), religious leaders, and activists. I was pleased to find my favorite niche categories, corporate trainers and fitness personalities, although they are far outnumbered by actors and television anchors. The most useful information included in *Who* are the titles and telephone numbers of celebrity agents. This directory puts "adore-me-but-don't-call-me" fan-directed Websites to shame by providing accessible contact information. *Who*, naturally, also suffers from its static print format; for example, 2004 elected officials, and hockey players sidelined during the 2004-2005 season are not uniformly included. [R: LJ, 1 Sept 05, p. 182]—**Polly J. Thistlethwaite**

United States

C, P

10.   **American National Biography, Supplement II.** Mark C. Carnes, ed. New York, Oxford University Press, 2005. 835p. index. $150.00. ISBN 0-19-522202-4.

This volume extends the coverage of the 24-volume *American National Biography* (ANB; see ARBA 2001, entry 17), which in itself was conceived as the successor to the *Dictionary of American Biography*. The over 400 subjects in *Supplement II* are a wildly disparate group of Americans, both those recently deceased and those from the past. There are more men than women, but there is a fairly generous representation of minorities. The preface clearly states that ANB's aim is "to show how [the entrants] were representative of American popular culture at a given moment in the country's history" (p. vii). There are indexes by birthplace and by occupation or "realm of renown," and a cumulative index that covers the entire series as well as both supplements I and II. The volume begins and ends with well-known, recently deceased figures: popular novelist Alice Adams, broadcast journalist Martin Agronsky, and Admiral Elmo Zumwalt. At midpoint is German-born cartoonist Charles Kahles, who arrived in the United States as a child, died in 1931, and whose *Hairbreadth Harry* was the first adventure comic strip. Each entry includes a very selective bibliography that usually includes information about archival holdings (e.g., blues singer Joe Williams' papers can be found in the archives of Hamilton College), major obituaries (e.g., openly gay Harlem Renaissance writer Richard Bruce Nugent's obituary can be found in the *Washington Post*), and important biographies about the entrant or the entrant's circle (e.g., Connecticut artist Mary Way, who died in 1833 and whose work was rediscovered in 1992). Every entry is well written and leaves no doubt about why a subject is worthy of inclusion. The ANB is also available electronically by subscription at http://www.anb.org/ (see ARBA 2004, entry 19), but libraries that already have the ANB in print will no doubt want to continue the set. The ANB Website has a freely available "biography of the day" containing clickable links (although access to the links' contents requires a subscription) that will give the uninitiated a feel for the world of knowledge available in the ANB.—**Martha E. Stone**

C, P

11.   **Who's Who in America 2006.** 60th ed. New Providence, N.J., Marquis Who's Who/Reed Reference Publishing, 2005. 2v. $749.00/set. ISBN 0-8379-6990-5. ISSN 0083-9396.

As with previous editions, *Who's Who in America 2006* contains a great deal of well-organized biographical information. The biographical directory, with its concise yet informative summaries, takes up most of this two-volume work. These listings include the subject's family relations, educational background, and accomplishments as well as their other noteworthy achievements. These subjects comprise a cross section of American life and professions. For the readers' benefit, the editors spell out their "Criteria for Admission," which each subject passed before inclusion in the work. For this edition, the editors included indexes pertaining to the subjects' occupations and locations (state and city). In addition, another listing of subjects without regional affiliations appears in this work. Other than the editors placing librarianship with the humanities, these listings follow the expected placement within their subject fields. The editors also mention that there is a *Who's Who* Website.

This set updates the *Who's Who in America* from previous years and should go alongside its counterparts in library reference collections. This set is recommended for public, special, corporate, and academic libraries.—**David J. Duncan**

DICTIONARIES AND ENCYCLOPEDIAS

P, S

12.   **Encyclopedia Americana.** international ed. Danbury, Conn., Grolier, 2005. 30v. illus. maps. index. $749.00/set. ISBN 0-7172-0138-4.

P, S

13.   **Encyclopedia Americana. http://auth.grolier.com/cgi-bin/authV2.** [Website]. Price negotiated by site. Date reviewed: Jan 06.

If time and longevity are any indication of the popularity of a reference title than the fact that *Encyclopedia Americana* is now in its 176th year is surely a good indicator of the respect this encyclopedia has found in U.S. and Canadian libraries. In general, this encyclopedia remains much the same from year to year; however, it is updated each year with new subjects never seen in previous editions and updated articles that have been revised by the original author or the editorial staff. No expansive revisions have been made to this latest edition of *Encyclopedia Americana*.

This encyclopedia provides more than 45,000 articles contributed by hundreds of subject experts. It is arranged in the standard A-Z format, with each article being signed by its original contributor. The language used for entries will be easily understood by general lay readers, high school students, and undergraduates. The volumes provide many research aids to help users navigate the encyclopedia, including an index with more than 350,000 terms, cross-references within articles and at the end of the articles, a table of contents at the beginning of the longer articles, and bibliographies at the end of articles. Some special features of the *Encyclopedia Americana* that are not seen in all large encyclopedia sets include: separate articles for each of the centuries (e.g., Twentieth Century), which provides an international perspective in the areas of politics, society, and culture; separate articles on each book of the Bible; articles on important historical documents (e.g., Declaration of Independence); and articles on specific areas of education (e.g., Medical Education, Business Education). This encyclopedia is filled with maps (1,200), photographs and illustrations (15,000), and sidebars and charts (3,800), some of which are in color. Although the illustrations are not as extravagant as those found in other notable encyclopedias, such as *World Book Encyclopedia* (2005 ed.; see entry 17), they do add significantly to the text.

The online edition contains the same data available in the print version with some added advantages. First, users can search for information by article title, word, or phrase. Stemming and Boolean options are available to make searching easier. A hyperlink to search tips is available to aid users in finding the information they are looking for. Second, more than 1,200 maps and 270 flags are available to print out in full color. Lastly, there are quarterly updates to the articles and monthly updates to the hyperlinked text.

This resource will continue to be a significant tool at the reference desk of academic and public libraries. Available in both print and electronic form libraries will have their choice of how to retrieve its information.—**Shannon Graff Hysell**

S

14. **The New Book of Knowledge.** Danbury, Conn., Grolier, 2005. 21v. illus. maps. index. $489.00/set. ISBN 0-7172-0539-8.

S

15. **New Book of Knowledge Online. http://go.grolier.com.** [Website]. Danbury, Conn., Grolier. Price negotiated by site. Date reviewed: Oct 05.

What makes *The New Book of Knowledge* unique is that it is designed specifically for children and young adults grades K-12. Unlike other encyclopedias, such as *Encyclopedia Americana* and *Encyclopaedia Britannica*, *The New Book of Knowledge*'s entries were selected by teachers, children's and school librarians, and cultural specialists who know school curriculum and the educational needs of students. This 2005 edition provides an A to Z listing of entries presented in 21 volumes. Each entry is written by a specialist in the field and includes the name of the author, while many also include the name of an article reviewer as well. Some of the newer, more timely articles provided in this year's edition include: Terrorism, War on; Volunteerism; ADHD; Homeland Security, United States Department of; J. K. Rowling; and Bush, George W. The articles are written to be easily understood by young children, although those entries that are more technical in nature will most likely only be understood by young adults. Illustrations, photographs, maps, charts, and informational sidebars accompany nearly every entry and the publisher stresses that each has been double-checked for accuracy and readability. More than 25,000 illustrations and 1,300 maps are presented in this set.

This encyclopedia is designed to be easy to search by including guidewords at the bottom of each page. Most of the entries also provide cross-references and *see also* references at the end of entries. The set also features "Wonder Questions," which are designed to grab the interest of students and inspire further research. As an added feature the encyclopedia provides a paperbound "Home and School Reading and Study Guides" volume that provides a bibliography to thousands of topics covered in the encyclopedia. Each recommended title is grouped by reading level—primary, intermediate, and advanced.

What makes this encyclopedia so outstanding are the full-color illustrations, the well-written text, and the fact that the information provided works well with current curriculum standards. This work is also available in an online edition from Grolier Online at http://go.grolier.com. The search function is typical of what is available on most Websites with Boolean options. Users can specify their search within a particular subject area (e.g., arts, geography, history, philosophy, religion, science and math). Under the browse function users can browse articles alphabetically or by subject. Lesson plans that include worksheets, activities, and critical thinking exercises are included specifically with elementary and middle school age children in mind.

This encyclopedia will be an ideal addition to school and public libraries. Compared to that of many other comparable encyclopedias, the price is quite reasonable.—**Shannon Graff Hysell**

C, P, S

16. **The New Oxford American Dictionary.** 2d ed. Erin McKean, ed. New York, Oxford University Press, 2005. 2051p. $60.00 (w/CD-ROM). ISBN 0-19-517077-6.

The 1st edition of this title was well received (see ARBA 2002, entry 34). The major innovation accompanying the 2d edition is that the entire contents can be downloaded from a disk to a PDA or a smartphone. As before, the dictionary has some 250,000 entries, 2,000 of which are new to this edition. The approach is to provide "core meanings" with related senses, followed by submeanings. Editor Erin Mckean has not shied away from the full range of words used in American English, providing a rich explanation for the various uses of slang words.

Biographical and place-name entries are included. The text is illustrated, and includes photographs, all of which are in black and white. In an era where color is expected, these look somewhat dated. There are publishers who are providing richly illustrated, full-color dictionaries and encyclopedias, and they are setting a standard that has not yet been adopted by the traditional dictionary powerhouses, such as Oxford University Press. Clearly the addition of color adds cost, but in the era of full-color Internet screens, can publishers really ignore the competition?

The bottom right of every other page includes a pronunciation key. Individual entries in the dictionary are designed to be simple and easily grasped. Reading a wide variety of words indicates that the entries are clear and well written. The title is without compare in terms of the resources drawn upon to create it—the full *Oxford English Dictionary* and a 200 million-word database. This work is highly recommended. [R: LJ, July 05, p. 124]—**Graham R. Walden**

C, P

17. **The World Book Encyclopedia.** 2006 ed. Chicago, World Book, 2005. 22v. illus. maps. index. $989.00/set. ISBN 0-7166-0106-0.

In publication since 1917, this well-known and well-respected encyclopedia now comprises 22 volumes, including a special research guide and index volume. With each new edition a significant amount of material is revised and many new entries are added. Many of the updates are to be expected because of the vast amount of new information that has emerged about them within the past year, such as the entries on Arabs and Jupiter. New entries this year include those on computer viruses, eating disorders (which is hard to believe since this has been a topic of interest for years), and search engine. Contributing to this update, more than 27,500 illustrations, photographs, and maps are presented here, including reproductions of fine art and well-drawn illustrations of the human anatomy.

Another key element of the *World Book Encyclopedia* is the plethora of research aids provided. Some examples include: "Facts in Brief" tables, which highlight important facts on counties; "Tables of Terms," which define highly technical entries; "Table of Important Dates," which provide a chronology of historical dates; lists of "Additional Resources" (arranged by difficulty); and a listing of "Related Articles."

World Book has a roster of over 3,000 experts who work as contributors, authenticators, reviewers, and consultants. Content of the encyclopedia is determined by what the publisher refers to as the Classroom Research Project. This project allows for the publisher to poll students in 250 kindergarten through high school classrooms and find out what they are researching, how they are researching, and if the *World Book Encyclopedia* is useful in their research. This encyclopedia is based on the schools' curriculum needs and national and state standards. For this reason, this *Encyclopedia* is most useful in K-12 school media centers and children's reference departments of public libraries.

The *World Book Encyclopedia* is available on an Internet version (by subscription) so libraries will have a choice of the most useful format for their library. Although the print version is bulky, it does provide stunning illustrations and will teach young users valuable research skills.—**Shannon Graff Hysell**

DIRECTORIES

C, P

18.   **The Grey House Homeland Security Directory, 2006: Federal Agencies, State Agencies, Products & Services and Information Resources.** 3d ed. Millerton, N.Y., Grey House Publishing, 2005. 874p. index. $195.00pa. ISBN 1-59237-084-5.

One of four titles in the Grey House 2006 Safety and Security Reference Collection, *The Grey House Homeland Security Directory, 2006* is updated and expanded from the 2d edition published in 2005 with hundreds of new entries (2d ed., see ARBA 2005, entry 43; and 1st ed., see ARBA 2004, entry 41). It is also available online by subscription. This book appears to be unique in its approach to the topic of homeland security—it is a resource guide as well as a directory of people and agencies. Contents of the book were culled from telephone calls and interviews with federal and state agency officials and industry professionals. Two introductory articles comment on the state of United States homeland security preparedness and discuss challenges and issues of facilities, administration, and staff management related to setting up Emergency Operations Centers. A hefty 888 pages (with introduction), the directory is arranged in five sections: Federal Agencies (descriptions and contact information, including names, telephone numbers, and e-mail addresses for top personnel in the Department of Homeland Security and the several sub-agencies within the department, other relevant departments, offices, and commissions plus a directory of the U.S. House of Representatives and Senate and pertinent committees within those bodies); 2) State Agencies (a directory of state executive offices and security-related state agencies arranged similarly to the federal agency listings); Company Listings (a directory of more than 1,900 companies doing business in security industries, preceded by a list of 675 products and services provided by the companies); Industry Resources (arranged in subcategories of associations, periodicals, directories and databases, and show and seminars); and Indexes (arranged by main entry, key personnel, or products and services). Federal and state agencies created to address homeland security concerns have proliferated over the past four years and this directory pulls those resources together in one well-indexed volume and simplifies the task of identifying offices and people responsible for a range of security activities.—**Polly D. Boruff-Jones**

C, P

19.   **Headquarters USA, 2006: A Directory of Contact Information for Headquarters and Other Cent4ral Offices of Major Businesses & Organizations ....** Detroit, Omnigraphics, 2006. 2v. index. $212.00/set. ISBN 0-7808-0804-5. ISSN 1531-2909.

C, P

20.   **HQ Online. http://www.headquartersonline.com.** [Website]. Detroit, Omnigraphics, 2005. $185.00 (single user) to $4,480 (more than 1,000,000 users). Date reviewed: Oct 05.

Formerly published under the titles *National Directory of Addresses and Telephone Numbers* and then the *Business Phone Book USA*, this edition contains more than 114,500 listings in two large volumes. Arranged much like a telephone directory, it is easy to use. Volume 1 is an alphabetic listing of organization names, and volume 2 is a listing by subject. The title covers a great variety of businesses and organizations in the United States and Canada. For-profit businesses, nonprofit organizations, government agencies and offices, colleges and universities, libraries, publications (such as magazines, newsletters, and newspapers), military bases, political organizations, sports organizations, television programs, Internet resources, and more than 4,000 high-profile people can be accessed through this work. Contact information includes a mailing address, telephone number, fax number, toll-free number, Web address, and stock symbols for each organization listed.

Research and verification are ongoing. Published criteria for inclusion are scattered throughout the subject volume. Selection criteria include industry rankings from lists compiled by associations and found in business publications. Most ranking schemes are based on annual sales. Other criteria are used for other listings. For example, libraries are chosen on the basis of population (public libraries) or by volumes owned.

Special features offered by this work are a U.S. map showing time zones and various charts and tables listing abbreviations, area codes, and conglomerates. The index contains useful *see* and *see also* references.

Users also have the option of purchasing this product in an online format. Organization of *HQ Online* is simple and straightforward. Users can conduct a basic search for organizations by company name or stock symbol or they can conduct an advanced search by providing city, state, zip code, or area code numbers. Searches can also be limited to show only companies listing telephone numbers, fax numbers, or Website addresses. For each company the following information is provided: address, telephone and fax numbers (often with toll-free number included), stock exchange and ticker symbol, and a link to the organization's Website (if available). Subject categories are also provided that link to lists of other organizations that fall into the same category. The site also offers a "download" feature that allows the user to download up to 25 company profiles at a time and save them in either text or spreadsheet format.

Both the print and online versions of this directory can be recommended for public and academic libraries. Several online or print sources would have to be consulted for the information found in this one reference set.—**Lois Gilmer**

C, P

21.   **Web Site Source Book, 2005: A Guide to Major U.S. Businesses, Organizations, Agencies, Institutions ....** 10th ed. Detroit, Omnigraphics, 2005. 2176p. index. $160.00pa. ISBN 0-7808-0755-3. ISSN 1089-4861.

The *Web Site Source Book* delivers much more than its title promises. It provides an extensive directory of U.S. organizations, institutions, agencies, businesses, and prominent individuals (such as actors, artists, journalists, fashion designers and models, and political leaders, among many others). Each entry lists the name of a business, an institution, an agency, an organization, or a person, and provides complete contact information, including the mailing address, telephone and fax numbers, and toll-free numbers (if available), as well as the Website address. More than 93,400 entries are included.

The organization of this volume is comparable to that of previous editions (see ARBA 2002, entry 1525 and ARBA 2001, entry 1504). Most entries are arranged alphabetically within specific subject categories. Some categories are subdivided geographically. For example, the "Colleges and Universities-Four-Year" category organizes institutions by state. This edition includes eight new subject categories: "Animation Companies," "Biometric Identification Equipment and Software," "Community Foundations," "Factors," "Flash Memory Devices," "Point-of-Sale and Point-of-Information Systems," "Smart Cards—Manufacturers," and "Swimwear—Manufacturers." Most subject categories provide cross-references to other relevant headings. The volume also includes a selected list of abbreviations used throughout the text, an alphabetic index of individual entries, an index to classified subject headings (listing the various subject categories), and listings of area codes. This well-organized directory is recommended for public, academic, and special libraries.—**Sharon Ladenson**

GOVERNMENT PUBLICATIONS

C, P

22.   **Local and Regional Government Information: How to Find It, How to Use It.** Mary Martin, ed. Westport, Conn., Greenwood Press, 2005. 239p. index. (How to Find It, How to Use It). $65.00. ISBN 1-57356-412-5.

A part of the How to Find It, How to Use It series, this work focuses specifically on local and regional government information. As the editor states in the preface, this book attempts to "provide a framework for understanding how local governments are organized, how they produce information, where that information may be located, and how to go about finding it and using it" (p. xiii).

Composed of 19 separate chapters, the first two provide a general introduction to local and regional government information and the structures of local governments in addition to listing resources for locating general information. The other chapters focus on more specific topics, including: archives; municipal and county codes; courts; census; genealogy; health services; crime; maps; parks and museums; education; environment; planning and zoning; transportation and public works; budgets and taxes; and small business loans, grants, and financial assistance. Each chapter follows a standard format with the bulk of the chapter giving an overview of the topics discussed and an annotated listing of the major relevant resources, including a wealth of Websites. The goal of the authors is not to provide a comprehensive listing of resources, but to list the major resources and give examples of other useful sources of information.

A quick spot check of Websites found that most of the addresses are still functional with only a small minority being broken. In most cases, a simple search using any search engine will find the desired Website. Surprisingly, several items listed as print resources, such as the budget of New York City, are also readily available on the Web. The index is serviceable and lists mainly the titles of the resources and the organizations mentioned in the text.

For most libraries, both academic and public, this will be a welcome addition to their collections. For academic libraries serving programs in public policy or public administration, it is a mandatory purchase and will prove well worth its cost.—**Gregory A. Crawford**

HANDBOOKS AND YEARBOOKS

C, P, S
23.   **The Facts on File Guide to Research.** By Jeff Lenburg. New York, Facts on File, 2005. 560p. index. (Facts on File Library of Language and Literature). $45.00. ISBN 0-8160-5741-9.

Although the author aims to include "valuable tips for beginners and more experienced students of all ages," *The Facts on File Guide to Research* best supports essays and term papers. Some useful items include chapters on evaluating and citing sources; a list of free journals on the Web; and appendixes that give sample citations in APA, MLA, and Chicago styles.

Lenburg's work acknowledges more sources than many guides do, including separate chapters on archival collections, associations and societies, online discussion groups, and libraries. Users must consult the index, since relevant items are found throughout the work, not just in the appropriate "Finding Resources by Subject" chapter. Unfortunately, the *Guide* is not as helpful as it could be for applied projects or topics. For instance, the "Psychology" section (pp. 450-458) does not mention sources (such as the *Mental Measurements Yearbook*), which help clinical students locate testing instruments; and the "Science and Technology" section (pp. 469-480) does not include handbooks or standards. "Treatment of Education" resources is noticeably poor. There is no chapter dedicated to education sources, no education organization listed in the associations chapter, and only three titles (one ceased in 1985) in the magazines and journals chapter.

Although each subject guide begins with an introductory paragraph, this and many other works lack a thorough explanation of how knowledge is produced and disseminated in each discipline. Also, few guides describe how a discipline's scope, vocabulary, and emphasis have changed over time; or tell users which source to consult first according to their particular task. The best research guides balance background information, research approaches, and source lists, such as Stephen Elias' *Legal Research: How to Find and Understand the Law* (13th ed.; Nolo, 2005).

The Facts on File Guide to Research may be a helpful text for English composition classes, or other situations where a one-volume guide to the most important literature sources is needed. However, libraries should supplement it with titles from Libraries Unlimited's Guide to Information Sources series and similar works from other publishers. This work is an optional purchase. [R: SLJ, Dec 05, p. 92]—**Bernadette A. Lear**

C, P, S

24.   ***The New York Times* Guide to Essential Knowledge: A Desk Reference for the Curious Mind.**
New York, St. Martin's Press, 2004. 1096p. index. $35.00. ISBN 0-312-31367-5.

This book is just what you need when you are trying to remember the difference between fusion and cool jazz, Romanesque or Gothic architecture, if you need to know the population of Bangkok, who won the Super Bowl in 1971, or are just looking for a conversational tidbit for the next office party. For instance, did you know, 20 percent of the U.S. workforce earns $8.23/hour or less? The editors provide a broad overview of the arts, economics and business, history, law, literature and drama, mathematics, the media, medicine, mythology, philosophy, science and technology, religion, and sports. Each subject area includes a "Times Focus" article that offers a more contemplative commentary on these broad topic areas. For example, the essay in the technology section discusses how to differentiate human intelligence from machine intelligence. In addition, there are glossaries, histories, and lists (e.g., the world's major rivers and canals). You will also find a grammar review, tips on doing crossword puzzles, demographic data for the American states, U.S. cities and all the countries of the world, primers on food and wine, and nutritional guidelines. The winners of the major awards for the arts and journalism as well as the Nobel Prize are listed by year. This reference ends with a biographical dictionary that covers personalities from pop culture to politics, science, and industry. This handy guide brings together the collective knowledge of *The New York Times* and is a ready-reference source for the general reader with a passion for intriguing facts and figures. [R: LJ, 15 Nov 04, p. 90]—**Adrienne Antink Bien**

INDEXES

C, P

25.   **Book Review Index: 2005 Cumulation.** Dana Ferguson, ed. Farmington Hills, Mich., Gale, 2005. 1042p. $350.00. ISBN 0-7876-7841-4. ISSN 0524-0581.

This 2005 cumulative volume of *Book Review Index* (BRI) covers book reviews featured in reviewing sources in the year 2004. Approximately 81,000 titles are covered and 135,500 reviews are cited. Reviewing sources that are cited here include reviewing journals/annuals (e.g., *Choice*, *Library Journal*, *American Reference Books Annual*), national publications (e.g., *Newsweek*, *Time*), scholarly journals, and electronic reviewing publications (e.g., *Reference Reviews*, *H-Net*, *Humanities and Social Sciences Online*). Each of the 400 publications is listed in the beginning of the volumes with their abbreviation, frequency of publication (e.g., quarterly, biannual), ISSN, postal address, and Website (if available). Reviews are accessed by the author of the book being reviewed or, if the author is unknown, by the title index in the back of each volume. Each citation includes the author's name, book title, illustrator (if applicable), age code or type of book code, abbreviation of the reviewing periodical, volume number or date of issue, page the review appears on, and number of words the review contains. The editor has recently started indicating whether the review is small (1 to 50 words), medium (51-500 words), or large (more than 501 words), as this can be helpful for users of BRI.

The print of this volume is small and the abbreviations for the reviewing journals take some getting used to but, overall, this source is very user friendly. This is a highly recommended resource for academic and public libraries. School libraries (especially elementary and middle schools) may want to consider the *Children's Book Review Index* instead (see ARBA 2005, entry 1032). This title can be purchased in three volumes that come out periodically throughout the year or in this cumulative edition. This resource is available in diskette and online formats as well.—**Shannon Graff Hysell**

MUSEUMS

C, P

26. Danilov, Victor J. **Women and Museums: A Comprehensive Guide.** Walnut Creek, Calif., Alta Mira Press, 2005. 285p. illus. index. (American Association for State and Local History Book Series). $119.95; $49.95pa. ISBN 0-7591-0854-4; 0-7591-0855-2pa.

Although limited geographically to the United States, this directory covers more than 1,000 museums and related facilities founded by, named for, and/or devoted to women. Danilov, the former director of the Museum Management Program at the University of Colorado, is also the author of *Corporate Museums, Galleries, and Visitor Centers* (see ARBA 92, entry 129) and *Museums and Historic Sites of the American West* (see ARBA 2003, entry 83).

Most entries provide information about a museum's history and collections, as well as contact information, a Website address (if available), and museum hours. However, several sections include a subsection of "other" museums; Danilov only provides a brief paragraph about these museums, and fails to include addresses, physical or virtual. The "Other Historic Houses" subsection alone provides information about more than 100 museums. The *Directory of Historic House Museums in the United States* (Alta Mira, 1999), in addition to providing contact information, also covers some "Women's History" house museums that are not covered by Danilov. *The Official Museum Directory* (see ARBA 2003, entry 56) includes information about a museum's publications and attendance, whereas Danilov does not.

The volume is arranged by museum type, such as "Art Museums," "Museums Honoring Exceptional Women," and "Historic Farms and Ranches," which makes finding many of the entries cumbersome. For instance, 22 of the 24 entries in the "Sculpture Garden" section provide nothing more than a cross-reference to another section. The reader still must go to the index to locate the appropriate page number. Individuals wanting information about all museums covered in a specific state will also be frustrated. Although indexes covering museum names, subjects, and "Founders, Donors, and Honorees" improve access, arrangement by state with a more extensive subject index would have been preferable. Better yet, an online edition that would not only let the user decide how the information is presented, but would also address the issue of keeping Website addresses current.

The volume also includes an excellent introduction by historian Susan Armitage, 30 photographs, and a bibliography. Despite the criticisms noted above, Danilov provides a wealth of descriptive information that museum professionals, historians, and the general public will find quite useful.—**Ken Middleton**

PERIODICALS AND SERIALS

C, P

27. **Periodical Title Abbreviations.** 16th ed. Leland G. Alkire Jr. and Cheryl Westerman-Alkire, eds. Farmington Hills, Mich., Gale, 2005. 2v. index. $290.00/set. ISBN 0-7876-9918-7 (v.1); 0-7876-9919-5 (v.2). ISSN 0737-7843.

With the 16th edition of *Periodical Title Abbreviations*, Leland G. Alkire Jr. and Cheryl Westerman-Alkire update a central resource for library reference, adding 8,000 new abbreviations to the 230,000 entries in this 2-volume work. As with earlier versions, this resource's separate abbreviation and title listings provide both patrons and librarians alike with convenient access points to journal citation information. Furthermore, the editors' introductory sections provide users with the entire context surrounding this information's scholarly importance, a user's guide, and a listing of other major abbreviation sources. The editors' product focuses on journals from all disciplines, including the humanities, social sciences, physical sciences, law, religion, health sciences, and business, as well as the Arts and other disciplines. The only question that I might have concerns format. While hard sources of this nature remain valuable for quick and ready-reference collections, perhaps a companion database might be a worthwhile project for Gale and/or the editors to put together. In any event, the books remain valuable tools in themselves.

These books are well worth purchasing either individually or as a set. As noted above, they grant ready access to journal titles and abbreviations. These books are highly recommended for academic, research, and large public libraries.—**David J. Duncan**

QUOTATION BOOKS

C, P

28. **Dictionary of Contemporary Quotations, Volume 10.** 5th rev. ed. John Gordon Burke and Ned Kehde, eds. Evanston, Ill., John Gordon Burke; distr., Manhattan Beach, Calif., PMA, the Independent Book Publishers Association, 2004. 336p. $60.00. ISBN 0-934272-59-X. ISSN 0360-215X.

The purpose of the Dictionary of American Quotations continues to be "to record contemporary quotations which are historically, sociologically, and politically significant" from representative prominent current persons. Thus, the coverage obviously leans very heavily toward political and social issues and less so to the cultural ones.

The fact that this volume is simultaneously called the 5th revised edition and volume 10 exemplifies the publishing complexity of the series. This edition supplements both the foundation volume of the series, volume 5 (which itself contains all the quotations published in volumes 1 through 4), as well as volumes 6 through 9 (see ARBA 2000, entry 54). Volume 10 and all future volumes are supposed to be supplemented via an electronic database, the details of which are not explained in the volume.

The quotations new to this volume were culled from approximately 175 metropolitan newspapers and popular magazines from 1999 to 2004. Thus, since approximately 20 percent of the quotations have been replaced from the earlier volume, the content contains relevant items from the 1970s onward as well as from last year.

The dictionary is arranged into two sections: author and subject. The author component contains the speaker's name, quote, explanation (if necessary), and source. The quotations chosen by prominent Americans are not what one would normally expect to find in a work of this kind. For example, Clinton's weaseling of what "is" is, Carter's lusting in his heart, or Ford's declaration of the absence of subjugation of Eastern Europe are not included, even if those quotes eventually made it later into the press. Interestingly enough, however, we find some older classics: Kennedy's "Ask not" zinger from his inaugural address, Goldwater's defense of extremism, the fatwa against Rushdie, Hitchcock's scorn for actors as "cattle," and Reagan's quip that trees produce air pollution. The subject section is more usable; for those looking for a quote about any of a far range of current topics—football, bureaucracy, love, God, conduct of life, and of course politics—they are likely to find it. The subject index is less complete in providing access to all named speakers. The category "Actors and Actresses," for example, includes some but not all of the included entries; for those not listed here, the user is referred to a *see also* list. Besides the obvious use as a possibly useful, but limited, addition to the quotations collection in an academic or public library, this volume might also be effectively used by students in need of a catchy lead-in phrase for a paper or by speech writers.—**Lawrence Olszewski**

C, P, S

29. **The Oxford Dictionary of American Quotations.** Hugh Rawson and Margaret Miner, comps. New York, Oxford University Press, 2006. 898p. index. $39.95. ISBN 0-19-516823-2.

This moderately priced work features almost 6,000 quotations on over 500 aspects of American life and culture, deriving from expected sources (e.g., Martin Luther King, Jr., John Gunther, Adlai Stevenson, Abraham Lincoln, Ralph Waldo Emerson) and those not-so-expected (Yoko Ono on love, the Grateful Dead on travel). The *Dictionary*, which the introduction states "records our national experiences as viewed by Americans from all walks of life" and also includes selected "foreign observers" (p. vii), is arranged alphabetically by topic (covering such diverse areas as Complaints, Danger & Dangerous People, Seasons, Usefulness, and Cities and States). The acknowledgments list the sources consulted, ranging in publication date from 1945 to 2004, but mostly from the 1990s onwards. There are numerous *see* and *see also* references, and the provenance of every quotation is clearly stated. For example, the quotation "Underpromise. Overperform." in the topic "Boasting" is attributed to "Michael Eisner, saying, quoted on National Public Radio, Morning Edition, Mar. 2, 2004" (entry 85.6). There is a keyword index and a complete author index, which also includes birth and death dates, and a word or two of biography. It should be noted that http://www.bartleby.com/, freely available as of the date of this review, is the "largest collection of quotations ever assembled in print or electronic form" and "contains 86,000 entries." Nine years have passed since the 1st edition of *The Oxford Dictionary of American Quotations*, which contains about 5,000 quotations, many of which leaned toward icons of American history and literature up to the 1980s. Large academic and public libraries, institutions where Internet access is problematic, and libraries needing to add a new source of quotations, will want to purchase this edition; libraries with the previous edition may wish to skip this volume.—**Martha E. Stone**

C, P, S

30.   **The Oxford Dictionary of Humorous Quotations.** 3d ed. Ned Sherrin, ed. New York, Oxford University Press, 2005. 525p. index. $40.00. ISBN 0-19-861004-1.

    For the past eight years, *The Oxford Dictionary of Humorous Quotations* has provided reference librarians with insightful and witty insights into various topics. For the 3d edition, Ned Sherrin eliminated some material, replacing those quotes with others like them from all periods including modern figures. (See ARBA 2002, entry 72, and ARBA 97, entry 71 for reviews of the 1st and 2d editions.) Each section's quotes vary in number but not in their ability to strike at their intended target. As they read through these entries, the audience cannot help but recall the context in which something happened. For entries from the past, the literary work in question comes to mind. Those items from the recent past recall memories of the person expressing themselves either in print or verbally. Sherrin organized his material by subject, allowing his audience easy access. Subject and author indexes provide guidance to specific quotes' locations.

    Sherrin has given us a work with insightful quotes, refreshing the contents for this new edition. As outlined in the introductions to the various editions, the standards are high for this work. While some entries may be more humorous than others, their irony, wit, and sarcasm give readers a perspective on art and life while bringing a smile to their faces. Ironically enough, the front cover quotes Mark Twain: "Classic. A book which people praise and don't read." On the contrary, readers will benefit from this reference work cover to cover, soaking in the insights while smiling and chuckling to themselves along the way. This work is recommended for public, school, and academic libraries' reference desks.—**David J. Duncan**

Part II
SOCIAL SCIENCES

2 Social Sciences in General

GENERAL WORKS

C, P
31. **The Statesman's Yearbook 2006: The Politics, Cultures, and Economies of the World.** New York, Palgrave Macmillan, 2005. 2112p. illus. maps. index. $200.00. ISBN 0-4039-1482-6. ISSN 0081-4601.

The 2006 edition of this standard title continues the publishing tradition begun in 1864 as a premier guide to political and economic information about the countries of the world. The first section contains information about major international organizations, such as the United Nations and the European Union. The second part features an alphabetic listing of the nations of the world, each with paragraphs on the nation's territory, population, government, economy, defense, social institutions, energy and natural resources, and so on. There is also a section with a political map of the world and the flags of all the countries and major international organizations. There are no major innovations in format or content over the previous year's edition. Except in countries that have experienced major upheavals, the statistics and names have simply been updated in the established format and text.

The Statesman's Yearbook is more comprehensive than the *World Almanac and Book of Facts* (2005 ed.; see ARBA 2005, entry 4) or other similar reference resources. In comparison to the *Europa World Yearbook* (2005 ed.; see ARBA 2006, entry 45), *The Statesman's Yearbook* is stronger in descriptive and background text, while the other source has more directory information and statistics. For those readers needing simply the basic facts on each country, the many official government sites on the Internet and the Internet version of the CIA's *World Factbook* (2005 ed.; see entry 32) could be sufficient. *The Statesman's Yearbook* retains its value for convenient overviews so that topics such as education, justice, health, broadcasting, agriculture, trade, and the like can be consulted or compared across various countries. Reflecting its origins, the *Yearbook*'s section on the United Kingdom is particularly strong.—**Henry E. York**

3 Area Studies

GENERAL WORKS

C, P, S

32. **The World Factbook 2005.** By Central Intelligence Agency. Dulles, Va., Potomac Books, 2005. 698p. maps. $54.95. ISBN 1-57488-942-7.

The World Factbook lists 192 counties and several other special interest areas (such as the Antarctica) for a total of 268 entries. Each entry is a list of basic facts and includes information on geography, people, government, economy, communications, transportation, military, and transnational issues. The average entry is about two pages long. There are also six appendixes covering abbreviations, international organizations and groups, selected international environmental agreements, and cross-reference lists. The cross-reference lists consist of country data codes, hydrographic data codes, and geographic names.

The only differences between the Central Intelligence Agency produced volume and the Potomac Books volume are that the CIA version is softbound and has color maps and flags, while the Potomac Books version is hardback and is in all black and white. This is an excellent resource for all reference collections, although redundant for those with the official CIA version.—**Robert M. Lindsey**

UNITED STATES

General Works

C

33. **The Encyclopedia of New England: The Culture and History of an American Region.** Burt Feintuch and David H. Watters, eds. New Haven, Conn., Yale University Press, 2005. 1564p. illus. index. $65.00. ISBN 0-300-10027-2.

Feintuch, director of the Center for Humanities, and Watters, director of the Center for New England Culture, both at the University of New Hampshire, have compiled and edited the contributions of over 1,000 scholars to produce this nearly 1,600-page encyclopedia containing information on all things New England. It is organized alphabetically in 22 different categories: agriculture, architecture, art, cities and suburbs, education, ethnic and racial identity, folklife, gender, geography and environment, history, images and ideas, industry, technology and labor, law, literature, maritime New England, media, music and performing arts, politics, religion, science and medicine, sports and recreation, and tourism.

Each category contains a 15- to 20-page introduction followed by entries on people, places, events, and more arranged in alphabetic order. A brief bibliography of five or more sources is provided at the end of each signed entry. The text is supplemented with 514 black-and-white photographs that take up an average of less than one-eighth of a page, a small number of maps, and a variety of tables and lists that contain such information as population, Pulitzer Prize winners, rivers, disastrous weather, U.S. postage stamps issued with a New England theme, and the largest newspapers arranged by state. The 49-page index provides adequate access to the encyclopedia's entries.

The title would have been improved by including color photographs, more maps, and useful Websites in the bibliography of each entry. That being said, this is a highly recommended resource at the affordable price of $65. It easily supplants Greenwood Press's *New England* (2004) and replaces Facts on File's 1985 *The Encyclopedia of New England*. This work is recommended for all school, public, and academic libraries. [R: LJ, 1 Oct 05, p. 110; BL, 1 & 15 Jan 06, p. 19]—**John J. McCormick**

S

34.   **Internet Sources on Each U.S. State: Selected Sites for Classroom and Library.** Carol Smallwood, Brian P. Hudson, Ann Marlow Riedling, and Jennifer K. Rotole, comps. Jefferson, N.C., McFarland, 2005. 375p. index. $39.95pa. ISBN 0-7864-2108-8.

An attractive, reasonably priced Web directory likely to be of significant interest and value to students of all ages, parents and senior citizens, teachers and professors, and all types of libraries and librarians is a rarity. The compilers of this volume have gathered and organized an easy-to-use numbered set of 2,583 Websites complete with URLs and interested descriptions of each site's content. The 50 chapters treat each individual state, appendix A offers 50 "Sites for all States," and appendix B provides 15 "Sites for Washington, D.C." Within each state chapter, the approximately 50 Website entries appear alphabetically. Each "official" state site appears in bold typeface. Concise notes detail unique or special features of each Website, including mention of the relevant curriculum areas for K-12 classes. Users will appreciate the Website selection criteria: readily accessible, reasonably stable, frequently edited, noncommercial, and password or registration free sites. Specific site content ranges widely, from history and statistics to animals, art, music, museums, and native peoples.

The compilers aim at an audience ranging from pre-kindergarten children through college students as well as educators, but general readers will find this book useful as well as a shortcut to important state and national Web-based information. Adult searchers, especially those new to computer use or interested in travel, will find that it functions as a focused, trustworthy searching aid, especially given its excellent, detailed index. Parents of school-age children may wish to procure a copy for home use. This handbook to online state information should become a standard reference tool for school, public, and undergraduate academic libraries, especially if the publisher and compilers choose to produce revised editions on a regular basis to avoid outdated entries, a common problem for all Internet source-based reference books. [R: LJ, July 05, p. 126]—**Julienne L. Wood**

AFRICA

General Works

C, P

35.   Kalck, Pierre. Xavier-Samuel Kalck. **Historical Dictionary of the Central African Republic.** 3d ed. Lanham, Md., Scarecrow, 2005. 233p. maps. (Historical Dictionaries of Africa, no.93). $65.00. ISBN 0-8108-4913-5.

Most of the structure of this reference is identical to the contents of its 1980 and 1992 editions: chronology, introduction, maps, abbreviations and acronyms, note on spelling, dictionary, and bibliography. There is a substantial amount of new material and the year entries in the chronology, which covers 1800 through 2003, have gotten significantly longer since the last edition.

Although there were some corrections, many of the same editing and content errors that were noted for the previous editions were still not corrected in this edition. In this edition there is a lack of information for some specific dates that fall within a year; for example, the entry for March 20, 1991 says "Important cabinet changes," but it does not explain what they are. Also, any new "people" entries in the dictionary had no date in the entry, making it difficult to place that person in the country's chronology (e.g., Amadou Toumani Toure). The quality of the supplemental grayscale maps could also be improved, as they were difficult to read with no clearly distinguished boundary between the Central African Republic and the surrounding countries. Even with the errors, this historical dictionary contains much substance about a little-known area and is an important resource for anyone beginning study of this country.—**Shelly McCoy**

C

36.   **Reference Guide to Africa: A Bibliography of Sources.** 2d ed. Alfred Kagan, ed. Lanham, Md., Scarecrow, 2005. 222p. index. $55.00. ISBN 0-8108-5208-X.

This work revises and updates *Reference Guide to Africa* by Kagan and Yvette Scheven, published in 1999 (see ARBA 2000, entry 84). The dynamics of research and bibliography more than justifies the effort. In all the work includes nearly 800 formal entries, with many others noticed in passing within them. These are divided into 23 categories by subject and/or format, and a significant portion of the whole represent titles published more recently than the 1st edition. All of Africa, including that north of the Sahara, is included. In addition to print materials, there are inevitably frequent references to Internet sources of information. The work concludes with excellent author/title and subject indexes.

What once might have been a solid and longstanding contribution to African studies now must be looked at somewhat differently. While print remains both the preferred and the most practical format for large chunks of scholarly communication networks, certain genres are only rendered less useful by being published in print. The appearance of *Reference Guide to Africa* and works like it afford the occasion for wondering whether their future lies, almost entirely, as Web-based compilations that can be updated frequently and painlessly. On a Website this work would look like the print version only momentarily, after which it would become more and more useful. Since its main utility should be for introducing undergraduates to the elements of African studies, it especially makes sense to offer it in a form that is both more attractive to this presumed audience and that permits it to remain current on a continuing basis. It could also easily be expanded indefinitely. Publishers must be fully aware of this and we can only hope that within a short time the transformation from print to virtual takes place, at least where the arguments support it.—**David Henige**

C, P

37.   **Research, Reference Service, and Resources for the Study of Africa.** Deborah M. LaFond and Gretchen Walsh, eds. Binghamton, N.Y., Haworth Press, 2004. 290p. index. $39.95; $29.95pa. ISBN 0-7890-2508-6; 0-7890-2509-4pa.

This is a guide to the resources available for the study of Africa, with emphasis on the difficulties that doing research on Africa can entail. It recognizes that librarians want to pass skills along to students. There is considerable attention to the changing technological nature of doing research, such as electronic databases and Web-based sources of information, along with the concerns about it. It has nine articles, each by a different author, divided into two sections. The first is on African studies in the United States, with its long first article, partially using an effective question-and-answer technique, to discuss the hazards frequently encountered while doing African research. There is an article on teaching African studies bibliography and on selected Internet resources for African business and economic information. The second section is on collaboration and innovation in Africa and the United States. Two articles address how reference librarians can help scholarly research as electronic resources influence reference services and collection development, and expand the study of African women writers in U.S. universities. There are three articles relating to how professionals in the United States can assist African efforts in curriculum development, a discussion of the question of African studies collections in Africa, and how to support libraries and indigenous publishing in Africa, all while recognizing that often the environment is tumultuous. This monograph is published simultaneously as *The Reference Librarian*, volume 42, numbers 87/88. While this book may appear to be aimed at those in research libraries, it contains valuable information for finding what patrons want about to know about Africa at any library.—**J. E. Weaver**

ASIA

General Works

C, P, S

38. Hanks, Reuel R. **Central Asia: A Global Studies Handbook.** Santa Barbara, Calif., ABC-CLIO, 2005. 467p. illus. index. (Global Studies, Asia). $55.00; $60.00 (e-book). ISBN 1-85109-656-6; 1-85109-661-2 (e-book).

   With the breakup of the Soviet Union at the end of the Cold War, more people became gradually aware of these struggling new nations (formerly Soviet Republics) in Central Asia. They received diplomatic recognition and more exposure in the Western press. This attention dramatically increased with the establishment of American bases in this region to support the invasion of Afghanistan. While previous entries in this series have focused on only one country, this item covers Uzbekistan, Kazakhstan, and Kyrgyzstan. For each country there is a thoroughly subdivided descriptive narrative of the geography, history, economy, society, institutions, and contemporary issues. This is followed by a reference section that contains a chronology; information about significant people, places, and events; a discussion of national languages; food and etiquette in the country; a short directory of related organizations; and an annotated bibliography of important monographic and periodical publications. While one can find similar or related information in other encyclopedias or reference books, such as the expensive Europa publications, this work collects a lot of varied information in one place, similar to the old Country Studies series from the Library of Congress. Hanks (Professor of Geography, Oklahoma State University) also compiled an annotated bibliography on Uzbekistan as part of ABC-CLIO's World Bibliographical Series (1999). As this item covers multiple countries, it is suitable for the reference collections of all academic and public libraries. It is also available as an e-book through netLibrary.—**Daniel K. Blewett**

China

C

39. **China Today: An Encyclopedia of Life in the People's Republic.** Jing Luo, ed. Westport, Conn., Greenwood Press, 2005. 2v. illus. index. $199.95/set. ISBN 0-313-32170-1.

   Focusing on economic reforms and social changes of the People's Republic of China (PRC) since its establishment in 1949, *China Today* provides a critical view of Chinese communism in transition from Mao, Deng, Jiang, to the fourth generation leadership, Hu Jiangtao and Wen Jiaobao. The encyclopedia begins with a chronology of the PRC, followed by a guide to related topics, 239 entries, selected bibliography, and an index. The entries are arranged in alphabetic order, each containing an essay, a *see also* reference, and a bibliography for further reading. The guide to related topics contains 22 categories covering agriculture and rural China; arts and literature; diplomacy and foreign relations; economy, trade, and business cultures; education; ethnic groups and issues; government, law, and administration; individuals; intellectuals; labor and human resource management; media; medicine and health; military, criminal justice, and human rights; political campaigns and leaders; population issues; regions; religion and spiritual life; social issues; Taiwan; United States and China; urban China; and women. It would be helpful if the entries under the guide were given corresponding page numbers for quick reference. The selection of entries is uneven, with "economy, trade, and business cultures" enlisting 45 entries while "religion and spiritual life" and "women" have only five entries each. However, the quality of the essays is generally good with interesting illustrations throughout. The title in two volumes is priced very high at $199.95 for the set. This work is recommended for academic libraries. [R: LJ, Aug 05, pp. 120-122]—**Karen T. Wei**

AUSTRALIA AND THE PACIFIC AREA

C, P

40.   Quanchi, Max, and John Robson. **Historical Dictionary of the Discovery and Exploration of the Pacific Islands.** Lanham, Md., Scarecrow, 2005. 299p. maps. (Historical Dictionaries of Discovery and Exploration, no.2). $70.00. ISBN 0-8108-5395-7.

This is the second book in the series Historical Dictionaries of Discovery and Exploration, and measures up to the high standard of the first volume, *Historical Dictionary of the Discovery and Exploration of Australia*, by Alan Day, two years ago (see ARBA 2004, entry 468). If the exploration of the Pacific can seem to us the most exciting in the annals of exploration, the editors make it clear that it was to those who undertook it extremely dangerous: so many men died young from illness, scurvy, or hostile clashes with natives. Contacts between the very different cultures were frequently disastrous for both Europeans and indigenous people.

With the history of Pacific exploration rewritten less nationalistically, the editors record exploration by Portuguese, Spanish, and Dutch earlier than by British. They emphasize the importance of imperial rivalry in exploration, even into the twentieth century with the Dutch/British competition to be first to reach and climb the highest mountains of New Guinea. In the Dutch expedition, 80 of 800 men lost their lives. Another important factor always acting as an undercurrent was the myth of South Seas paradises, first spread by Bougainville concerning Tahiti in the last third of the eighteenth century, a romantic fantasy that captured and held the European imagination even to the present. (In fact, one finds often enough in present-day Tahiti precisely the kind of rudeness one used to encounter in France in the 1970s.)

The book has a comprehensive series of appendixes: postulated estimates of the times of the migration of the peoples of the Pacific, a chronological listing of European voyages and of first discoveries by European, and an extensive bibliography of over 100 pages. The bibliography focuses specifically on the islands of the Pacific, not on the Pacific Rim. This is a valuable, extremely interesting work of scholarship.
—**John B. Beston**

EUROPE

General Works

C, P, S

41.   **Eastern Europe: An Introduction to the People, Lands, and Culture.** Richard Frucht, ed. Santa Barbara, Calif., ABC-CLIO, 2005. 3v. illus. maps. index. $285.00/set; $310.00 (e-book). ISBN 1-57607-800-0; 1-57607-801-9 (e-book).

This set gives a thorough overview of the social, political, and economic histories of most countries in Eastern Europe, written by scholars specializing in that area. Here, Eastern Europe includes nations such as Estonia, Latvia, Greece, and Albania, but curiously does not include Belarus and Ukraine, two very important nations that certainly play a major role in Eastern European politics and society—arguably more so then the nations on the periphery that rarely identify themselves as Eastern Europe. The stated purpose of this encyclopedia is to act as a companion to the superb *Encyclopedia of Eastern Europe: From the Congress of Vienna to the Fall of Communism* (see ARBA 2001, entry 438). The coverage of each nation is lengthy yet clearly written and easy to understand for the nonspecialist, while at the same time of sufficient depth to satisfy the needs of researchers in the field. In addition to the overviews, which range in length from 40 to 80 pages, each section has a number of additional articles on related topics. Particularly useful are sections explaining the differences between the Serbian and Croatian languages—both the linguistic and the political explanations. There are also a series of historical maps and a large number of photographs (sadly none in color) to add to the appeal and usefulness of the text. Each section ends with a selected bibliography as well as an extensive historical chronology. A thorough index rounds out the work. [R: SLJ, June 05, p. 90; LJ, 1 April 05, pp. 122-123]—**Terri Tickle Miller**

Germany

C, P

42.   Buse, Dieter K. **The Regions of Germany: A Reference Guide to History and Culture.** Westport, Conn., Greenwood Press, 2005. 290p. illus. maps. index. $59.95. ISBN 0-313-32400-X.

Buse has provided readers with an overview of Germany by region both culturally and historically—a resource that has been absent from the English language for a long time. The volume is divided into 16 chapters, one for each region, beginning with Baden-Wuerttemberg, and ending with Thuringia. Black-and-white photographs are used throughout, and although they are of varying quality and clarity, they do provide quick highlights of architecture and landscape.

Each chapter follows a basic outline, including the following elements: special aspects, regional traits, geographic features, history, economy, main cities, capital, attractions, customs, cultural attributes and contributions, visual arts, literature, music, film, theater, customs and festivals, leisure and sport, opera, museums and galleries, civics and remembrance, and cuisine. A brief seven-page chronology is included as an appendix, starting with 9 C.E. The review of history is succinct and would be a quick read for anyone seeking an overview. The selected bibliography contains references for both print and Web resources. The 20-page index is quite detailed, and would be very helpful for quick reference work.

Author Buse notes in his acknowledgements that this work is the culmination of 30 years of "working with the history of Germany." Clearly this work is not intended as a substitute for the many multivolume histories of Germany, but it does adequately cover the whole country, region by region, with a consistently applied outline that would be very useful for undergraduate students in German courses as well as overview courses in European history and culture. This work is highly recommended. [R: LJ, 1 Sept 05, p. 176]—**Graham R. Walden**

LATIN AMERICA AND THE CARIBBEAN

Mexico

P, S

43. **Junior Worldmark Encyclopedia of the Mexican States.** Farmington Hills, Mich., U*X*L/Gale, 2004. 336p. illus. maps. index. $58.00. ISBN 0-7876-9161-5.

The *Junior Worldmark Encyclopedia of the Mexican States* presents readable and well-organized introductory information on each state, as well as the entire country of Mexico. The volume begins with an overview of the content and organization of the entire text as well as a description of selected sources consulted. The editors also include a 19-page glossary of frequently used terms and an index. Separate entries focusing on individual states and the Federal District are arranged alphabetically, followed by an article on Mexico itself. The state profiles begin with information about the origin and pronunciation of the state name, the date of entry into the country, the capital, official holidays, a description of the coat of arms, and the standard time (in relation to Greenwich Mean Time). Each state entry also indicates that individual Mexican states do not have their own flags. Entries cover 27 topics, such as (among others) the environment and wildlife, history, economics, agriculture, education, travel and recreation, media, sports, and famous people from the past and present. Entries also include maps of each state, and a bibliography of selected print and Web resources. Students at the secondary level should find this text especially useful. This work is recommended for public and school libraries. [R: SLJ, Feb 05, p. 84]—**Sharon Ladenson**

MIDDLE EAST

General Works

S

44. **Middle East Conflict Reference Library.** By Tom Pendergast, Sara Pendergast, and Ralph G. Zerbonia. Farmington Hills, Mich., U*X*L/Gale, 2006. 3v. illus. maps. index. (Middle East Conflict Reference Library). $172.00/set. ISBN 0-7876-9455-X.

This comprehensive series provides a look at the complex political, social, and military turmoil of the Middle East. The simple format provides the intended juvenile audience with objective information that helps to untangle the numerous conflicts and make them and the Middle East more comprehensible. Each of the three volumes: *Almanac*, *Biographies*, and *Primary Sources* contain the same reader's guide, timeline, and "Words to Know", helping each volume stand on its own. The *Almanac* explores the motivations of the conflicts in an easy-to-read manner, although the format of the "Country Facts" would be easier to read if the headings and subheadings were not all bold and in the same font. *Biographies* provides essays on 26 prominent figures involved in conflicts, while *Primary Sources* offers official documents, political philosophies, and personal accounts related to conflicts, then explains them and what happens next in a way for all to understand. Sidebars, of mostly vocabulary definitions, are included to help throughout all volumes. The paperback cumulative index, while helpful, would be best added to each volume or at the end of one volume for maximum durability and usefulness. Educators will appreciate that the "Research and Activities" section in the *Almanac* gives suggestions for classroom projects and all volumes include citations of books, periodicals, and Websites so that the beginning scholar can learn more.—**Shelly McCoy**

Israel

C, P

45.	**Dictionary of the Israeli-Palestinian Conflict: Culture, History, and Politics.** New York, Macmillan Reference USA/Gale Group, 2005. 2v. illus. maps. $270.00/set. ISBN 0-02-865977-5.

For the greater part of the twentieth century and spilling into the twenty-first century, Jewish/Israeli-Arab disputes have agitated the Middle East and have shaken the foundations of global balance. Efforts to end these discords depend largely on a full understanding of how this conflict originated, developed, and intensified. Part of the problem is the approach that sees the history of the Middle East in the form of a tapeworm that grinds forth period after period, and the other is the theory that considers the Middle East culture self-contained with a life-cycle as predetermined as that of a eucalyptus tree. Also reactionary are viewpoints obsessed by images of Arab and Jewish nationalism driven along a collision course toward a no-return summit. Arguably, the undercurrent of the Israeli-Palestinian conflict are the misunderstanding between the belligerents generated by self-pride in a nation's past, the lack of empathy to the outsider, realized fears and prejudice, and the inability to commit to a trust in *Shalom-Salam*. To explain the history and current malaise of Israeli-Palestinian realpolitik is the focus of the *Dictionary of the Israeli-Palestinian Conflict*. Major shapers and shakers, ideology and issues, movements, organizations and political parties, events, and treaties are offered in 1,140 cross-referenced entries, which are enhanced by a glossary, images and maps, and selected bibliography. This is a reader-friendly and a reliable reference tool.—**Zev Garber**

4 Economics and Business

GENERAL WORKS

Dictionaries and Encyclopedias

C, P

46. Folsom, W. Davis. **Understanding American Business Jargon: A Dictionary.** 2d ed. Westport, Conn., Greenwood Press, 2005. 364p. $79.95. ISBN 0-313-33450-1.

Buzzwords or business jargon can make communicating in the business world difficult or even impossible. Therefore, this 2d edition of a handy reference guide will help businesspeople, researchers, and students gain understanding of not only the buzzword-laden business-speak but business culture. The over 2,500 colorful terms and concepts include "alpha geek," "golden handcuffs," "800-pound gorilla," "eleventh hour," "cube farm," "Yettie," and "echo bubble"—terms which have evolved and transformed theories, practices, and procedures into catchy phrases or even acronyms that can puzzle novices. Folsom, a marketing and economics professor at the University of South Carolina, understands that jargon can be exclusionary; but if your audience knows the jargon, it can be a succinct, efficient way of conveying your thoughts and message. Folsom's work itself attempts to capture the essence of the business world in the new millennium. Each entry briefly defines words and phrases used and many contain examples of usage from a wide variety of popular business publications. Cross-references and a list of acronyms are also included. A short bibliography provides additional resources. Useful in all areas of business communications, Folsom's work will really help students whose first language is not English. This well-written, entertaining glimpse into the ever-evolving American business culture and environment is a worthwhile purchase for academic and large public libraries. [R: BL, 1 & 15 Jan 06, p. 155]—**Susan C. Awe**

C, P

47. **Harrap's Spanish and English Business Dictionary.** New York, McGraw-Hill, 2005. 1v. (various paging). $27.95. ISBN 0-07-146337-2.

This latest entry to the Spanish-English business dictionary market was prepared with assistance from PricewaterhouseCoopers Spain. Its 40,000 entries cover all facets of business and industry, including marketing, accounting, insurance, law, and telecommunications, with a particularly strong emphasis on computing technology, a quality that distinguishes it from its competitors. This volume has many favorable features: large font, indication of gender and part of speech, usage notes, geographical labels and, best of all, price. The editors make it clear, for example, that *ordenador* is used for "computer" in Spain, but *computadora* in Latin America. Communication guides and a listing of nations of the world, each in Spanish and English, supplement the dictionary. The examples, spelling, and monetary terms, however, show a very British slant, and the poor binding will not stand up to repeated use. Although it pales in comparison with the 100,000 entries of the *Routledge Spanish Dictionary of Business, Commerce, and Finance* (see ARBA 99, entry 146), it more than compensates for it with its attractive price and currency.—**Lawrence Olszewski**

C, P

48.   Krismann, Carol H. **Encyclopedia of American Women in Business: From Colonial Times to the Present.** Westport, Conn., Greenwood Press, 2005. 2v. index. $175.00/set. ISBN 0-313-32757-2.

The *Encyclopedia of American Women in Business: From Colonial Times to the Present* is an excellent resource for students, teachers, scholars, and librarians to browse and explore the contributions women have made to business and industry, as well as gain an understanding of notable successful women. This 2-volume encyclopedia provides details on the lives of over 300 women executives, women entrepreneurs, or women business owners, from the early 1600s to the present. Entries are arranged alphabetically and provide information on all aspects of the woman's life, such as education, positions held in companies, businesses owned or managed, personal struggles, and accomplishments in business. Profiles provide both historical and current facts and are written in a fairly balanced manner with only some editorial comments. Women included are only those involved in profit-making occupations and endeavors, not those involved in founding or running nonprofit organizations, or those who are primarily actresses, musicians, interior or jewelry designers, or government officials. Entries are an average of one to two pages in length and are easily readable for all users. Suggestions for further reading, significant Websites, and cross-references to other subjects and entries are found at the end of each entry.

The *Encyclopedia of American Women in Business* also includes separate entries on topics related to American businesswomen such as childcare, affirmative action, salaries, flexible work arrangements, and work-life balance. Other general business topics on significant legislation, industries, and organizations are also covered.

This encyclopedia is further enhanced by an alphabetic list of entries provided at the beginning of the first volume. Also included in the set is a chronology of events from colonial times to the present as an easy way to browse for women and accomplishments by time period. Appendixes include "*Fortune Magazine*'s Fifty Most Powerful Women in American Business from 1998-2003," businesswomen by ethic heritage, businesswomen by time period, businesswomen by profession, and businesswomen in Junior Achievement's Global Business Hall of Fame. An extensive bibliography and a thorough index are also included, making the *Encyclopedia of American Women in Business* a solid addition to public, academic, and business library collections. [R: LJ, 1 April 05, p. 124]—**Kara JoLynn Gust**

Directories

C, P

49.   **BizStats.com. http://www.bizstats.com/.** [Website]. Free. Date reviewed: 2005.

In this easy-to-use Website users can find profitability and operating ratios for S corporations, partnerships, and sole proprietorships for industries like furniture stores, electronics, gas stations, and sporting goods stores. Users can find "Retail Industry Benchmarks" like sales per foot (SPF), average sales per foot in malls, and SPF for a three-year trend. You can find lists of the "Most Popular Small Businesses," "Current Ratios and Balance Sheet Ratios by Industry," and "Industry Profitability for Sole Proprietorships," for example. This site has financial and operating ratios for 30,000 industry segments. Even if the industry one is looking for is not here, this site will show users how to do a financial and industry analysis using the figures they have gathered. CPA Patrick O'Rourke has produced the data on this well-organized, comprehensive site for small business statistics.—**Susan C. Awe**

C, P

50.   **Hoover's Handbook of American Business 2005.** 15th ed. Austin, Tex., Hoover's, 2005. 950. index. $225.00. ISBN 1-57311-101-5. ISSN 1055-7202.

One of the Hoover's line of popular business references, the *American Business* edition provides standard business and financial profiles for 750 of America's "largest and most influential companies," plus information on more than 50 of America's largest privately owned companies. Other titles in Hoover's series include *Hoover's Handbook of Emerging Companies* (see entry 51), *Hoover's Handbook of Private Companies* (see ARBA 2006, entry 133), and *Hoover's Handbook of World Business* (see entry 72).

Companies have been selected based on size, growth rate, and visibility. Additionally, the editors have sought to include a diverse range of types of businesses. Entries for the businesses profiled include company overview, history, officers, locations, products/operations, and identification of competitors. Additionally, a chart details historical financials plus 10-year annualized annual growth rate. The Hoover's handbooks are known for the informative and engaging nature of the company overviews, and this edition continues that tradition.

Supplementing the alphabetically arranged company entries are a terrific collection of lists, such as "The 300 Largest Companies by Sales" and its unfortunate opposite, "50 Shrinking Companies by Employment Growth." A handful of indexes (by industry, headquarters location, and executives' names) further enhance the handbook's usefulness.—**G. Kim Dority**

C, P

51. **Hoover's Handbook of Emerging Companies 2005.** Austin, Tex., Hoover's, 2005. 527p. index. $140.00. ISBN 1-57311-104-X. ISSN 1069-7519.

As one part of a four title series that covers American business (see entry 50), private companies (see ARBA 2006, entry 133), world business (see entry 72), and emerging companies, this 2005 edition offers one-page, alphabetic company profiles and some 600 short, alphabetic summaries of important emerging public companies. This handbook, like others in the series and on the Internet (http://www.hoovers.com), represents an important source of information on companies the general public has read or heard about in the news. The longer profiles combine an overview of performance with brief history, basic data (e.g., officers, locations, competitors), and six years of financial and employment information. The short reports, the largest section in the handbook, include the basics (e.g., name, address, officers) with sales figures for 2003, names of three competitors, and a one-paragraph summary of company status and developments. Some companies are listed in both sections of the easy-to-read and easy-to-use profiles and statistics. Section contents and making the best use of data are clearly explained. Separate indexes by industry, headquarters location, and brands/company/people names are provided. In addition, there are tables of the top companies for different factors (e.g., top 100 in 5-year sales growth) and reports on the hot, fastest-growing, and best companies as identified by key business journals such as *Business Week*, *Fortune*, and *Forbes*.

For the amount of information provided, the price is attractive. This volume and the others in the series are recommended for all libraries serving undergraduates or a public interested in investment opportunities that do not have access to the online version through Hoover's.—**Sandra E. Belanger**

C, P

52. **Hoover's Masterlist of Major U.S. Companies 2006.** Austin, Tex., Hoover's, 2005. 990p. index. $285.00. ISBN 1-57311-107-4.

As with its other directories, Hoover's presents this material in an attractive format with alphabetically arranged entries printed in bold, easy-to-read fonts. This 2006 edition of *Hoover's MasterList of Major U.S. Companies* packs a lot of information into 1 volume, listing over 5,000 companies and organizations in the United States. Public companies with sales over $125 million are included in the directory. Entries are brief due to the large number of listings in one volume. Each entry includes a summary of the company's products and operations, the mailing and Web address of the firm, the top three executives (CEO, CFO, and human resources contact), an indication if the company is publicly traded or privately held, and a selection of recent company financials. The financial information, when available, includes sales, net income, market value, and number of employees for the previous five years, and also indicates the percentage change from the previous year for each category.

Valuable features include company rankings lists arranging the top 500 U.S. companies by sales, employees, 5-year sales growth, and market value. Useful indexes include the "Index by Industry," which allows one to browse for companies by major and specific industry grouping, and the "Index by Headquarters," which lists by state and city the corporate headquarters of each of the companies included in the directory. Another less useful listing, "Index by Stock Exchange Symbol," shows the stock exchange and lists the page number of the entry for each of the public companies listed in the directory.

A unique quality of this publication, the directory lists many private companies and nonpublic entities, such as foundations, sports teams and leagues, universities, not-for-profits, and major government-owned entities such as the United States Postal Service. This inclusion of many organizations that would not normally be listed in a business directory provides a scope of content rarely seen in similar publications. This guide is recommended for all libraries, especially those with small business reference collections in need of a current directory.—**Glenn S. McGuigan**

C, P

53. **National Directory of Minority-Owned Business Firms.** 13th ed. Washington, D.C., Business Research Services Inc., 2006. 1v. (various paging). index. $295.00. ISBN 0-933527-82-9.

The directory lists minority-owned businesses throughout the country. It is organized by SIC code number and encompasses virtually all codes. Within each SIC code, users find a geographic classification. Firms are indexed by name and may be listed under multiple SIC codes. Entries include firm name, address, telephone number, contact person, and a description of the services performed. Most entries identify the type of minority owner and alert the user if the business has government contract experience or is certified. A number of entries include other information, such as Web address, general sales and employee information, and date of incorporation. Although the prefatory material explains the criteria for the listings, it is unclear exactly how the list was compiled. Thus, the directory's comprehensiveness is questionable.

The directory is in its 13th edition and, despite its limitations, serves the useful purpose of providing users with guidance regarding minority-owned businesses. If a library's patrons request this type of information, the directory is a credible and convenient source. It would be difficult to compile a list of minority-owned businesses without the aid of this directory.—**Holly Dunn Coats**

C, P

54. **National Directory of Woman-Owned Business Firms.** 13th ed. Washington, D.C., Business Research Services Inc., 2006. 700p. index. $295.00. ISBN 0-933527-83-7.

This useful title brings together information on businesses in the United States where one or more of the principal owners or the majority of shareholders are women. Additionally, the directory notes if a business is also minority-owned, although the specific minority (black Americans, Hispanic Americans, Asian Americans, Native Americans, Native Hawaiians, or Hasidic Jews) is not given. The main section of the volume is arranged according to the four-digit Standard Industrial Classification (SIC) business descriptions, then alphabetically by state, zip code, and company name. The information was compiled by using various federal, state, and regional organizations and from the listees themselves.

As in earlier editions, each entry includes name, address, telephone and fax number, a contact person, and a very brief description of the product. Some entries also include sales information and references. There is a company name index and an alpha industry class index. There is no information given regarding the amount of changes since the last edition. Although users might wish for more consistency in the information given for each entry, this directory serves its purpose well.—**Michele Russo**

Handbooks and Yearbooks

C

55. **Business Statistics of the United States, 2005: Patterns of Economic Change.** 10th ed. Cornelia J. Strawser and Mark Siegal, eds. Lanham, Md., Bernan Associates, 2005. 545p. index. $147.00. ISBN 1-886222-24-X. ISSN 1086-8488.

Business Statistics of the United States: Patterns of Economics Change presents statistical data, largely from World War II through 2003, on the U.S. economy by means of some 3,000 time series. The comprehensive collection of data series is conveniently displayed in a single volume, supported by pertinent explanatory comments. Thus, basic statistics become meaningful information that can be extremely useful in understanding economic trends of the last half-century and in providing bases for forecasting the future. Roughly half of the volume provides essential series on the U.S. economy (e.g., national income, gross domestic product, industrial production, income, savings, investment, governmental receipts and outlays, foreign trade, prices, employment, energy, financial markets, international comparisons). The data sets reflect revisions made in 2003 to the National Income and Production Accounts. Other series include industry data utilizing the North American Industry Classification System, summary historical data by quarter and month, and selected state and regional data. Most of the series have been drawn from government sources, organized and presented in a manner that offers easy access to the vast spectrum of economic data. Contact information and relevant publications are given for major sources. In addition to statistical tables, each chapter contains graphs, commentary, definitions, and notes (data availability, references, supplements, and revisions). Also included are a preface, an overview of U.S. economy, an explanation of expanded historical statistics, special notes, comparison of employment trends as measured by the Bureau of Labor Statistics household and payroll surveys, table of contents, and an index. This is a comprehensive and convenient reference for researchers, practitioners, and students.—**William C. Struning**

C, P

56. Mishel, Lawrence, Jared Bernstein, and Sylvia Allegretto. **The State of Working America 2004/2005.** Ithaca, N.Y., Cornell University Press, 2005. 484p. index. $24.95pa. ISBN 0-8014-8962-8.

Since 1988, the Economic Policy Institute (EPI) has prepared an examination of the effect of the economy on the quality of life and living standards of America's working families. Lawrence Mishel, President of the EPI, has contributed research to all of the previous editions of this work; Jared Bernstein has contributed to five previous editions, and Sylvia Allegretto joined the EPI in 2003. Using a broad spectrum of data gathered from various sources, the authors evaluate family income, taxes, wages, wealth ratios, unemployment, and poverty.

In the previous edition from the summer of 2002, the economy did not seem promising for working families. The unemployment rate was high, job growth was low, wages were low, and the number of long-term unemployed was growing. Although the job growth rate has improved since mid-2004, early signs indicate that wage inequality is returning to a level not seen since the 1980s. The data point to the fact that the U.S. economy is capable of generating more wealth than any other developed nation, but there is little evidence that this wealth is reaching the working families responsible for generating this wealth (i.e., doing the work).

This volume consists of an executive summary, a section describing the comprehensive documentation and methodology used to derive the eye-opening results of this study, and seven chapters of data and charts. Chapters include: "Family Income"; "Wages"; "Jobs"; "Wealth"; "Poverty"; "Regional Analysis" (showing a labor market slump in most states); and "International Companies." Appendix A details family income data series, and appendix B demonstrates wage analysis computations. A complete, 8-page bibliography begins on page 463, and a 12-page index begins on page 471.

The authors' analysis points to an economy at a crossroads. Will the benefits of faster recovery and productivity flow freely to all income classes? Or will declining wages and high average unemployment keep living standards stagnant for working families? They believe the documented evidence shows the economy is moving in the wrong direction. They maintain that policy-makers and citizens can make a difference—that the economy is not determined by fate. In fact, they "firmly reject that notion [fate] and maintain that we can . . . we must wield public policy most effectively to push the economy toward the better path." This book is recommended for corporate, public and academic libraries. [R: LJ, 1 Feb 05, p. 118]—**Laura J. Bender**

ACCOUNTING

C, P

57.   Siegel, Joel G., and Jae K. Shim. **Dictionary of Accounting Terms.** 4th ed. Hauppauge, N.Y., Barron's Educational Series, 2005. 506p. $13.99pa. ISBN 0-7641-2898-1.

Accounting is the language of business. Accounting concepts such as profit and loss, assets and liabilities, and return on investment measure the financial success of business enterprises. Owners, managers, lenders, and investors all depend on the accuracy of timely financial statements. Managers and manufacturers require detailed cost accounting to make decisions about what to produce and what prices are required to ensure a reasonable profit.

The 4th edition of Barron's Educational Series' *Dictionary of Accounting Terms* is a handy 500-page lexicon of modern accounting. Many entries have examples and illustrations. Cross-references within the definitions point to related entries. For example, the entry on *depreciation* explains that the term refers to both the decline in value of an economic asset as it ages and spreading the original cost of fixed assets, such as plant and equipment, over their estimated useful lives. Cross-references are made to common methods of depreciation such as *straight-line depreciation* and *accelerated depreciation*. Explicit examples of depreciation accounting are given in related entries on the Double Declining Balance Method and Sum-Of-The-Year's—Digits (SYD) Method.

From Activity-Based Costing (ABC) and Generally Accepted Accounting Principles (GAAP) to Zero-Based Budgeting, the whole panoply of accounting regulation and rules are defined. Contemporary developments, such as the passage of the Sarbanes-Oxley Act (SOX) in 2002, are covered. Passed in response to the recent accounting scandals involving Enron and WorldCom, SOX established the Public Company Accounting Oversight Board (PCAOB) to oversee the auditors of public companies to ensure that the interests of investors are protected. All of the most important accounting-related organizations are covered: The American Institute of Certified Public Accountants (AICPA), the Financial Accounting Standards Board (FASB), the Securities and Exchange Commission (SEC), and the International Accounting Standards Board (IASB). Notable publications such as the *Accounting Review* and the *Journal of Accountancy* also have entries.

Legal, finance, investment, management, mathematical, tax, and other business terms are included as part of the vocabulary an accountant must be acquainted with. For example, the Capital Asset Pricing Model, Correlation Coefficients, and Simple Regression all have entries because they are used to value financial assets. Many computer-related words are defined because of the ubiquity of information technology in recording, analyzing, and reporting accounting information. A list of acronyms and abbreviations appears at the end of the work along with an appendix presenting compound value, present value, and t-statistic tables. This new edition of the dictionary is an excellent, affordable source of brief definitions of key accounting and related terms for students, educators, practitioners, and librarians.—**Peter Zachary McKay**

BUSINESS SERVICES AND INVESTMENT GUIDES

C, P

58. **Plunkett's Investment & Securities Industry Almanac 2005.** Jack W. Plunkett, ed. Houston, Tex., Plunkett Research, 2004. 449p. index. $249.99pa. (w/CD-ROM). ISBN 1-59392-016-4.

Plunkett's Investment & Securities Industry Almanac 2005 covers part of what was formerly included in the broader *Plunkett's Financial Services Almanac* (see ARBA 2003, entry 169). The latter title has been divided and expanded into three separate new titles: *Plunkett's Banking, Mortgage, and Credit Industry Almanac* (see entry 62); *Plunkett's Insurance Industry Almanac* (see ARBA 2006, entry 196); and, the subject of this review, *Plunkett's Investment & Securities Industry Almanac 2005.*

Where the *Financial Services Almanac* covered the "Financial Services 500," the more specialized *Investment & Securities Almanac* covers 328 companies (referred to as the "Investment 300") in the investment industry and related industry segments. Industry segments include brokers, investments, asset management, exchanges, services, and technology. Most of the companies profiled are based in the United States, but 79 firms are headquartered elsewhere. All were selected for inclusion because of their prominence in the investment industry.

Company information is presented in the same format found in the earlier Plunkett's title. Listed alphabetically, a full page is devoted to each entry. The amount of white space on each page varies with the company. A standard company profile includes: types of businesses the company is involved in; brands, divisions, or affiliates; contact information and Website; short lists of company officers; summary financial information; salary and benefit information; locations in which the company has a presence, including international; and a "Growth Plans/Special Features" section that provides several paragraphs of narrative information about the companies' business activities, position in the industry, and recent events. Each company entry also shows its ranking within its industry group by sales and profits. An accompanying CD-ROM provides company profiles in electronic format.

In addition to company-specific information, the *Almanac* continues to provide some useful industry data. "Major Trends Affecting the Investment & Securities Industry" provides a 20-page environmental scan and touches upon such topics as offshoring, the convergence towards "one-stop shopping" for consumers, and challenges facing traditional exchanges. "Investment & Securities Statistics" offers 20 pages of tables of data produced by the Securities Industry Association, stock exchanges, and the Treasury and Commerce Departments of the U.S. government. Other sections include a 15-page "Investment & Securities Industry Glossary," a short directory of "Important Investment & Securities Industry Contacts," and several special indexes. These include geographical indexes of firms with operations outside the United States and non-U.S. headquarters by country, an index of "Subsidiaries, Brand Names, and Affiliations," and an index of "Firms Noted as Hot Spots for Advancement for Women & Minorities."

The introduction states that *Plunkett's Investment & Securities Industry Almanac* is "intended to be a general guide to a vast industry" and suggests that researchers start with this volume for an overview and, if more information is needed, consult the companies themselves or other resources for more in-depth research. It meets its stated goal. Serious researchers often need to dig further to find the company or industry information they need, but the Plunkett's almanacs fill an important niche by combining basic industry overview information and basic company information in one package. This work is recommended for all reference collections serving users with academic or personal interests in the investment industry. —**Gordon J. Aamot**

CONSUMER GUIDES

P

59. **The Grey House Safety & Security Directory.** 2006 ed. Millerton, N.Y., Grey House Publishing, 2006. 1082p. index. $225.00pa. (print edition); $385.00 (online database). ISBN 1-59237-104-3.

Now in its 4th edition, *The Grey House Safety & Security Directory* was published for over 50 years by the AM Best Company. Grey House has maintained the format developed by AM Best. The current directory's 16 chapters are organized to match the most important OSHA safety regulations such as Electrical and Lighting Safety, Employee Health Maintenance and Ergonomics, Facilities Monitoring and Maintenance, Fall Protection, Fire and Rescue, and Food Services. Each chapter begins with the OSHA requirements and follows with training articles. Most chapters also include self-inspection checklists and product buying guides. Each volume includes alphabetically arranged company profiles, with addresses, Websites, brief descriptions, and product listings; industry resources, including listings of associations, newsletters, magazines and journals, trade show directories, and databases and industry Websites; a glossary; and advertiser, brand name, geographic, and product indexes.

The addition of training articles and checklists written by experts in the field makes this much more than a standard product/service directory. Also included is a listing of the top 50 OSHA violations. A condensed table of contents is included in this edition. Tabs make thumbing through the *Directory* for a particular chapter and section much easier.

Grey House Publishing provides access to an accompanying Website that follows the arrangement of the *Directory* and is easy to navigate. Users can search the database either by entering a keyword or by conducting a step-by-step category search, which includes selecting a key category from a drop-down menu, selecting a product from the next list, and then selecting a subcategory if needed. Competing online products include *All About OSHA* (http://www.allaboutosha.com/osha-regulations.html) and *SafetyInfo* (http://www.safetyinfo.com) as well as OSHA's Website (http://www.osha.gov).

This continues to be the standard reference tool for safety professionals. It is appropriate for special and public libraries as well as academic collections supporting programs such as building construction, engineering, food services management, and safety management.—**Colleen Seale**

P

60. **The Purple Book: The Definitive Guide to Exceptional Online Shopping.** 2005 ed. Hillary Mendelsohn, ed. Westminster, Md., Bantam Dell Publishing Group, 2004. 655p. index. $25.00pa. ISBN 0-553-38283-7.

The 1st edition of *The Purple Book: The Definitive Guide to Exceptional Online Shopping* was published in 2003. With the vast changes in the World Wide Web from year to year, this 2d edition is a much-appreciated update. The author has painstakingly gone through tens of thousands of sites to find the 1,600 sites that are recommended in this directory. In her introduction Mendelsohn explains exactly how these retailer (or "e-tailer") sites were selected. Each site must offer secure credit card transactions, each must offer a customer service number on the site, and each must offer "open browsing" where searchers are not required to provide credit card or other personal information before searching the site. If the site has these three requirements it is then judged by its ease of use, visual appeal, product selection, and special offers on shipping and handling fees.

What makes this work so convenient to use is its well-organized layout. The work is organized in chapters according to 19 categories, including "Art & Collectibles," "Health & Beauty," "Home & Garden," "Pets," "Sports & Outdoors," and "Travel," just to name a few. The sites are arranged alphabetically by store name and each provides a four to five sentence description of the goods sold. Mendelsohn also includes many icons that further explain the usefulness of the site, including whether they accept or sell gift cards, whether they ship overnight, shipping costs, and user-friendliness of the site. Customer service numbers have been included with each site as well. The work concludes with a product index, a company name index, and a URL index, all of which make this guide extremely user friendly.

This guide will be useful to both those new to shopping online as well as those who have been doing it for years. There are many online retailers listed here that will be new to consumers. Of course, there are many that did not "make the cut" that will be missed by the Internet savvy. Overall, this guide is highly recommended for all public libraries.—**Shannon Graff Hysell**

FINANCE AND BANKING

Dictionaries and Encyclopedias

C, P

61. Hafer, R. W. **The Federal Reserve System: An Encyclopedia.** Westport, Conn., Greenwood Press, 2005. 451p. index. $95.00. ISBN 0-313-32839-0.

Virtually everyone has heard of the Federal Reserve System but how many really understand it? Hafer, an economist formerly at the Federal Reserve Bank in St. Louis and now at Southern Illinois University, offers approximately 280 articles of up to 3 pages in length on all facets of the Fed to expand our understanding. It is preceded by a 13-page historical overview of monetary policy focusing on the why, how, and history of the Fed. Articles are strong in personalities (like Marinner Eccles, Paul Volcker, and Alan Greenspan), U.S. Presidents and their relationship to the fed, policy issues (gold standard), international agreements or agencies (Bretton Wood, IMF), court cases, events (Black Monday, Panic of 1907), and federal policies. Terms or concepts (like moral hazard) used in the text that have their own entries are printed in bold type in each article. Every article also has a list of current scholarly citations for further reading. Three appendixes cover the Federal Reserve Act, members of the Board of Governors from 1913-2004, and federal regulations. No math is included. Hafer's writing style is straightforward and clearer than most economists, but many articles will be difficult for high school students. A decent index and separate list of articles by topic assists access, but a separate list of article entries is redundant. According to WorldCat, no other encyclopedia on the Fed exists, although there are encyclopedias for banking and finance. Better done than most of the Greenwood topical encyclopedias, this work is recommended for undergraduate and graduate libraries serving economics, banking, and finance users.—**Patrick J. Brunet**

Directories

C, P

62. **Plunkett's Banking, Mortgages, & Credit Industry Almanac 2005.** Jack W. Plunkett, ed. Houston, Tex., Plunkett Research, 2004. 470p. index. $249.99pa. (w/CD-ROM). ISBN 1-59392-015-6.

This is the 1st edition of *Plunkett's Banking, Mortgages, & Credit Industry Almanac*. The introduction states that this work was designed to be broad in scope so that it can have value for a diversity of researchers. The organization and content of the *Almanac* support this objective.

The work is divided into two main sections: the "Banking Industry" and the "Banking & Lending 350." This structure allows a researcher to easily locate the specific type of information they are seeking. Also facilitating access are several indexes in the following categories: alphabetical; industry sectors; headquarters by state; non-U.S. headquarters by country; regions of the United States; firms with operations outside the United States; firms that are hot spots for women and minorities; and brand names, affiliates, and subsidiaries.

The first section is a compilation of somewhat disparate industry information. This includes a glossary of financial services industry terms; industry statistics; trends impacting the three sectors; and a short directory of trade associations, Websites, publishers, government agencies, and other organizations that intersect these sectors. The second and lengthiest section of the *Almanac* contains one-page profiles of the "Banking & Lending 350" (335 actually profiled). These are primarily U.S. companies that operate in the banking, mortgage, and credit industry sectors. Companies were selected based on their dominance in their industry sectors. In addition to basic directory information, such as ticker, address, and telephone and fax numbers, company profiles can also include industry designations, brands, divisions, and affiliates, lines of business, key executives, number of employees, up to five years of sales and profit statistics, growth plans, and compensation for the top executives.

While the content in the first section is valuable, the strength of the work is the "Banking & Lending 350" section. A specific aim of the *Almanac*'s design is to support market research, employment searches, and mailing list creation utilizing the CD-ROM. The "Banking & Lending 350" section will be an excellent tool for these pursuits. This moderately priced almanac is recommended for public libraries as well as academic libraries on limited budgets.—**Susan Shultz**

Handbooks and Yearbooks

C, S

63. **Cash and Credit Information for Teens: Tips for a Successful Financial Life.** Kathryn R. Deering, ed. Detroit, Omnigraphics, 2005. 407p. index. (Teen Finance Series). $65.00. ISBN 0-7808-0780-4.

C, S

64. **Savings and Investment Information for Teens: Tips for a Successful Financial Life.** Kathryn R. Deering, ed. Detroit, Omnigraphics, 2005. 370p. index. (Teen Finance Series). $65.00. ISBN 0-7808-0781-2.

This new series from Omnigraphics is similar in format to the publisher's Teen Health Series, only for these volumes the focus is on responsible management of money and finances. The works consist of documents and excerpts written by various government, nonprofit, and for-profit organizations and agencies, including the Department of the Treasury, the United States Securities and Exchange Commission, the American Savings Education Council, the National Association of Securities Dealers, and Visa, Inc.

Cash and Credit Information for Teens provides information on being a wise consumer from everything from cars to cell phones, understanding how banks and debit cards work, getting the most from your paycheck and understanding how taxes work, understanding credit cards and loans, and avoiding financial risks (e.g., gambling, Internet scams, identification theft). One of the most valuable chapters in this book, titled "Use Your Card—Don't Let It Use You," is especially timely for today's youth. It discusses using a credit card to build your credit rating, how to avoid college credit debt traps, and how to choose a debt management plan if your debt gets too high to handle. This work concludes with a chapter for more information that includes Websites for more information about handling money and a directory of financial organizations.

In *Savings and Investment Information for Teens* there are chapters discussing money basics, basic investing for teens, stocks and bonds, and advanced investing for teens (e.g., financial advisors, researching for investments, leveraged trading). The chapter on "Stocks, Bonds, and Mutual Funds" will be especially useful as many of this information will be new to teens. The work concludes with a chapter for more information that provides Websites about saving and investing money, a directory of investment organizations, and books and magazines the provide useful information on investing.

This series will prove useful for high school and undergraduate students. Both school libraries and college reference collections should add them to their collections.—**Shannon Graff Hysell**

INDUSTRY AND MANUFACTURING

Directories

C

65.   **High-Volume Retailers, 2006: The Alternate Channel Sourcebook.** Wilton, Conn., Trade Dimensions, 2005. 620p. index. $260.00pa.

With this excellent resource on over 600 retailers (with 4 or more stores) in 90,000 locations, services suppliers, manufacturers, and others can locate corporate headquarters, buying offices, and key personnel. The introductory material explains volume use, key terms (e.g., supercenters), and major news events for the year. For each of 49 areas, as defined by major population centers in seven U.S. regions (e.g., West Central), Canada, and Puerto Rico, the market profile offers a map, list of industry leaders, and company description for drug store chains (e.g., Longs, Walgreens) and mass merchandisers (e.g., Wal-Mart, Sears, Best Buy). The detailed profiles describe basic company information (address, Website), along with corporate status (public, number of stores), operating data (square feet, checkouts, states of operation), three years of financials, industry data (advertising media use, suppliers, warehouse locations, key personnel), and recent events (acquisitions). Excluded companies (e.g., the Good Guys) are identified along with the reason they were eliminated.

Four indexes and numerous tables complete the volume. The indexes delineate operating names, retail operations by state, retailers by category (e.g., close out stores), and retailers alphabetically. The category index identifies retailers in eight categories. Here is where Wal-Mart (Wholesale Clubs) is differentiated from Longs (Chain Drug Stores). Amongst the tables are those ranking market areas by population and headquarters, and the top 100 high-volume retailers by category and number of stores. Who would expect that the most headquarters (60) could be found in New Jersey, the most stores are Blockbusters (9,000), and that Wal-Mart leads in two separate categories (Discount, Supercenters).

This work is recommended for academic business libraries and other libraries serving large business clientele. Reference is made to the publishers Website, the availability of monthly updates, and the availability of a CD-ROM version that, although more costly, facilitates complicated searches and exporting of data for analysis. These features are nice but what the patrons will really want is subscription access to the publisher's database.—**Sandra E. Belanger**

Handbooks and Yearbooks

C

66.   **Industrial Commodity Statistics Yearbook, 2002: Production Statistics (1993-2002). Annuaire de Statistiques Industrielles par Produit.** By the Department of Economic and Social Affairs, Statistics Division. New York, United Nations, 2004. 835p. $150.00. ISBN 92-1-061209-4. ISSN 0257-7208. S/N E/F.04.XVII.11.

This volume, the 36th compilation in this UN series, provides a 10-year span of annual production data for over 500 commodities from 200 countries covering the years 1993-2002. The tables are arranged by commodity and show 10 year's worth of annual production figures for different countries. Weights and measures are shown in metric terms.

Commodity tables are grouped by ISIC classification number (International Standard Industrial Classification of All Economic Activities [ISIC] Rev.2). The first four digits of the six-digit ISIC number refer to the broad industry group. The last two digits indicate the more specific commodity. For example, the table for ISIC number 3140-01 shows production information for "Tobacco, prepared leaf" and that for

3140-07 shows production information for "Cigarettes." Within each commodity table, countries are displayed in continental and regional order—Africa, America North, America South, Asia, Europe, and Oceania. The last line of each table shows total world production for that commodity.

The volume has two useful annexes. Annex 1 is an "Index of Commodities in Alphabetical Order." Users will begin their search here to find the appropriate ISIC number. Annex 2 is table showing the correspondence between ISIC codes and other commodity codes; for example, SITC (Standard International Trade Classification) and Harmonized System codes.

The *Industrial Commodity Statistics Yearbook* is held by hundreds of North American libraries and remains a must have for reference collections. This yearbook is highly recommended for all reference collections serving researchers with interests in international business and economics.—**Gordon J. Aamot**

C, P

67. **Plunkett's Biotech and Genetics Industry Almanac.** 2006 ed. Jack W. Plunkett, ed. Houston, Tex., Plunkett Research, 2005. 560p. index. $299.99pa. (w/CD-ROM). ISBN 1-59392-033-4.

Plunkett's Biotech & Genetics Industry Almanac is one more example of the fine publications offered by Plunkett Research. This reference book is particularly timely given the considerable interest in biotechnology and genetics from scientific, investment, and entrepreneurial audiences. Although primarily a detailed directory of companies in this industry, the *Almanac* has many additional features that provide an overview to both the financial and research sides of biotechnology, including genomics, proteomics, biopharmaceuticals, business development, and commercialization. With coverage of the 450 major firms in the sector, the *Almanac* presents a comprehensive source for researchers and the general reader.

There are many special features at the beginning of the *Almanac*. The volume begins with a glossary of commonly used biotechnology and genetics terms. There is a short introduction to the volume that explains some of its special features and the methodology that was used in compiling information. This is followed by a guide to using the book, with details on how to read the individual company listings. Chapter 1 provides an overview of trends affecting the biotechnology and genetics industry that is interesting and well written, while chapter 2 offers a generous number of charts and graphs with statistics on the industry. Chapter 3 lists important industry contacts, including associations, publications, and investment companies and databases, which include mailing address, fax and telephone numbers, Web address, and a brief description. Finally, chapter 4 provides specific information on the 450 companies, including rankings, NAIC codes, and alphabetic and geographic indexes. These indexes are complemented by indexes of firms that are noted for advancing women and minorities, and a comprehensive index of subsidiaries, brand names, and affiliations, which are located at the end of the volume.

Individual company entries comprise the bulk of the *Almanac* and are in Plunkett's usual format of easy-to-use boxes and tables. Even though the amount of information for each entry is considerable, entries are attractively presented and easy to use. There are individual boxes for type of business, brands, divisions and affiliates, top officers, and contact information. A shaded box on the right side of the page provides a concise description of the company. Reading just a few of these company descriptions provides an appreciation for the complexity of the work they do, the amount of technology transfer with government and university-sponsored research, and the fast-changing nature of the industry as a whole. Boxes at the top of the page indicate business activities, which are divided into five categories and rankings. The bottom section of the entries contains financial information, stock ticker, number of employees, and fiscal year date. Another box provides information on salaries and benefits, with additional boxes on the company's competitive advantage, location, and ratings for the company's opportunities for women and minorities. Entries have been artfully designed to provide a considerable amount of detail that is still easy to find and that does not overwhelm the reader.

In addition to the two indexes mentioned in the back of the volume, the *Almanac* also has an appendix on research techniques, along with illustrations of various elements that are significant in research, such as DNA, protein, and adenovirus. These illustrations are beautifully done and are particularly helpful in understanding the kinds of research that is done by the companies featured in the *Almanac*.

Plunkett's Biotech & Genetics Industry Almanac will be an excellent reference source for nearly any kind of library. Certainly it is appropriate for academic and health sciences libraries, along with corporate libraries that support companies either working in or investing in the biotechnology and genetics industry. Finally, many public libraries may find that this book is a useful volume for patrons interested in either the scientific or the investment side of this industry.—**Sara Anne Hook**

C

68.   **Plunkett's InfoTech Industry Almanac.** 2006 ed. Jack W. Plunkett, ed. Houston, Tex., Plunkett Research, 2006. 650p. index. $299.00pa. (w/CD-ROM). ISBN 1-59392-053-9.

The Plunkett series of directories are well known for providing company and industry information on clearly defined subject areas. The 2006 edition of this book on the Infotech industry focuses on information technology that moves or manages voice, data, or video, whether the mode is wireless, Internet, satellite, fiber optics, traditional copper wire telephony, computer network, or emerging technology. Companies that manufacture or provide products or services in these fields, including relevant computer hardware and software, are included. The layout of the company profile page is similar to that used in the Hoover's company directories. Each one-page company profile includes a rank by industry group code and within the company's industry group; types of business, brands, divisions, and affiliations; contact information of up to 27 top officers; the company's address; annual sales and profits figures for the latest fiscal year; number of employees; some indication of salaries of the top executive and what fringe benefits are available to employees; and a statement of the company's competitive advantage. Some companies will be noted for providing advancement opportunities for women and minorities.

In addition to the profiles of 500 companies, the user will find such information as: a glossary of terms; a discussion of the 15 major trends facing the InfoTech industry; 17 industry statistical tables; a list of related associations, government agencies, and Websites; an index of companies noted for advancement of women and minorities; and an index listing subsidiaries and brand names. This material comprises just over 20 percent of the book.

The combination of company profiles and the material related to the industry makes this a very useful acquisition for libraries since information on many of the companies included are not readily available in other sources. The industry information provides a framework in which to locate additional material at a later time. The publisher provides a free CD-ROM of the corporate profiles, enabling a user to export data for such activities as a mail merge.—**Judith J. Field**

C

69.   **Plunkett's Retail Industry Almanac.** 2006 ed. Jack W. Plunkett, ed. Houston, Tex., Plunkett Research, 2006. 624p. index. $279.99pa. (w/CD-ROM). ISBN 1-59392-055-5.

This is a directory of U.S.-based and mostly publicly held retailers, where retailers are broadly defined to include retail chain stores and retail service companies as well as the growing number of nonstore retailers. Given the pervasive significance and influence of consumer spending, this is an industry that clearly has a meaningful effect on both the U.S. economy and American culture. Accordingly, this is a useful and informative guide to current conditions in U.S. retailing rather than merely for select firms or for particular retailing activities. It provides statistical and descriptive information for 500 companies. It consolidates into one general reference guide information on acquisitions and consolidations, data on sales and profits, the numbers of personnel in various occupations, and the names and addresses of officers and other significant contacts, as well as the names and descriptions of brands, divisions, and affiliates for these firms.

This reference work also helps provide a historical context to American retailing. There is a brief descriptive passage for each of the 500 profiled retailers, outlining growth plans and other special features of the firm. Appendixes to the guide also include three years' worth of monthly retail trade surveys along with the Web addresses needed to retrieve current census surveys. The almanac also contains a glossary of retailing terms, definitions of the business classification used by the Department of Commerce, a short list of notable industry-wide retail and retail-related contacts (postal and Web addresses, telephone numbers), along with state and regional indexes of company headquarters. This is an easy-to-use and informative reference work that will be helpful to a variety of users.—**Timothy E. Sullivan**

INSURANCE

C, P
70.   **Weiss Ratings' Guide to Life, Health, and Annuity Insurers, Fall 2005: A Quarterly Compilation of Insurance Company Ratings and Analyses.** Jupiter, Fla., Weiss Rating's, 2005. 380p. $249.00pa. (single edition); $499.00pa. (4 quarterly editions). ISBN 1-58773-214-9. ISSN 1079-7815.

The purpose of the Weiss insurance guides is to provide the consumer with information about various insurance companies that will enable them to make wise choices for their insurance needs. The Weiss Guides cover only U.S. companies and are updated on a quarterly basis. Weiss Ratings do not accept money for recommendations. Therefore, the ratings are unbiased and are recognized as the insurance industry's leading consumer advocate. The Weiss Ratings range from A-F, with "A+" being the best rating and "F" signifying failure of the company. The volume is divided into "Index of Companies"; "Analysis of Largest Companies"; "Weiss Recommended Companies"; "Weiss Recommended Companies By State"; "All Companies Listed By Rating"; "Rating Upgrades and Downgrades"; an appendix with state guaranty associations, risk-adjusted capital, and recent industry failures; and a glossary of terms. This rating guide is recommended as a priority purchase for public libraries and academic libraries.—**Kay M. Stebbins**

INTERNATIONAL BUSINESS

Dictionaries and Encyclopedias

C
71.   **Encyclopedia of World Trade.** Cynthia Clark Northrup, ed. Armonk, N.Y., M. E. Sharpe, 2005. 4v. illus. index. $425.00/set. ISBN 0-7656-8058-0.

A more accurate title for this four-volume set would be the "Historical Encyclopedia of World Trade" as the emphasis of its approximately 445 articles is how trade developed globally and its effect on societies and politics. Entries include commodities (such as jute, guano, and minerals), overviews of countries, trade routes (the Silk Road, Santa Fe trail), individuals (Keynes, Richard Haklyut), cities (Petra, Venice), and trade issues (slavery, globalization). While most of the contributors are U.S. academics, the article coverage is truly international. Presented in double-column format on oversized pages, each entry has a one- or two-sentence summary heading the text of the signed article, which can run from half a page up to 10 pages, but the average is about a page and a half. There is an illustration on about every third page but only 17 maps (such as the Indian Ocean trade). Select bibliographies are found at the end of every article; while short, they are current and the citations are much more current than most multivolume encyclopedias. Writing quality is also much better and stylistically more consistent than similar reference works; although the long article on the Atlantic trade is both repetitive and needs to be reconciled with information found in other articles that deal with slavery. Articles on contentious topics like globalization fairly discuss differing views. Volume 4 contains an appendix with 57 whole or partial documents that are important to the history of trade, such as the charter of the British East India Company or the medieval Papal Edict on Usury. Each volume contains the 41-page general subject index, the 7-page biographical index, and the 13-page geographic index that provides access to all four volumes. Overall, the quality of the writing, indexing, and bibliography make this a recommended title for any library interested in the topic, from upper secondary grades to graduate school, but the most likely users will be undergraduates in history, economics, international trade, or political science. [R: SLJ, Aug 05, p. 76]—**Patrick J. Brunet**

Directories

C, P

72. **Hoover's Handbook of World Business 2005.** 12th ed. Austin, Tex., Hoover's, 2005. 385p. index. $180.00. ISBN 1-57311-103-1. ISSN 1055-7199.

This is the 12th edition of this handbook, which fills a need for the small academic and public libraries that have occasional queries about non-U.S.-based companies. In this edition they have identified some 300 of the world's most influential companies. Some of the industries included are telecommunication firms, banks, chemical firms, petroleum companies, and airlines. The contents of the book include a two-page description of the elements that are included in the profile template used for the companies; a 50-page compendium of various lists of the largest, most profitable companies by assets within their industries; the 2-page profile of each company; and 3 indexes.

The profiles provide an informative snapshot of each company. One of most popular sections in the profile is a short list of major competitors. Other information included in the profile include a brief overview of the company, some history about the company, a list of officers, their corporate location, a list of their major product lines and operations, and some financials. There is an index by industry; by headquarters location; and a very detailed index by brands, people, and companies.

This can be purchased separately or as part of a four-title series available as an indexed set. The other titles in the set are *Hoover's Handbook of American Business* (see entry 50), *Hoover's Handbook of Emerging Companies* (see entry 51), and *Hoover's Handbook to Private Companies* (see ARBA 2006, entry 133). Whether purchased individually or as a set, smaller business collections will find that this title is well worth the money.—**Judith J. Field**

Handbooks and Yearbooks

C, P

73. **World Economic Factbook 2005/2006.** 13th ed. London, Euromonitor International, 2005. 450p. $545.00. ISBN 1-84264-379-7.

Euromonitor is a respected publisher of international business and marketing reference works. The *Factbook* presents a selection of key economic, political, and demographic data in a standardized format for 204 countries, making it easy to compare countries on these variables. The data in the 2005/2006 edition cover the years 2004, 2003, and 2002. Data sources include national statistical bureaus and multilateral agencies, such as the International Monetary Fund and the United Nations. For each country there is a two-page report. The first page is a textual summary providing the currency unit, the location and area of the country, the Head of State and the Head of Government, the Ruling Party, the Political Structure, the results of the last elections, a quick assessment of political risk, highlights of international disputes, a paragraph summarizing economic developments, a paragraph highlighting the main industries, and an overview of the energy situation.

The numerical data provided are primarily economic measures and population statistics. Economic data include the rate of inflation, the U.S. dollar exchange rate, real GDP growth, GDP in U.S. dollars and the home currency, total and per capita consumption, exports and imports, and tourism receipts and spending. There is also a table listing major trading partners with percentage share of exports and imports and value in U.S. dollars. Population data includes total population, population density, population by age groups, total male and female population, urban population, birth and death rates, male and female life expectancy, infant mortality, and number of households. After a brief introduction that explains the content and layout of the reference work, the first section contains maps of the continents with outlines for individual countries and their capitals. Section 2 contains comparative world rankings with separate tables for rankings by area, population, and economic measures.

Given the breathtaking price of the work ($545) users may wish to check some of the excellent authoritative sources of data available for free on the Internet such as the CIA's *The World Factbook* (http://www.cia.gov/cia/publications/factbook/), *globalEDGE* (http://globaledge.msu.edu/ibrd/ibrd.asp), and the *World Development Report* (http://econ.worldbank.org/wdr/).—**Peter Zachary McKay**

LABOR

General Works

Dictionaries and Encyclopedias

C, P, S

74. **Encyclopedia of Careers and Vocational Guidance.** 13th ed. New York, Facts on File, 2005. 5v. illus. index. $249.95/set. ISBN 0-8160-6055-X.

This title, now in five volumes, has been a standard acquisition for school, public, and academic libraries for over 30 years to requests regarding career information. Most career counseling centers also acquire this book to use in consultation with their clients. Volume 1 provides general information for selecting a career, including information on writing résumés, interviewing, and 95 articles on career fields that average 4-5 pages. Each article concludes with some recommendations on where to locate additional information. Many articles provide a short glossary and others provide an interesting bit of trivia related to the specific career field. The appendixes in volume 1 provide the reader with career resources for individuals with disabilities; a general guide to internship programs within the government; organization and Website index; and four indexes that index the career articles by commonly used government classification systems. Some 738 career articles, including 63 new articles, reviewed and updated as needed, comprise the content of volumes 2-5. These articles provide educational requirements, general description of the duties, outlook for the profession, some quick facts, and places to contact for additional information. While much of this information is similar to that found in *Occupational Outlook Handbook* (2004-2005 ed.; see ARBA 2005, entry 236) it is found here in greater detail. This remains a must-have acquisition by school, public, and academic libraries where career information is needed. [R: LJ, 1 June 05, p. 180]—**Judith J. Field**

Directories

C, P

75. **The Almanac of American Employers.** 2006 ed. Jack W. Plunkett, ed. Houston, Tex., Plunkett Research, 2005. 748p. index. $229.00pa. (w/CD-ROM). ISBN 1-59392-045-8.

The Almanac of American Employers is a directory of successful corporate businesses focused on the job-seeker, whether they are a new college graduate or an employee considering a change in employment. The main section of the directory describes 500 companies with name, address, voice and fax number, and industry group code information. Details on professional degrees they hire, salary and benefit rankings, and the company's ranking within its industry group are also included. Descriptions continue with the company's plans for expansion and special features, such as new plant locales, special benefits for employees and their families, the corporate financials, a list of officers, and a statement of the company's competitive advantage. An indication of whether the company complies as a "Hot Spot for Advancement for Women/Minorities" and data on the "Number of Women Officers and Directors" are also provided.

The "Seven Keys for Job Seekers" guides readers in locating information about a company. The "Important Contacts" chapter provides names of organizations and associations that will provide job-seekers with a network of professionals. The 500 companies listed in the almanac are not the same list as the Fortune 500. The companies were chosen because they offered more job openings or long-lived jobs to the greatest number of employees. This guide is a must-purchase for career collections.—**Kay M. Stebbins**

C

76. **Internships 2005.** Lawrenceville, N.J., Peterson's Guides, 2004. 764p. index. $26.95pa. ISBN 0-7689-1498-1.

This directory, an annual volume, updates the information on thousands of short-term, learning-oriented positions in many career fields. The fields are broad and include arts; health care/social assistance; manufacturing; and information, professional/scientific, and technical services. For each entry, the sponsor is fully identified with a brief description of the nature of the organization, followed by the internships available and the benefits anticipated for the intern. Generally, the listing identifies the number of positions, the nature of the work, and skills required.

Introductory material includes extensive information describing the internship experience in general, how to apply for an internship, and what sponsors are seeking from interns. Indexes, invaluable in a source like this, include geographic, field of interest, and academic level. Lists of paid internships and those that have the possibility of permanent employment are also included.

The extensive material included is very compacted and requires the ability to cross-reference to the various sections to find what is needed. Yet it is not the kind of tool that career and guidance counselors would peruse. Rather, it is intended for the strongly motivated internship-seeker who is willing to expend some time to glean the most salient information needed. The long history of this volume has given a base of experience and interest, particularly in academe, to perpetuate its use.—**Barbara Conroy**

C, P

77. **Plunkett's Companion to the Almanac of American Employers: Mid-Size Firms.** 2004-2005 ed. Jack W. Plunkett, ed. Houston, Tex., Plunkett Research, 2004. 722p. index. $199.99pa. (w/CD-ROM). ISBN 1-891775-81-2.

As indicated by its title, *Plunkett's Companion to the Almanac of American Employers: Mid-Sized Firms* is intended to complement its volume covering firms with more than 2,500 employees. This volume emphasizes mid-size firms, defined as those with 150 to 2,500 employees, that are primarily U.S.-based, for-profit companies with publicly held stock. The volume's purpose is to assist job-seekers in finding quick and meaningful information about potential employers, with individual company entries and supplemental materials that permit comparison within and across industry groups. *Plunkett's* can also be differentiated from other sources of information on corporations because this volume's view of companies is tailored to what potential employees need to know rather than to the information needs of investors, accountants, or financial analysts.

Each entry in this guide is presented on a single page, divided into segments that make it easy to find and compare the information. The top box provides the industry group code, the URL for the company's Website, a ranking of sales and profits within the industry groups, and a salary and benefits rating. The second box lists a variety of subject backgrounds, such as technical writing and hardware development, arranged into six categories, with an indication of whether the company hires people with these types of backgrounds. On the left side of the page, a series of boxes contain information on type of business, brands, divisions and affiliates, and names and titles of top officers and their telephone numbers, along with the company's toll-free number, fax number, and address. On the right side of the page, a brief, concise narrative provides information on the growth potential of the company and any special features of the company that would bode well for future employees. The bottom of the page contains boxes for financial information.

A "Salaries/Benefits" box lists the various plans available to employees, along with the salaries and bonuses for the top and second executive positions. A separate box includes comments on the company's competitive advantage, with another box for additional thoughts about the company. There is also a space for the number of women officers or directors, a space to note whether the company is a "hot spot" for the advancement of women and minorities, and boxes to check the location of the company that are divided regionally rather than by state. The information presented in the entries is clear and well organized and will be useful to job-seekers in targeting the employers that will offer the best opportunities for long-term career growth and stability.

In addition to the individual company entries, this guide has a number of special features that make it a particularly valuable research tool for job-seekers and others who have a particular interest in a company or industry group. Beginning chapters not only cover how to use the volume, but discuss major trends affecting the employee marketplace and ideas for doing research on potential employers. A directory of contacts for job-seekers and a composite view of 498 companies included in the volume and why they were selected are also provided along with an industry list with codes, a ranking of the companies within industry groups, an alphabetic list of the companies with industry codes, and three geographical indexes. Additional indexes are provided at the end of the volume. All of these indexes make it simple to find information on specific companies and to see how they compare to companies within and outside of their own industry groups. *Plunkett's* also includes a number of interesting tables, including one on female CEOs and another on the top 20 employers with women officers and directors.

This work will be a useful addition to nearly any public or academic library, as well as libraries that serve companies or agencies that assist people looking for jobs. The page-long entries will be easy for patrons to photocopy and the supplemental directory and statistical information will be handy for ready-reference. The chapters covering major trends that will affect those seeking new jobs and techniques for effective job hunting are particularly timely and well written.—**Sara Anne Hook**

Handbooks and Yearbooks

C

78.   Beik, Millie Allen. **Labor Relations.** Westport, Conn., Greenwood Press, 2005. 302p. index. (Major Issues in American History). $65.00. ISBN 0-313-31864-6.

Following the Financial Panic of 1873, a deep depression began in the United States that resulted in the collapse of many banks, thousands of business failures and bankruptcies, and widespread unemployment, hunger, and destitution. Among the hardest hit industries was the railroad industry, which had enjoyed unprecedented expansion following the Civil War. In 1877, when the Baltimore & Ohio Railroad announced its second 10 percent reduction in wages, railroad workers in Martinsburg, West Virginia, halted the freight trains. Local militia failed to break the strike. Many of them had friends and relatives among the strikers. The governor requested President Rutherford B. Hayes to call in federal troops. Across the country spontaneous strikes erupted in Baltimore, Pittsburg, New York, St. Louis, Chicago, San Francisco, and other cities. Locomotives and freight cars were destroyed, tracks were pulled up, and buildings burned. The nation's transportation network was completely disrupted. The worst violence took place in Pittsburg where 26 people died. The strikes ended in August after being violently put down.

The Great Railroad Strike of 1877 was the first nationwide strike and marks the beginning of the modern labor movement. Millie Allen Beik's reference work on labor relations discusses nine key labor conflicts, beginning with the New England Shoemaker's Strike of 1860 and ending with the Professional Air Traffic Controllers Organization (PATCO) Strike in 1981, to explain the history of labor relations in the United States. Each chapter presents an overview of the strike and its significance in labor history. The overview is supplemented with excerpts from several primary source documents. The chapters conclude with briefly annotated bibliographies featuring books, articles, Websites, and videos. The other strikes covered are: the Pullman Strike and Boycott of 1894; the Lawrence Textile Strike of 1912; the Miners' Program, 1919-1923; the General Textile Strike of 1934; the General Motors Sit-Down Strike of 1936-1937; and the Memphis Sanitation Strike of 1968. Chapter 9 examines the Labor Management Relations (Taft-Hartley) Act of 1947 that redefined labor relations after World War II.

This work is the latest addition to Greenwood Press' Major Issues in American History series. The series focuses on key themes in American history. *Labor Relations* follows the established format of the series. A series Foreword explains the event-driven approach taken to study the issues. A chronology dates landmarks in labor history. The introduction briefly surveys the development of workers' rights in the United States and the impact of major historical events on the labor movement including the Civil War (end of slave labor), the transformation of the economy to an industrial nation, the Progressive Era, the Great Depression, the Taft-Hartley Act, civil rights legislation, and the PATCO strike, which has become emblematic of the decline of organized labor in the post-World War II era. The first chapter looks at the beginnings of the labor movement from 1827 to 1837.

Beik, who is an independent labor historian, colors her account with phrases like "shoe bosses" and sentences such as "…capitalism is a dynamic, historical, and even a revolutionary economic system that is motivated, first and foremost, by the notion of profit, not human needs." Nonetheless, the work is a useful reference on the labor movement that can help students and researchers study the development of labor relations in the United States.—**Peter Zachary McKay**

C, P

79. **Employment, Hours, and Earnings: States and Areas, 2005.** Diane Werneke and Mary Meghan Ryan, eds. Lanham, Md., Bernan Associates, 2005. 1185p. $95.00pa. ISBN 1-886222-25-8.

This is called a special edition of the *Handbook of United States Labor Statistics: Employment, Earnings, Prices, Productivity and Other Labor Data*. It is based on Bureau of Labor Statistics (BLS) data. It is similar to in content to the discontinued BLS publication titled *Employment, Hours and Earnings: States and Areas*, last published in 1994. This work provides data on state and local labor markets, while the *Handbook of United States Labor Statistics* focuses on national labor market trends. It presents the industry employment data under the new North American Industry Classification System (NAISC), which are not compatible for data prior to 1990 that is available from BLS. The statewide, District of Columbia, and major metropolitan areas data on employment by industry are given monthly and annually from 1990 through 2003. Average weekly hours, average hourly earnings, and average weekly earnings by industry are for 2001 through 2003. Data are not available for all of the metropolitan areas for which there are employment data. In addition, for each state and the District of Columbia, population from the 2000 census, 2003 total nonfarm employment, change in total nonfarm employment and compound annual rate of change for total nonfarm employment for 1990-2003, 1990-2001 and 2001-2003, and the unemployment rate for 1990, 2001, and 2003 are provided. There are carefully written technical notes to guide the users of this data and assist them if more information on BLS methodology and data is desired. This volume's contents have a variety of uses, such as seeing how employment and changes in it varied in different states, conditions in specific states that might indicate the need for activity by state and/or local government, and to see where businesses might find better conditions for future activity. Apart from the technical notes, it contains little more than the data. Thus, users need to know what data they want and how to make good use of what is included here. [R: LJ, Aug 05, p. 120]—**J. E. Weaver**

C, S

80.   Hinds, Maurene J. **The Ferguson Guide to Résumés and Job-hunting Skills: A Step-by-Step Guide to Preparing for Your Job Search.** New York, Ferguson/Facts on File, 2005. 248p. index. $45.00. ISBN 0-8160-5792-3.

A comprehensive coverage of résumé types, content, and style along with cover letters and their use, this handbook is directed to the person who has not had extensive experience in a job search. There are many varied examples of résumés provided here. Interviewing is more briefly covered with key emphasis on preparation and practice to assure clarity and a solid personal presentation suitable to the situation. An index improves access beyond the brief table of contents. The volume would be useful in high school and college libraries as well as in a personal collection.—**Barbara Conroy**

Career Guides

Handbooks and Yearbooks

S

81.   **Career Ideas for Teens Series.** By Diane Lindsey Reeves, with Gail Karlitz, Don Rauf, and Anna Prokos. New York, Facts on File, 2005. 8v. maps. index. $320.00/set; $40.00/vol. ISBN 0-8160-5287-5.

With an overwhelming number of career options available for young adults these days, it is no wonder they often feel overwhelmed when it comes to narrowing down their career choice. In high school a student will likely have no idea what they will be interested in pursuing for a career for the next 30 years. These volumes are designed to help them pinpoint their skills, their particular interests, and their priorities when it comes to working.

The eight volumes in this series cover different career clusters as defined by the U.S. Department of Education: Health Sciences, the Arts and Communications, Information Technology, Law and Public Safety, Manufacturing, Education and Training, Architecture and Construction, and Government and Public Service. The first 30 pages of each volume begin with the same material in a section titled "Discover You at Work." This section provides questions that will help students identify their strengths and weaknesses, discover their preferences (e.g., relating to others, decision-making skills), explore their values, and figure out their work personality. Section 2 of each volume explores in two to three pages various career options within the field. For example, in the Health Sciences volume there are discussions on athletic trainers, chiropractors, dieticians, massage therapists, morticians, and veterinarians, just to name a few. Each of these discussions focuses on the key responsibilities of the job, people skills required, education required, salary, and career paths. Each also includes a sidebar with Websites that discusses the field further, a "Get Started Now!" box that gives tips on how to prepare for the career through education and volunteer work, and a "Hire Yourself" section that gives ideas for how to prepare for the job. The final section, "Experiment with Success," provides comments from real-life professionals working in these jobs, as well as questions students might ask professionals if they were to conduct their own interview. The appendix provides additional Websites that students can research to find out more about the featured professions.

This set would be valuable in a high school library or high school counselors office. There is a lot of information packed within each volume and a lot of practical tips to get students truly thinking about their career options.—**Shannon Graff Hysell**

C, P, S

82.   Echaore-McDavid, Susan. **Career Opportunities in Aviation and the Aerospace Industry.** New York, Facts on File, 2005. 305p. index. $49.50. ISBN 0-8160-4649-2.

This volume of over 300 pages is neatly arranged. Its layout is very clear and the easy-to-use format is appropriate for career-seeking readers. The contents are divided into 14 subject areas with 80 careers described. The selection of careers is comprehensive, including traditional pilot, flight attendant, astronaut, and maintenance technician jobs as well as the less traditional, such as airport planner, federal air marshal, aviation curator, skydiving instructor, and aerospace engineer. Both aviation and aerospace are well represented; those searching for career information will find this volume very useful.

Each of the 80 career entries is 2 or 3 pages in length. Each entry has a consistent format: Career Profile, Career Ladder, Position Description, Salaries, Employment Prospects, Education, and so forth. The final paragraphs, "Tips for Entry," contain useful suggestions to prepare for entry into the specific career. These few well-organized pages give concise but sufficient information for someone seeking preliminary career information.

Several appendixes give additional information about pilot certification, education, professional associations, federal government agencies, and resources on the World Wide Web. The appendixes are thorough and provide excellent supplemental information. A glossary is followed by a bibliography, which is followed by the index that completes the book.

This hardbound volume is a good resource for the young person seeking career information. Echaore-McDavid has done a creditable job in gathering and presenting this industry information. The volume is strongly recommended for high school, public, and university libraries.—**Jim Agee**

C, P

83.   Farr, Michael. **America's 101 Fastest Growing Jobs: Detailed Information on Major Jobs with the Most Openings and Growth.** 8th ed. Indianapolis, Ind., JIST Works, 2005. 393p. $15.95pa. ISBN 1-59357-070-8.

In this volume Michael Farr discusses the best job prospects in the coming decade using the Bureau of Labor Statistics' *Occupational Outlook Handbook* (OOH), a biennial guide to the job market. Word for word, sentence for sentence, entry for entry, the 101 occupational descriptions that comprise the main part of the book are taken directly from the 2004-2005 edition of the handbook, which is available for free on the Internet (http://www.bls.gov/oco/home.htm). The BLS Website offers both HTML and PDF versions for all 271 occupations. Sometimes information really is "all on the Internet."

The first section of Farr's book begins with a list of the 101 fastest growing jobs, advice on how to use the book effectively, and important trends in the labor market affecting career planning. A table in the introduction provides a ranked list from first to last showing each job with its growth rate in percentage over the 10-year period 2002-2012 and the total numerical growth of job openings. His top five are: postsecondary teachers (38 percent, 602,700); computer systems analysts, database administrators, and computer scientists (42 percent, 16,000); computer software engineers (45 percent, 307,200); medical assistants (59 percent, 214,800); and social and human service assistants (49 percent, 214,800). Additional tables rank all 271 jobs covered in the OOH by percent growth and by number of openings and then combines them using a scoring method devised by the author.

Next are his top 101 detailed profiles. Arranged alphabetically, each occupational profile follows a standard format: key points about the occupation; a discussion of the nature of the work; a description of typical working conditions; the number of jobs in 2002 with key industries and number of self-employed, if any; training and qualifications required for the job and advancement opportunities; job outlook; typical earnings; related occupations; and sources of additional information.

Section 2 offers "The Quick Job Search: Seven Steps to Getting a Good Job in Less Time." Farr, who founded JIST Publishing and conducts workshops on self-directed career planning and job search, distills his job-searching advice into brief, easy-to-follow steps with worksheets. This is a valuable time-saver that keys on the most important things to do to prepare for and seek employment. The "Seven Steps" are a skills assessment; identifying the most suitable job; effective job search techniques; preparing résumés; time management tips; interviewing; and pursuing leads. Example résumés are included. Section 3 concludes with two articles that briefly review the most important trends in both jobs and industries. These are adapted from OOH and the *Career Guide to Industries*, another BLS publication that is also available for free (http://www.bls.gov/oco/cg/home.htm>).—**Peter Zachary McKay**

C, P

84.   Farr, Michael. **America's Top 101 Jobs for College Graduates.** 6th ed. Indianapolis, Ind., JIST Works, 2005. 407p. $15.95pa. ISBN 1-59357-071-6.

The 6th edition of this title provides descriptions and the latest salary information for 101 of the highest paying jobs for college graduates. The job information provided in this book has been taken from the *Occupational Outlook Handbook* (2004-2005 ed.; see ARBA 2005, entry 236). The book is divided into three sections. Section 1 describes jobs in three categories: those requiring a professional or doctoral degree, those typically requiring a master's degree, and those typically requiring a bachelor's degree. The description of each job title includes salient information about the type of work and its future prospects, a detailed description of the nature of the work, typical working conditions, the number of jobs in this category and the type of employer, training/qualifications required with a discussion of advancement potential, the job outlook, earning potential, related occupations, and sources of additional information. Section Two provides a seven-step plan for getting a job as quickly as possible. This includes identifying your skills and strengths, defining your ideal job, finding job openings, developing contacts, writing a résumé and cover letter, and interviewing. Section 3 covers trends in jobs and industries. The information in the first essay, called "Tomorrow's Jobs" is, again, taken from the *Occupational Outlook Handbook*. The second essay in this section discusses the advantages a college degree gives to job applicants. It is convenient to have job descriptions, job search advice, and information about trends in employment all in one place. However, since all of the information in this volume is available elsewhere, at little or no cost, one wonders why anyone would pay to own this book, even at its modest price.—**Joanna M. Burkhardt**

P, S

85.   **People at Work! A Student's A-Z Guide to 350 Jobs.** Indianapolis, Ind., JIST Works, 2005. 424p. illus. $27.95pa. ISBN 1-59357-078-3.

This guide to careers is designed for middle and high school students. Published by a leading source of career information, the editors provide up-to-date information on both the well-known as well as the less-well-known career options available today. Because this is a source for students, the editors have gone out of their way to present this guidebook in an entertaining and conversational style. In order to do this the work is presented from the viewpoint of "Dez the Dog" who is currently researching career options. The 350 jobs are presented in alphabetic order, with each job listed on one page. Along with a description of the job duties, hours of work, and benefits of the job, the guide also provides information on salary, potential job growth up to 2012, required education, and school subjects that students should study in order to do well at the job. A wide variety of jobs are presented here, many which students will turn to immediately (e.g., professional athlete, model, pilot, firefighter), and some which will be new to them (e.g., actuary, CAD technicians, Hospice workers). Some of the information provided may surprise some students; for example, the average salary listed for professional athletes is only between $25,001 and $50,000 a year, while investigators typically earn over $50,001 a year.

The final section of the book lists jobs into "job families," making it easier for students to consider a wider range of jobs requiring similar skills. After a list of potential jobs are listed there are sections on how to "get a head start" (including researching the job family or trying it out first hand), a glossary of words related to the job, and directory information on where to find out more about the industry.

This is a well-thought-out guide for young adults about the career world. Although the job descriptions are a little vague, it is useful to have so many jobs described in one place, and by providing ideas on where to gain more information the publisher has developed a useful research tool. *People at Work!* is highly recommended for middle school and high school libraries, as well as public library collections.
—**Shannon Graff Hysell**

MANAGEMENT

C, P

86. **All Business. http://www.allbusiness.com.** [Website]. Free. Date reviewed: 2005.

This huge site contains articles and advice on any area of business law, including legal structure, property leases, patents, trademarks, employment law, taxes, and even how to work with a lawyer. Links to many directories are also provided as well as news and business information sites. Forms and agreements are covered in detail. The helpful checklists (e.g., contract checklist, issuing stock checklist) are very thorough. The tax articles discuss things like barter tax and accounting issues and tax strategies for keeping the family business in the family. This well-organized, functional Website will be used by small and large business owners often.—**Susan C. Awe**

C

87. **Encyclopedia of Management.** 5th ed. Marilyn M. Helms, ed. Farmington Hills, Mich., Gale, 2006. 1003p. index. $290.00. ISBN 1-4144-0478-6.

This 5th edition of the *Encyclopedia of Management* is just over 1,000 pages. More than 300 essays by 45 contributors explain a wide variety of topics. Essays are arranged alphabetically in the table of contents and throughout the volume. There are also 18 "Functional Areas" described, such as "Emerging Topics in Management," "International/Global Management," and "Performance Measures and Assessment" that guide readers to relevant essays within the topic of interest. While some essays are only a few paragraphs, many extend to several pages.

"International Management" is 6 pages, includes 3 tables (which are scarce throughout the volume), and has 10 subheadings. Immediately following the essay are *see also* terms, as well as a further reading list. A 13-page index completes the volume. *See also* terms and acronyms are used extensively in the index.

This volume has an easy-to-use structure. Previous editions, such as the 4th (see ARBA 2001, entry 201) provided more contributors, and likely more illustrations and tables. This is, altogether, a very comprehensive and current collection of management essays. The 5th edition is highly recommended for any academic, special, or large public library. It is an excellent resource for undergraduate or graduate students, or anyone who wants to better understand business topics. Helms has edited a noteworthy business resource.—**Jim Agee**

C

88. **Encyclopedia of the History of American Management.** Morgen Witzel, ed. New York, Continuum Publishing, 2005. 564p. index. $195.00. ISBN 1-84371-131-1.

The *Encyclopedia of the History of American Management* contains biographies for nearly 260 business leaders, inventors, writers, and educators who have made significant contributions to the development of American business and management. General Editor Morgan Witzel collected the entries from the 1,130-page, two-volume set *The Biographical Dictionary of Management* (Thoemmes Press, 2001).

The *Encyclopedia* has a scholarly tone compared with *Business Leaders for Students* (see ARBA 2000, entry 118) or *American Business Leaders: From Colonial Times to the Present* (see ARBA 2000, entry 119). The contributors, mostly academics, offer a thorough assessment of each individual's work, in addition to biographical details. A selected bibliography rounds out most of the entries, offering a good starting point for conducting additional research.

The choice of entrants reflects a broad perspective of management. Psychologist Abraham Maslow is included for the influence that his theory, the hierarchy of needs, has had on both organizational behavior and marketing. Likewise, the work of economists Milton Friedman and John Kenneth Galbraith are examined with respect to the development of corporations.

The *Encyclopedia* provides cross-references along with a name index. Additional indexes by area of expertise, ethnicity, and gender would improve the work. Overall, the *Encyclopedia of the History of American Management* will be a useful addition for academic libraries that support an undergraduate and graduate management program.—**Elizabeth Kay Tompkins**

MARKETING AND TRADE

Dictionaries and Encyclopedias

C, P
89.   **History of World Trade Since 1450.** John J. McCusker, ed. New York, Macmillan Reference USA/Gale Group, 2006. illus. maps. index. $250.00/set. ISBN 0-02-865840-X; 0-02-866070-6 (e-book).
       Recently, two economic history encyclopedias have appeared: Cynthia Clark North's *The American Economy: A Historical Encyclopedia* (see ARBA 2004, entry 122), and Joel Mokyr's *Oxford Encyclopedia of Economic History* (see ARBA 2004, entry 127). To these two works is now added the excellent *History of World Trade Since 1450*, differentiating itself by taking the contemporary topic of world trade and treating it historically (covering over 500 years of history) and comprehensively.
       The *History of World Trade Since 1450* is arranged alphabetically, with over 400 entries that vary in length from 200 to 3,000 words. There is only slight overlapping with other encyclopedias, notably the *Oxford Encyclopedia of Economic History* (see, for example, entries under Capitalism, Henry Ford, Joint Stock Company, Mercantilism, and Population). At the beginning of volume 1, these 400-plus entries are thematically divided into 16 groups: "Business Families," "Cities," "Commodities," "Concepts and Ideas (Economic)," "Concepts and Ideas (General)," Corporations and Businesses," "Countries and Regions," Economic Agents," "Empires," "Industries," "Infrastructure," "Labor," "Organizations and Institutions," "People," "Phenomena," and "Shipping." This two-volume set is lavishly illustrated, filled with carefully chosen maps, graphs, historical images, and contemporary photographs, which enhance understanding of the entries.
       The volumes are "intended for general readers with a high school or college-level education" (p. ix). The contributors, experts in their respective fields, have abided by their instructions: neither jargon nor statistics mar the text; and each entry is written in plain English, easily accessible to anyone interested in the subject matter. Volume 2 also contains a glossary of terms readers might be unfamiliar with and 18 primary sources, including historical texts, speeches, agreements, treaties, and legislation.
       Most surprising, in this deeply researched and informative work, is the almost total lack of references to the Web. In contrast, the overzealous editor overuses the cross-reference function. Entries containing 20 or 30 cross-references are common; in an extreme case, the entry "United States," contains 138 cross-references.
       Still, these are minor quibbles. The *History of World Trade Since 1450* is an exceptional work of scholarship that easily meets its modest goal "to help in understanding the complex interactions between peoples over time as they sought to exchange goods and services to their own benefit" (p. ix). This set is recommended for all libraries.—**E. Wayne Carp**

REAL ESTATE

P
90.   **Plunkett's Real Estate & Construction Industry Almanac 2005.** Jack W. Plunkett, ed. Houston, Tex., Plunkett Research, 2005. 537p. index. $249.99pa. (w/CD-ROM). ISBN 1-59392-027-X.

This is the 2d edition of this work; the 1st edition was released in December 2003 (see ARBA 2004, entry 176). Users of other Plunkett industry almanacs will be familiar with the general format of this book. This book includes a brief glossary of real estate and construction terms, followed by four chapters. The first one discusses the major trends that are currently impacting the real estate and construction industry, including how the Internet has impacted the real estate business, the trend in designing and constructing "green" structures, and the trend away from rentals to home ownership. This is followed by a chapter on statistics gleaned from those U.S. government agencies that collect data on home ownership and public and private construction trends. The third section is a list of real estate and construction industry associations grouped by topic, such as alternative energy, career guidance, mortgage resources, and government agencies. Addresses, telephone numbers, Websites, and a brief distribution of each association's prime mission are given. The bulk of the book is devoted to detailed information of what Plunkett has labeled as "The Real Estate 400." This is a list of 408 prime movers in the industry, and how companies conduct business around the globe (although only 52 firms have headquarters outside of the United States). The companies listed are seen as prominent firms in the industry but may not be exclusively in the real estate or construction business. Financial data and vital statistics had to be available for the editors from the companies individually and from reputable statistic gathering agencies in order to be considered for inclusion.

The one-page profile of each company includes such information as types of business, list of brands divisions and affiliates, a list of their top executives, a five-year summary of sales and profits, geographic region where they primarily do business, and a section labeled "growth plans and other special features." The book includes an index of rankings within industry groups: an index by subsidiaries, brand names, and selected affiliations and an index of firms noted as "Hot Spots for Advancement" for women and minorities. The book comes with a CD-ROM that provides keyword searching and the ability to export information retrieved for all the companies to produce reports.

It would be difficult to easily find information on many of these companies included in this work; therefore, libraries in large business schools will find this a very useful acquisition. Companies in related fields will find this a useful ready-reference source.—**Judith J. Field**

5 Education

GENERAL WORKS

Dictionaries and Encyclopedias

C

91.   **Encyclopedia of Education and Human Development.** Stephen J. Farenga and Daniel Ness, eds. Armonk, N.Y., M. E. Sharpe, 2005. 3v. index. $349.00/set. ISBN 0-7656-1268-2.

While not as comprehensive as the recently published *Encyclopedia of Education* from Macmillan Reference (see ARBA 2004, entry 239), this focused, three-volume set nonetheless does an excellent job covering education, human development, and learning. The seven major sections of the encyclopedia address: constructs of learning; philosophical, social, and political issues in education; levels in educational practice; physical, motor, and cognitive domains; educational issues concerning diverse populations; people; and organizations. Every major section has numerous chapters (31 in all), each devoted to a key subtopic in the area. For example, section 2 includes essays within the field of Foundations of Education (i.e., philosophy, sociology, policy, equity and cultural issues, moral education, students at risk, achievement motivation), which is a welcome and appropriate addition to the *Encyclopedia*'s coverage. Similarly, section 3, "Levels in Educational Practice," has chapters on such subtopics as early childhood, middle level education, and higher education, among others. Section 4 covers the psychomotor domain, language development, semiotic principles, and the development of quantitative and spatial thinking. The signed essays are quite thorough and accompanied by a substantial list of references. There are a modest number of biographies and organization profiles in sections 6 and 7, with the former being selected after surveys of educational colleagues. Overall, there is appropriate attention both to the content and process of learning, as well as the social and structural contexts within which it takes place. An index provides fairly detailed access to subjects, but more selective access to names and titles. This is a sophisticated and worthy addition to the reference literature on education and is suitable for students and professionals in the field. [R: BL, 1 & 15 Jan 06, pp. 132-149]—**Stephen H. Aby**

Directories

C, P

92.   **Educators Resource Directory, 2005/06.** 6th ed. Millerton, N.Y., Grey House Publishing, 2005. 761p. index. $145.00pa.; $195.00 (online edition); $280.00 (print and online editions). ISBN 1-59237-080-2.

A thick and thorough volume, the *Educators Resource Directory* is a useful but concise resource for any educator at any level in the educational process. Like its predecessors, the *Directory* covers several different types of resources, including, but not limited to, associations, conferences and trade shows, publications, and testing resources. A new addition to the *Directory* comes in the form of a section devoted entirely to resources pertinent to the No Child Left Behind Act of 2001 (NCLB). This section also includes a listing for entries in the rest of the *Directory* related to the NCLB.

The *Directory* provides a user's guide to reading entries. The entries themselves include the title of the company or product; contact information (e.g., mailing address, telephone number, fax number); URL (where appropriate); entry description (which provides a brief overview of the company or product); key persons in the company; and the year the company was established. In addition to the resource listings, the *Directory* provides a section on statistics and rankings in nine categories ranging from higher education to learning resources and technology. Specific topics include degrees, enrollment, and student behavior. The *Directory* provides four different indexes to assist users in finding the information they need: entry and publisher name index; geographic index; Web sites index; and a new index subject index, which is organized according to core academic subjects. Another new aspect of the *Directory* is its online counterpart—the *Directory* in a searchable database format. A valuable and user-friendly tool, the *Educators Resource Directory* is a recommended purchase for any library, at any level.—**Megan W. Lowe**

Handbooks and Yearbooks

C, P

93.　***U.S. News & World Report*** **Ultimate Guide to Becoming a Teacher.** By Ben Wildavsky and the Staff of *U.S. News & World Report*. Naperville, Ill., Sourcebooks, 2004. 519p. index. $18.95pa. ISBN 1-4022-0291-1.

U.S. News & World Report Ultimate Guide to Becoming a Teacher is the latest foray of the magazine into education guides. This book fills a unique niche in that it provides information for college graduates without education degrees who want to become teachers. The book contains six short discussion chapters, an "Insider's Index" comparing education graduate schools, a directory of these schools, an alphabetic index of school names, and a section about the authors. The book begins with a discussion of the current state of education and then moves on to more practical matters, such as alternative certification programs, financing a graduate degree, and licensing requirements for each state. The comparative index and the directory of education graduate schools are organized alphabetically by school name within state sections. The comparative index looks at acceptance rates; average GRE scores; number of masters, specialists, and doctoral students; pass rates for state certification examinations; and teacher salaries. The directory provides information on graduate school Websites, degrees offered, admission fees, required tests, assistant positions available, tuition rates, and areas of specialization. This book is especially useful for those wanting to make a career change and wishing to understand the education culture. This book is a good complement to *A Guide to College Programs in Teacher Preparation*, written by the National Council for Accreditation of Teacher Education, and *Graduate Programs in Education 2004*, published by Peterson's Guides. This book is recommended for academic and public libraries. [R: Choice, Jan 05, p. 839]—**Cynthia Crosser**

ELEMENTARY AND SECONDARY EDUCATION

Directories

P, S

94.   **Summer Opportunities for Kids & Teenagers 2006.** Lawrenceville, N.J., Peterson's Guides, 2005. 987p. index. $29.95pa. ISBN 0-7689-1891-x.

These days there are summer camps for acting, chess, space, sports, the arts, academic subject specialties (e.g., mathematics, science, languages), and anything else one might imagine. This guide identifies more than 3,000 such camps around the United States and abroad, with useful descriptive information and a variety of ways to identify camps of interest.

The guide is organized into chapters arranged alphabetically by state and, following that, by country. Within a state or country, camps are listed alphabetically by name. For each camp one can find an address, general information, program information (i.e., dates, costs, availability of financial aid), contact information, application deadlines, available jobs, Websites, e-mail addresses, and lists of offerings (including arts, sports, wilderness/outdoors, trips, academics, and special interest areas). As with other Peterson Guides, there is an accompanying section of full, two-page advertisements provided by some of the camps; this is noted in the camp's brief entry. These provide much more information on camp offerings, its staff, and its philosophy and background, among other things.

There are supplementary directories that provide alternative means of identifying appropriate camps. The specialized directory lists camps by name, then location, under 12 categories covering academic programs, adventure, arts, bible, community service, cultural, family, outdoor, special needs, sports, traditional, and wilderness. There is also a travel programs directory, a special needs accommodations directory (subdivided by type of need), a religious affiliations directory, a sponsor directory, a substantial primary activity directory (arranged alphabetically by topic), and a program directory arranged alphabetically by program name. An introductory quick-reference chart lists general and program information for camps in each state. This is a wonderful resource for those students who have the time, resources, and specialized interests to pursue the opportunities. Public and school libraries should have this available for families.—**Stephen H. Aby**

Handbooks and Yearbooks

C, S

95.   Harmon, Deborah A., and Toni Stokes Jones. **Elementary Education: A Reference Handbook.** Santa Barbara, Calif., ABC-CLIO, 2005. 261p. index. (Contemporary Education Issues). $45.00; $50.00 (e-book). ISBN 1-57607-942-2; 1-57607-943-0 (e-book).

In *Elementary Education: A Reference Handbook* Harmon and Jones, professors of education at Eastern Michigan University, have provided a "one-stop" experience for everyone interested in elementary education. Teachers, parents, education students, and education researchers will all find something useful in this reference resource. It is divided into broad chapters ("Elementary Schools," "Foundations of Elementary Education," "Development of the Elementary Student," "The Elementary Learner," "Elementary School Curriculum," "Technology and Elementary Education," "Special Programs in Elementary Education," and "Print and Non-Print Resources in Elementary Education") , and within each chapter are more specific categories, including learning theories, language, foundations, current trends, diversity, technology and literacy, and legal issues in special education. Entries are succinctly and clearly written, and charts and tables are provided to summarize information when appropriate. Obvious attention to clarity and authority are present in the entries.

Each chapter has a general summary of the material contained, and a list of references is provided for further research. The chapter on print and nonprint resources is fairly complete, and the Internet links appear to be up to date. The authors have provided a reasonably detailed glossary to help novice users decipher the sometimes confusing educational acronyms and "buzz words." A detailed index is also provided to allow easy access to relevant information. *Elementary Education: A Reference Handbook* is an outstanding reference resource, and the price is even reasonable (although why the e-book is more expensive is a mystery to this reviewer). Large public libraries, academic libraries supporting programs in education, and even school media centers with professional development collections should be sure to buy this book.—**Mark T. Bay**

HIGHER EDUCATION

General Works

Directories

C, P

96.   **Barron's Guide to Graduate Business Schools.** 14th ed. By Eugene Miller and Neuman F. Pollack. Hauppauge, N.Y., Barron's Educational Series, 2005. 848p. index. $16.99pa. ISBN 0-7641-3198-2. ISSN 1043-190X.

    Barron's profiles more than 600 U.S. and Canadian schools that offer graduate business programs in this guide. Each profile states the school's name, address, telephone number, admission contact, Web address, and a short institutional history. The student body statistics include the school's retention rate, while the faculty section describes credentials and average class size. The library and computer lab facilities are discussed. Monetary factors are enumerated in the sections on cost and financial aid. Academics are covered in the sections on admissions, programs offered, course requirements, and average GMAT of accepted applicants. The placement section states the number of companies recruiting on campus, the degrees most in demand, the average and the range of starting salaries, and the percentage of graduates employed within three months of graduation. Preceding the profiles is a sample GMAT, a narrative about pursuing an MBA, and how to choose an institution to fit one's needs. This is a must-have resource for any library that has patrons who are considering graduate business studies.—**Holly Dunn Coats**

P, S

97.   **Barron's Guide to the Most Competitive Colleges.** 4th ed. Hauppauge, N.Y., Barron's Educational Series, 2005. 970p. illus. index. $18.99pa. ISBN 0-7641-3197-4.

    From Amherst to Yale, this is a collection of descriptive essays on nearly 70 of the most competitive American undergraduate colleges and universities. The essays, 10-15 pages in length, were written by current or recent graduates and include such basics as an introduction, admission requirements, academic life in its various aspects, social life and activities, financial aid, and lists of prominent graduates. These essays definitely give the reader a feel for life on each campus; they comprise more than 900 of the book's 970 pages.

    Inclusion was based on the standards of Barron's Selector Ratings in the comprehensive *Profiles of American Colleges* (26th ed.; see ARBA 2005, entry 291). A check of that publication reveals median test scores at these colleges are generally between 655 and 800 on the SAT I and 29 and above on the ACT. The acceptance rate at these colleges would not exceed 35 percent at the most; most acceptance rates range from the low teens (13 percent at Stanford) to 30 percent. Many fine colleges, such as Occidental (44 percent), did not make the cut. The guide is not strong on illustrations; there is one black-and-white photograph of each college and a beautiful front cover photograph.

The main body of the text is followed by smaller sections on "Strategies" (e.g., application, essay writing, financing, study). A chart shows how the colleges compare in acceptance numbers, test scores, and costs. The "College Summaries" section has capsule descriptions of each college. The "Biographies" section contains brief biographical sketches of the student contributors. This is a most unique volume in the crowded college guide field. It deserves a place in all libraries.—**Marshall E. Nunn**

C, S

98. **The College Board Book of Majors.** New York, College Board, 2004. 1252p. index. $24.95pa. ISBN 0-87447-701-9.

As with other College Board publications, this title, in its 1st edition, exists to help promote the mission of the Board: to connect students to college success and opportunity. Following the *College Board Index of Majors and Graduate Degrees* (24th ed.; see ARBA 2002, entry 268) and the *College Board Guide to 150 Popular College Majors*, it combines features of those two titles to become a more complete reference source.

Each description of the over 900 majors listed is composed of results of student questionnaires submitted by university professors. The book is divided into two parts: "The Majors," arranged alphabetically in broad subject fields; and the nationally accredited colleges offering the majors. Each listing indicates the degree level of the major.

MyRoad, a Website devoted to providing in-depth information about majors and careers and to compiling personal profiles, is described as a companion to the print guide. The glossary provides definitions of words and phrases associated with the academic experience with which high school students may be unfamiliar. The "Brief Descriptions of Majors" page, which gives one-sentence definitions of majors, is a good place for the novice to begin the process of learning what various majors are all about before they begin the in-depth study of the major. Any student seriously considering a major field of study will find helpful guidance in the pages of this book.—**Lois Gilmer**

C, S

99. **College Board College Handbook 2006.** 43d ed. New York, College Board, 2005. 2200p. index. $28.95pa. ISBN 0-87447-750-6.

The College Board College Handbook 2006, the 43d edition of this excellent reference work, is indispensable in providing students, their advisors, parents, and any interested parties with the most current information available on more than 3,600 accredited 2-year and 4-year colleges and universities in the United States. The material is divided into nine detailed, easy-to-use sections that include a planning workbook, information on college admission and placement tests, community colleges, early decision/early action plans, student life, and four-year and two-year colleges (alphabetically divided by state then school), and, finally, a section with tables and indexes. The most useful section is the detailed descriptions of each college. Information included for each college covers key facts, general information, freshman class and student body profiles, the basis for admission selection, the 2005-2006 annual costs, financial aid information, the application procedure, academics, honor college/programs, majors, most popular majors, computing on campus, student life, athletics, student services, and contact information. This work is an invaluable resource in the field of higher education directories that is recommended for all libraries.
—**Scott R. DiMarco**

C, P, S

100. **Four-Year Colleges 2006.** 36th ed. Lawrenceville, N.J., Peterson's Guides, 2005. 3087p. illus. index. $32.00pa. (w/CD-ROM). ISBN 0-7689-1749-2. ISSN 1544-2330.

The latest edition of this well-known reference guide provides complete and accurate information on more than 2,000 undergraduate institutions in the United States and Canada. Easy-to-use indexes under majors, school names, and geographic locations are included. Details on academic programs and degrees awarded; tuition, fees, and housing costs; entrance requirements and application procedures; student-faculty ratios; and campus life are only a few of the many frequently asked questions dealt with in this edition. Practical information on taking the SAT, ACT, and TOEFL tests is provided as well. A bonus college resources CD-ROM that features in-depth descriptions of approximately half of the institutions listed in the print edition, SAT and ACT practice tests, links to financial planning information at http://www.key.com, and access to BestCollegePicks.com (a new kind of search engine that lets users compare colleges based on their own goals and aspirations) is also included.—**Bradford Lee Eden**

C, P

101.   **Guide to Distance Learning Programs 2005.** Lawrenceville, N.J., Peterson's Guides, 2004. 879p. index. $29.95pa. ISBN 0-7689-1398-5.

Public and academic libraries seeking a reasonably priced, up-to-date, one-volume guide for readers interested in distance education will find that this compilation of basic advice and descriptions of degree and certificate programs will meet the needs of students seeking traditional correspondence courses as well as courses and degrees delivered via audio, video, or Internet technology. The publisher solicited most of the information directly from more than 1,100 accredited U.S. and 31 Canadian institutions, but the editors correctly caution prospective students to check specific institutional Websites for current tuition and fee figures. Brief profiles of each institution precede two-page overviews of course and program content. Most readers will likely go directly to the three very useful indexes organized by institutions, individual courses, and geographic area. Given the rapid, recent growth of distance education offerings and evolving course delivery technology, potential students will also benefit from closely examining the Websites of the Distance Education Clearinghouse (http://www.uwex.edu/disted/home.html) and the United States Distance Learning Association (http://www.usdla.org/).—**Julienne L. Wood**

C, P

102.   **Professional Degree Programs in the Visual and Performing Arts 2006.** Lawrenceville, N.J., Peterson's Guides, 2005. 569p. index. $29.00pa. ISBN 0-7689-1751-4.

This Peterson volume was published to aid students in the visual and performing arts select appropriate academic or conservatory programs that will help them achieve their vocational goals. Good advice is offered in terms of the comparative advantages and disadvantages of conservatory versus academic programs, as well as the pros and cons of B.A. and B.F.A. programs. There is also an essay dealing with the realistic appraisal of the employment opportunities in the visual and performing arts. There follows a section on college costs and sources of financial aid, as well as tips on procuring monetary help.

The heart of the volume is a detailed profile of the various U.S. and Canadian training programs in the visual and performing arts. This material is preceded by a quick reference chart that actually is a state-by-state table of degrees offered by the various programs. This table also provides quick reference information about each institution's enrollment size, tuition, summer programs, and the page numbers in the detailed program descriptions that supply very specific information. The layout of this table makes program comparisons easy for the reader. The detailed program descriptions are alphabetically presented in four segregated groups: arts, dance, music, and theater. Each citation consists of the institution's name and location. Further information is provided on total enrollment; undergraduate and graduate degrees available; accreditation; current enrollments; particulars about art, music, dance, and theater student profiles; and particulars about the faculty. There are some details about student life in each of the performance areas. Expenses and financial aid information is supplied and application procedures are described. Website and contact person information is also provided.

All of this information is followed by a very useful index of majors. All of the schools that offer programs in a particular visual or performance art specialty are listed here. The index is divided into the four sections (art, dance, music, and theater) and each section is further divided into subsections. The final part of the volume is a school index that lists every school and the programs offered by that institution.

This volume is a must have for high school and college counselors, art and performance department libraries, and students who want to pursue careers in these areas. The use of this work is indispensable and the necessary first step in career planning. The ability to so easily compare programs is certainly a vocational planning luxury. Peterson's should be congratulated for their modest pricing of this 569-page volume. —**Charles Neuringer**

Handbooks and Yearbooks

C

103.   Levinson, David L. **Community Colleges: A Reference Handbook.** Santa Barbara, Calif., ABC-CLIO, 2005. 255p. index. (Contemporary Education Issues). $45.00; $50.00 (e-book). ISBN 1-57607-766-7; 1-57607-767-5 (e-book).

With the publication of *Community Colleges*, ABC-CLIO's Contemporary Education Issues series grows to 24 "reference handbooks" (more have appeared since), addressing such topics as charter schools, bilingual education, assessment, and school vouchers. Users of earlier volumes in the series will recognize familiar features employed to provide both a review of major issues and trends and a guide to the research in yet another area of current interest in education. The greater part of *Community Colleges* consists of a series of analyses in essay form, beginning with an introduction to the topic with overviews of the major features and key concepts, and followed by a chronology and examination of the development of the community college movement. Subsequent chapters are devoted to discussion of specific issues such as the tensions between access and quality and between career/vocational and transfer curricula. Questions related to lifelong learning and distance learning are also addressed, and each chapter concludes with a list of references. Final chapters offer an annotated directory of organizations, associations and government agencies, and a bibliography of selected print and nonprint resources for further research and study. A glossary and index complete the volume.

With its high proportion of current references, up-to-date directory listings, and clearly written analyses of the history and issues, *Community Colleges* appears to have succeeded very well in its aim to provide an introduction to, and analysis of, its topic as well as a guide to further research. Because of its static format as a book publication, however, students and researchers will increasingly need to supplement it with more current literature as time goes by. Despite its subtitle, it is not a ready-reference source, and librarians will serve its potential users best by allowing it to be signed out for the extended study its contents require.—**Gregory M. Toth**

Financial Aid

Directories

C, P, S

104.   **The College Board Scholarship Handbook 2006.** 9th ed. New York, College Board, 2005. 600p. index. $26.95pa. ISBN 0-87447-752-2.

There are many scholarship directories currently available. This publication is not one of the larger ones, but it does direct students to some of the most promising sources of scholarship money, including state administered programs. It is probably also one of the most authoritative since the College Board, the organization that produces the SAT and an organization that is known to be dedicated to preparing students for college, publishes it.

There are useful opening sections with practical information about paying for college. They are followed by extensive eligibility indexes. The body of the work is alphabetically arranged. Descriptions of individual scholarships include information about the basis for selection and application requirements and deadlines. All state scholarships, even when privately funded, are listed under the name of the state in this alphabetic arrangement. There are also shorter sections on internships and loans that provide similar information. The work ends with sponsor and program indexes. This directory belongs in every scholarship collection.—**Christine E. King**

C, P, S

105.   Schlachter, Gail Ann, and R. David Weber. **Directory of Financial Aid for Women, 2005-2007.** El Dorado Hills, Calif., Reference Service Press, 2005. 528p. index. $45.00. ISBN 1-58841-131-1.

This title remains a well-organized, comprehensive, and easy-to-use guide for women seeking financial aid for undergraduate to postgraduate studies. Information on over 1,500 scholarships, fellowships, loans, grants, personal grants-in-aid, awards, and internships designed primarily or exclusively for women is given in the directory. The main section describes each funding source and lists sponsoring agency, address, purpose, eligibility, financial data, duration, limitations, number awarded, and deadline. Programs that supply more than one type of assistance are listed in all relevant subsections. The directory also provides indexes by program title, sponsoring agency, residency, tenability, subject, and calendar along with brief instructions for optimal use of each index.

The introductory section is quite thorough. Besides providing the obligatory purpose and sample entry explanation, it includes the extent of updating in this edition (it was completely updated with every item checked before inclusion), plans to update the directory in two years, and a list of other related publications. This work is highly recommended for all public, high school, and college libraries.—**Michele Russo**

C

106.   Schlachter, Gail Ann, and R. David Weber. **Financial Aid for Studying and Training Abroad, 2006-2008.** El Dorado Hills, Calif., Reference Service Press, 2006. 354p. index. $39.50. ISBN 1-58841-094-3.

This directory is a response to the National Security Act of 1991 and other programs that emphasize the importance of foreign-language study and undergraduate scholarships for study abroad. Included in the information provided for both structured and independent study are eligibility requirements, financial data, duration of the funding, special features and limitations, number of awards given, and application date. While other financial aid directories exist, this one is recommended for current and comprehensive coverage of more than 1,000 programs.

A currency conversion table identifies currency used in key countries covered by this directory and is to be used as a guide to the approximate value of the support offered. Additional assistance is provided by an annotated bibliography of general financial aids such as scholarships, fellowships, loans, grants, internships, awards and prizes, and financial assistance to special population groups.

Programs are identified and listed in several separate indexes: program titles, sponsoring organizations, geographic, subject, and calendar (deadline dates). The calendar index is divided into four major sections (the four categories addressed by this work): high school and undergraduate students, graduate students, postdoctorates, and professionals and other individuals. Other sections also indicate level of study covered.—**Lois Gilmer**

C, P, S

107.   Schlachter, Gail Ann, and R. David Weber. **Financial Aid for Veterans, Military Personnel & Their Dependents 2004-2006.** El Dorado Hills, Calif., Reference Service Press, 2005. 418p. index. $40.00. ISBN 1-58841-097-8.

According to the information presented in the introduction to this book, more than one-third of the U.S. population today has either direct or indirect ties with the armed services and billions of dollars a year have now been set aside for financial aid to these veterans, military personnel, and their dependents. Obviously there is a need for a comprehensive and user-friendly resource to enable those qualified for these funds to locate and access them. This directory is designed to meet that need and does so in a way that is indeed both convenient and sufficient for most users. It provides the right information, complete and accurate (to the degree that is possible in such a rapidly changing environment). To meet the challenge of escalating change, an online source is listed for updates and new information.

A clear explanation of how to use the directory and a sample entry are given. The directory is divided into 4 major sections: financial aid programs for veterans, military personnel, and their dependents (scholarships, fellowships/grants, loans, grants-in-aid, and awards); state sources of information on benefits; annotated bibliography of financial aid directories; and indexes. The indexes are worth noting. They are intuitive and greatly increase the convenience of the directory. Included are a program title index, a sponsoring organization index, a residency index, a tenability index, a subject index, and a calendar index.

It seems as though this particular resource would be exceptionally useful for high school counselors and college advisors in schools where there is a high proportion of students searching for financial aid. It provides information on sources that are not as widely known as others and, of course, if it does not provide desired information, the directory provides an annotated bibliography of financial aid directories.
—**Karen D. Harvey**

C, P, S
108.   **Scholarships, Fellowships, and Loans: A Guide to Education-Related Financial Aid Programs for Students and Professionals.** 22d ed. Farmington Hills, Mich., Gale, 2006. 1142p. index. $240.00. ISBN 0-7876-8821-5. ISSN 1058-5699.

A tradition of excellence continues in the 22d edition of *Scholarships, Fellowships, and Loans*. Detailed information on more than 5,400 awards is listed for students ranging from undergraduate and vocational/technical education to post-doctoral and professional studies. The preface includes three pages of useful tips on how to find financial aid that students should be encouraged to study.

The main body of the text includes entries that are alphabetically arranged by administering organization. In addition to contact information, each entry provides information about purpose, qualifications and restrictions, selection criteria, award amounts, number of awards granted, and application details.

The addition of six extremely useful indexes makes this resource stand out above similar sources. The vocational goals index is arranged by levels of study and broad subject categories to give the reader a quick overview of each award's purpose and eligibility requirements. Other indexes classify awards by fields of study, legal residence and place of study requirements, special recipients, and sponsors. These indexes allow users to further refine their search for appropriate awards.

While *Scholarships, Fellowships, and Loans* does not discuss financial aid programs administered and funded by individual colleges or universities, it does include useful information about state and federal programs, including the AmeriCorps. Although not inexpensive, *Scholarships, Fellowships, and Loans* is a valuable resource for anyone seeking financial aid. It is highly recommended for all libraries.—**Michele Russo**

INTERNATIONAL EXCHANGE PROGRAMS AND OPPORTUNITIES

C
109.   **Study Abroad 2006.** 13th ed. Lawrenceville, N.J., Peterson's Guides, 2005. 616p. index. $29.00pa. ISBN 0-7689-1894-4.

Now in its 13th annual edition, this extensive guide to overseas study opportunities is intended primarily for students at U.S. colleges. It provides information on over 1,900 semester- or year-long programs that are sponsored by accredited institutions, accepted for credit at U.S. colleges and universities, and not restricted to students enrolled at the sponsoring school.

The program descriptions, which make up the largest section of the book, are arranged by host country and include sponsoring and host institutions, focus and nature of each program, eligibility requirements, application deadline and term dates, living arrangements, costs, and contact information. The descriptions are well indexed by field of study, sponsoring institution, host institution, and availability of internships.

A "Guidance" section at the front of the volume provides a series of helpful essays addressing such topics as preparing and paying for study abroad, opportunities and considerations for persons with disabilities, internship and volunteer options, and health and safety tips. There are other titles that provide this kind of advice at greater length; even *Study Abroad for Dummies* (Wiley, 2003) and the UNESCO *Study Abroad 2004-2005* (32d ed.; see ARBA 2005, entry 312) provide more directory listings, although compiled for an international audience. For U.S. students, however, this Peterson's title surely represents the most useful and comprehensive directory.—**Gregory M. Toth**

LEARNING DISABILITIES AND DISABLED

C, P, S

110.   **Learning Disabilities Information for Teens: Health Tips About Academic Skills Disorders and Other Disabilities that Affect Learning.** Sandra Augustyn Lawton, ed. Detroit, Omnigraphics, 2006. 400p. index. (Teen Health Series). $58.00. ISBN 0-7808-0796-0.

Although ostensibly targeted at teenagers, this book provides a wealth of information for any reader interested in the signs, causes, and consequences of learning disabilities, as well as related legal rights and educational interventions. The book includes 52 chapters that are arranged under eight parts: overview; types of learning disabilities; co-occurring disorders; other disabilities and chronic conditions that affect learning; academic issues; living with a learning disability; legal rights; and more information. Within these categories, there can be upwards of 10 chapters on specific topics. For example, part 2, discussing types of learning disabilities, has chapters on dyslexia, dysgraphia, dyscalculia, speech and language disorders, impaired sensory and motor skills, processing disorders, and gifted students with learning disabilities. The chapters themselves, excerpted from other sources, are generally well written and include occasional factoids, quick tips, and reminders. At times, an author is suitably cautious about the causes of some conditions. For example, conduct disorder associated with attention deficit disorder is noted to be "subjective" in its determination and potentially easily confused with adolescent rebellion. Other times, such as in the discussion of attention deficit hyperactivity disorder (ADHD), the chapter talks of the legitimate incidence of the condition but avoids discussing the precipitous increase in its behavioral diagnosis in schools. This unevenness in depth of coverage is not surprising given the assembled nature of the chapters.

The last two chapters identify additional readings as well as list learning disabilities organizations with addresses, telephone numbers, Website addresses, and e-mails. A comprehensive name/title/subject index provides additional access to an already well-delineated chapter organization. Public and academic libraries should want this title for both students and general readers.—**Stephen H. Aby**

NONPRINT MATERIALS

S

111.   **Educators Guide to Free Videotapes, 2005-2006: Elementary/Middle School.** 6th ed. Kathleen Suttles Nehmer, ed. Randolph, Wis., Educators Progress Service, 2005. 292p. index. $37.95pa. ISBN 0-87708-428-9.

S

112.   **Educators Guide to Free Videotapes, 2005-2006: Secondary Edition.** 52d ed. Kathleen Suttles Nehmer, ed. Randolph, Wis., Educators Progress Service, 2005. 295p. index. $37.95pa. ISBN 0-87708-418-1.

Educators Progress Service publishes 16 educators' guides to free materials. Each of these two video guides lists a significant number of new titles each year (1,299 titles in the current elementary and middle school edition; nearly 2,000 titles in the current secondary and adult edition). The videos are from governmental, organizational, and corporate agencies contacted annually by the publisher. Main entries include the title, a brief annotation, availability, suggested grade levels, an order number, the production date, the format, the running time, any special notes, terms of borrowing, and the source contact information. The publisher includes a sample letter of request, a list of suggestions on how to cooperate with the agencies who provide materials, and an evaluation form that may be returned to sponsoring agencies to guide the development of other educational materials.

Educators Progress Service has a long history of providing these guides. Libraries that have found use for these guides in the past or who have demand for this type of information will want to subscribe to have the most current editions on hand. These titles are recommended for libraries serving teachers and other educators and trainers.—**Rosanne M. Cordell**

6 Ethnic Studies

ANTHROPOLOGY

C

113. **Anthropology Review Database. http://wings.buffalo.edu/ARD/.** [Website]. Free. Date reviewed: Jan 06.

Published by Department of Anthropology, University of Buffalo, the *Anthropological Review Database* (ARD) provides signed full-text reviews or citations to reviews of books, audiovisual materials, software, multimedia, exhibits, tourist sites, conferences, and online resources in anthropology. Published online since September 1997, ARD aims to publish reviews as they are written and edited, usually approximately two months after the reviewed item's publication. In practice, many ARD reviews appear later. In addition, it include reviews published in 12 other print and electronic anthropological journals or Websites, including, for example, *American Antiquity*, *American Journal of Physical Anthropology*, and *Current Anthropology*. Coverage varies across the journals but extends as far back as 1990 for *American Antiquity*. As of July 2005, ARD included almost 2,400 reviews, including 270 written for ARD. Hugh Jarvis, an anthropologist at the University of Buffalo, is editor-in-chief, and the database has an editorial board and an editorial review board; the latter includes 13 editors for anthropology areas. The ARD reviews are written primarily by faculty members in anthropology. Brief biographies of some reviewers are available at the Website. ARD solicits reviews by listing materials to be reviewed at the Website; the site also includes guidelines for reviews, which address both content and style. Reviews are accessible via both search and browsing modes. Search provides access by title, author, subject, year, medium, and reviewer; searching by no entry retrieves the entire database. Browsing is limited to ARD reviews or reviews published within the last 90 days. A database on publishers, providing contact information and addresses, is available through a separate search with access by keywords. This is a useful Website but access to the full-text of older reviews is available through *Jstor* in most academic libraries in more core journals.
—Marilyn Domas White

ETHNIC STUDIES

General Works

S

114. Downing, Karen, Darlene Nichols, and Kelly Webster. **Multiracial America: A Resource Guide on the History and Literature of Interracial Issues.** Lanham, Md., Scarecrow, 2005. 253p. index. $35.00pa. ISBN 0-8108-5199-7.

America is almost to the point in its contentious racial history where interracial marriages and interracial children no longer merit unabashed shock, hushed gossip, or even a quizzical look. Over the past two decades, the number of interracial marriages has doubled, culminating in a population explosion of inter-racial children. As interracial relationships become commonplace, a vast array of books and materials on the subject has appeared. This book is the first attempt to systematically categorize this growing body of scholarship. Although not completely comprehensive, this literature review is nevertheless substantial. The strength of the book is that it is geared toward parents, youth, and high school teachers. For example, parents and teenagers are given a quick tutorial in chapter 1 on how to access interracial literature. Another chapter is devoted entirely to books for children and young adults, ranging from picture books to fiction and nonfiction for older children. In chapter 2, teachers are given a first-person account on how to teach an interracial issues course. Teachers also will be interested in chapter 4, which provides the core historical literature, including fiction, personal and family accounts, early social and scientific studies of interracial matters, laws and politics, and social commentary. Other chapters discuss politics and being interracial, dating and marriage, families, transracial adoption, multiracial identity development, the intersection of race and queer sexuality, and interracial relationships in the motion pictures. The text also provides a cou-ple of useful appendixes for parents and adolescents, particularly a vocabulary and definition of terms used in interracial literature. For teachers, another appendix provides a course outline, required texts, a course pack, and weekly course outlines.—**Paul Gerard Connors**

C, P

115. **Multiculturalism in the United States: A Comparative Guide to Acculturation and Ethnicity.** rev. ed. John D. Buenker and Lorman A. Ratner, eds. Westport, Conn., Greenwood Press, 2005. 435p. in-dex. $75.00. ISBN 0-313-32404-2.

This new, significantly expanded edition of a work that first appeared over a decade ago (Green-wood Press, 1992) reflects an ever-increasing focus on the phenomenon of multiculturalism in American life, particularly some of its current manifestations. The editors have added seven socio-historic essays to their original 10, each devoted to an immigrant group of recent importance, raising the total number of pages from 271 to 435. New groups covered are Arab Americans, Asian Indian Americans, Dominican Americans, Filipino Americans, Haitian Americans, Korean Americans, and Vietnamese Americans. Re-maining essays on more traditional groups such as German Americans or Mexican Americans have been revised and their bibliographies updated. The same holds true for the essays on African Americans and American Indians. A substantial bibliographic essay at the end of the volume listing items on immigration in general has received a five-page "Addendum for the Second Edition."

The professors and scholars who contributed these essays provide solid, but never dry, academic in-formation on various aspects of each group's experience, pointing out both similarities with and differ-ences from other groups. As they explain in an updated introduction, the editors encouraged flexibility within certain guidelines. The six-volume *Encyclopedia of Multiculturalism* (see ARBA 95, entry 396) is more inclusive but the depth of analysis and overview of secondary literature found here, not to mention its updating of a timely subject, make this a desirable purchase for academic libraries.—**Willa Schmidt**

C, S

116. **Peoples, Nations, and Cultures: An A-Z of the Peoples of the World, Past and Present.** John M. MacKenzie, ed. London, Weidenfeld & Nicolson; distr., New York, Sterling Publishing, 2005. 672p. maps. index. $49.95. ISBN 0-304-36550-5.

This book covers "diverse, dominant and prolific" human species. It is organized into five sections: the Americas, Africa, Europe, South and Central Asia and the Middle East, and East and Southeast Asia and Oceania. Each section lists ethnic groups, including subgroups and tribes, in alphabetic order. Over 2,000 entries of peoples are given. An introduction on the historical development of the human species and on selected terminology is useful. At the end is an index of entries from A to Z.

It describes well each entry. A number of cultures have separate entries, such as Acheulian, Aurig-nacian, Bandkeramik, Bell Beaker, Great Zimbabwe, Sangoan, and Yayoi, but the book in general prepon-derates in historical not cultural aspects. Many maps are provided. In some entries a number of sub-ethnic groups and tribes are listed in boxes. But, not all are profiled. For instance, in the entry of "Gauls" (p. 336), 35 main tribes are listed in a box, only one-third of them have entries. Again, 3 out of the 20 main ethnic groups in a box in the entry of "Chinese" (p. 581) do not have separate entries. All groups listed in the boxes but not justified for separate entries should be given at least a one- or two-line description.

An error may be noted in the entry of "Hong Kong Chinese" (p. 592). Hong Kong is a special administrative region of China. There is no capital called "Victoria." The book has an extensive coverage and is a fine reference guide. A subject index will enhance its usefulness. [R: LJ, 15 June 05, p. 104]—**Tze-chung Li**

African Americans

Dictionaries and Encyclopedias

C, P

117. **Africana: The Encyclopedia of the African and African American Experience.** 2d ed. Kwame Anthony Appiah and Henry Louis Gates Jr., eds. New York, Oxford University Press, 2005. 5v. illus. maps. index. $500/set. ISBN 0-19-517055-5.

Although the 1st edition is only 6 years old, librarians and scholars will want to invest in the 2d edition of this title. Under the editorship of Appiah and Gates, two of the greatest names in contemporary black studies scholarship, the new 5-volume edition features over 4,400 articles, including over 1,200 brand-new entries and hundreds that have undergone extensive revision. Almost every article has been penned by a specialist in the field, and the advisory board boasts itself is impressive. Articles range from a couple of paragraphs to 10 or more pages, depending on the topic, and most feature cross-references and secondary bibliographies. Material is presented for the most part matter-of-factly, without the one-sided commentary that has marred otherwise fine recent reference tools. Excellent full-color photographs, maps, and other illustrations complement the text, and charts and large graphs are scattered throughout. The new edition also includes a comprehensive index, missing from the 1st edition, along with a lengthy bibliography and topic list. The large typeface should attract browsers, although the slick pages also make for unusually heavy volumes. The only complaint one might have with this edition is that a portion of the articles are not original but rather are culled from other standard reference sources, such as the *Dictionary of American Negro Biography* (1982). Some of the subject headings also are a bit awkward (e.g., "Black Towns"), but that does not detract from the overall excellence of the work. This title is highly recommended for all libraries, to replace the 1st edition. [R: LJ, Aug 05, p. 119; SLJ, Dec 05, p. 89; BL, 1 & 15 Jan 06, p. 19]—**Anthony J. Adam**

C, S

118. **Encyclopedia of African American Society.** Gerald D. Jaynes, ed. Thousand Oaks, Calif., Sage, 2005. 2v. illus. index. $295.00/set. ISBN 0-7619-2764-6.

Although the market seems flooded with black studies reference material, Jaynes' new work focusing on social events and issues of consequence that provide "the source of continuing cohesiveness" of an "African American society" should find a home in most collections. The approximately 700 unsigned alphabetically arranged entries cover social issues, humanities, people, and places, with most articles ranging from half to a few pages in length. Some of the general articles (e.g., "Academy Awards") are not as up-to-date or complete as they could be, but the more specific entries are for the most part solid. The topics themselves will be found in the average quality African American encyclopedia, and the presentation is primarily straightforward and factual, rather than interpretive. However, the sparse commentary plays against Jaynes' goal, in that the reader often cannot sense the significance within a cultural continuum of many events and individuals. Perhaps this problem arises from the nature of the contributors, 8 (of 18) of whom are "independent scholars" rather than working academicians. Also, the breadth of topical coverage, although welcome, suggests the existence of numerous African American "societies" rather than a cohesive "society." Some small black-and-white illustrations highlight the text, and a good index concludes the work. Appendixes include a list of "African Americans in Halls of Fame," colleges with black studies programs, and an extensive secondary bibliography. Despite these criticisms, Jaynes will find an audience seeking basic African American information, alongside Salzman's *Encyclopedia of African-American Culture and History* (see ARBA 97, entry 331), Mack's *African American Encyclopedia* (2d ed.; see ARBA 2002, entry 309) and Altman's *Encyclopedia of African American Heritage* (2d ed.; see ARBA 2001, entry 287). This work is recommended for secondary school and undergraduate libraries. [R: SLJ, June 05, p. 90; LJ, Dec 04, p. 166]—**Anthony J. Adam**

Arab Americans

P, S

119.   Kayyali, Randa A. **The Arab Americans.** Westport, Conn., Greenwood Press, 2006. 177p. illus. index. (The New Americans). $45.00. ISBN 0-313-33219-3.

As one volume in The New Americans series, which focuses on updating readers on the "newer" waves of immigrants over the last 30 years, *The Arab Americans* is published in a post-September 11th time where most of us either want or should want to know more about the ethnic group that many incorrectly stereotype as terrorists. The book provides the general reader with an easy-to-read overview of the Arab American community—who they are, why they have come to the United States, how well they have integrated into mainstream society—as well as providing some in-depth details on their religion, politics, employment, customs, and impact on U.S. society.

We learn that beginning in 1880 the first wave of Arab immigrants were largely Christian men from Lebanon. Now, the more diverse Arab American community, which is still more than one-third Lebanese, includes more Muslims, and many are from Egypt, Iraq, and Jordan. *The Arab Americans* explores the different identities of Arab Americans, but also discusses the commonalities, including their struggle in being recognized as a minority group. Filling a gap in literature on this topic for which there were only books for children or for academic researchers, this book also includes brief biographies of notable Arab Americans, tables with immigration facts, a short bibliography and glossary, and a few black-and-white photographs. —**Shelly McCoy**

Indians of North America

Dictionaries and Encyclopedias

C, P, S

120.   **American Indian Culture.** Carole A. Barrett and Harvey J. Markowitz, eds. Hackensack, N.J., Salem Press, 2004. 3v. illus. maps. index. (Magill's Choice). $188.00/set. ISBN 1-58765-192-0.

American Indian Culture joins three other Magill's publications relating to Native North Americans from the sixteenth century to the present day. The essays in *American Indian Culture* add 275 entries to the more than 800 covered in the companion publications. Bibliographies and essays have been updated and/or revised and 16 new essays were commissioned for this publication. Arranged alphabetically by topic, each of the essays addresses a cultural phenomenon characteristic of the indigenous peoples of North America. The essays range in length from 250 to 3,000 words and cover the range of culture from lifeways, religious rituals, and material culture to art forms and modern social phenomena. There are 20 separate essays that cover both "Architecture" and "Arts and Crafts" in 10 North American culture areas.

Each essay contains the keyword of the topic, tribe or tribes affected (often but not always pan-tribal), a brief synopsis of topic's significance, and a description and discussion of the topic's importance in American Indian culture. All essays are cross-referenced and end with further study lists, including Web resources. The media includes movies, but unaccountably fails to mention *When the Legends Die* or *Light in the Forest*, both acclaimed as important novels and motion pictures dealing with acculturation difficulties. All three volumes use consecutive page numbers but show only the alphabetic range of content on the spine.

Only volume 3 contains a comprehensive subject index of all three volumes. The index contains only page numbers, rather than both volume and page numbers, which makes its use more difficult. The black-and-white illustrations break no new ground and vary in value.

American Indian Culture's three volumes are excellent for browsing and contain some interesting tribal folktales, but students researching a particular cultural aspect of a single tribe must do a lot of page-turning to find pertinent information. Those libraries needing the latest information on North American Native American culture will probably find *American Indian Culture* a welcome addition.—**Kay O. Cornelius**

Handbooks and Yearbooks

P, S

121.   **American Indian Contributions to the World Series.** By Emory Dean Keoke and Kay Marie Porterfield. New York, Facts on File, 2005. 5v. illus. maps. index. $175.00/set; $35.00/vol. ISBN 0-8160-5392-8.

The authors of this work previously collaborated on a well-received reference book for adult readers, the *Encyclopedia of American Indian Contributions to the World* (see ARBA 2002, entry 324), that addressed the same general topic. While it would be logical to assume that the content is similar, this series has been developed for a special market—young people. The content, reading level, organization, and format are designed to interest the intermediate reader and meet the demands of typical school curricula.

Keoke is American Indian and Porterfield has extensive experience working with American Indian people, having taught, for example, at Oglala Lakota College. Their respect for Indian ingenuity and cultures and sensitivity to Indian issues is evident throughout each book in the series. They acknowledge, "that there has been no intention to speak on behalf of any tribe or to pretend knowledge in the ways of all Indian people." The titles of the five volume in the series are: "Buildings, Clothing, and Art"; "Food, Farming, and Hunting"; "Medicine and Health"; "Science and Technology"; and "Trade, Transportation, and Warfare."

The books are organized in logical themes. For example, in one volume there are chapters on "Clothing from Hides" and "Clothing from Fiber," which extend the reader's knowledge of the importance of the environment in the development of cultures as well as telling about how clothes were made. There are numerous sidebars that provide interesting information and enhance the text. The sidebars are black and white, as are the many photographs. The authors explain that the quality of historical photographs is not equal to the quality of contemporary photographs, but that they greatly contribute to readers' understanding.

To supplement the text, each volume includes the following: a glossary of ancient cultures of the Americas, a listing of tribes organized by culture area, 15 maps of the culture areas (including Mesoamerican, Circum-Caribbean, South American culture areas, and Ancient Civilizations of the Americas), suggested further reading, and an extensive index. A notable feature in every chapter is a small timeline, inserted when appropriate and important.

The cover of each individual book is illustrated by the work of a prominent artist. The back of each cover introduces the content of each book, which is helpful. This is a series that should be a part of public, elementary, and middle school libraries. [R: SLJ, June 05, pp. 90-92]—**Karen D. Harvey**

Indians of South America

S

122.   **Early Civilizations in the Americas Reference Library.** By Sonia Benson. Farmington Hills, Mich., U*X*L/Gale, 2005. 3v. illus. maps. index. (Early Civilizations in the Americas Reference Library). $110.00/set. ISBN 0-7876-9252-2.

In these three volumes written for young adults, it is evident that the author and publisher were knowledgeable of the particular needs of middle and high school students and classrooms. The organization of each volume is unusual and exceptionally practical for students of this age and their teachers and is worthy of special note.

The first two volumes tell the story of the development of the earliest known societies in South America and Mesoamerica from their beginnings to the Spanish conquest. Included are dates, locations, sites, history, arts and sciences, religions, economies, governments, and the decline of these ancient civilizations. A third volume presents 23 biographies and primary sources. Included in this volume are excerpts from the memoirs and histories by indigenous writers and Spanish missionaries and conquerors following the conquest.

The first volume begins with a "Reader's Guide" and introduces the purpose and organization of the series. A timeline of events and a thorough "Words to Know" or glossary section place these ancient civilizations in a larger historical context and prepares the reader to understand the information that follows. A section on research and activities suggest ideas for complementing the series. Teachers will appreciate this useful section.

This framework is further extended by providing an introduction to early American civilizations with a broad overview of the world's first civilizations. The next chapter begins with an overview of human life in South America and Mesoamerica before the development of civilizations. The tricky term *civilization* has been carefully defined here.

The content in volume 2 is focused on the Mesoamerican civilizations from the Olmecs through the Aztecs. A paperback cumulative index is another useful part of this collection. Once criticism of this book is its title. At first glance, the assumption is made that the ancient cultures of North America are included. An additional volume, in a similar format, is needed for North American civilizations such as the Ancestral Puebloans, Hohokam, Mogollan, and other ancient cultures of North America.

All three volumes and the index could easily support an engaging high school class. Currently, however, few high schools have a social studies/history curriculum that includes an in-depth study of ancient South American and Mesoamerican cultures. A class like this would be exciting and appropriate, and perhaps engage our increasing number of Hispanic students. These volumes should have a place in middle school, high school, and public libraries.—**Karen D. Harvey**

Irish Americans

C, P

123.   **The Columbia Guide to Irish American History.** By Timothy Meagher. New York, Columbia University Press, 2005. 398p. index. (Columbia Guides to American History and Cultures). $45.00. ISBN 0-231-12070-2.

The purpose of this book is to provide a general introduction to the experience of the Irish in America for readers beginning to study it for the first time. The author is associate professor of history and curator of the American Catholic History Collections at Catholic University of America. Two of his previous books, *New York Irish* and *Inventing Irish America: Generation, Class and Ethnic Identity in a New England City, 1880-1928*, won the James Donnelly prize for best books in Irish American history. He is also author of *From Paddy to Studs: Irish American Communities in the Turn of the Century Era, 1880-1920* and other works on the Irish and Catholicism.

This Columbia Guide contains five parts: "History of Irish Americans from the Seventeenth to the Twenty-First Century," "Issues and Themes in Irish American History," "Important People, Organizations, Events, and Terms," "Chronology of Irish America," and a bibliography. There is a dictionary-type index. The first part occupies nearly half of the work; is very well done, as we would expect from a scholar with the author's credentials and previous achievements, and is an excellent starting point for readers new to the topic. The chapters in part 2, on Irish American gender/family, politics, nationalism, and race, could have been incorporated into part 1 giving the story more depth and complexity. The only comparable work in the reviewer's reference department is Michael Glazier's *Encyclopedia of the Irish in America* (University of Notre Dame Press, 1999). This is a larger work, with signed entries by over 200 writers edited by Glazier, a co-editor of the *Encyclopedia of American Catholic History* (see ARBA 99, entry 1286), who is interested in Irish American genealogy. The Glazier work's entries each conclude with a number of further reading references, unannotated. The Irish in each of the 50 states are considered, in addition to biographical and topical articles. *The Columbia Guide* has a chronology, while Glazier's does not. *The Columbia Guide*'s bibliography has nice annotations. Glazier's contains more entries overall than *The Columbia Guide*'s part 3 on important people, organizations, events, and terms, but does not offer the fine narrative history of *The Columbia Guide*. Were a person to do a paper on Richard J. Daley, mayor of Chicago from 1955-1976, one would use the entries in both these works to good profit. This is a nice addition to reference collections for those that have space to add a reasonably priced, quality work. If there is no room in reference, libraries are encouraged to buy it for their circulating collections.—**Agnes H. Widder**

Jews

C

124.   **Antisemitism: A Historical Encyclopedia of Prejudice and Persecution.** Richard S. Levy, ed. Santa Barbara, Calif., ABC-CLIO, 2005. 2v. illus. index. $185.00/set; $200.00 (e-book). ISBN 1-85109-439-3; 1-85109-444-X (e-book).

This 2-volume set contains over 600 articles on antisemitic incidents (e.g., the Kielce Progrom), persons both historical (e.g., Vincente Ferrer, a fourteenth-century Spanish priest) and current (e.g., David Duke, Louis Farrakhan), political groups and organizations (e.g., American Nazi Party, Liberty Lobby), publications (e.g., Protocols of the Elders of Zion), and 28 countries/regions. Each signed article contains a bibliography and *see also* references, and many of the entries were written by recognized authorities on the subjects, such as Geoffrey Cocks on Psychoanalysis, Peter Hayes on German Big Business, Jeremy Jones on Australia, John T. Pawlikowski on several Roman Catholic topics, and Roni Stauber on both Holocaust denial and David Irving. Articles range in length from a few paragraphs to several pages; other features include numerous black-and-white photographs and illustrations, and an index. While several topics can elicit strong opinions among the public (e.g., Poland, Jedwabne, Popes Pius IX and XII), they are treated here with balance and objectivity. Although many of this book's entries are treated in historical, Judaica, and religious reference books, it is convenient to have them discussed in depth in one set. This well-written and thoroughly researched encyclopedia should become the standard reference source in the field. [R: LJ, 15 Sept 05, p. 89; BL, 1 & 15 Jan 06, p. 19]—**John A. Drobnicki**

Latin Americans and Caribbeans

Dictionaries and Encyclopedias

C, P, S

125.   **Encyclopedia Latina: History Culture, and Society in the United States.** Ilan Stavans and Harold Augenbraum, eds. Danbury, Conn., Grolier, 2005. 4v. illus. maps. index. $499.00/set. ISBN 0-7172-5815-7.

This encyclopedia, designed for students and scholars, presents a broad panorama of the Hispanic experience in the United States and contributions of Latinos to American history, society, and culture. Its scope is broad, covering the sixteenth to twenty-first centuries. It is multidisciplinary in content, including broad, overview articles, as well as entries on specific individuals and events. There are about 150 biographical entries (23 percent of the total), representing, according to the editors, a balance between the individual and the community. It is important to emphasize that the focus of the encyclopedia is on Latinos in the United States, not Hispanic civilization in general or Latin America in particular.

Entries, arranged alphabetically, vary in length, from about 500 to 5,000 words. They are signed and include a list of related articles that point the reader to other parts of the encyclopedia where the topic is expanded or considered in another context. They also include a short bibliography of print and electronic resources. Cross-references are provided. The contributors are mostly Latino or Latina academics. Special features include excerpts from literature, poetry, speeches, and recipes. Maps and statistical charts show the distribution of the Latino population in the United States. An appendix includes primary documents of historical significance reproduced in their entirety, statistical tables, and a chart of Latino and Latina representation in Congress from 1822 to 2004. Illustrations in black and white appear throughout the text, in addition to a section of impressive color plates in each volume. The paper is good quality, with clear, easy-to-read type. Other useful features include the alphabetical listing of all entries at the beginning of volume 1, and a listing of entries by subject category at the end of volume 4, along with an extensive, detailed index. The introduction serves to clarify terminology issues, as well as provides a background and description of the process of preparing the encyclopedia. Overall, this work is an important contribution to Latino history, culture, and society that will enrich and enhance reference collections in school, academic, and public libraries. [R: LJ, 15 June 05, p. 100; SLJ, Dec 05, p. 94; BL, 1 & 15 Jan 06, p. 19]—**Susan J. Freiband**

C, P

126.   **The Oxford Encyclopedia of Latinos and Latinas in the United States.** Suzanne Oboler and Deena J. González, eds. New York, Oxford University Press, 2005. 4v. illus. maps. index. $525.00/set. ISBN 0-19-515600-5.

Oxford's four-volume encyclopedia dedicated to the Latino experience in the United States is a welcomed resource. Cross-disciplinary in nature, it examines not only important figures in Latino history but also Latino cultural, economic, social, and political achievements. Instead of casting Latinos as a homogeneous group, the editors cogently acknowledge the diverse cultural and social backgrounds of the peoples collectively referred to as Latino. As a result, this extensive undertaking encompasses a wide swath of peoples including Chicanos, Puerto Ricans, and Cubans.

The encyclopedia contains more than 900 alphabetically arranged entries that are made up of four general types of essays—historical, thematic, issue, and biographies. Historical essays examine the social and cultural backgrounds of the various ethnic groups represented in the encyclopedia, while the thematic essays are interdisciplinary in nature and provide general information on these groups including discussions of important individuals and events. Issue essays elaborate on specific topics raised in the thematic essays, while biographies, naturally, focus on individuals who have contributed significantly to the Latino experience in the United States. These essays work well together, allowing the reader to transition from the general to the more specific with ease. They are clearly written and most offer sufficient detail to spark further study. There are many tools to assist students and researchers in using the encyclopedia. Cross-references, bibliographies, a systematic outline, and an index make it accessible to a wide audience.

Students, faculty, or general readers alike will find that this encyclopedia is a valuable tool for researching Latino history, culture, experiences, and contributions to the United States. Although no work is perfect, this one is well executed and is as close to comprehensive as possible given the breadth of its subject matter. [R: LJ, Jan 06, p. 162; BL, 1 & 15 Jan 06, p. 20]—**Melvin Davis**

7 Genealogy and Heraldry

GENEALOGY

Directories

P

127.   **The Genealogist's Address Book.** 5th ed. By Elizabeth Petty Bentley. Baltimore, Md., Genealogical Publishing, 2005. 783p. index. $49.99pa.; $19.99 (CD-ROM edition). ISBN 0-8063-1757-4; 0-8063-9850-7 (CD-ROM).

The 5th edition of the print volume of this work is 49 pages shorter than the previous edition (see ARBA 2000, entry 328). The scope is genealogical addresses within the United States. The information contained in this edition was gathered from direct mail questionnaires, e-mail inquiries, and some Internet resources. In her questionnaire, the author asked for the name and address of the institution, voice and fax numbers, e-mail addresses, Website URL, the contact person with title, the hours of operation, periodical title produced (if any), frequency of publication, cost of subscription, cost of membership, research by mail fees, and comments about the organization's specialties. Some listings, however, have only name and address. Some organizations requested that they not be included simply because of the additional workload that genealogists generate.

The book is divided into four parts. Part 1 lists national organizations, including federal government offices, vital records offices, historical and genealogical societies with national focus, and independent publications unrelated to a geographical region. Part 2 is the major section of the work. It lists state resources arranged alphabetically within each state. Part 3 lists ethnic and religious organizations, archives, libraries, and societies. Part 4 lists special resources, including lineage, hereditary, and patriotic societies; surname registries; radio programs; and other miscellaneous organizations. There is also a comprehensive index. The CD-ROM version of this title provides all the information in the print version but in a easy-to-search database format.

There were a few mistakes found in the work. However, this would be much more useful if it were broken down geographically to at least the county, if not city level, since most genealogists are interested in local resources for finding their family. This will be useful in most collections. [R: BL, 1 & 15 Jan 06, p. 151]—**Robert L. Turner Jr.**

Handbooks and Yearbooks

P

128.   Carmack, Sharon DeBartolo. **Carmack's Guide to Copyright & Contracts: A Primer for Genealogists, Writers & Researchers.** Baltimore, Md., Genealogical Publishing, 2005. 119p. index. $15.95pa. ISBN 0-8063-1758-2.

This exceptionally concise, well-written work will be gratefully received by the book writing public. A guide of this type has been a long time coming, and will certainly be appreciated by the genealogical community to which it is addressed.

Among the topics that are addressed the reader will find" "Copyright Basics"; "Fair Use and the Public Domain"; "Illustrations, Photos, and Maps"; "Works for Hire"; "Collaboration Agreements"; "Journal/Magazine Contracts"; and contracts for books, electronic works, and self publishing. Those who serve as editors of genealogical and/or family surname magazines will learn from the topics covered, and will surely benefit from the suggestions that are offered.

Although the author does not proclaim to offer legal advice, she does provide enough common sense information to assist the reader in finding more, or to ask intelligent questions if an attorney is needed. This work is highly recommended for individuals seeking more information, and it should be added to all good genealogical library collections.—**Carol Willsey Bell**

Indexes

P

129.   Bockstruck, Lloyd deWitt. **Denizations and Naturalizations in the British Colonies in America, 1607-1775.** Baltimore, Md., Genealogical Publishing, 2005. 350p. index. $35.00pa. ISBN 0-8063-1754-X.

The introduction to this work explains that British citizens continued to be British citizens in their American colonies, and colonists' children born in America were considered British citizens as well. The British could not entice enough of their citizens to move to the colonies. In turn, they invited foreigners to become citizens via either naturalization or denization. The later included civil rights. Only naturalization, which was costly and harder to obtain, included both civil and political rights. There were, over the years, also numerous changes in these laws. The last five pages of the introduction contain the numerous sources used to create this noteworthy list of persons.

Each entry consists of one or two lines. There are approximately 11,800 entries, which represent 4 percent of 1775s approximately 316,000 population of the American colonies. Entries are in alphabetic order by surname, with given names and a few middle names. The place is stated where the oath was taken, the date thereof, and occasionally a name of the place of residence and/or nationality. Many entries also include the colony and county from which the person came or his nationality, if not British. The index includes only the names of children, spouses, and parents that may be included in entries. Bockstruck's index is recommended for all American history and genealogical reference and circulating collections. —**J. Carlyle Parker**

P

130.   **Germans to America—Series II: Lists of Passengers Arriving at U.S. Ports in the 1840s. Volume 7: October 1848-December 1849.** Ira A. Glazier, ed. Lanham, Md., Scarecrow, 2004. 506p. index. $90.00. ISBN 0-8420-5087-6.

Germans to America-Series II succeeds an earlier 67-volume series of the same title providing passenger lists of Germans arriving at U.S. ports between 1850 and 1897. Series II, in seven volumes covering January 1840 through December 1849, fulfills the need for German immigration information during the crucial 1840s. Indeed, P. William Philby, former director of the Maryland Historical Society, points out in his foreword that the year 1840 was chosen as a point of departure because it marked the beginning of a swell of immigration to the United States " . . . touched off by the departure of political refugees, liberals, and intellectuals and by stories about a better life sent back by those who had emigrated previously." Furthermore, the editor, Ira A. Glazier, Director of the Temple-Bach Institute Center for Immigration Research, insists that the 1840s " . . . are an excellent starting point from which to observe the course of

German immigration, which underwent four phases in the nineteenth century: an introductory phase between the 1820s and the 1830s, a growth phase from 1845 to 1854, a saturation phase from 1867 to 1893, and a regression phase from 1895 to 1914."

This volume provides introductory sections outlining the historical background of German migration in the nineteenth century, accompanied by three tables: "German Immigration to the U.S. and the Total German Emigration, 1820-1914"; "Geographic Origins of German Emigration, 1871-1910 (percentages)"; and "German Arrivals at U.S. Ports, 1840-90 (Percentages)." Additionally, there is information on ports of embarkation, debarkation, and passenger manifests. Most significantly, Glazier points out in the conclusion to his introduction that in utilizing the information in the seven volumes of *Germans in America—Series II* researchers" . . . will be able to go beyond gross statistical profiles to study these movements at the level of micro-history and to follow individuals and families from their places of origin to their destination and to focus on their personal circumstances. This, in turn, will enable scholars to access the push-and-pull factors that contributed to the migration phenomenon and to give a more human dimension to the mass movement."

The bulk of the volume is divided into two sections: the passenger lists in chronological order from October 22, 1848 to December 22, 1849, and a surname index. The passenger list section provides the following information for each ship arrival: the ship's name, port of embarkation, port of debarkation, date of arrival, alphabetic list of passengers by surname, and age, sex, occupation, province, village, and destination of passengers. The surname index refers readers to the page on which a passenger's name appears.

This seventh volume of *Germans to America—Series II* follows the previous *Series I* in providing absolutely essential statistical information on one of this country's most significant immigrant populations, both for scholars in the fields of history and genealogy, as well as for laypeople interested in family genealogy. It is most highly recommended for public and academic research libraries.—**Mark Padnos**

HERALDRY

P, S

131. **World Book's Encyclopedia of Flags.** Chicago, World Book, 2005. 12v. illus. maps. index. $339.00/set. ISBN 0-7166-7900-0.

This entire set is arranged by the world's countries in alphabetic order, except for volume 20, which includes flags for international organizations, regions, international alphabet flags, heraldry, symbols, and a 21-page index for the set. Pages 5-7 of each volume contain instructions on "How to Use This Set," "The Parts of a Flag," "Flag Shapes," "Raising the Flag," "Heraldry," and "Key to Color Bars."

Each entry usually has a single-column essay about the nation, state, province, or territory and a column about its flag. A third column contains a map and the subject data concerning the place; for example, capital, national anthem, form of government, head of state, head of government (title), largest cities, land area, language(s), ethnic/national groups, and major religion(s).

Under each flag, which is printed in excellent colors, is a statement of "Flag Data." End pages contain a Robinson projection map of the globe. The author's evaluation of the users interest level is "grades four and up." Each volume is 8-x-10 inches and hardbound. This work is recommended for all library collections. [R: SLJ, Oct 05, p. 92]—**J. Carlyle Parker**

PERSONAL NAMES

P

132. Delahunty, Andrew. **Goldenballs and the Iron Lady: A Little Book of Nicknames.** New York, Oxford University Press, 2004. 254p. $17.95. ISBN 0-19-860964-7.

In this compact volume, Andrew Delahunty pulls together more than 800 nicknames of contemporary figures and explains the history behind them. While nicknames often are affectionate, others express ridicule or contempt. As the editor notes in the introduction they are a way to "poke a little fun at our public figures and cut them down to size" (p. vii).

This work is alphabetically organized beginning with "Action Man," a name given to Prince Charles in the early 1980s due to his love of adventurous activities, to "Zoot," a name given to tenor saxophonist John "Zoot" Sims. Not only focusing on people, Delahunty also includes nicknames of places, events, and organizations as well. For each entry the author provides a one-paragraph description of how the person or institution got their nickname and an indication of whether it was favorable or not quite so favorable. An example of some of the nicknames featured here are: "Broadway Joe" (given to football legend Joe Namath for his glamorous image), "Elvis the Pelvis" (given to Elvis Presley for his suggestive dancing), "The Equality State" (given to Wyoming because it was the first state to grant voting rights to women), "The Man in Black" (given to Johnny Cash for his penchant for that color), and "Dubya" (given to President George W. Bush in order to distinguish him from his father). Throughout the volume users will also find black-and-white cartoons explaining the origin of certain nicknames and sidebars with groups of nicknames (e.g., film stars, jazz musicians, red heads).

This work is both entertaining and informative. It would be a useful point of reference for someone researching specific people, places, or institutions. [R: LJ, 1 June 05, pp. 174-176]—**Shannon Graff Hysell**

8   Geography and Travel Guides

GEOGRAPHY

General Works

Atlases

C, P, S

133.   **Chambers Reference Atlas.** 8th ed. Boston, Chambers, 2005. 320p. maps. index. $16.95 flexibinding. ISBN 0-550-10163-2.

This book is more reference than atlas. Its dimensions (9.25-x-6.25 inches) suggest that it is to be kept close by in the home office or book bag to provide convenient but brief information. The first section contains a number of world thematic maps and some tables of top and bottom ranking countries on various topics. Country entries are arranged alphabetically by continent. Each section has a continent map, and each country has a map showing relief, major cities, roads, and water features. Most maps are between 9 and 16 square inches. A regional map also shows the location of the country in a larger context.

Chambers pulls together statistics from such sources as the World Bank, United Nations Food and Agricultural Organization, and International Monetary Fund. Each country can be compared on such topics as infant mortality rate, annual inflation rate, energy generation, tourist revenue, cars per 1,000 inhabitants, and size of armed forces. A list of key dates in history varies widely from country to country: Iran's list begins in 2,000 B.C.E., but Saudi Arabia's list begins in 1930 C.E. with the discovery of oil. Most countries are described on one page, although some entries are longer, such as China, India, Russia, United Kingdom, Spain, Canada, and United States.

This reference will be a delight to have close at hand for quick reference. When size and cost are not an issue, Gale's *Countries of the World* (see ARBA 2003, entry 683), the CIA's *World Factbook* (see entry 32), Palgrave's *Stateman's Yearbook* (see entry 32), and *The Europa World Year Book* (see ARBA 2006, entry 45) provide more data, although with inferior maps.—**Kathleen Weessies**

P, S

134.   **DK First Atlas.** New York, DK Publishing, 2004. 128p. illus. maps. index. $15.95. ISBN 0-7566-0231-9.

In the *DK First Atlas*, DK Publishing provides a very good resource for young children who want to get a glimpse at life around the world. The *DK First Atlas* begins with an eight-page "Our World" section, explaining simple geographic features, continents, and climates. The two-page spread, "Maps and Atlases," would be especially useful in teaching the concept of maps to young children.

Each geographic region or nations is presented in a series of graphic and picture-laden pages beginning with a physical map shaded to represent terrain and landscape. Capital cities are noted. A small globe highlights the relative positive of each map on the Earth. Maps are decorated with color drawings representing what someone might expect to see if visiting the region. For example, the Midwest of the United States is decorated with a bison, Mount Rushmore, a wheat harvesting machine, and a tornado. Several pages of colorful photographs and text follow each map. These pages focus on culture and daily life. "Getting Going" graphics encourage and instruct in simple geography and culture-based exercises. An informational question (with answer) appears on the bottom of each page. The "Reference Section" at the end of the book contains thumbnail-sized flags and a thorough index.

The *DK First Atlas* is presented in the colorful, graphic-intensive style of other DK Publishing books. A typical page contains four or five photographs and drawings presented in collage style. This style is certainly appealing to young children, the *DK First Atlas*' target audience. Someone spending a few minutes on this resource would certainly learn about the country or region.

Educators planning to use this work as a teaching resources should be aware of its Euro-centric viewpoint. The "Europe" section is 40 pages long, while "Africa" gets fewer than 10 pages and "The Americas" about 20 pages. Also, on some pages the colorful photographs provide an overly busy background making text sections very difficult to read. The minute yet graphic text about Aztec human sacrifice is out of place in a work intended for small children, and some educators and parents might be uncomfortable with references to alcoholic beverage production and consumption. Also worth noting, the book binding is not reinforced.

These minor caveats aside, the *DK First Atlas* succeeds in the task of educating elementary-aged children about the regions and cultures of the world. It would be a welcome addition to any library children's department, elementary media center, or primary school classroom. [R: SLJ, Feb 15, p. 81]—**Keith Kyker**

C, P

135.   **Dorling Kindersley Concise Atlas of the World.** 3d ed. New York, DK Publishing, 2005. 350p. illus. maps. index. $34.95. ISBN 0-7566-0966-6.

DK Publishing's atlas is very colorful and lives up to the publisher's reputation of providing colorful and interesting maps with their atlases and tour guides. The atlas starts out with a section in the front on how to use the atlas. After that it has different world maps, such as physical, political, languages, and religions. It also includes many of small color photographs throughout the book. From there it goes to the various continents starting with North America. From continental maps it goes to regional and national maps. The physical maps have cross-sectional ones and flat colored maps. There are also oblique view maps of the landscape that are interesting. Many political maps of countries show local administrative divisions like states, provinces, and more. There are short charts with the maps on various subjects that relate to the particular map. The index is long and includes place names with their page number in the atlas and its coordinates where to find it on the map(s). There is a glossary of terms included in the end of the atlas. The atlas is not as extensive as a National Geographic atlas would be, but for its price it is worthwhile and attractive for academic and especially public libraries.—**Benet Steven Exton**

C, P, S

136.   **Firefly Great World Atlas.** New York, Firefly Books, 2005. 224p. maps. index. $39.95. ISBN 1-55407-121-6.

Atlases are getting better all the time. With breakthroughs in computer and digital technology and cartography, atlases have become sharper and visually powerful. A case in point is the *Firefly Great World Atlas*. This magnificent atlas provides authoritative coverage of the globe with maps of exceptional quality that provide balanced coverage of the continents while highlighting densely populated or economically and strategically important areas. The physical maps combine relief shading with layer-colored contours to give a stunning visual impression of the earth's surface while accurately charting physical features and boundaries. The eye-catching maps are complemented by a 55,000-name index. Thee stunning images of the Earth section show satellite views of major cities and regions. The 48-page introduction to world geography has maps, charts, graphs, and diagrams explaining the solar system, the structure of the earth, environment, climate, population, resources, standards of living, trade, and tourism. Reasonably priced, the *Firefly Great World Atlas* is recommended for both public and personal libraries.—**George Thomas Kurian**

C, P, S

137.   **National Geographic Atlas of the World.** 8th ed. Washington, D.C., National Geographic Society, 2005. 1v. (various paging). maps. index. $165.00. ISBN 0-7922-7543-8.

Top tier atlases range in price from $80 to $250 and are comparable on many features. The *National Geographic Atlas of the World* belongs in the top tier due to its size, scope and features. It contains the expected world thematic maps on such topics as climate, culture, and communication. These are followed by detailed maps of the world at varying scales. Map color schemes, peppered with informative blurbs and tables, will be familiar to users of other National Geographic map products. The distinctive style of cartography firmly emphasizes political boundaries, which can be quite subtle in other atlases. The atlas also contains maps of constellations, the solar system, the galaxy, and the known universe. A URL with user ID and password allow the user to access interactive maps, animations, and updates ("patches") to the atlas. The patches are prefaced with commentary explaining changes made to the map. This atlas is recommended for public libraries, schools, and as part of an academic atlas collection. [R: LJ, 1 Oct 04, p. 112]—**Kathleen Weessies**

S

138.   **National Geographic United States Atlas for Young Explorers.** updated ed. Washington, D.C., National Geographic Society, 2004. 176p. illus. maps. index. $24.95. ISBN 0-7922-6840-7.

Like the earlier edition (see ARBA 2000, entry 340), this book is typical of the excellent work done by National Geographic. This atlas is accessible and appealing, even to young children. From the instructions on how to use the atlas and through the whole work, this book is an essential tool for anyone who wants to give children a sense of our country's geography. The format is similar to the earlier edition; physical and political maps as well as state and regional maps are included. The illustrations are outstanding and all of the factual information has been updated. The index and glossary are also very helpful. [R: SLJ, Dec 04, pp. 85-86]—**Jeanne D. Galvin**

C, P

139.   **Oxford Atlas of North America.** New York, Oxford University Press, 2005. 320p. maps. index. $125.00. ISBN 0-19-516993-X.

This large-format (approximately 11⅜-by-14⅞- inches) atlas provides detailed cartographic, textual, and statistical coverage of North America as a whole, then of the United States, Canada, and Mexico in order. After a two-page section of tables giving comparative statistics on countries in North America, each section first focuses on satellite images, then on maps of the whole, and then, in the country sections, on regional maps covering states and provinces and then on the region's largest and most important cities. The North America section is a thematic section addressing political, physical, historic, economic, and social topics, such as climate and weather, immigration and population change, land use, highways and railroads, indigenous peoples, and languages and religions. Along with the maps are texts, charts, and graphs, which together combine to give a sense for the region or topic. The textual summaries focus on the geography, history, and industry of each political unit. A total of 154 pages of maps are included, some with more than one map per page: North America (35 pages), United States (77), Canada (24), and Mexico (18). In addition, after each country's maps, a separate gazetteer is included for each country with separate one-page entries for each state or equivalent unit. Each gazetteer entry has a small map and gives basic factual information about the geographical region: for example, historical geography; physical geography;

capital; motto; and official bird, flower, and tree. A separate "At a Glance" section for each entry provides statistics for both the unit and the country about population (for example, for the United States, by age, ethnic background, education, place of birth, home ownership, median household income), business (for example, employment, number of establishments by type), and geography (land area and persons per square mile). The data are similar but vary slightly by country. The data are from the U.S. Bureau of the Census, Statistics Canada, and the Instituto Nacional de Estadística Geografía e Informática.

The cartography and place-name index is by Philip's, a division of Octopus Publishing Group, which has provided similar cartography for the *Oxford Atlas of the World* (see ARBA 2005, entry 376). The maps are accurate, legible, have good gradations of coloring to show geographic features, and contain an appropriate level of detail; the scales vary but allow for legibility. Separate sections for each country identify map symbols. The table of contents lists the maps (and scales for the larger maps). In addition, a comprehensive index covering all countries lists over 40,000 place-names and geographical features and includes latitude and longitude coordinates and alphanumeric grid references for locating them easily. The book is bound carefully so that all sections of each map (including two-page maps) and pictures are clearly visible. The book opens easily for photocopying. Both the maps and textual content are excellent, and the atlas is reasonably priced for its content. H. J. DeBlij, the editor, is a Distinguished Professor of Geography at Michigan State University and prolific author. A seven-person Board of Advisors, consisting of professors in geography from universities in all three countries, assisted him. [R: SLJ, Aug 05, p. 74]—**Marilyn Domas White**

Dictionaries and Encyclopedias

C, S

140.   **Encyclopedia of World Geography.** R. W. McColl, ed. New York, Facts on File, 2005. 3v. illus. maps. index. (Facts on File Library of World Geography). $250.00/set. ISBN 0-8160-5786-9.

A guide to geography on a broad level, the *Encyclopedia of World Geography* includes brief signed articles (few of them more than two to three pages) on all aspects of geography history, concepts, and practice. The set includes country and place information—the sort of material found in many sources in every reference collection—along with articles about concepts such as alluvium, bases of trade, climate classifications, energy geography, glaciation, jet stream, orogeny, riparian, and vegetation zones.

Comparable sources include Peter Haggett's *Encyclopedia of World Geography* (see ARBA 2002, entry 357), which has a regional structure and presentation of concepts and *World Geography* (see ARBA 2002, entry 361), which has a separate volume covering basic concepts and additional volumes focusing on the various world regions. All are suitable for high school or lower-level undergraduates. Because each presents the information in a different way, they complement each other nicely. Most libraries, however, will not need to have all three. [R: LJ, Jan 06, p. 158]—**Michael Levine-Clark**

Handbooks and Yearbooks

S

141.   **Discovery & Exploration Series.** John S. Bowman and Maurice Isserman, eds. New York, Facts on File, 2005. 10v. illus. maps. index. $40.00/vol.; $400.00/set. ISBN 0-8160-5255-7.

This series sketches the history of world exploration—from the ancient Greeks to the astronauts. The authors of each volume integrate the individual stories to show how each effort connects and builds on previous voyages. We see each explorer's experience within the larger context and not in isolation as usually portrayed in school texts. By starting with the ancient world, the editors go beyond the more commonly known stories of the fifteenth-century voyages to the New World and European imperialism. For example, we learn about Pytheas who in 315 B.C.E. sailed from the Greek colony Massalia (Marseilles) past the Pillars of Hercules (Straits of Gibraltar) to record the coastline of Britain. At the time little was known about Britain, even though it was the major source of tin—a key ingredient in the manufacture of bronze. Although he was probably not the first to sail beyond the Pillars of Hercules, Pytheas was the first to record his travels—a distinguishing characteristic of an explorer. During the Middle Ages the Chinese and Arabs were extensively exploring. The Chinese discoverer, Admiral Zheng He, sailing in the 1400s, used advanced navigational aids unknown in Europe at the time to travel extensively throughout Asia, Africa and possibly even to Australia. Religion was a strong motivator for Muslims to study geography during the Middle Ages. The faithful are required to pray five times a day facing Mecca and to make a pilgrimage to this city once during their lifetimes. It was religion and the Crusades that caused the Arab world to retreat from exploration. This entrenchment caused the European nations to look for other trade routes to the Far East. Each chapter features sidebars with interesting sidelights that complement the narrative. Photographs from the nineteenth and early twentieth century are used throughout the books to show locations before the encroachment of modern development. Generous use of quotes from original sources adds to the learning experience. Each volume ends with a glossary and suggestions for further reading that includes not only nonfiction works and Websites but also novels and movies to better bring the times alive so that the school-age reader can make his or her own voyage of discovery. [R: SLJ, Aug 05, pp. 73-74]—**Adrienne Antink Bien**

PLACE-NAMES

C, P

142. Room, Adrian. **Placenames of the World: Origins and Meanings of the Names for Over 6,600 Countries, Cities, Territories, Natural Features and Historic Sites.** 2d ed. Jefferson, N.C., McFarland, 2006. 433p. $75.00. ISBN 0-7864-2248-3.

Ever wonder how a city or geographic feature got its name? Adrian Room can tell you. The 2d edition of *Placenames of the World* has 6,600 entries, ranging from Aachen (from the Old High German term, aha, "water") to Zyrardów (named for Philippe de Girard, the French owner of a factory located in this Polish town, with the slavic possessive suffix –ów appended). In between are explanations for the names of rivers, mountains, towns, oceans, lakes, and islands. This edition includes over 1,500 new entries not included in the last edition. Many of the new entries are for places in Asia, somewhat neglected in the previous edition. Older definitions have been expanded and errors have been corrected. There are three appendixes covering "Common Placename Words and Elements," "Major Placenames in European Languages," and "Chinese Names of Countries and Capitals." These replace a lengthier, and still useful, list of appendixes in the 1st edition (see ARBA 98, entry 401). Other than Isaac Taylor's *Names and Their Histories: A Handbook of Historical Geography and Topographical Nomenclature* (1898) there are no books that attempt to provide an overview of toponymy on a global scale. This is a useful reference source that should be in all collections.—**Michael Levine-Clark**

9　History

ARCHAEOLOGY

C

143.	**The Giza Archives Program. http://www.gizapyramids.org/code/emuseum.asp.** [Website]. Free. Date reviewed: June 05.

Intended to be the "centralized online repository for all archaeological activity at the Giza Necropolis" (homepage), *The Giza Archives* is based at the Museum of Fine Arts (MFA) in Boston and funded by the Mellon Foundation. It is an evolving resource, building initially on documentation from the joint Harvard–MFA excavations from 1902-1947. It includes about 22,000 black-and-white photographs of artifacts, expedition diaries, object registers (with almost 20,000 individual object records), and 10,000 maps and plans. This collection has been supplemented by searchable .pdf files of about 200 journal articles and books on Giza, many in publications not readily available in electronic form. Other excavation records will be added in time and additions are noted in the "News" section of the site.

The search mechanism is not as meritorious as the collection. It is cumbersome, divided into quick and advanced strategies. The quick search allows for keyword searching of all records except for the scholarly publications in the library. The latter are divided into several groups and are browsable by author across all groups, chronologically in the "Bulletin of the Museum of Fine Arts" and "Ancient Egypt Research Associates Aeragram Newsletters," and by series order in the "Giza Mastaba Series." The advanced search permits searching by field separately for the document/item categories: finds, diaries, plans and drawings, people, tombs and monuments, and photographs. The number of fields varies by category from two to five. It is possible to combine fields within a particular category but not across categories in the advanced searching; fields are sometimes replicated across categories (e.g., "people" appears in diaries, plans and drawings, people, tombs and monuments, and as photographers in the photographs category; tombs/monuments in diaries, plans and drawings, and tombs and monuments). Diary pages are available in .pdf and in transcription so it is possible to search full-text of diaries. The site is also experimenting with immersive photography and other interactive technologies for access, including, for example, zoomable plans of the Giza site and 360-degree interactive panoramas of Giza and Museum Giza collections. The objective and collections at the Website are admirable, but access does not match their quality.—**Marilyn Domas White**

AMERICAN HISTORY

General Works

P, S

144.   **Development of the Industrial U.S. Reference Library.** By Sonia G. Benson. Jennifer York Stock, ed. Farmington Hills, Mich., U*X*L/Gale, 2006. 3v. illus. maps. index. (Development of the Industrial U.S. Reference Library). $180.00/set. ISBN 1-4144-0174-4 (set).

This attractive set composed of three hardcover volumes and a paperback cumulative index will be of particular value to middle and high school students and teachers exploring the standard history or social studies units on industrialization in the United States. However, the crisply written text, well-chosen black-and-white photographs and illustrations, and up-to-date bibliographies of selected books and Websites (the latter all current as of July 8, 2005) make it useful for college students and the general reading public as well. The editors have made a noteworthy effort to include the historical voices of women, workers, and critics of industrialization.

Although the individual volumes may be purchased separately, together they convey "the combined spirit of individualism, greed, and innovation" characteristic of this era. Most users of this set probably will begin with the *Almanac*. Its 14 concise chapters survey the history of American industrialization from about 1780 through World War II and the "computer age" beginning in the 1950s. As in the other two volumes, readers will find an introduction, a timeline, sample research and activity ideas, and suggested readings. *Biographies* features 8- to 14-page articles on 26 mid- to late nineteenth-century persons ranging from Andrew Carnegie to A. Philip Randolph and Chinese railroad workers. Brief bibliographies accompany each article and the glossary is helpful. *Primary Resources* introduces and analyzes, in 18 chapters, significant documents as varied as congressional reports, speeches, letters, song lyrics, political cartoons, and novels. The cumulative index supplies alphabetically arranged entries coded to page numbers in the individual volumes. Bold type clearly identifies persons included in *Biographies* and documents found in *Primary Resources*.—**Julienne L. Wood**

Atlases

C, P

145.   Woodworth, Steven E., and Kenneth J. Winkle. **Atlas of the Civil War.** New York, Oxford University Press, 2004. 400p. illus. maps. index. $85.00. ISBN 0-19-522131-1.

The *Atlas of the Civil War* is the best reference works of its kind to be published in many years, if ever. Written and compiled by three leading historians of the Civil War era, it is superior in the quality and authority of its narrative sections, the variety and choice of its illustrations, and the quality and selection of its maps. Moreover, the broad content provides users much more than the title indicates, going beyond the four years of the war to cover pertinent events and factors relating to and affecting the war between 1781 and 1900. The book's large size, sturdy construction, and overall attractiveness permit this work to serve additionally as an attractive coffee-table book for the home.

The primary organization follows the war chronologically, with each year, 1861-1865, serving as separate sections. Within each, the period is presented in maps with lengthy narrative histories accompanying each, as well as selected photographs and artwork. This is particularly true in 1862 through 1864 sections, which are devoted primarily to the military campaigns and battles of that year. Interspersed within each section are essays, charts, and illustrations devoted to such noncombat and nonmilitary topics as the Emancipation Proclamation, political parties, national elections, the Confederate and Union governments, the location of prison camps, costs of the war, the state of the armies, and tactics, strategies, and engineering. Similarly titled essays are presented within each section to allow readers to follow changes as they occurred during the war years. The beginning and concluding 1861 and 1865 sections differ primarily in the time spans covered. The former treats those events and activities beginning in 1781 and ending in 1861 that would affect the cause and course of the war. The latter treats the last months of the war itself as well as the aftermath or consequences of the war into the 1890s. Well-treated in both essay and cartography form are such topics as earlier wars, territorial expansion, immigration, slavery and emancipation, the status of African Americans, the development of the U.S. Army, railroad construction, cotton and agriculture, industry, significant national elections, disfranchisement laws in the South, and much more.

The *Atlas of the Civil War* is supplemented by a detailed table of contents and subject index that provide good access to information, as well as a current list of major Civil War battlefield sites, a separate chronology of the war, a seven-page dictionary of terms, and a brief bibliography. Many photographs, some rarely seen, are interspersed between narrative sections and more than 40 specially commissioned three-dimensional color maps that detail campaigns, battles, terrain, and troop movements. These and numerous additional maps trace the history of the Civil War era. Also included are numerous graphs, charts, and lists.

There are criticisms that should be noted. While this book is to be commended for the many minor battles included, there are battles of equal and larger scale that have been omitted. For example, the Battle of South Mills, North Carolina, which is little-known even within its own state, is included, while excluded is the Battle of Plymouth, the second largest in the state, that nearly resulted in the end of the Union occupation of eastern North Carolina. Similar examples can be found throughout. While such omissions may be understood in a work of this scope and size, they nevertheless exist.

This reviewer, a Civil War historian and former reference librarian himself, is greatly impressed by this book. Given its moderate price, superb treatment of the Civil War era, and its overall quality, this book is highly recommended for any library that devotes a significant portion of its collection to nineteenth-century American history and to those in the general public that enjoy the study of the Civil War. [R: SLJ, June 05, p. 94]—**Donald E. Collins**

Biography

C, P, S

146.   Monroe, Dan, and Bruce Tap. **Shapers of the Great Debate on the Civil War: A Biographical Dictionary.** Westport, Conn., Greenwood Press, 2005. 405p. index. (Shapers of the Great American Debates, no.6). $75.00. ISBN 0-313-31745-3.

What were the issues that brought about the American Civil War? Dan Monroe and Bruce Tap have taken on the task of explaining this simply and effectively in *Shapers of the Great Debate on the Civil War*. For the most part, this is typical of the many biographical dictionaries of the Civil War era. Beginning with an introductory essay that places the issues over which the conflict was fought in perspective, it follows with two separate biographical sections, the first containing 20 extended articles treating the so-called "shapers" of the thinking that brought on the war, followed by numerous shorter entries for other Civil War figures. A nine-page subject index brings the two sections together in a single alphabet and leads users to information within the longer biographies. Unlike most biographical dictionaries, the contents are well documented with numerous endnotes.

Monroe and Tap selected as primary biographies men and women who were not only leaders, but who represented the varied and often conflicting positions within the political, social, literary, military, and economic spheres of society of the day. These include authors such as Harriet Beecher Stowe; newspaper editors such as Horace Greeley; military men such as Union General George McClellan and Confederate General Robert E. Lee; former slave Frederick Douglass; radical guerilla leader John Brown;

pro-slavery theorist George Fitzhugh; presidents Abraham Lincoln, Andrew Johnson, and Jefferson Davis; Radical Republican Senator Thaddeus Stevens; Northern Copperhead Clement Vallandigham; secessionist firebrand William Yancey; and nine others. The biographical sketches of these individuals provide readers with a superb view of the thoughts and reasoning of Northern and Southern leaders that helped bring about the Civil War.

Each of the 20 primary biographical entries consists of 5 parts: Life (i.e., biography), Principle Ideas (of the individual in regard to the issues that tore the country apart), Notes (that document the narrative sections), Conclusion (or significance of the person to the debate on the issues), and Further Reading. The biographies are accurate and well written, although their chief contribution is to provide background material relative to the "Principle Ideas" section, which is what makes this work distinctive and valuable. This latter section details the thoughts of the individual on the issues in brief essays of from one to several pages in length.

As good as this book is, it has faults. This is particularly true in the authors' failure to include in the biography of Abraham Lincoln any treatment of his position on state and national sovereignty, and how and from where his thinking on these issues evolved. This is a major oversight since it was the issue of sovereignty rather than slavery on which Lincoln based his decision to prevent secession and thus to go to war. The authors instead present only the president's thinking on slavery and the economy. And while the book includes only men and women who lived during the period, it would have benefited from the inclusion of such by-then-deceased persons as John C. Calhoun, whose political theories on the nature of the Union had great influence on Southern thinking in regard to secession.

This book has double significance as outside reading to accompany high school and college history courses, and as a library reference work. It should also find a place among Civil War buffs. It is highly recommended for high school, public, and college libraries with an interest in the American Civil War.—**Donald E. Collin**

C, P, S

147.   Morton, Joseph C. **Shapers of the Great Debate at the Constitutional Convention of 1787: A Biographical Dictionary.** Westport, Conn., Greenwood Press, 2006. 368p. index. (Shapers of the Great American Debates, no.8). $75.00. ISBN 0-313-33021-2.

This new offering from Greenwood Press is the eighth installment of the publisher's Shapers of the Great American Debates series. Written by Joseph C. Morton, a long-time colonialist and early American history specialist (now Emeritus) at Northeastern Illinois University, this work is a scholarly, interesting, well-researched compilation of 55 biographies (one for each delegate) that will make an excellent companion volume for collections that recently acquired John R. Vile's superb two-volume encyclopedic addition to American historiography—*The Constitutional Convention of 1787: A Comprehensive Encyclopedia of America's Founding* (see entry 150).

Articles cover a wide-range of topics—state's rights, slavery, fiscal programs, Native American relations, treaties, laws, British relations, banking, agriculture, and many others—each written from a biographical perspective. The strength of this work is in the skill and care Morton gives to the biographies of the less-renowned, say Abraham Baldwin or Jonathan Dayton, as he does to the more celebrated Hamilton, Madison, or Franklin. The result is a comprehensive collection of intriguing facts and little-known information that will serve as an important reference source for the interested reader and students of American history. Features worthy of note include a bibliography (annotated with insightful observations), a solid index providing subtopics that facilitate its ease of use, and two appendixes that provide the full text of the Articles of Confederation and the Constitution, respectively. The book comes in an attractive, sturdy package produced from high-quality materials and is offered at a reasonable price. The only significant flaw is the omission of illustrations, particularly portraits accompanying the biographies. Nonetheless, Morton's book is enjoyable, informative, and a valuable contribution to the American history reference literature.
—**Vincent P. Tinerella**

Chronology

S

148. **Decades of American History Series.** New York, Facts on File, 2005. 10v. illus. index. $350.00/set; $31.50/vol. ISBN 0-8160-6489-X.

Each decade of American history has had its own memorable "firsts" that make it unique and interesting to young readers. This series takes a look at each decade of the twentieth century and explains the history, inventions, wars, and people that made that decade unique. Each decade has its own volume, with volume 10 being of a comprehensive "Chronology of Twentieth-Century America." The chapters of the books themselves are organized two years at a time, so that students will begin reading about the onset of the decade and end with final year. The chapters are written in prose style and include black-and-white photographs, sidebars with interesting facts, quotations, and definitions of important words of the day. For example, while reading the volume on the 1920s students will learn about the rise in the general public's standard of living, prohibition (and the underground force that fought it), the nineteenth amendment granting women the right to vote, the resurgence of the Ku Klux Klan, the popularity of jazz music and dancing, and the crash of the stock market in 1929 that marked the beginning of the Great Depression. Students will enjoy reading about more current decades as well, such as that of the 1990s, which discusses the Persian Gulf War, Generation X, the World Wide Web, O. J. Simpson, and the impeachment of President Clinton. The works conclude with a glossary of terms and lists for further reading and of Websites.

This set will ignite the interest in young readers about the history of the United States. The text is engaging and the photographs and layout will provide much insight into the time being discussed. Although the volumes can be bought separately, this series works best as a set as each volume ties in nicely with the next in the series. This series is highly recommended for middle and high school libraries.—**Shannon Graff Hysell**

Dictionaries and Encyclopedias

C, P

149. Mays, Terry M. **Historical Dictionary of Revolutionary America.** Lanham, Md., Scarecrow, 2005. 379p. (Historical Dictionaries of U.S. Historical Eras, no.3). $70.00. ISBN 0-8108-5389-2.

Beginning with a chronology from 1733 to 1790, Mays focuses on the economic, social, and political aspects of the period from 1763 to 1789. The military aspects are covered in the author's companion volume, *Historical Dictionary of the American Revolution* (see ARBA 2000, entry 415). There are 1,140 entries, covering people, places, institutions, events, and industries. Persons included range from the prominent (e.g., Samuel Adams, George Washington) to the more obscure (e.g., John Heckewelder, a Moravian missionary). Articles range in length from one sentence to several pages, and although the author did not attempt to write an encyclopedia, one wishes that in some instances there was more depth, especially for the lesser-known persons. For example, rather than just saying that "William Peery represented Delaware in the Congress of the Confederation in 1786," one would have liked to have briefly known what Peery accomplished and why he was chosen to represent his state. Other features include cross-references, *see*, and *see also* references; 10 black-and-white portraits; and four appendixes that list the signers of the Articles of Confederation and the Declaration of Independence, the attendees of the Constitutional Convention of 1787, and the Presidents of Congress prior to 1789. The 60-page bibliography is well chosen, including monographs and scholarly articles, and is arranged by broad subjects (for example, "British Colonial Acts and the American Reaction") , subdivided by more specific topics ("Boston Tea Party") . This work is a well-researched volume.—**John A. Drobnicki**

C, S

150.　Vile, John R. **The Constitutional Convention of 1787: A Comprehensive Encyclopedia of America's Founding.** Santa Barbara, Calif., ABC-CLIO, 2005. 2v. illus. index. $185.00/set; $200.00 (e-book). ISBN 1-85109-669-8; 1-85109-674-4 (e-book).

Distinguished historian Daniel Boorstin has made the observation that only 20 days after the Constitutional Convention adjourned, 55 of the 80 newspapers publishing in the colonies at the time had provided the full-text of the proposed Constitution, a remarkable achievement considering the length of the document, the scarcity of paper, the high cost of printing, and the small size of the presses. Even then, Americans understood that they were witnessing one of the most profound moments in the history of the United States. Still a popular and controversial topic, students of the era will now have an impressive new two-volume, A-to-Z reference from ABC-CLIO—the first encyclopedic treatment of the events and personalities that came together over four months in 1787 to produce one of the world's most venerable documents.

John R. Vile, professor and chair in the Department of Political Science at Middle Tennessee State University, has produced a superb encyclopedia that is scholarly, insightful, engaging, and packed with information in an easily accessible format. The strength of this work's 350 entries rests with its author, who provides first-rate analysis and writes with the authority of an accomplished constitutional scholar. Sidebars, illustrations, primary documents, maps, charts, graphs, bibliographies, appendixes, chronologies, and photographs highlight a long list of features that add to the set's comprehensiveness and ease of use. Unrivaled in its field, this exhaustive encyclopedia is indicative of ABC-CLIO's commitment to providing superior reference sources in the attractive, sturdy packages readers have come to expect. A work with this much depth and quality is easy to recommended for all libraries that support history, political science, and law students, scholars, researchers, and interested readers. [R: SLJ, Dec 05, p. 94]—**Vincent P. Tinerella**

Handbooks and Yearbooks

C, S

151.　Burg, David F. **The Great Depression.** updated ed. New York, Facts on File, 2005. 444p. illus. index. (Eyewitness History). $75.00. ISBN 0-8160-5709-5.

The Eyewitness History series provides excellent sources that demonstrate how important periods and events in American history were seen and interpreted by the people who experienced them. In this updated edition, the author expanded both the narrative and the eyewitness testimonies, and brought the extensive bibliography up to date. The structure of the volume consists of chapters by chronological periods that include a very fine narrative followed by scores of commentaries from the period. The latter include contemporary sources, such as excerpts from novels, histories, newspaper articles, popular magazines, memoirs, diaries, radio broadcasts, speeches, and many other sources. The chapters include detailed chronologies of events and abundant pictures. The pictures alone justify the acquisition of the volume. The appendixes include the texts of 24 valuable documents, biographies of major personalities of the period, and an array or graphs and charts. The biographies are especially useful. The bibliography and index are both outstanding. This is an exceptionally fine reference source that would be of significant value in any library. —**Joe P. Dunn**

C, P, S

152.　Dooley, Patricia L. **The Early Republic: Primary Documents on Events from 1799 to 1820.** Westport, Conn., Greenwood Press, 2004. 375p. illus. index. (Debating Historical Issues in the Media of the Time). $65.00. ISBN 0-313-32084-5.

In teaching history to students, using primary sources remains a key concern. This activity involves two steps: introducing students to the concerns contained within these materials and allowing them to weigh the sources' differing viewpoints. In this regard, *The Annals of America* (see ARBA 2005, entry 27) and the source editions accompanying American Decades do well. With its coverage of newspaper articles from 1800-1820, *The Early Republic: Primary Documents of Events from 1799 to 1820* illustrates both the sources and the opposing viewpoints.

This book has many great qualities. The introduction overviews the early development of newspapers in late eighteenth-century America in addition to examining the attitudes toward these information sources. Dooley utilizes a wide variety of newspapers in her coverage. She chose important events and topics for her discussions. Each section has its own overview as well. In each section, the articles give in-depth coverage to the divergent viewpoints as expressed by the nineteenth-century writers. Each area has its own set of questions. The timeline and bibliography provide still more assistance to readers.

The Early Republic is a useful book for a wide audience. While the questions in each chapter would seem to target a secondary school audience, the sources and the wider discussions span both secondary schools as well as college and university survey courses. This work and the rest of the Debating Historical Issues in the Media of the Time series are recommended for public, high school, college, and university libraries.
—**David J. Duncan**

P, S
153.   **Industrial Revolution in America.** Kevin Hillstrom and Laurie Collier Hillstrom, eds. Santa Barbara, Calif., ABC-CLIO, 2005. 3v. illus. index. $185.00/set; $200.00 (e-book). ISBN 1-85109-620-5; 1-85109-625-6 (e-book).

Industrial Revolution in America is a well-put-together set of books that covers a pivotal time in American history. The set covers different aspects of the development of the country's industries. Each set covers related industries and how they complemented or competed with each other. The books have excellent bibliographic entries, one at the end of each volume and one at the end of each chapter within the books. The illustrations are generally very clear and are placed in strategic areas that complement the text. Each volume contains a series introduction as well as an introductory note that gives a general outline of the importance of that volume's topic on the industrial revolution. The volume then begins with the history of the industry and proceeds to a thorough and, happily, an interesting narration about the industry and its impact on America. There are insets scattered throughout the volumes that add spice to the books. They provide entertaining and interesting supplemental tidbits of information on topics related to the subjects under discussion. The credentials of the contributing authors are listed at the beginning of each volume and are excellent; each one is an authority in his or her field. The author of each chapter is listed at the beginning of the chapter.

The stated objective of the set is to provide "information on historical impact of various industries on the nation's workers, families, and communities." It also gives insight on the industries' effects on "U.S. politics, corporate practices, philosophies of natural resource use and stewardship, and cultural development." This set does an excellent job of reaching the stated objective and would be a good choice for both public school and public libraries.—**Diana Caneer**

AFRICAN HISTORY

C, P
154.   **Encyclopedia of African History.** Kevin Shillington, ed. New York, Routledge/Taylor & Francis Group, 2005. 3v. illus. maps. index. $495.00/set. ISBN 1-57958-245-1.

The *Encyclopedia of African History*, a three-volume set, is full of historical information about Africa. It covers the earliest days of Africa to the present. The editor, Kevin Shillington, has brought together many international scholars on African history to create this encyclopedia. There are articles about countries, the past and present, peoples, cities, places, and many other topics connected with Africa. The articles vary in length. Topics of importance have more than two articles on it. The writing styles of the articles make them easy to read. There are many cross-references and further reading references, which are not only in English. There are a lot of black-and-white illustrations. There are also several shaded maps. The maps of countries could have used a symbol to designate the capital. Each volume starts off with the thematic list of entries. The index to the set is in volume 3. This set is an excellent addition to any library's African collection. Do not get this set mixed up with the revised edition of the *Encyclopedia of African History and Culture* from Facts on File (see ARBA 2006, entry 461). [R: LJ, 1 Feb 05, p. 114; BL, 1 & 15 Jan 06, p. 19]—**Benet Steven Exton**

ASIAN HISTORY

Handbooks and Yearbooks

C, P, S
155.   Deal, William E. **Handbook to Life in Medieval and Early Modern Japan.** New York, Facts on File, 2006. 415p. illus. index. (Handbook to Life). $70.00. ISBN 0-8160-5622-6.

This volume is the result of thorough research done by William E. Deal, who obtained his Ph.D. in religious studies from Harvard University. The book deals with Japanese history from 1185 to 1868, commonly referred to as the medieval and early modern periods. This was a time when military rulers, warriors, religious leaders, wealthy merchants, protesting peasants, and scholars shaped a society's culture, which in turn influences today's Japanese traditions. Deal takes a topical approach to the periods, devoting 12 chapters to subjects such as history, government, society and economy, language and literature, performing arts, travel and communication, and everyday life. The book's format helps the reader to understand the two periods covered, with each chapter divided into several sections to enhance and deepen the reader's understanding of topics. The chapters on history and literature give brief biographies of important figures in these fields, and the former chapters also include a chronology of events during the periods. The list of readings at the end of each chapter points the reader to further resources. The 5 maps, 85 illustrations (including many photographs that the author took), 17 tables and charts, and the bibliography and index are all informative and useful. Detail and even minutiae demonstrate the degree of care Deal devotes to elucidating Japanese culture; he explains the finer points of weaponry, pronunciation, the dating of sub-periods, geographical features, and the romanization of Japanese words. This book is recommended for high schools, general libraries, and colleges and universities.—**Seiko Mieczkowski**

EUROPEAN HISTORY

General Works

Dictionaries and Encyclopedias

C, P, S
156.   **Exploring the Middle Ages.** Tarrytown, N.Y., Marshall Cavendish, 2006. 11v. illus. maps. index. $329.95/set. ISBN 0-7614-7613-X.

In a 10-volume set, *Exploring the Middle Ages* contains 253 entries that target the history and culture of the European Middle Ages (500 to 1500 C.E.). Even though this work centers on Europe there are many entries specifically about the peoples, places, and cultures of the non-European world.

This encyclopedia is aimed at an upper-elementary and middle school audience. In addition to its alphabetic organization the entries are helpfully organized into eight distinct groups: biographies; dynasties; civilizations and peoples; places; art, culture, history, law, and literature; philosophy and religion; science and technology; and cross-cultural articles. In an attempt at a third organizational structure the individual articles are color coded by geographical region; however, this work does not actually contain a list of articles divided by region. Each article in this work is conveniently separated into sections for easy reading and every article contains a supplementary informational panel, wonderful illustrations from period sources, and cross-references to other articles. Where appropriate articles may also contain a timeline of historic events or a regional map. Each volume has its own glossary and index, but an 11th index volume caps this set, providing a great deal of supplementary information. Included in this volume are several indexes, a timeline, a glossary, and several lists of resources for further study. Upon further inspection of the resource list aimed at elementary and middle school students one discovers a few Websites that are not strictly appropriate for a work of this type; however, most of the resources are appropriate and will be useful for students conducting further research.

Be aware that this encyclopedia is not a true cross-cultural study of the Middle Ages. Some of the cross-cultural articles focus very heavily on Europe and give only cursory treatment to other civilizations or marginalize them by setting them off from the main European entry. Nevertheless, it must be noted that nowhere did this encyclopedia claim that it would give equal treatment to all cultures. Europe by design is the primary focus of this work and overall the topics covered by this work appear to be well chosen. However, there are a few entries that are more obscure than might be appropriate for a work targeted at such a young audience. Another entry on torture is unnecessary and perhaps inappropriate; marring slightly what is otherwise a useful and informative resource.—**Larissa Anne Gordon**

C, P

157.   **The Oxford Dictionary of the Classical World.** John Roberts, ed. New York, Oxford University Press, 2005. 858p. index. $40.00. ISBN 0-19-280145-7.

The Oxford Dictionary of the Classical World is an abridgement of *The Oxford Classical Dictionary* (3d rev. ed.; see ARBA 2004, entry 477), containing just over one-third of the content of the venerable 1st edition (1949), with no scholarly apparatus such as bibliographies or signed articles and in a format designed to be more user-friendly to laypersons. The print is somewhat larger, Archaic and Classical Greece and the era of the Roman Republic are emphasized, while the Hellenistic period and the later Roman Empire are de-emphasized. *The Oxford Dictionary of the Classical World* retains the dictionary format of *The Oxford Classical Dictionary* and its broad coverage, and there are many cross-references. John Roberts, the editor, is the former Head of Classics at Eton College.

The Oxford Dictionary of the Classical World is a handy volume for users and libraries who feel intimidated by *The Oxford Classical Dictionary* and its price ($125.00), and is recommended for home users or for libraries that cannot afford *The Oxford Classical Dictionary* and do not own *The Oxford Companion to Classical Civilization* (1998), another spin-off that is slightly more expensive, more scholarly, and larger than the volume under review. No other general "classics" dictionaries in English can compete with the Oxford line.—**Jonathan F. Husband**

Greek

C

158.   **Encyclopedia of Ancient Greece.** Nigel Wilson, ed. New York, Routledge/Taylor & Francis Group, 2006. 800p. index. $150.00. ISBN 0-415-97334-1.

A revision of the *Encyclopedia of Greece and the Hellenic Tradition*, edited by Graham Speake (see ARBA 2001, entry 448), this work provides a greater concentration on the classical world than did the original. With over 540 articles written by almost 170 contributors, this single volume provides an excellent introduction to the world of ancient Greece. Articles are arranged alphabetically, although the prefatory material includes both a thematic list of entries and a chronological list of individuals so that relevant articles may be found quickly. While the bulk of the work is devoted to the classical period, entries span the time period from prehistory to the Roman and Christian eras. Topics covered include events and wars, cities and regions, cultural and political history, science and medicine, and literature and philosophy. Coverage is a diverse as abortion and aesthetics, Homer and Josephus, and Athens and the Ukraine.

Most articles are short, averaging less than a page each. A few topics rate longer articles, such as those on Athens, Sparta, the Persian Wars, and the Peloponnesian War. The longest article focuses on architecture and has individual sections devoted to subtopics such as domestic architecture, fortifications and military buildings, palaces, and public works, with each section being written by a specific contributor. While the work seems very complete, there are some unexplained omissions. As one example, Xerxes, the Persian ruler who led the invasion of 480 B.C.E. does not rate an individual article, yet he is mentioned in at least 16 other articles. The index is serviceable, yet lacking. For example, the Oympieion in Athens is mentioned in the article on the Roman emperor Hadrian, but it is not included in the index. Additionally, the library of Pergamum is listed under the index entry for Pergamum, but not under the entry for libraries. There are no illustrations or maps, a serious flaw that detracts from the overall quality of the work as a whole.

For libraries that own the original two-volume encyclopedia, this is not a critical purchase. For academic libraries that serve students in classics and ancient history, this will be a welcome addition to the reference collection.—**Gregory A. Crawford**

C, P, S
159.   Sacks, David. **Encyclopedia of the Ancient Greek World.** rev. ed. Revised by Lisa R. Brody. New York, Facts on File, 2005. 412p. illus. index. (Facts on File Library of World History). $75.00. ISBN 0-8160-5722-2.

This revised edition maintains the original format of the 1995 edition, but many entries have been edited or rewritten to emphasize new scholarship and several new entries have been added. Arranged alphabetically, the entries cover topics such as political history, social conditions, warfare, religion, mythology, literature, art, philosophy, science, daily life, and biographies of major leaders, artists, and philosophers. The text is enhanced by over 60 illustrations and 9 maps, although more maps would have been helpful. The 2,500 entries range in length from the very short with around 100 words to those that are several pages in length. For example, the article on the Peloponnesian War is six pages long and the one on the Persian Wars is two pages. Sparta rates almost five pages, while Athens inexplicably receives only three. Most attention is given to topics from the Classical era of the 400s and 300s B.C.E., although the encyclopedia does cover the period from the Minoan civilization to the Roman domination of Greece.

As a tool for high school and college students and for general readers, this encyclopedia amply fulfills its purpose. The entries are well written and provide enough detail to answer most basic questions. The structure of each entry provides for additional information through ample *see also* references and through embedded references within the text. The bibliographies attached to each article list major books, articles, and reports from the past as well as current material. The author has also included a six-page general bibliography as an appendix. The index is complete and includes relevant *see* and *see also* references. The chronology included in the prefatory material helps put Greek history into context.

For libraries seeking a good, general encyclopedia of the ancient Greeks, this one will be a wise purchase. For academic libraries serving students of the classics, the new English translation of the standard Brill's New Pauly *Encyclopaedia of the Ancient World* (Brill, 2002-), although expensive, will be the best purchase. [R: SLJ, Dec 05, p. 94; BL, 1 & 15 Jan 06, p. 149]—**Gregory A. Crawford**

Spain

C, S

160.   **History in Dispute, Volume 18. The Spanish Civil War.** Kenneth W. Estes and Daniel Kowalsky, eds. Farmington Hills, Mich., St. James Press/Gale Group, 2005. 440p. illus. index. $135.00. ISBN 1-55862-494-5.

This volume represents the eighteenth of St. James Press's excellent series on major controversial events in modern and ancient history. *History in Dispute, Volume 18: The Spanish Civil War* offers the same incisive point/counterpoint format with essays on such topics as the American volunteers in Spain (Abraham Lincoln Battalion), Franco as national leader, German and Italian intervention, and the bombing of civilians at Guernica, the tragic event that unleashed the wrath of the world and the artistic fury of Picasso in his eponymous mural painting.

Each entry begins with a brief statement of two or more opposing points of view on the topic, followed by a short essay summarizing the issue and outlining the controversy. A full-length signed essay by an expert in the field follows this introduction. Each section also includes a bibliography of works related to the topic, as well as a primary source document and photographs or illustrations. The opposing view format is designed, according to the publisher, to foster critical thinking skills and to serve as a valuable research tool for class discussions and assignments. I would concur with this assessment based on my own experiences in teaching the Spanish Civil War, one of the most complex and hard to explain struggles of the twentieth century. The value of such an approach is that it promotes active, participatory learning on the part of students, making the classroom experience both richer and more meaningful.

The Spanish Civil War is enriched by a well-organized set of bibliographic references at the end of the volume, copious illustrations, and an extensive index. Moreover, historians Kenneth Estes and Daniel Kowalsky's preface is particularly illuminating and complements well the chronology of events, which immediately follows it. One of the hallmarks of their chronology is that they trace the war all the way back to 1898 and the Spanish-American war, a conflict that propelled the United States onto the world stage and marked the ultimate demise of the Spanish empire. In addition, they conclude their diachronic survey with the 2001 publication of Javier Cerca's bestseller, *Soldados de Salamina*, in which the central figure is a fascist who escapes a Loyalist firing squad. Clearly, the legacy of this bloody struggle still haunts modern Spain.

The editors' introductory remarks are one of the most cogent statements I have every read about this war, its origins, and its outcomes. I will use it in future classes in which students need a succinct background to the Spanish Civil War. This volume will provide a wealth of useful material for educators and students from the secondary school through university levels. Researchers and scholars will benefit immensely as well.—**John B. Romeiser**

MIDDLE EASTERN HISTORY

C, P

161.   McIntosh, Jane R. **Ancient Mesopotamia: New Perspectives.** Santa Barbara, Calif., ABC-CLIO, 2005. 395p. illus. index. (Understanding Ancient Civilizations). $75.00; $80.00 (e-book). ISBN 1-57607-965-1.

This volume does a very nice job of presenting ancient Mesopotamia, the land between the rivers, much of which is today's Iraq. Opening with a terse but comprehensive overview, the author initially discusses the environmental setting followed by a chapter on the history of investigations of this land. She then addresses the civilization's origins, growth, and decline over six and a half millennia, describing holistically its general developments; for example, shifting power blocs, the rise of kings, and Assyria's heyday. Following this long chapter, the reader encounters a series of contextual chapters that examine the civilization's economics, aspects of social organization and structure, politics, religion and ideology, material cultures, and intellectual accomplishments. The various subsections of these chapters address topics like language, literature, art and artifacts, and warfare. Overall, this volume provides an interesting and creative contextual view of this ancient civilization, showing its warts as well as its glories. It concludes with a chapter on Mesopotamia today, including issues around archaeological fieldwork, controversies over artifacts, and of course the wars that have plagued the area with the consequent destruction of its—and our—heritage.

With bibliographies at the ends of each chapter and at the ends of the glossary; a detailed chronology and a comprehensive one for the whole book by topic (which includes a list of useful Websites); and a list of the journals that address the field the reader is left with many places to go for further study. These bibliographies, along with the excellent maps that open the volume and the many black-and-white photographs illustrating the text, make this well-written text an excellent addition to public and college libraries, and it may serve some well as a college textbook.—**Susan Tower Hollis**

WORLD HISTORY

Atlases

C, P

162.   McKitterick, Rosamond. **Atlas of the Medieval World.** New York, Oxford University Press, 2003. 304p. illus. maps. index. $45.00. ISBN 0-19-522158-3.

This resource is more than just an atlas. It has a lot of color illustrations and articles. It also is not only about medieval Europe, but also contains information on medieval Asia and Africa. The maps are in color with nations or other divisions shown by using different colors. There are maps of various battles that occurred during the Middle Ages. There are portraits and photographs of statues, buildings, and other physical items from the Middle Ages. This atlas covers the years 700 to 1500. The articles introduce the reader to various medieval topics and persons. The contributors to this atlas are scholars mainly from England and Wales who are professors at Cambridge and Oxford. The atlas has a timeline that helps the reader keep track of when in time the particular pages they are occurring. There is a glossary in the back of the book. The bibliography is in very small print. This atlas is a good addition to a medieval history of the world in academic or public libraries. [R: LJ, 1 June 05, p. 174; SLJ, Dec 05, p. 92]—**Benet Steven Exton**

Chronology

C, P

163.   **Cassell's Chronology of World History: Dates, Events and Ideas that Made History.** By Hywel Williams. London, Weidenfeld & Nicolson; distr., New York, Sterling Publishing, 2005. 767p. index. $39.95. ISBN 0-304-35730-8.

Underpinning this chronology is an overarching narrative of world history conceptualized by author Hywel Williams. The chronology is divided into four historical sections—Ancient and Modern, Early Modern, 19th Century, and Modern World—each with an introductory essay. Interspersed throughout these sections are a few more one-page descriptive essays, such as "Turkic Power: The Ottoman Challenge to the West." This book also includes 100 short biographical profiles, whom Williams considers the "key thinkers in world history." Unfortunately, there is no index just to these profiles. The list is predominantly made up of Europeans and is focused on Western civilization.

The chronology itself is easy to follow. Entries under the arts and humanities tend to list particular individuals or pieces. Political entries are longer and occasionally suggest the author's views. Likewise, entry selection, like any work, shows the author's interests. The modern period has a little more emphasis. Also, the arts are well represented, including some movies of dubious durability, while sports get scant attention outside the Olympics. The book jacket considers this a work for the family reference shelf. Indeed, it is eminently readable and reliable, although as an earlier review (*Library Journal*, July 2005) points out, it is unfortunate that no bibliography was included. Even with that caveat, this chronology is recommended for libraries. [R: LJ, July 05, p. 126]—**Allen Reichert**

C, P

164.   **Great Events from History: The 17th Century, 1601-1700.** Larissa Juliet Taylor, ed. Hackensack, N.J., Salem Press, 2006. 2v. illus. maps. index. $160.00/set. ISBN 1-58765-225-0.

This extensive 2-volume reference work, a revision of the 12-part *Great Events from History* series (1972-1980), lists and discusses important world events from 1600-1700. Each decade of the seventeenth century is subdivided into approximately 25 to 35 major events. Each event contains locale, categories, key figures, and summary of the event, with a further reading list, *see also* references, and related articles section. A keyword list of contents; list of maps, tables, and sidebars; and maps of the seventeenth century are also provided. There is a personages and a subject index, as well as a number of appendixes with a timeline, glossary, bibliography, electronic resources, chronological list of entries, geographical index, and category index.

Because each book in this series focuses on one century of world history, they contain detailed and interesting historical documentation outside of the traditional Western/European historical framework, and thus are more international in scope. This is a definite important addition to any library's reference section.—**Bradford Lee Eden**

C, S

165.   Roberts, J. M. **Ancient History: From the First Civilizations to the Renaissance.** New York, Oxford University Press, 2004. 911p. illus. maps. index. $70.00. ISBN 0-19-522148-6.

This reference work, a completely revised edition of the author's *History of the World* (first published in 1976 and revised in 2002), is beautifully illustrated with color maps and pictures. Arranged chronologically, beginning with prehistoric times over 2,000,000 years ago, the book documents major time periods, events, and discoveries, from the rise of *Homo erectus* to the beginnings of the Renaissance. Examples of topics include Byzantium, Sumer, Greek life, medieval Christendom, the Mediterranean world, the Roman world, ancient China, Aegean civilization, and many others.

This book is an excellent reference source on ancient history for K-12 and college-level students. It is lavishly illustrated, the text is understandable yet scholarly, and it is comprehensive. The price is very reasonable, given the size of the volume and the wealth of color maps, photographs, and pictures. [R: SLJ, Aug 05, p. 78]—**Bradford Lee Eden**

S

166.   **Timelines of History.** Danbury, Conn., Grolier, 2005. 10v. illus. maps. index. $249.00/set. ISBN 0-7172-6003-8.

This 10-volume chronology covers prehistory to the twenty-first century. The timelines in each volume contain varying numbers of year, ranging from 500 years (e.g., 3000 - 2500 B.C.E. to decades in the twentieth century. Each of the timelines covers main events for six geographic regions: the Americas, Europe, Africa, Western Asia, South/Central Asia, and East Asia/Oceania. Broad topics, such as politics, religion, technology, and conflicts are reported in each timeline.

Each of the volumes contains a table of contents that lists the main timelines of that particular period as well as essays covering main events. Topic examples in volume 5, the end of the Middle Ages

(1250-1500 C.E.), range from the Incas to the printing revolution to China's Ming Dynasty. These articles are easy to read and are enhanced with maps, pictures, and topic timelines.

One of the nicest features of this collection is the "How to Use this Book" section, which is located at the beginning of each volume. While most reference books contain a preface that provides this type of information, these are frequently overlooked because they tend to be text-heavy. However, in this collection the information is provided in an easy-to-read and visually effective manner. Since this set is geared for young adults, it can be assumed that many of these young learners do not know how to use a chronology. This feature provides a simpler mechanism for these readers to navigate the monograph. These provide text as well as diagrams that highlight the important features of the book, including symbols, maps, subject-specific timelines, text, and information boxes. Other important features in each volume include a Facts at a Glance section, which addresses important facts from each time period. A cumulative set index as well as additional reading recommendations are at the end of each volume.

This informative chronology is a wonderful resource for middle school students or a public library young adult reference section. Social studies instructors may also want to add this set to their classroom collection.—**Carol Anne Germain**

Dictionaries and Encyclopedias

C, P

167.   Chisick, Harvey. **Historical Dictionary of the Enlightenment.** Lanham, Md., Scarecrow, 2005. 512p. (Historical Dictionaries of Ancient Civilizations and Historical Eras, no.16). $85.00. ISBN 0-8108-5097-4.

As the author correctly notes in his preface, why have another work on the Enlightenment after the recent publication of two multivolume, well-received reference works both named the *Encyclopedia of the Enlightenment* (see ARBA 2003, entry 878, and ARBA 2002, entry 915)? Chisick answers this question by citing the need for a single volume and the coherence provided by having a single author (even though an occasional entry is written by someone else). He also lauds the structure of the Scarecrow Press dictionary for providing chronologies, concentrated bibliographies, a substantial introductory essay, and moderately sized factual summaries for each entry.

Fortunately, Chisick's observations about his own work are correct. The introductory essay is over 50 pages and is a thorough overview of the period, highlighting the key social and philosophical elements. Although a bit dry, this essay could serve admirably as required reading for a survey course. The entries, on the other hand, are a pleasure to read and are reminiscent of Slominsky's entries in *Baker's Biographical Dictionary of Musicians.* In particular, see the entry on Bentham. Chisick succinctly details the role of individuals and ideas, while wryly including his learned observations. All entries are cross-referenced. The comprehensive bibliography runs 70 pages and thoroughly references works based on broad topics of the Enlightenment. The chronology is moderately useful, providing a year-by-year grid divided between individuals, politics and society, and scholarship. This dictionary is highly recommended, especially for smaller libraries that could not afford one of the multivolume encyclopedias. [R: LJ, 15 Oct 05, p. 81]—**Allen Reichert**

C, P, S

168.   **The Encyclopedia of World War I: A Political, Social, and Military History.** Spencer C. Tucker, ed., with others. Santa Barbara, Calif., ABC-CLIO, 2005. 5v. illus. maps. index. $485.00/set; $530.00 (e-book); $770.00 (print and e-book editions). ISBN 1-85109-420-2; 1-85109-425-3 (e-book).

This is another in a series of encyclopedias on major wars published by ABC-CLIO and edited by Spencer Tucker, and a fine addition it is. It is rich in features: four volumes of A-Z entries covering both battlefronts and homefronts as well as individual biographies and art and literature; several sidebars examining historical controversies, such as the performance of African American troops; a fifth volume of the texts of nearly 200 documents; a set of general maps included in each volume plus maps within entries for easy reference; numerous photographs; overview essays on the origins, conduct, and legacy of the war; an extensive general bibliography; a month-by-month chronology; a glossary; an index; a historiography on recent trends in research and interpretation; and an annotated selective list of Victoria Cross and Medal of Honor recipients. The list of contributors and the entries reflect a comprehensive scope. There are entries on subjects not well covered in more traditional surveys, such as the role of and impact on children and women and the war in Asia and Africa. Although, of necessity, the entries are short (three pages on the homefront in Britain hardly do justice to the topic), they are supplemented by *see also* references and suggestions for further reading. This encyclopedia is not only an excellent reference source for secondary and undergraduate students and the general reader but its many special features make it a useful starting point for advanced researchers. It is highly recommended for public and academic libraries.—**Helene Androski**

C, P, S

169.   **Encyclopedia of World War II: A Political, Social, and Military History.** Spencer C. Tucker, ed. Santa Barbara, Calif., ABC-CLIO, 2005. 5v. illus. maps. index. $485.00/set; $530.00 (e-book). ISBN 1-57607-999-6; 1-57607-095-6 (e-book).

This is a noteworthy entry in a well-represented field, edited by an acknowledged authority in military history, numbering many eminent World War II historians among its contributors. The first four volumes of the set contain some 1,700 pages of descriptive entries, while the fifth volume provides a selection of over 200 contemporary documents.

While political and social aspects of World War II do receive coverage (in particular, the participation of women in the war is discussed thoroughly), military aspects predominate. Entries are global in scope, with all major and most minor powers featured. The focus is on campaigns, battles, and individual biographies as opposed to military hardware, which is treated in synoptic surveys (e.g., major types of aircraft, warships, and land weapons). The standard of writing is clear and readable, making this an ideal entry point for further study of any of the topics addressed, since all have cross-references and further reading suggestions (most of which aggregate recent and highly regarded sources). The maps are clear and effective; apart from individual portraits, the photographs are more impressionistic in quality.

A wide variety of effective access aids enhance the utility of this resource for either ready-reference or background study: each volume has a list of entries, *see* references are copious in conjunction with running heads, and the extensive index enables easy retrieval of detailed information. A select glossary and a brief chronology provide additional informative context.

Compared to the venerable *Simon and Schuster Encyclopedia of World War II* (Simon and Schuster, 1978, with 700 pages) the ABC-CLIO set has fewer entries (4,000 vs. 1,500), largely because of its aggregated treatment of weapons systems, which are addressed individually in the older work, whereas the average entry length is much greater in the ABC-CLIO set. Compared to the *Oxford Companion to World War II* (Oxford University Press, 1995, with 1,300 pages) the ABC-CLIO set has fewer entries (the Oxford title has 1,700), with some of the entries in one of the two being more extensive, and others being less extensive. In terms of total word count (excluding the documents volume), the Simon and Schuster book contains 700,000 words, the Oxford volume 1,000,000 words, and the ABC-CLIO set 1,600,000 words, enabling depth of coverage.

While the overall quality of the contents is acceptable, the occasional inaccuracy creeps in. Some of these are simple misprints, the most serious of which is on page 1133, where the stockpile of supplies for the Normandy invasion is given as 2.5 tons, an error of several orders of magnitude. Some mistakes are outright errors (e.g., KM *Scharnhorst* is described as a "pocket battleship" on page 18, or the photograph caption on page 541 purporting to describe a picture of French cruisers, when the ships depicted are clearly British Dido class anti-aircraft cruisers). In addition, despite the size of this work, the occasional omission can be cited (e.g., in the entry for "Fighter Aircraft," neither the French MS-406 type nor the Italian Regianne series are mentioned, although both were relatively important and numerous in those nation's armouries). When considering the total scope of these volumes however, such flaws may be overlooked.

Sturdily bound with good quality, acid-free paper and clear, cleanly printed type, this title deserves careful consideration from any library serving patrons interested in the Second World War. [R: SLJ, Aug 05, p. 78; BL, 1 & 15 Jan 06, p. 20]—**John Howard Oxley**

C, P

170.   **Great Events from History: The Renaissance & Early Modern Era, 1454-1600.** Christina J. Moose, ed. Hackensack, N.J., Salem Press, 2005. 2v. illus. maps. index. $160.00/set. ISBN 1-58765-214-5.

This set is the third in the series, following *The Middle Ages, 477-1453* (see ARBA 2005, entry 516). Like the rest of the series, this set revises the first *Great Events from History* (12 volumes, 1972-1980) while incorporating essays from *Chronology of European History: 15,000 B.C. to 1997* (see ARBA 98, entry 462), *Great Events from History: North American Series* (see ARBA 98, entry 497), and *Great Events from History: Modern European Series* (1973). Besides the 88 core essays, 242 completely new essays have been written for the work. Entries are divided into sections: a statement of introduction, locale, categories, key figures, summary of event, significance, further reading, *see also* references, and related articles. The expanded and redesigned appendixes at the end of volume 2 consist of a timeline, a glossary, an extensive bibliography, electronic resources (with a note of caution about changing URLs), a chronological list of events, a geographical index, a category index, a personages index, and a subject index.

Coverage begins with the founding of the House of Saud in the mid-fifteenth century and ends with the granting of the East India Company's charter by Queen Elizabeth I of England. The maps and illustrations are clear and add to the attractiveness of the volumes. The scope of the set is global, with events from Oceania, North and South America, and Africa as well as Europe and the Middle East. This is a great resource for school students, undergraduates, and general users that are beginning their research and is recommended.—**Michael W. Handis**

S

171.   **Reformation, Exploration, and Empire.** Danbury, Conn., Grolier, 2005. 10v. illus. index. $389.00/set. ISBN 0-7172-6071-2.

This informative encyclopedia set covers 200 of the most significant years,1500-1700, of world exploration, the changes brought about by the reformation, and the impact these significant occurrences had on the empire. The text in each one- to five-page essay is easy to read and includes language a young adult reader can comprehend. Brief explanations for lesser-known facts (e.g., Armada—navel ships) are unobtrusively placed within the essays so readers do not have to go back and forth between the glossary and the content. Attractive pictures and drawings enhance each entry. Sidebars provide additional information that youngsters will appreciate. For example, the sidebar in the anatomy entry is anatomy's dark past, which outlines the difficulties with acquiring corpses for dissection. At the end of each essay, a *see also* box contains cross-referencing information. Topic headings range from very broad (e.g., Architecture) to very narrow (e.g., Antwerp). The index is essential for locating particular subjects (e.g., Plague), which do not have headings of their own, but are addressed in other entries (e.g., Sickness and Disease). Each volume contains a table of contents, a timeline highlighting the most important events of this era, and a cumulative index and glossary.

This 10-volume set is a wonderful resource for higher level elementary and middle school students. It is a wonderful addition to the children's library collection or a social studies classroom library.—**Carol Anne Germain**

C, S

172.   **World War I: A Student Encyclopedia.** Spencer C. Tucker, ed., and others. Santa Barbara, Calif., ABC-CLIO, 2006. 5v. illus. maps. index. $485.00/set; $530.00 (e-book). ISBN 1-85109-879-8; 1-85109-880-1 (e-book).

The five-volume *World War I: A Student Encyclopedia* is an impressively comprehensive study of this complex conflict. The text is written at a high school or college level, and would be suitable for any researcher, from the casual to the scholarly. All entries include cross-references and a bibliography as well as the author's name. Volume 1 commences with some initial general essays on the origins, outbreak, fighting, and outcomes of the war. Entries are arranged alphabetically, and a list of entries is included in the first few pages of each volume. There is seemingly no topic too arcane for the encyclopedia, including a wonderful discussion of the role of dogs in the war. There are sections entitled "Historical Controversy" that are set aside from the main text and discuss such topics as Germany's U-Boat policy. Each volume is replete with fascinating photographs, and opens with several maps that help the reader grasp the war on both a battlefield and continental level. Maps are also embedded within the text of volumes, laying out the positions of various key battles. There are statistical tables within larger entries, covering topics like the top aces of the war, and there are a variety of bar and pie charts detailing numeric information in a readily accessible way. The final volume consists of primary documents arranged by topic with introductory essays. Volume 5 ends with an alphabetic index of topics and a numerical index of military unit numbers. *World War I: A Student Encyclopedia* is highly recommended for all libraries.—**Philip G. Swan**

C, S

173.   **World War II: A Student Encyclopedia.** Spencer C. Tucker and others, eds. Santa Barbara, Calif., ABC-CLIO, 2005. 5v. illus. maps. index. $485.00/set; $530.00 (e-book). ISBN 1-85109-857-7; 1-85109-858-5 (e-book).

A publicity release for *World War II: A Student Encyclopedia* frame its significance as follows: "It was the pivotal event of the 20th century, the last world war, and the culmination of long-running animosities and aggression. Nothing about our 21st-century world can be understood without reference to World War II. And now, the entire scope of World War II is within reach in this richly illustrated publication." Rather than slick hyperbole to tout virtues that are non-existent or not readily apparent, the publisher's words are fully borne out by this magnificent, painstakingly researched, and eminently readable contribution to the study and understanding of the Second World War.

The first four alphabetically organized volumes cover every important battle and weapon system; individual nations and geographic locations; and political, social, and military leaders who played significant roles in the coming of the war, its course, and aftermath. Featured essays offer analyses of crucial events such as Pearl Harbor, the Holocaust, the decision to drop the atomic bomb, and other fascinating topics such as code breaking and the breakthrough role of women in war. One of the major attractions of World War II study for the secondary and post-secondary classroom is the wealth of issues still relevant today. Students interested in the evolution of weaponry will find plenty of treasures in these volumes, as will those researching the role of African American soldiers, the history of mass movements, and political intrigue among the Allies.

The final volume in this series offers a host of official documents and excerpts from oral histories recorded by World War II veterans. These primary sources, the raw materials of history as the editor calls them, begin with documents from the mid 1930s dealing with pacifism in post War I Great Britain and the territorial ambitions of Italian dictator Benito Mussolini and conclude in 1945 with the Marshall Plan for post-war Europe and a prophetic call for the independence of the Democratic Republic of Vietnam by Ho Chi Minh. While World War I arbitrarily reordered the map of Europe and the Middle East, sowing seeds of discord for future conflicts, World War II's legacy was less bleak. Europe was set back on its feet economically, democratic institutions were established, and despite the decades long stand-off between the West and the Soviet bloc, another global war was averted. However, the legacy of World War II in terms of Indochina was less glorious, especially for France and the United States, as the eloquent statement by Ho Chi Minh makes painfully evident. Ironically, the future Vietnamese leader, already at the Paris Peace Conferences in 1919, sought a place in the sun for his country, which would not come until several generations of bloody warfare later.

This multivolume series is an indispensable resource for libraries of all stripes. There is also an e-book version available, and given the electronic media expectations of students today, many schools will want to consider adopting it in tandem with, or perhaps in place of, the print version. While its title seems to target exclusively a student audience, especially at the middle school and secondary school levels, *World War II: A Student Encyclopedia* would be an invaluable asset for community libraries as well as post-secondary institutions.—**John B. Romeiser**

Handbooks and Yearbooks

C

174. **The Avalon Project at Yale Law School: Documents in Law, History and Diplomacy.** **http://www.yale.edu/lawweb/avalon/avalon.htm.** [Website]. Free. Date reviewed: Feb 05.

The Avalon Project, sponsored by the Yale Law School since 1996, has created a collection of approximately 690 key electronic primary documents relevant to diplomacy, economics, government, history, law, and politics. The documents are scanned and stored by the Project and are not just represented by links to other sites. The electronic collection is comparable, for American coverage, to the highly used and useful print publication, Henry Steele Commager and Milton Cantor's *Documents of American History* (10th ed.; Prentice Hall, 1988). The emphasis is on primary documents related to the United States, but, besides the treaties, which by their nature cover at least one other country, the collection also covers materials from several other countries and from international agencies, such as the United Nations. Lists of documents are available for browsing by: 5 date-based collections (pre-eighteenth century, and then by century); 64 broad subject collections; more specific subject headings; authors or parent organization (e.g., United Nations); and titles, including official title for all documents and common and official names for treaties and other international agreements. Within each section, documents are arranged alphabetically by author/title, subject, date, or event, depending on the type of list. In addition, any document mentioned in the text of the primary documents is also linked to others in the collection "to facilitate study and navigation" (Statement of Purpose, Avalon Project Helpdesk). A search engine provides natural language access to all fields, including the full text, with the possibility of confining the search to one or all collections. The aim is to present a balanced, accessible, easily navigable collection that is complete in regards to including not only primary sources but also documents mentioned within sources. Some controversial documents, such as those dealing with Nazi-Soviet Relations 1939-1941, are included for balance and completeness. Documents included are deemed "of sufficient importance as primary material" (Document Selection, Avalon Project Helpdesk) or are referred to in a document already in the collection. Some odd choices, such as the Ancient, Medieval, and Renaissance legal documents, are included at the request of individuals "to learn more about a particular time period or subject" (Document Selection, Avalon Project Helpdesk). The broad subject collections are selective: President's annual messages, for example, include annual messages for only Washington, Adams, and Jefferson, but additional documents by these and other presidents are included in Presidential Papers (which includes papers only from 13 presidents although 37 presidents are listed with no documents; missing from the list are Presidents Tyler, Fillmore, Johnson, Arthur, and Ford). The collections need more specific statements of the scope of each collection. A text comparison feature allows for side-by-side comparisons for different versions of six American documents, including the Articles of Confederation. Permission to use the documents is freely granted with the stipulation that notification be sent to the project. The Avalon Project is affiliated with the International Relations and Security Network ISN (http://www.isn.ethz.ch/).—**Marilyn Domas White**

C, P, S

175. **Chambers History Factfinder.** New York, Houghton Mifflin, 2005. 666p. index. $13.95pa. ISBN 0-550-10143-8.

This reference book provides a comprehensive overview of historical events that have shaped the world, from prehistory to the present. It is divided into three sections. Section 1 is a chronology of world events from prehistory to the twenty-first century, a year-by-year overview of major historical events. Section 2 is a collection of individually themed timelines that provide a more in-depth examination of major episodes in history, such as World War I, medicine, technology, the Vikings, and more. Section 3 provides a number of history lists, showing the world's rulers of various countries throughout history, as well as short biographical entries for topics such as religion, warfare, and politics. This is an excellent resource of quick facts related to historical and political personalities, events, and places.—**Bradford Lee Eden**

C, P, S

176. Ferguson, Rebecca. **The Handy History Answer Book.** 2d ed. Detroit, Omnigraphics, 2006. 640p. illus. index. $39.00. ISBN 0-7808-0925-4.

For those readers who want a concise yet comprehensive historical overview, Rebecca Ferguson's *The Handy History Answer Book* will be useful. As with the 1st edition (see ARBA 2001, entry 504), she poses and then answers questions pertaining to historical highlights from across time. For this edition, she added new information and updated several entries. In her "answers," Ferguson gives the reader insights not just on the topic but its social context as well. The work is subdivided into the following areas: "Eras and their Highlights," "Religion," "Exploration and Settlement," "War and Conflict," "Government and Politics," "Law and Famous Trials," "Economics and Business," "Political and Social Movements," "Natural and Man-Made Disasters," "Medicine and Disease," "Philosophy," "Science and Invention," and "Culture and Recreation." The bibliography contains a mixture of scholarly and popular works. A comprehensive index will guide its users to the answers' location. For several entries, Ferguson provides illustrations for her audience's benefit.

To her credit, Ferguson advises her audience of the work's shortcomings in the introduction: it has a mainly western emphasis with eastern influences and that she did not intend for it to be truly comprehensive. While the entries are factually correct for the most part, there are a few places where the coverage could have been better. Perhaps Omnigraphics might wish to consider breaking the work's scope into different regions or eras so as not to grant readers more perspective while not overtaxing a single author. Given the scope and subject matter, Ferguson did an admirable job in crafting this work. It is recommended for public, school, and academic libraries.—**David J. Duncan**

10 Law

GENERAL WORKS

Biography

C, S
177.   Wright, Jonathan A. **Shapers of the Great Debate on the Freedom of Religion: A Biographical Dictionary.** Westport, Conn., Greenwood Press, 2005. 266p. index. (Shapers of the Great American Debates). $75.00. ISBN 0-313-31889-1.

That religion played some part in the settling of the American colonies and continues to this day to exercise considerable influence is undeniable. That Americans have never agreed fully on religion's precise role, especially where it has intersected with politics, is just as undeniable. The disestablishment of the churches and the subsequent ratification of the First Amendment were major hallmarks of the revolutionary era, but exactly what the Founding Fathers meant by "Congress shall make no law respecting an establishment of religion, or prohibiting the free exercise thereof" has been the subject of endless debate. And even if "original intent" could somehow be divined, are contemporary Americans obligated to act accordingly without any consideration to the enormous changes within the nation since the 1780s? This fine volume by an Oxford University educated student of American and European religious history offers insightful and timely assistance to Americans interested in and concerned about the ongoing debate over church and state. But the author hastily cautions that disappointment awaits anyone who expects definitive answers, for the boundary between the sacred and the secular is fluid and often eludes absolute definition.

Adding to this work's popular appeal is its biographical approach. Arranged chronologically by date of birth, the author gives extended treatment (10 to 15 pages) to 20 key figures, emphasizing their significance to the debate on religious freedom. There are no surprises here, as one encounters the likes of John Cotton, Anne Hutchinson, Roger Williams, Thomas Jefferson, Ralph Waldo Emerson, Joseph Smith, Earl Warren, and Jerry Falwell. Two appendixes follow, the first containing brief sketches of 54 other contributors to the debate. Arranged alphabetically, one finds such persons as Richard Allen, William C. Brann, Charles Coughlin, Clarence Darrow, Ben Franklin, Elijah Muhammad, Billy Sunday, and Paul Weyrich. Appendix 2 consists of Supreme Court decisions, sensibly organized under either the First Amendment's free exercise or establishment clause. Although one could easily quibble over some of the author's choices, this is nonetheless a good and useful study for a general audience, and it would be a worthwhile addition to high school and college libraries.—**John W. Storey**

Dictionaries and Encyclopedias

C, P

178.   Boczek, Boleslaw A. **International Law: A Dictionary.** Lanham, Md., Scarecrow, 2005. 477p. (Dictionaries of International Law, no.2). $110.00. ISBN 0-8108-5078-8.

International Law: A Dictionary provides a well-organized and thorough treatment of the burgeoning area of international law. The purpose of the volume is to introduce the basic tenets of public international law in a language understandable to the layperson and it has fulfilled this purpose admirably. The author has had a stellar career studying, teaching, and writing about international law and is currently a faculty member at Case Western Reserve University. *International Law* clearly benefits from his expertise in this area as well as his obvious passion for the project as a whole. This volume is the second in a series of dictionaries of law published by Scarecrow Press and fills a niche between scholarly sources meant for those with legal training and the more general versions of legal materials available for the public.

International Law is divided into nine separate chapters and covers a wide variety of topics falling under the broad headings of the enforcement of international law, jurisdiction, individual human rights, environmental law, law of the sea, treaties, use of force, and international humanitarian law. Individual entries are extensive, with some more than a page in length. Although the entries may seem daunting at first glance, they are well written, informative, and interesting to read. While the text can easily be read by people without a legal background, the entries still retain all of the detail required to thoroughly explain the topic and are not watered down in tone, content, or writing style. Readers will particularly enjoy the entries about historical events that have shaped international law as well as entries on geography and the environment. The text also contains cross-references to other entries, designated by the entry number rather than by the term, a method that is less distracting for the reader. Although it is called a dictionary, the volume reads more like a history book and readers may find that they want to explore additional entries even after they have found the answer to their original question.

There are several extra features in *International Law* that add to its value as a reference source. The front of the volume has a list of acronyms and abbreviations, a glossary of Latin phrases, and a chronology of the development of international law from 3100 B.C.E. to 2004. It also contains a table of cases, arranged by specific courts and tribunals, and a detailed list of entries within each of the nine chapters. The back of the volume contains an extensive bibliography that is organized by type of material. Although the volume is called a dictionary, the substantial length of its entries makes it more like an encyclopedia and thus an index would have been helpful. There are no illustrations, although some maps or charts would have enhanced the content. The pages of the volume are densely packed with single-spaced text, but the content is well organized and attractively printed.

Many libraries will find *International Law* to be an excellent addition to their collections. It is a natural choice for academic and law libraries as well as government and nonprofit libraries in agencies and organizations that deal with international issues. It may also fill an important need in public libraries, particularly with the heightened interest that citizens now have about international matters.—**Sara Anne Hook**

C, P

179.   **Encyclopedia of Law Enforcement.** Larry E. Sullivan and Marie Simonetti Rosen, eds. Thousand Oaks, Calif., Sage, 2005. 3v. index. $295.00/set. ISBN 0-7619-2649-6.

The *Encyclopedia of Law Enforcement* is an excellent resource for those beginning research in this area. The *Encyclopedia* discusses a wide variety of subjects that are placed into three separate volumes: State & Local, Federal, and International. Entries in the first two volumes are alphabetically arranged by subject, while entries in the international volume are organized by country. This allows readers to easily identify and access the information needed. Each entry provides a "For Further Reading" section that lists detailed references.

The *Encyclopedia* would be a wise investment for academic libraries that support a law enforcement curriculum as well as medium and large public libraries. One of the best qualities of this resource is the efforts taken by the editors to ensure credibility. Detailed information about each editor is provided, along with the names and professional affiliations of contributors. This allows the reader to investigate their credentials. In addition to providing this information, the *Encyclopedia* adds to its credibility by providing a wide variety of references in the "For Further Reading" section at the end of each entry. Case law, journal articles, books, and government resources are some of the resources cited, in varied combinations, in each entry. Entries are structured in a logical format and are interesting and easy to read. The *Encyclopedia of Law Enforcement* is a user-friendly resource that provides a good starting point for law enforcement research. [R: BL, June 05, p. 1850; LJ, Aug 05, p. 122]—**Stefanie S. Pearlman**

C, P

180.   **The Oxford Companion to the Supreme Court of the United States.** 2d ed. Kermit L. Hall, James W. Ely Jr., and Joel B. Grossman, eds. New York, Oxford University Press, 2005. 1239p. illus. index. $65.00. ISBN 0-19-517661-8.

This title's 2d edition remains a most useful compilation of information on the U.S. Supreme Court, the ultimate interpreter of the U.S. Constitution and a tribunal with worldwide influence. The A-Z entries cover biographies, concepts, practices and procedures, major court decisions with analyses, vocabulary, and a thorough essay on the "History of the Court." The appendixes are especially handy for Court details and trivia; the cross-references and illustrations add value to the volume.

The 13 years since the 1st edition have witnessed two new justices and over 800 decisions, including several landmark opinions. The 2d edition adds 86 entries and updates many others. A new entry is the controversial 2000 election decision, *Bush v. Gore.* Surprisingly, index searches (topical and case name) for "Gore" do not lead to the case. The page listed for "Gore, Al" in the topical index does not mention the Vice President. In the case entry under *Bush v. Gore* two justices' names are not capitalized and the dissenting votes are not clear. The entry's author cites only his own book, when two equally important books by Alan Dershowitz and Richard Posner merit mention. Fortunately, the quality of the *Bush v. Gore* entry is not representative, and the *Companion* remains a valuable source of scholarly information on the Supreme Court for law and large public libraries.

Libraries wanting a shorter work for the layperson should consider CQ's *The Supreme Court A-Z* (3d ed.; see ARBA 2004, entry 534). Also of interest is the three-volume *Encyclopedia of the U.S. Supreme Court* (see ARBA 2002, entry 529) and the two-volume *Guide to the U.S. Supreme Court* (4th ed.; see ARBA 2005, entry 556). [R: LJ, 15 May 05, p. 150]—**Georgia Briscoe**

C, P

181.   Schwabach, Aaron. **Internet and the Law: Technology, Society, and Compromises.** Santa Barbara, Calif., ABC-CLIO, 2006. 395p. illus. index. $95.00; $100.00 (e-book). ISBN 1-85109-731-7; 1-85109-736-8 (e-book).

The horrific "howling wastes of the Internet" as one person once called it, never cease to amaze. While one can find the occasional useful tidbit, one can also find hate sites, pornography and its ever-increasing perhorrescence, and finally the dumb, the dumber, and the dumbest. Of course, this is the entity that "will eventually make libraries obsolete." Given that the Internet has everything from fascinating geological sites to the irrepressible flat earth society, it should come as no surprise that the law figures in prominently. Not necessarily as a presence mind you, although it does from time to time, but as the arbiter elegantiae of intellectual property. Schwabach has put together, not on the Web but in those curiosities we once called books, a most useful tool. *Internet and the Law* brings together all things legal with all things cyberspace. In short but highly informative entries, users will be regaled with descriptions of abandonware, child pornography, the Digital Millennium Copyright Act, fair use, courts cases involving everyone from Adobe to Yahoo!, open source, phreaking and phishing, Zombie, and more.

A useful overview of the subject matters commences the book, followed by brief chronological history. Even the half dozen pages about how to use this volume will provide readers with helpful tips and suggestions. While the table of contents identifies the subjects and their pages, and a "topic finder" identifies topics treated, specific items that do not appear as main entries require access through the index.

Users will find most of what they are looking for when it comes to the Internet and legal matters. Whatever is not treated exhaustively is treated well enough so that an inquirer will have either all he or she needs or enough to know where else to look. Schwabach points out that, although most of the major case laws are on the Web, committed users will have to make a trip to the library! Does he mean to say that not everything is on the Web? Imagine that.—**Mark Y. Herring**

Directories

C, P

182.   BNA's Directory of State and Federal Courts, Judges, and Clerks: A State-by-State and Federal Listing. Catherine A. Kitchell, comp., with the BNA Library Staff. Washington, D.C., BNA Books, 2004. 696p. index. $185.00pa. ISBN 1-57018-473-9. ISSN 1078-5582.

This standard reference provides current contact information for 214 federal and 2,113 states and territories courts, 14,708 judges, and 5,311 clerks. Over 70 percent of the court entries contain changes in this edition. Court structure charts are provided for the federal and the state courts at the beginning of each section. Court structure charts for each state are prepared by the National Center for State Courts.

The *Directory* begins with the federal courts, followed by an alphabetic arrangement of the states. Within each federal or state section, it is organized to follow the three jurisdictional levels of the courts, from the court of last resort down. For example, level 1 in federal court is the Supreme Court of the United States, level 2 comprises the United States Court of Appeals, and the third level includes the United States District Courts, United States Tax Court, United States Court of International Trade, United States Court of Federal Claims, United States Court of Appeals for Veterans Claims, and Courts of Criminal Appeals for the United States military.

The *Directory* includes contact information for federal and state administrators, individuals who report judicial decisions, and nominations for Federal Court Judgeships. It includes a directory of electronic public access services to automated information in the United States Federal Courts and a listing of Internet sites for federal and state courts. The *Directory* includes two geographic jurisdiction indexes and a personal name index.

The online version of the *Directory* (http://www.onlinebnabooks.com/dsc.htm)can be searched by personal name (judges, clerks, and other officials); courts (federal, state, and territory); federal, state, and territorial officials; and by state. It contains a wealth of information that is easy to use and is highly recommended for all general collections and law libraries.—**Ladyjane Hickey**

P

183.   The Sourcebook to Public Record Information: The Comprehensive Guide to County, State, & Federal Public Records Sources. 6th ed. Tempe, Ariz., BRB, 2005. 1924p. $85.95pa. ISBN 1-879792-77-X.

In its 6th edition, the *Sourcebook* now also includes material previously published in *The Guide to Background Investigations* (see ARBA 98, entry 640). Section 1 describes the various categories of public records and how to search for them both online and on-site at over 20,000 public agencies. Birth, death, marriage, divorce, and business records; voting registrations; state licenses; court decisions; federal securities filings; aviation and military documents; motor vehicle records; commercial liens; and criminal records are discussed. Contact information, including Website addresses, for federal and state agencies and courts holding these public records are arranged by state in section 2. Under each state the information is organized by the type of record sought, providing specifics about mail, fax, and in-person access (including any limitations), available modes of searching, and fees for various services. Very brief information is given for Canada and its provinces as well as for U.S. territories. A fee-based online database, updated weekly, at http://www.publicrecordsource.com and a CD-ROM, updated annually, are also available. This continues to be a valuable resource for both public and research libraries.—**Deborah Jackson Weiss**

Handbooks and Yearbooks

P

184.   **The American Bar Association Guide to Credit and Bankruptcy.** New York, Random House, 2006. 299p. index. $16.95pa. ISBN 0-609-80926-1.

It is well known that many Americans are suffering from credit and debt problems. The abundance of credit card offers, variety of home and car loans, and the increasing standard of living along with inflation and hard economic times have taken their toll on the American public. This guide, published on behalf of the American Bar Association, will help those with credit problems navigate through their options. The book is divided into two sections—"Consumer Credit" and "Bankruptcy." "Consumer Credit" discusses in 15 short chapters such topics as how credit works, choosing the right credit card, credit records and your rights under the Fair Credit Reporting Act, identity theft, dealing with debt, debt collection and the law, and the up- and downside of credit counselors. Throughout the chapters users will find relevant sidebars that discuss such topics as discrimination, when to talk to a lawyer, and knowing your rights. The second section deals with bankruptcy and includes information on the new requirements of the Bankruptcy Abuse Prevention and Consumer Protection Act of 2005. Chapters in this volume discuss such topics as what to do when your swimming in debt, both Chapter 7 and Chapter 13 bankruptcy and how to decide which is right for you, and how to save your home when going through a bankruptcy. A concluding appendix gives step-by-step instructions on how to resolve a credit dispute as well as where to go for additional information on specific topics.

This is an inexpensive book that offers a lot of advice in an easy-to-read style. Both large and small public libraries should consider its purchase.—**Shannon Graff Hysell**

C, P

185.   Aust, Anthony. **Handbook of International Law.** New York, Cambridge University Press, 2005. 505p. index. $90.00; $43.00pa. ISBN 0-521-82349-8; 0-521-53034-2pa.

According to the preface, the *Handbook of International Law* is intended to be a short and helpful guide to international law that can be kept close at hand for quick answers. The purpose of the book is to explain international law principles and rules in a clear and concise way. This purpose is admirably fulfilled with a handy, attractive, and well-organized volume that is reasonably priced. The author of the *Handbook of International Law* is well qualified to write this book, having served as a solicitor, a consultant, a deputy legal advisor for the Foreign and Commonwealth Office in London, and a visiting professor at the London School of Economics.

The volume is nicely and logically arranged into 19 chapters, beginning with an overall chapter on international law. Individual chapters span a wide variety of subjects, such as territory, treaties, diplomatic privileges and immunities, human rights, the law of the sea, the environment, civil aviation, and the European Union. The book is well organized with a lot of headings and subheadings so that the reader can find information on specific issues. However, the book makes for interesting reading from cover to cover as well. The text is beautifully written, concise, and interesting without being heavy or laden with legal jargon. It is particularly helpful to have a quick source that can be used to decipher the treaties, international agencies, protocols and other documents, and bodies that dictate international relations. The book is also useful in that it describes the relationship between countries in terms of settling disputes, responsibilities of individual countries with respect to their borders, neighbors, the seas and outer space, and in determining which country's law applies in specific situations.

The *Handbook of International Law* has some additional features that add to its value as a reference source. It includes a table of treaties, a table of memorandum of understanding, and a table of cases. A glossary of legal terms and a list of abbreviations are also provided and there is a detailed index. Each chapter includes references to major premier legal texts, treaties, and Websites, as well as liberal footnotes to additional materials.

The primary audience for the *Handbook of International Law* will be attorneys, diplomats, faculty members, and law school students, Thus, the book would be an appropriate choice for academic libraries, law firm libraries, and libraries that serve various government and nonprofit agencies concerned with international matters. It would also be a good choice for public libraries. It is organized and written in a way that will be appealing and understandable to the general public. Many citizens are eager to know more about international law, particularly in the wake of 9/11 and with the increasingly global nature of economics and environmental issues, and this book would be an excellent starting point.—**Sara Anne Hook**

P

186.   **Flying Solo: A Survival Guide for the Solo and Small Firm Lawyer.** 4th ed. K. William Gibson and others, eds. Chicago, American Bar Association, 2005. 679p. index. $99.95pa.; $79.95pa. (ABA members). ISBN 1-59031-480-8.

When opening a solo or small-firm law practice, an individual "graduates" from being an attorney to becoming a business owner. Many lawyers who are considering starting their own practice have no idea about the ramifications of such a decision and the myriad of responsibilities they will be required to undertake. *Flying Solo: A Survival Guide for the Solo and Small Firm Lawyer* is a comprehensive introduction to the issues involved in starting a small law practice. The book is a compilation of essays written by legal administrators, legal consultants, law professors, and others experienced in law practice management.

The book covers the entire process of starting a law practice. The process includes whether the attorney should start a practice in the first place, areas of practice, creating a business plan, managing finances, selecting office space, managing staff, creating office procedures, managing technology, marketing, and quality-of-life issues. Every chapter has valuable information that gives even the most experienced business manager new ideas about how to manage a practice. The book boasts that each expert has, "distill[ed] their years of experience in law practice management into a few pages of easy-to-read prose" (p. xi). I would agree that the book is extremely easy to read, and any attorney will have no problem opening the book and obtaining valuable information during short breaks within a very busy schedule. However, what this book delivers in breadth of information, it lacks in depth. It gives a person with little or no experience in business management a comprehensive overview of the issues involved but does not delve into the details of how to effectively manage the business on a daily basis. Some contributors have included additional references at the end of their chapters that may provide the details not covered in the synopsis set forth in the chapters. Other authors do not offer such references, leaving readers on their own to research the essential details. *Flying Solo* is a valuable reference for anyone considering starting a solo or small law practice and a good starting point to help an attorney make informed decisions about whether and how to get started.—**Seth Ryan**

C, P

187.   Gershman, Gary P. **Death Penalty on Trial: A Handbook with Cases, Laws, and Documents.** Santa Barbara, Calif., ABC-CLIO, 2005. 265p. (ABC-CLIO's On Trial Series). $55.00; $60.00 (e-book). ISBN 1-85109-606-X; 1-85109-611-6 (e-book).

This book is primarily a legal history of the death penalty in the United States. While other aspects of this hot-button issue are touched upon, the main emphasis is on constitutional considerations as they have been treated by the U.S. Supreme Court. An early chapter traces the history of capital punishment in the ancient world, as well as in medieval and modern Europe, and emphasizes that death was the standard penalty for even the most trivial of crimes (e.g., being in the company of Gypsies for one month, under England's "bloody code") . And clearly the American founding fathers accepted the death penalty as a given. But as the criminal justice system developed and imprisonment became far more common, reformers increasingly called into question the morality, efficacy, and constitutionality of the death penalty. The constitutional arguments have centered on the Eighth Amendment prohibition of cruel and unusual punishment and procedural issues under the Sixth (right to a fair trial) and Fourteenth (equal protection and due process of law) Amendments. In the seminal case of *Furman v. Georgia* (1972), the Supreme Court declared Georgia's death penalty statute unconstitutional, effectively calling into question the statutes of other states and voiding the death penalty. However, the statutes have been rewritten in an attempt to pass constitutional muster and the legal arguments continue to rage. Gershman provides a readable account of these developments and adds excerpts from the key cases, short definitions of "key people, laws, and concepts," a chronology, table of cases, and an annotated bibliography. He acknowledges at the outset that he is opposed to the death penalty, but his account is fair and balanced. Occasional slips in grammar, word usage, syntax, and spelling notwithstanding, this will be a useful source for public and academic libraries. [R: LJ, 15 Sept 05, p. 90; SLJ, Dec 05, p. 90]—**Jack Ray**

C, S

188.	Maddex, Robert L. **State Constitutions of the United States.** 2d ed. Washington, D.C., CQ Press, 2006. 529p. index. $125.00. ISBN 1-933116-25-0.

This resource provides seven- to nine-page profiles on the constitutions of each of the 50 states, 3 territories, and the District of Columbia. It does not reprint the full text of the constitutions; instead, readable summaries of constitution articles or sections with some excerpts are used with informative material on the dates the articles or sections were enacted. This 2d edition includes the District of Columbia as well as over 500 new amendments enacted since the 1998 edition (see ARBA 2000, entry 656).

State Constitutions is designed for easy comparisons between the states and territories, with an introductory section highlighting specific topics followed by three tables providing data on those topics for each state or territory. The table of "State Government Structure" is divided into the executive, legislative, and judicial branch and lists such things as the term of the office, term limits, veto power, item veto power, the number of house members, and whether advisory opinions are issued by the judicial branch. The table of "State Constitutions and Amendments" provides the date of statehood, current constitution, number of constitutions, number of amendments, and legislative processes. The third table of "New State Rights and Special Provisions" delineates whether provisions for the following topics are included: privacy, sexual discrimination, disabled persons, victims, taxpayers, balanced budget, direct democracy, health and welfare, home rule, environment, official language, abortion, and definition of marriage.

The appendix contains the United States Constitution, a table of cases, a glossary, sources, and Websites. An index is included. The profiles are arranged with the states listed first, then the territories. Within each section, the states are generally arranged alphabetically except the District of Columbia is filed at the end of the states. It is easy to read, easy to locate information within the tables and profiles, and is highly recommended for high school and college students as well as researchers.—**Ladyjane Hickey**

C, P, S

189.	Telgen, Diane. **Brown v. Board of Education.** Detroit, Omnigraphics, 2005. 246p. illus. index. (Defining Moments). $38.00. ISBN 0-7808-0775-8.

As the President, Congress, and their financial backers prepare for another pitched battle over the nomination and confirmation of a U.S. Supreme Court justice, the prologue of this history of *Brown v. Board of Education* (347 U.S. 483, available online or at public libraries) further reminds the reader how powerful the U.S. Supreme Court is, for good or for evil: "Although the U.S. Constitution promised equal rights to all Americans, a series of Supreme Court rulings relentlessly eroded the civil rights and social standing of African Americans."

Anecdotes, photographs, and biographies animate a shameful American story that is so familiar that students of any race often resist reading it. Fortunately, the author's engaging, simple style, combined with a visually enticing layout, will appeal to young readers, or to older readers who want a quick review. Excerpts from primary sources (a staple in recently published histories for teenagers) encourage young students to read these sources—when the full texts would otherwise be too daunting. A brief summary and analysis precedes each document. A bibliography gathers references suitable to the book's target audience—high school students—but also sources that would be useful to college students. Other study tools include a glossary and a chronology.

Adult lay readers and college students looking for a more detailed discussion of the case and its context may also want to read *Brown v. Board of Education: A Documentary History*, which includes briefs and oral arguments (updated ed.; Markus Wiener Publishers, 2004). Telgen's book is recommended for public, school, and academic libraries.—**Nancy L. Van Atta**

C, P

190.   Walzer, Lee. **Marriage on Trial: A Handbook with Cases, Laws, and Documents.** Santa Barbara, Calif., ABC-CLIO, 2005. 307p. index. (On Trial). $55.00; $60.00 (e-book). ISBN 1-85109-610-8; 1-85109-615-9 (e-book).

Marriage on Trial introduces students and general readers to the "contradictions, conflicts and disparities" of marriage in American society. "The intent of the On Trial series is to present a framework for understanding how the law shapes modern life." This is achieved for all books in the series with two parts: part 1 is four well-written explanatory chapters; part 2 reprints selective supplemental documents.

Anyone interested in a very basic understanding of how the American courts have shaped the history of marriage will find this book interesting. Chapter 1 summarizes the many issues involved: religion, divorce, and the roles of women, men, homosexuals, polygamists, racial minorities, and political groups. Chapter 2 delves into the historical background of each issue. Chapter 3 briefs important cases that challenge the basic civil right to marry. A few cases are analyzed in depth such as *Loving v. Virginia* (1969) on interracial marriage and *Baker v. Vermont* (1999) on same-sex marriage. Chapter 4 discusses the future of marriage as legislation and religious ideas evolve.

Documents in part 2, which support the discussion in part 1, include parts of six key cases and statutes of Vermont. Also included is a ten-page glossary of key people, laws, and concepts; a five-page timeline; a one-page table of cases; a three-page annotated bibliography; and a four-page Index. These aids, plus the reference lists at the end of each chapter in part 1, make the book very useful and handy.—**Georgia Briscoe**

CRIMINOLOGY AND CRIMINAL JUSTICE

Dictionaries and Encyclopedias

C, P

191.   Champion, Dean John. **The American Dictionary of Criminal Justice: Key Terms and Major Court Cases.** 3d ed. Lanham, Md., Scarecrow, 2005. 513p. index. $57.95. ISBN 0-8108-5406-6.

First published in 1998 by Fitzroy Dearborn as the *Dictionary of American Criminal Justice* (see ARBA 99, entry 576), the 2d edition (retitled as the work under review) appeared in 2001 from a new publishers, Roxbury. The current 3d edition is published by Scarecrow Press. Although publishers have changed, the quality and usefulness of this essential reference source has not. Champion, professor of criminal justice at Texas A&M International University, has since 1970 authored some 30 books in this and allied fields. He has witnessed firsthand the evolution of U.S. Supreme Court law and is a recognized authority on criminal justice, policing, and corrections. More ambitious in scope and format than its predecessors, this title has added a large number of new terms and key concepts from criminal justice and its allied fields. The more than 5,000 definitions are concise and clearly written. New to this edition is the inclusion of charts, graphs, and statistical tables. As stated in the earlier review, the strength of the book rests in its impressive review of over 125 significant U.S. Supreme Court cases. Entries include a background of the case and its significance for criminal justice. A "Case Index by Topic" permits a researcher to find similar cases within a legal concept ("Border Searches," "Free Speech") . Appendixes include Internet sources and contact information for federal and state probation and parole agencies. This is the finest one-volume dictionary for American criminal justice and relevant landmark U.S. Supreme Court cases. The material is so well written and presented that it is an essential purchase for public, college, and university libraries.—**David K. Frasier**

C

192.   **Encyclopedia of Criminology.** Richard A. Wright and J. Mitchell Miller, eds. New York, Routledge/Taylor & Francis Group, 2005. 3v. index. $395.00/set. ISBN 1-57958-387-3.

The encyclopedia under review is the fourth major criminology or criminal justice encyclopedia to be published over the past four years. This number is restricted to encyclopedias with a scholarly character, and does not include the various scholarly encyclopedias with a specialized focus, such as terrorism, white-collar crime, juvenile justice, or prisons. A number of crime or criminal justice encyclopedias directed at a broader popular readership have also been published during this period of time, including Jay Robert Nash's *The Great Pictorial History of World Crime* (see ARBA 2005, entry 566) and Carl Sifakis's *The Encyclopedia of American Crime* (see ARBA 2002, entry 567). Still another encyclopedia, Shirelle Phelps' *World of Criminal Justice* (see ARBA 2002, entry 568), falls somewhat between the scholarly encyclopedias and those intended for a more general audience. In certain respects this proliferation of criminological encyclopedias during an era when scholars, students, and general readers increasingly rely upon the Internet for specific information about crime and criminal justice phenomena is somewhat baffling. Presumably, publishers of these encyclopedias have reason to believe that libraries will want to continue acquiring such volumes. As one of those still biased toward print mediums, I personally welcome this on-going commitment to a traditional medium for making information accessible.

Richard A. Wright of Chicago State University was the original editor of the *Encyclopedia of Criminology*. Wright was an excellent choice for this assignment. He was perhaps best known for his series of citation studies, and he certainly knew the criminological terrain as well as anyone else. Tragically, Richard A. Wright died of a heart attack late in December, 2001, with the encyclopedia project far from completed and in a process of transition to a different publishing entity. A close professional and personal associate of Wright's, J. Mitchell Miller of the University of South Carolina, eventually assumed the task of finishing the editorial work initiated by Wright. The resulting three-volume work is a fitting tribute to its original editor, but small consolation for his premature death.

Of the scholarly encyclopedias recently published, the work under review, as its name suggests, is most attuned to the field of criminology, and should prove especially useful to students and scholars in that field. The over 525 entries in 3 volumes are arranged in alphabetic order, and are of varying length. Each entry ends with a list of references and further reading, and cross-references. A thematic list of entries at the beginning of the first volume, as well as a comprehensive index at the end of the third volume, provide users of the encyclopedia with helpful guidance. Some graphs and figures are scattered throughout the encyclopedia. The several hundred contributors range from doctoral students to prominent scholars in the field, with from 1 to as many as 9 or 10 entries by a single contributor.

The principal substantive areas addressed by this encyclopedia are as follows, with the number of entries provided: history of criminology (9); history of legal and criminal justice traditions (15); criminal law (61); types of criminal behavior (124); correlates of criminal behavior (30); victimization (8); measures of crime (15); theories of criminal behavior (49); the justice system (121); cross-cultural and global crime and justice (45); professional issues (8); and prominent figures in criminology and criminal justice

(44). The coverage here is most closely comparable to that of the four-volume *Encyclopedia of Crime and Punishment*, edited by David Levinson (see ARBA 2003, entry 566). This encyclopedia has many more entries with a historical focus than the Sage encyclopedia, and is alone among the scholarly criminology encyclopedias to include biographical entries on prominent figures. It also has many more entries on theories of criminal behavior than does the Sage work, and has a unique series of entries on professional issues. The encyclopedia under review also has a conspicuous international or global focus. The Sage encyclopedia has more entries on specific institutions, such as Attica prison. On the other thematic categories the two encyclopedias are somewhat more comparable. The four-volume second edition of the *Encyclopedia of Crime and Justice*, edited by Joshua Dressler (see ARBA 2003, entry 565) is especially strong on law-focused entries. The four-volume *Encyclopedia of Criminology and Deviant Behavior*, edited by Clifton D. Bryant (see ARBA 2001, entry 551), is especially strong—as its title suggests—on varieties of deviant behavior. Of course there is substantial overlap between all of these encyclopedias, but they also complement one another in some noteworthy ways.

Altogether, the *Encyclopedia of Criminology* is a highly commendable addition to an increasingly crowded field, with well-written and well-informed entries on the topics addressed. It would seem to be an especially appropriate acquisition for libraries at universities or colleges offering a strong undergraduate or graduate program in criminology. One has to hope that it will be widely consulted by criminology students and scholars in the field for many years to come. [R: LJ, 15 April 05, p. 117]—**David O. Friedrichs**

C, P

193.   **Encyclopedia of Rape.** Merril D. Smith, ed. Westport, Conn., Greenwood Press, 2004. 301p. index. $75.00. ISBN 0-313-32687-8.

This history of rape, from antiquity to present, focuses on the United States, but also describes notorious attacks in other countries, such as the raping of Chinese men and women by the Japanese during the Rape of Nanking. The encyclopedia is not an investigation into the causes, but the recording of acts of rape offers some insight into the reasons for this unusually brutal crime; for example, the greater incidence against smaller men in prisons or against the mentally disabled are noted. The reader will quickly see a pattern of the stronger victimizing the weaker, with the criminals at times clearly demonstrating this intent to humiliate (as was the case with the rape of Jews by the Nazis). Indeed, the entry for the Nazis illustrates the risk of writing about rape without careful analysis. The entry recounts the likelier fate of sexual humiliation, in concentration camps, for Jewish women, rather than actual rape, because of the Nazi law against sexual intercourse with "other races" and the soldiers' fear of punishment by officers' enforcement of this law. Yet another explanation for the low incidence of rape is dropped *into the middle of* this line of thought: "Women in the camps were also often physically unattractive to the Nazis . . .." At no point is the distinction between the conflicting theories of sexual assault as sex and sexual assault as assault more apparent than when the author of this entry failed to recognize it. However, the overall quality of the research and presentation of this and other entries is very high, and the *Encyclopedia* is an excellent source of facts about rape not easily found. Making the information even more accessible are a timeline of rape-related events from the Code of Hammurabi to the modern-day rapes of Air Force servicewomen by Air Force servicemen, a topical index, and a bibliography. The more than 75 contributors to this work reflect the variety of source material: historians, of course, but also experts in art, literature, and films, as well as attorneys, anthropologists, and other scholars. For readers who are interested in the history of the U.S. laws about rape, Greenwood Press has also published by the same editor *Sex Without Consent: Rape and Sexual Coercion in America* (2001). The *Encyclopedia of Rape* is recommended for public, high school, and undergraduate libraries. [R: LJ, 1 Nov 04, p. 120]—**Nancy L. Van Atta**

P

194.   Sifakis, Carl. **The Mafia Encyclopedia.** 3d ed. New York, Facts on File, 2005. 510p. illus. index. (Facts on File Crime Library). $65.00. ISBN 0-8160-5694-3.

The Mafia Encyclopedia is an informative and entertaining look at the world of organized crime. Arranged alphabetically, the *Encyclopedia* covers people, places, practices, and terminology associated with the Mafia. It includes black-and-white photographs, an index, and a timeline of important dates associated with the Mafia.

Yet, while informative, the *Encyclopedia* lacks some of the objectivity that one would expect in a reference work. The author includes, in addition to the verifiable facts and figures, rumors and gossip as they relate to the people and events he recounts in the *Encyclopedia*. In some cases this makes for more interesting reading, but in some cases it is mere speculation or observation on the author's part. Furthermore, the cross-referencing of entries is inconsistent. Where one might expect cross-referencing, there is none; also, while some entries have brief definitions before the actual entry begins, others do not. It would be more helpful to the lay reader if all entries had such a definition.

Enlightening and engaging, the *Encyclopedia* is a good resource for those uninitiated to the topic of the Mafia. This work is recommended for public libraries. [R: LJ, 15 Sept 05, pp. 93-94]—**Megan W. Lowe**

C, P

195.   **World of Forensic Science.** K. Lee Lerner and Brenda Wilmoth Lerner, eds. Farmington Hills, Mich., Gale, 2005. 2v. illus. index. $185.00/set. ISBN 1-4144-0294-5.

The *World of Forensic Science* is a superb two-volume encyclopedia set. Both volumes emphasize innovative forensic applications from diverse scientific disciplines. One is immediately impressed with the appealing hardbound cover and professional presentation. Readers will be receptive to the encyclopedia's creative approach and format. The book's design serves it well, especially for readers with minimal preparation in the field of forensic science.

The composition, production, design, and photographic illustrations offer insight and enhance presentation. The carefully selected forensic photographs in the first volume are superior (e.g., a 600-year-old mummy, missing children software, rigor mortis). Additional appropriate photographic illustrations are found in the second volume, which supplement the theories and concepts (e.g., the "I Love You" computer virus, numerous other illustrations). Furthermore, the visual images assist in motivating and capturing the reader's imagination.

The contributing advisors are outstanding professionals in their respective fields. The authoritative writing of expert contributors offers a collective and comprehensive contribution for readers seeking forensic science information. The clarity of writing and topic organization increases retention and reader interest. This notable collection of readings consists of approximately 600 well-researched and well-documented entries.

The A-Z range of forensic topics is too numerous to cite. Some sampling of articles might peak the reader's interest—The 2001 Anthrax Investigation, The Peruvian Ice Maiden, and The Identification of Tsunami Victims. The entries are arranged alphabetically and the text includes references, historical chronology, and a comprehensive general index. The boldface type and cross-references assist in the explanation of topics and offer the reader an opportunity to explore selected entries.

Scientific leaps in forensic science continue to revolutionize crime scene investigation. This essential twin-volume encyclopedia set would be an essential edition to libraries, universities, and community college collections. In addition, federal, state, and local law enforcement agencies would characterize the *World of Forensic Science* as relevant when appraising investigations. The reader will appreciate the syntax, editing, and writing. The text is an excellent resource for anyone interested in the topic forensic science.—**Thomas E. Baker**

Handbooks and Yearbooks

C, P, S

196. Altschiller, Donald. **Hate Crimes: A Reference Handbook.** 2d ed. Santa Barbara, Calif., ABC-CLIO, 2005. 247p. index. (Contemporary World Issues). $50.00; $55.00 (e-book). ISBN 1-85109-624-8; 1-85109-629-9 (e-book).

The present volume is yet another addition to ABC-CLIO's thoroughly admirable Contemporary World Issues series, with over 20 volumes now published. These volumes are intended to serve as a basic starting point for more focused research on a timely topic, with current volumes addressing such matters as environmental activism, nuclear weapons, immigration, and the like. The books are attractively produced, and embrace an exceptionally user-friendly format. They are certainly accessible to high school students and members of the general public, but more advanced students and even scholarly specialists on the topics addressed may well find them useful.

The author of the present volume, on hate crime, is a Boston University librarian who has edited a number of reference books and has also contributed to newspapers, encyclopedias, and library journals. The topic itself has been a contentious one in recent years. The 1st edition of this book was published in 1999 (see ARBA 2000, entry 533), but the author argues that a 2d edition is now warranted, in light of some significant developments since that date. Perhaps 9/11 in 2001 was the most important event relevant to hate crimes, as it inspired a measurable outbreak of hate crimes against Muslims, or those perceived to be part of the culture of the 9/11 terrorists.

The first chapter of this book explores the origins of hate crimes legislation, the major relevant laws, the role of different governmental entities in these laws, the critics of hate crime laws, and some of the major targets of hate crimes. This chapter provides a broad overview of the topic. A second chapter quite briefly reviews some global dimensions of hate crimes. A fairly detailed chronology begins with the assassination of a civil rights activist in Mississippi in 1955, and ends 50 years later with two hate crime cases early in 2005. A chapter of biographical sketches contains brief entries on some of those who have been actively involved with the response to hate crimes or carried out significant research on the topic. One is a little surprised that some high-profile victims of hate crimes, such as Matthew Shepard, are not profiled here as well.

A fairly long section on "Documents and Reports" includes some statistical data on hate crimes, law enforcement strategies for combating it, and some attention to how it manifests itself on college and university campuses and on the Internet. Other sections include a directory of organizations (e.g., the Anti-Defamation League) relevant to hate crimes. Two final sections provide annotated guidance to important print and nonprint resources. In sum, this volume should prove helpful to a wide range of students of the hate crime phenomenon, from secondary school students to scholarly specialists. [R: LJ, 15 Sept 05, p. 89]—**David O. Friedrichs**

C, S

197. Banks, Cyndi. **Punishment in America: A Reference Handbook.** Santa Barbara, Calif., ABC-CLIO, 2005. 319p. index. (Contemporary World Issues). $50.00; $55.00 (e-book). ISBN 1-85109-676-0; 1-85109-681-7 (e-book).

Punishment in America constitutes an excellent addition in the Contemporary World Issues series. The books in this series enable beginning scholars to define a particular research topic. For more specific punishment topics in this series, for example, see *Cruel and Unusual Punishment* by Joseph A. Melusky and Keith A. Pesto (see ARBA 2004, entry 603) and *Capital Punishment* by Michael Kronenwetter (2d ed.; see ARBA 2003, entry 573). Banks divides her book into eight parts: a general history (e.g., corporal punishment, criminal law reform, chain gangs, the rehabilitative ideal); the identification of "problems, controversies, and solutions" (e.g., the right to punish, boot camps, mandatory minimum sentences); punishment trends worldwide (e.g., Australia, China, Germany, Italy); a brief but interesting chronology; biographical sketches of famous people (primarily in the eighteenth and nineteenth centuries) in punishment theory and practice (e.g., Beccaria, Bentham, Lombroso); some noteworthy facts and data; a directory of agencies and organizations (e.g., Federal Prison Policy Project, Prison Reform Advocacy Center, the Vera Institute of Justice); and a guide to print and nonprint resources. The book concludes with a useful, albeit introductory, glossary as well as an index. Overall, high school and college students will find this book a good place to begin their research on punishment. The subject is so broad, however, that no single volume could begin to address the vast literature that defines punishment in America. The bibliographies, for example, are extremely limited in number and scope. Still, the book is well written and clearly and coherently organized. *Punishment in America* is highly recommended for beginning researchers. [R: LJ, 15 Sept 05, p. 89]—**Michael A. Foley**

C, P

198.   **Crime State Rankings 2005: Crime in the 50 United States.** 12th ed. Kathleen O'Leary Morgan and Scott Morgan, eds. Lawrence, Kans., Morgan Quitno Press, 2005. 506p. index. $56.95pa. ISBN 0-7401-0944-8. ISSN 1077-4408.

Now in its 12th edition, this useful source has become a reference staple among interested individuals and librarians seeking quick, easy-to-understand statistical information on crime and criminal justice in America. As with earlier editions (see ARBA 2001, entry 556, and ARBA 2000 entry 536) the format remains the same; 506 state-by-state tables are presented with data in seven major sections—arrests, corrections, drugs and alcohol, finance, juveniles, law enforcement, and offenses (subdivided by urban/rural crime). Data are taken from state and federal sources listed at the bottom of each table. Much of the federal data has been extracted from the FBI's *Uniform Crime Reports* and covers 2003. Each table provides a national total for a specific population (e.g., "Prisoners in State Correctional Institutions") then presents the information in two side-by-side tables; alphabetical by state and rank. In each state, the raw number of the national total is given as is the state's percentage of the national whole. Also included is a useful section comparing crime statistics (and their percent change) from 1999 to 2003 for felony offenses like murder, rape, robberies, aggravated assault, and a wide variety of theft. An appendix offers information on national population subdivided by rural/urban and a small roster of sources with Websites, addresses, and telephone numbers is provided. An easy-to-use source for answers to the most commonly asked crime-related questions, this resource is ideal for the statistically challenged in all public and academic libraries.—**David K. Frasier**

C

199.   Henderson, Harry. **Gun Control.** rev. ed. New York, Facts on File, 2005. 316p. index. (Library in a Book). $45.00. ISBN 0-8160-5660-9.

Harry Henderson has authored over 30 books, 14 of which are part of the aptly titled Library in a Book series, including his titles on global terrorism, gun control, Internet predators, campaign and election reform, and privacy in the information age. This book is an update of Henderson's 2000 award-winning work ("2001 Outstanding Academic Titles" *Choice*) of the same title. Issues of gun control and Second Amendment rights, contentious topics in the best of times, have become even more heated and divisive in a post-9/11, post-Columbine high school world. Several excellent reference works on the topic have already been published in the twenty-first century, including Gregg Lee Carter's 2002 two-volume set *Guns in American Society: An Encyclopedia of History, Politics, Culture, and the Law* (see ARBA 2003, entry 582) and Glenn H. Utter's 2000 *Encyclopedia of Gun Control and Gun Rights* (see ARBA 2001, entry 571). What distinguishes Henderson's book is his emphasis on research strategy. Harry Henderson worked in the library field before he became an author and editor, which probably explains the book's depth of subject analysis and arrangement of material. Part 1 provides historical background, extended chronology, significant gun control case law analysis, biographical sketches, and a glossary. Three chapters comprise part 2: "How to Research Gun Control Issues"; "Annotated Bibliography"; and "Organizations and Agencies." These chapters outline gun control resources and suggest strategies in researching both print and online sources, including an introduction to legal research and finding case law. Part 3 contains four appendixes, some statistically based, and two more appendixes that briefly analyze two significant court cases: *United States v. Miller* (1939) and *United States v. Timothy Joe Emerson* (2001). The work concludes with an index.

Although aimed at the "9th grade and up" market, this work would be able to hold its own beside other gun control works on undergraduate college reference shelves. It earns its spot for its depth and breadth of specialized research materials and its particularly well-articulated strategy for finding and using those materials.—**Linda D. Tietjen**

C, P, S

200.   Henderson, Harry. **Internet Predators.** New York, Facts on File, 2005. 298p. index. (Library in a Book). $45.00. ISBN 0-8160-5739-7.

As an information source, the Internet may be the most dangerous form of information access libraries have ever made available. We need turn no farther than the recent and tragic horrifically devastating hurricanes of the 2005 season, Katrina and Rita, to see the Web's (and its victims) vulnerability to crime. Within hours of the Katrina tragedy, for example, scores of "donate here" sites had been uncovered that merely lined the pockets of their creators.

The current book is not limited to libraries alone but it does underscore that problem by treating all the Internet's ills and spelling out the giant enormity the Web has become. The book covers cybercrime, cyberfraud, scams, online gambling, fictive investment schemes, online shopping, identify theft, education scams, buy-a-bride, and of course pornography and its attendant sexual predators, mainly pedophiles.

While the list of potential crimes and victims are the easy part to describe, the book pays close attention to the law and the Internet as well as its policing. The news here is less sanguine as issues of due process and borderless crimes raise serious constitutionality issues. All the more reason, it would seem, to press on with not only punishment but also prevention. Also included in this volume are current laws and potential legislation. Part 2 is devoted to further research and includes a most helpful guide on how to research cybercrime. A 50-page bibliography follows and is itself followed by a list of agencies and organizations devoted to curbing Internet crime. Appendixes on what to do about identify theft, "dot. cons.," and portions of the Code which deal with the Web close out this most useful volume.

Only the most foolhardy among us (and, unfortunately, that category includes many librarians) do not want a safer, cleaner Internet. This book goes a long way to providing an opening discussion to that most important topic.—**Mark Y. Herring**

C, P

201.   Morgan, Kathleen O'Leary and Scott Morgan, eds. **City Crime Rankings: Crime in Metropolitan America.** 12th ed. Lawrence, Kans., Morgan Quitno Press, 2005. 408p. index. $49.95pa. ISBN 0-7401-0739-9. ISSN 1081-6453.

This useful reference, now in its 12th edition, utilizes the most recent nonpreliminary, full-year numbers available from the FBI to rank American cities and metropolitan areas by type of crime and overall safety. For each city and metropolitan area the following index crimes are examined: murder, forcible rape, robbery, aggravated assault, burglary, larceny-theft, and motor vehicle theft. The current edition boasts 90 tables of detailed statistical information on crime numbers, crime rates, and crime trends. There are also numerous charts and diagrams that enable users to track trends in crime over a 20-year period of time.

City Crime Rankings is organized into five sections. The first section provides the results of the Morgan Quitno Safest City and Metro Area survey, which ranks American cities and metropolitan areas in overall safety. The crime records of 369 cities and 330 metropolitan areas are measured against the national average, and, as in subsequent sections, data are displayed in both alphabetical and rank order. The second section presents an overview of crime in the United States for the year 2004. Definitions, basic facts, and brief summaries of violent crime and its subcategories and property crime and its subcategories provide important background information for the numbers and comparisons presented in sections 3 and 4. The third section features 40 tables comparing 338 U.S. metropolitan areas in numbers of crimes, crimes rates, and crime trends over one and five years. Metropolitan areas included in this comparison are those for which at least 75 percent of law enforcement agencies reported crime statistics and for which the central city/cities submitted a full 12 months of data. Several metropolitan areas did not meet these criteria in 2004 and thus are not included in the rankings. The fourth section features statistical tables showing crime rankings for 379 American cities of 75,000 or more population. Crime numbers, rates, and percent changes in crime rates over one and five years are provided. This section also presents tables showing numbers and rates of police patrolling American cities. The fifth and final section consists of appendixes that provide population data, descriptions of metropolitan areas, and charts showing rates for each crime category for the past 20 years.

The editors of this edition of *City Crime Rankings* provide a brief cautionary note about the use of crime rankings, stating that such information must be considered carefully and presented responsibly. They also acknowledge that crime levels are affected by many factors, such as population density, economic conditions, and strength of local law enforcement agencies. The editors do not, however, feel that such reasons for varying crime rates invalidate the comparisons made in this reference book. Altogether, the current edition provides a clear and comprehensive overview of crime in American cities and metropolitan areas. It is an important resource for those wishing to better understand and better respond to crime in their area and is strongly recommended for public and college libraries.—**James C. Roberts**

ENVIRONMENTAL LAW

C, P

202.   **The Environmental Regulatory Dictionary.** 4th ed. James J. King, comp. Hoboken, N.J., John Wiley, 2005. 507p. $99.95. ISBN 0-471-70526-8.

The laws that regulate the environment in the United States are codified in the 30 volumes that comprise Title 40, "Protection of the Environment" of the Code of Federal Regulations (CFR). These regulations are complicated and the same term may be defined uniquely in different contexts or sections of the code. The 4th edition of *The Environmental Regulatory Dictionary* provides an easy solution to these difficulties. It is not only a specialized dictionary with over 5,000 terms, but possibly more importantly, an index to where the terms exist in Title 40. Each alphabetically arranged entry has the section number where the definition occurs, as well as reproducing the definition from Title 40. The preface makes it clear that the dictionary is merely a reproduction from Title 40 and therefore "does not guarantee the correctness or validity of the definition."

The 4th edition title, *The Environmental Regulatory Dictionary*, is a more precise title than the previous editions' titles, which were simply, *Environmental Dictionary*. For further clarity, the book could be subtitled "Index to CFR Title 40." Since the general index to all 258 volumes of the Code of Federal Regulations indexes only to title and part (not section), *The Environmental Regulatory Dictionary* is extremely valuable to users of CFR Title 40. The only alternative is to do a search of the online full-text version of the CFR on the Internet (or on Lexis or Westlaw) or to use the older *Dictionary of Environmental Legal Terms* (McGraw-Hill, 1997) that has 10,000 statutory definitions from CFR Titles 40, 29, 10, and selected Environmental Protection Agency publications. This book will be of special interest to attorneys, consultants, compliance officers, and any person who must tackle the details of environmental regulations in America. —**Georgia Briscoe**

HUMAN RIGHTS

C, P, S

203.   Bales, Kevin. **New Slavery: A Reference Handbook.** 2d ed. Santa Barbara, Calif., ABC-CLIO, 2005. 273p. index. (ABC-CLIO's Contemporary World Issues). $50.00; $55.00 (e-book). ISBN 1-85109-815-1; 1-85109-816-X (e-book).

New Slavery: A Reference Handbook not only helps one better understand modern day slavery, a little-known and misunderstood phenomenon, but also provides resources to combat it. Several chapters of background information succinctly describe the extent and forms of modern-day slavery as well as solutions. A chronology of slavery from the ancient world to 2004 is presented, with an emphasis on recent events. Biographical sketches of contemporary abolitionists, many of whom are former slaves and not widely known, illuminate the people behind the cause. A chapter devoted to facts, data, and evidence includes powerful testimonies from former slaves around the globe. An annotated organizational directory covers global and regional associations, agencies, and organizations involved in anti-slavery activities. Each annotation describes the activities and publications of the organization and includes contact information. An annotated guide to print and nonprint resources follows. Books, teaching packs, reports, newsletters, exhibits, videos, digital images, and Websites are some of the types of resources detailed. The work concludes with a glossary and index.

As stated in the preface, the author's intent is for this book to serve as a starting point to understanding the new slavery. The work does this and more. *New Slavery: A Reference Handbook* should not only raise awareness and understanding about contemporary slavery, but should also act as a catalyst for change. This book is highly recommended for public, academic, and high school libraries.—**Danielle Marie Carlock**

C, P

204.   **Encyclopedia of Civil Liberties in America.** David Schultz and John R. Vile, eds. Armonk, N.Y., M. E. Sharpe, 2005. 3v. illus. index. $299.00/set. ISBN 0-7656-8063-7.

It is unfortunate, but it can no longer be said that the words "civil liberties" strike fear or angst in the hearts of many. Fifty years or so ago, such words would have been invoked only in the rarest of circumstances and for only the most serious of offenses. Rightly, the South learned the hard way that this one nation, indivisible, provided for life, liberty, and the pursuit of happiness with equal justice for all, not just for some. Again, rightly, the South is still paying for its sins of both omission and commission and may never find forgiveness.

Lamentably, however, "civil liberties" began to be invoked about everything, and I do mean everything: one's right to eat or not eat; one's right to be dense; one's right to be offended; one's right to wear short dresses or spill hot coffee; and on and on it went until this winsome phrase has been turned into a near-profanity. It is good to see such a volume as this come out to remind us that there really are serious omissions in the area of civil liberties, and to help us come to understand that not all of them are trivial as we are often made to believe they are.

Included in this volume are reminders about academic freedom, search and seizure, blacklistings, and boycotts. Articles expanding on abortion and pornography as well as rights to a host of things: appeal, counsel, education, travel, and the more recent right to die. (Oddly, however, there is no article or even a mention of "right to work" issues.) A slew of court cases pepper this volume throughout: *Skinner v. Oklahoma*, *Tinker v. Des Moines*, *Payne v. Tennessee*, *Katz v. United States*, *Gitlow v. New York*, *Buck v. Bell*, *Ashcroft v. Free Speech Coalition*, and many others. In all, there are more than 800 court cases treated in this volume.

While arranged alphabetically, an expanded tables of contents followed by a subject guide make using this volume quite easy. For example, if on is looking for cases or articles on the exclusionary rule, all 14 articles are grouped under that heading. The same is true for homosexual rights, the right to bear arms, religion, and many others. This volume could serve as a proof-texting cornucopia for would-be writers of *Law and Order* and its multitudinous offspring. But it also deserves to be on the shelf of libraries all across America. In point of fact, it doubtless would be helpful if it were found on the shelves of many laypersons. While we may not always like all the "penumbras" the courts claim to uncover, we are always pleased when we find ourselves protected by those shadows when it is our ox being gored. Moreover, knowing about those shadows might help us remain in the light. [R: LJ, 15 April 05, p. 117]—**Mark Y. Herring**

11 Library and Information Science and Publishing and Bookselling

LIBRARY AND INFORMATION SCIENCE

Reference Works

Dictionaries and Encyclopedias

C

205. Coakes, Elayne, and Steve Clarke. **Encyclopedia of Communities of Practice in Information and Knowledge Management.** Hershey, Pa., Idea Group Publishing, 2006. 601p. index. $275.00; $220.00 (e-book). ISBN 1-59140-556-4.

The field of information science is changing rapidly. Keeping up with these changes, and the impact they have on research and practical applications, is often a daunting proposition. This encyclopedia will help educators, researchers, and information science practitioners keep up with changes through a descriptive examination of all the facets of communities of practice (CoPs). The book is edited by Elayne Coakes and Steve Clarke, both of whom contributed articles on the subject of CoPs. They quote the American Productivity and Quality Center (APQC) definition of CoP: "As groups of people who come together to share and learn from one another face-to-face and virtually, communities of practice are held together by a common interest in a body of knowledge and are driven by a desire and need to share problems, experiences, insights, templates, tools, and best practices." The foundation of their research is based on the work of Etienne Wenger, considered to be the person who is most responsible for developing the concept of these communities. He said: "Communities of practice are a specific kind of community. They are focused on a domain of knowledge and over time accumulate expertise in this domain. They develop their shared practice by interacting around problems, solutions, and insights, and building a common store of knowledge." (See http://www.ewenger.com/tech for more information.)

In this volume, a total of 128 contributors from all over the world share insights and experiences with the concept of communities of practice in 100 separate articles. They all subscribe to the belief that technology is not the driver, but the enabler of actions that must be taken to deliver services that answer the needs of our twenty-first century communities. The articles are divided into seven categories: Generic Aspects of CoPs, CoPs and the Business Environment, Organizational Aspects of CoPs, Virtual Teams and the Role of Communities, The Role of Knowledge Management, Enabling Technology, and The Philosophy Theory of CoPs/KM. The book also contains a compendium of key terms and definitions, along with explanations of processes, associated concepts, and acronyms to help the reader understand the references provided by the scholars and authors responsible for the articles.

The *Encyclopedia of Communities of Practice in Information and Knowledge Management* is also available in e-book form. Electronic access is available only for libraries and is good for the life of the book. In short, this collection of articles sheds light on all facets of special communities of knowledge, including their advantages and challenges in the formation of a new world of research. The encyclopedia is highly recommended for large public, community college, and academic libraries.—**Laura J. Bender**

C, P

206.   **Encyclopedia of the Library of Congress: For Congress, the Nation, & the World.** John Y. Cole and Jane Aikin, eds. Lanham, Md., Bernan Associates, 2004. 569p. illus. index. $125.00. ISBN 0-89059-971-8.

Numerous books, articles, dissertations, and government documents have described the history and operations of the Library of Congress (LC). Over the past 30 years, many of them have been written by John Y. Cole. In addition to editing this *Encyclopedia*, Cole has recently published *Library of Congress: The Art and Architecture of the Thomas Jefferson Building* (Norton, 1997) and *On These Walls: Inscriptions and Quotations in the Buildings of the Library of Congress* (LC, 1995). Co-editor Jane Aikin is also a veteran researcher of library history (see *The Nation's Great Library: Herbert Putnam and the Library of Congress* [University of Illinois Press, 1993]).

Entries were written by more than 50 contributors, including Cole and Aikin. There are biographies of each Librarian of Congress, as well as detailed histories of important collections and services. One can also find essays on major themes, such as "The International Role of the Library of Congress." The *Encyclopedia* is notable for its insider's view, particularly of units that are relatively unknown to the general public (for instance, the Cataloging Distribution Service). In this respect, the *Encyclopedia* is superior to James Conaway's *America's Library: The Story of the Library of Congress, 1800-2000* (Yale University Press, 2000). Although the *Encyclopedia*'s mostly small, black-and-white illustrations pale in comparison to full-color versions found in *America's Library*, some show everyday activities that are not typically reproduced in coffee-table books. The *Encyclopedia* also includes appendixes that chart the Library's appropriations, names and tenure of key officials, the growth of the Library's collections, and resources for additional reading.

The *Encyclopedia* is an invaluable resource for library science students and scholars, cultural historians, library employees, book lovers, and others who have more than a passing interest in the nation's greatest library. Legislators, reporters, and writers may also find it helpful for fact-checking. This work is recommended for collections that serve these populations. [R: BL, June 05, p. 1852; LJ, Aug 05, p. 126]—**Bernadette A. Lear**

C, S

207.   Green, Jonathon, and Nicholas J. Karolides. **Encyclopedia of Censorship.** new ed. New York, Facts on File, 2005. 698p. index. (Facts on File Library of World History). $85.00. ISBN 0-8160-4464-3.

Nicholas J. Karolides has revised Jonathon Green's 1990 reference source, *Encyclopedia of Censorship* (1st ed.; see ARBA 91, entry 635). This new edition contains many of the fundamental articles originally published in the earlier version and adds new issues and examples on the subject. Sample entries include the USA Patriot Act, shock jocks (such as Howard Stern), and the Harry Potter materials. There are also entries for most of the top books and/or authors appearing in the top ranks of the American Library Association's 100 Most Frequently Banned Books. This one-volume edition highlights countries' freedom of expression and historical perspectives on censorship. These entries provide examples of books, Websites, movies, and other materials banned in respective countries, as well as court cases and other legislative actions.

In the tradition of the earlier version, the author provides an extensive bibliography of monographic resources. However, as noted in the 1991 ARBA review, important articles on the subject would be beneficial. Cross-referencing is provided and select entries include recommendations for further reading.

This easy-to-read source is an excellent addition to the library's reference section as well as a helpful source for high school and college students enrolled in political and information literacy programs. [R: SLJ, Dec 05, p. 90]—**Carol Anne Germain**

C, P

208.   **Harrod's Librarian's Glossary and Reference Book.** 10th ed. Ray Prytherch, comp. Burlington, Vt., Ashgate Publishing, 2005. 753p. $195.00. ISBN 0-7546-4038-8.

International in scope, this glossary lists over 10,250 terms related to the information and library science profession. The 1,700 new entries in the 10th edition focus on the relevant issues and concepts affecting librarianship and information specialists, such as intellectual property, copyright, electronic publishing, open access, and privacy. Other terms include the names of organizations, library projects and programs, and words related to publishing, conservation, preservation, printing, binding, classification, and cataloging. The 3,000 entries that appeared in the 9th edition (see ARBA 2001, entry 591) have been updated and revised for the latest version. Website addresses, if applicable, are listed for organizations that include institutions, libraries, associations, and more.

This resource was originally published in 1938 at the recommendation of the United Kingdom's professional library organization who proposed that library terminology be compiled into what became *Harrod's Librarians' Glossary*. Leonard Montague Harrod compiled and edited the glossary through the publishing of the 5th edition (1984). This resource is suitable for library professionals, information specialists, and others in the library and information science field.—**Maris L. Hayashi**

Directories

P

209.   **The Big Book of Library Grant Money 2006: Profiles of Private and Corporate Foundations and Direct Corporate Givers Receptive to Library Grant Proposals.** Chicago, American Library Association, 2006. 1564p. index. $275.00pa. $247.50pa. (ALA members). ISBN 0-8389-3558-3. ISSN 1086-0568.

This aptly titled, 1-volume compilation provides detailed information on nearly 2,400 philanthropic programs in the United States. Among these are 1,730 major private foundations, grant distributors who have contributed at least $100,000, about 515 corporate foundations, and more than 120 hard-to-identify corporate direct givers. All of the funding sources described support libraries and will consider unsolicited proposals.

The highly useful directory was compiled especially for the American Library Association by the Taft Group from its *Corporate Giving Directory* (26th ed.; see ARBA 2005, entry 810), and the *Foundation Reporter* (37th ed.; see ARBA 2005, entry 811). All entries are updated annually with reliable information from a variety of sources, such as the most recent IRS Form 990-PF, the foundations' annual reports, grants lists, questionnaire responses, press releases, and telephone interviews. Each entry includes the corporation or foundation name, sponsoring company information, content, contact information, giving histories, a financial summary, a contributions summary, corporate officers and directors, application procedures and restrictions, publications, an analysis of grants, and recent grants.

Other useful features are five specialized indexes: index to corporations and foundations by headquarters, index to corporations by operating location, index to officers and directors, index to library recipients by state, and a master index. Although impressive, the usefulness of this big book cannot be judged by size alone. Its true value lies in its information, currency, relevancy, and ease of use for all library fundraisers.—**K. Mulliner**

C, P

210.   **The Oxford Guide to Library Research.** 3d ed. By Thomas Mann. New York, Oxford University Press, 2005. 293p. index. $17.95pa. ISBN 0-19-518998-1.

The Oxford Guide to Library Research is an outstanding overview of research methodology at a time when electronic and print resources vie for relevance in our larger culture. Starting with the assertion that the Internet cannot hope to supplant books and "bricks and mortar" libraries, the author proceeds to examine a wide variety of research tools, emphasizing that electronic resources are a means to an end and not an end unto themselves. Reference sources, including an extensive exploration of encyclopedias, are championed, the utility of subject headings is considered, as are the joys and pains of browsing the stacks, as well as the use of indexes, citations, and bibliographies. There is an excellent examination of keyword searching and the use of Boolean logic, as well as a consideration of the factors in developing a literature review. The author encourages researchers to utilize people as sources of information, including experts in various fields, librarians, and unpublished but knowledgeable authors contributing to listservs. He also suggests that researchers not overlook underused formats like microforms, Web collections, and government documents. Methods of finding materials in other libraries are suggested, and there is a study of disparate formats, including maps, photographs, and book reviews. There are helpful illustrations throughout the text. The author takes great pains to explain how to use these research tools in a coherent way that will explore a subject both thoroughly and creatively, and continuously reminds the reader that wisdom lies in the ability to assess information from multiple sources.—**Philip G. Swan**

PUBLISHING AND BOOKSELLING

Directories

C, P

211.   **American Book Trade Directory 2005-2006.** 51st ed. Medford, N.J., Information Today, 2005. 1800p. index. $299.00. ISBN 1-57387-212-1.

The *American Book Trade Directory* (ABTD) has been published since 1915 and is clearly a standard tool housed either in the reference or in the acquisitions department of all but the smallest libraries. With over 25,500 retail and wholesale booksellers listed, the volume, while not necessarily exhaustive, is certainly comprehensive (the distinction being that entries are based primarily on voluntary responses to mailed questionnaires). A nonscientific review of some entries in multiple states demonstrates that even some very minor establishments have been posted. The information provided per entry is scant, but it is nevertheless what most libraries will be seeking. The following data elements are included: business name, address, telephone number and fax number (where appropriate), Web address, year established, the current owner's start year, square feet, subjects covered, and sidelines and services. An overall category is also assigned, such as general, antiquarian, or computer software.

Coverage is for the United States and Canada, and includes the following major areas: retailers and antiquarians; wholesalers of books and magazines; book trade information (such as auctioneers, appraisers, exporters, importers, and associations); dealers in foreign-language books; types of stores (a subject index by category, such as "German Language") ; and an index to retailers and wholesalers, which provides the city and state for the listed name. (The overall arrangement for the ABTD is alphabetical by state, and then similarly by city name.)

The directory is designed to fill a very specific function. While this information would be easier to access online, the market for the product might be too small to justify the expense associated with such an undertaking. Until an electronic version arises, the paper copy will continue to be needed by librarians and others associated with the book trade. This resource is highly recommended.—**Graham R. Walden**

P

212.   **Directory of Small Press/Magazine Editors & Publishers 2005-2006.** 36th ed. Len Fulton, ed. Paradise, Calif., Dustbooks, 2005. 348p. $25.95pa. ISBN 0-913218-11-1.

P

213.   **International Directory of Little Magazines & Small Presses, 2005-2006.** 41st ed. Len Fulton, ed. Paradise, Calif., Dustbooks, 2005. 796p. index. $55.00; $37.95pa. ISBN 0-913218-06-5; 0-913218-00-6pa.

Writers interested in submitting their work to small publishers or magazines have come to rely on these annual directories, as have many who work in the publishing and book-reviewing industry. *The International Directory* continues to list alphabetically both magazines and presses in entries that include publisher/editor name, contact information, date of founding, material published, editor's comments, circulation, annual number of books or issues, single-copy and subscription prices, magazine length or press run, percentage of manuscripts published, simultaneous submissions policy, payment arrangements, rights/copyright, subjects of interest, and advertising rates. A geographic index by state and country and a subject-area index help users narrow their focus. Up to 10 subject-matter categories as found in the index are listed at the end of each entry, which means users need not flip to the subject index as frequently as before. The *Directory of Small Press/Magazine Editors & Publishers*, a companion to *The International Directory*, alphabetically lists all the editors and publishers found in the latter, plus a number of self-publishers not found there. Thus, if users have only the personal name of an editor or publisher, they can locate the publication or press name, its addresses, and telephone numbers for that person and then turn to the larger directory for more information.—**Lori D. Kranz**

P

214.   **Literary Market Place 2006: The Directory of the American Book Publishing Industry with Industry Yellow Pages.** Medford, N.J., Information Today, 2005. 2v. index. $299.95/set. ISBN 1-57387-221-0. ISSN 0000-1155.

The 2006 edition of *Literary Market Place* provides users with directory information for nearly 14,000 publishers, editorial services, associations, trade magazines, book marketing specialists, book manufacturing companies, sales and distributions companies, and services and suppliers. In each new edition *Literary Market Place* provides contact information for new publishers, deletes those no longer in business, and provides thousands of updates to existing entries. Volume 1 provides information for publishers (including Canadian and small presses); editorial services and agents; associations, events, courses, and awards; and books and magazines for the trade. Volume 2 provides information on service providers to the book industry, including advertisers and marketing, book manufacturers, sales and distribution, and suppliers. Directory information includes the name of the company; address; telephone, fax, and toll-free numbers; e-mail and Website addresses; names of key personnel with titles; company reportage; branch offices; brief statistics; and a short description of the company. When appropriate Standard Address Numbers (SANs) and ISBN prefixes are provided. A variety of indexes will help users expedite their search. They include company and personnel indexes, a toll-free directory, an index to sections, and an index to advertisers.

The information provided in the print version of this directory is as accurate as one will find. The LMP staff contacts each publisher directly for updates on an annual basis and is continually researching to find new publishing or publishing-related companies. The directory also includes a six-page list of book trade acquisitions and mergers that occurred between June 2003 and July 2005. Those libraries considering this title should note that there is an online version available for an annual subscription rate of $399.00 per year, which includes access to the information in *International Literary Market Place* as well. Both are highly recommended for public and academic libraries.—**Shannon Graff Hysell**

12 Military Studies

GENERAL WORKS

Atlases

C, P, S

215. Murray, Stuart. **Atlas of American Military History.** New York, Facts on File, 2005. 248p. illus. maps. index. (Facts on File Library of American History). $85.00. ISBN 0-8160-5578-5.

Stuart Murray, author of *The Encyclopedia of War & Weaponry* (Franklin Watts, 2002) and *The American Revolution: Eyewitness Guidebook* (DK Publishing, 2002), has prepared an attractive and well-designed atlas that traces American military history from the colonial period to the wars in Afghanistan and Iraq. The 28 succinct chapters survey the significant wars, campaigns, and battles of the military history of the United States. More of an illustrated history than a conventional atlas, the book uses an array of color maps, photographs, and illustrations to support the narrative. Although not footnoted, the text is well written and highly readable. The book includes a detailed eight-page chronology and a useful index. However, the one-age bibliography consisting of only 23 entries and 32 selected Websites is inadequate for such a reference work. A more extensive bibliography would have much improved the utility of the book. This atlas employs a similar format as the *Atlas of American Military History*, edited by James C. Bradford (see ARBA 2004, entry 681). Libraries already owning Bradford's more detailed atlas may consider Murray's work, although more up to date with coverage of the war in Iraq, optional. A good introduction to the topic, Murray's *Atlas of American Military History* would be a useful addition for high school libraries, public libraries, and undergraduate collections.—**Bradley P. Tolppanen**

Chronology

C, P

216. Brune, Lester. **Chronology of the Cold War 1917-1992.** Edited by Richard Dean Burns. New York, Routledge/Taylor & Francis Group, 2006. 700p. illus. maps. index. $150.00. ISBN 0-415-97339-2.

The Cold War was one of the most defining ideological conflicts of the past century. It started with the Bolshevik Revolution of 1917 and ended with the fall of the Berlin Wall and the collapse of the Soviet Union. Through two World Wars and numerous smaller ones, this battle of ideologies was fought on many fronts. It did not really heat up until 1945 when the North Atlantic Treaty Organization (NATO), "probably the most successful alliance in history," was created to counter the aggressive post World War II Soviet Union. Thus this chronology explores this extremely important historical event.

These documents should be viewed as pieces of a much larger puzzle. If a particular event or document is either a major event or a mere blip on an individual's radar, it still had significance to this conflict.

This entire work should be seen as a useful tool for the historian checking a fact or a student looking to start a research project. An index, maps, and illustrations are present.

A typical example of an entry is on page 169—March 10, 1952. On this date, in Cuba, General Batista overthrew President Socarras and made himself Chief of State and Premier. A simple paragraph provides the reader with some of the background that galvanized the left-wing opposition to the Batista regime and ultimately swept Castro into power and created the first Communist state in the Americas. This work is highly recommended for all types and levels of libraries. [R: LJ, 15 Nov 05, p. 94]—**Scott R. DiMarco**

Dictionaries and Encyclopedias

C, P, S

217.   Axelrod, Alan. **Encyclopedia of the American Armed Forces.** New York, Facts on File, 2005. 2v. illus. index. (Facts on File Library of American History). $175.00/set. ISBN 0-8160-4700-6.

Some say that the price of freedom is never free and that the cost is paid for by the military. Well-known author and historian Alan Axelrod (author of the *Complete Idiot's Guide to the Civil War* and the *Complete Idiot's Guide to the American Revolution*) has authored this two-volume encyclopedia for Facts on File. His expertise is evident. This reference work is relevant and topical with a purpose of informing the novice on the basics of military life in today's armed forces.

Divided into four sections that are each devoted to a branch of the U.S. military—U.S. Army, U.S. Air Force, U.S. Marine Corp, and U.S. Navy—this fine work has approximately 1,200 entries. Each branch has an initial list of entries, a list of branch-specific abbreviations and acronyms, and a bibliography. Each section is alphabetized. Black-and-white photographs with captions are included. A general index is also provided.

Entries range across all military-related areas, from past to the current day. They include people, places, events, battles, equipment, structure, and life and traditions. A typical entry is in volume 1, under U.S. Army—"1st Infantry Division (ID) (The 'Big Red One')." This entry spans two pages (pp. 89-90) and has a photograph. The history of and actions involving the 1st ID is documented with other entries for easy reference. It is tight, but well written. This work is recommended for libraries and individuals. [R: BL, 1 & 15 Jan 06, pp. 149-150]—**Scott R. DiMarco**

C

218.   **Encyclopedia of Intelligence and Counterintelligence.** Rodney P. Carlisle, ed. Armonk, N.Y., M. E. Sharpe, 2005. 2v. illus. index. $199.00/set. ISBN 0-7656-8068-8.

Intelligence agencies, operations, and analysis have received extensive news coverage recently due to the recent U.S. intelligence community reforms produced by the 9/11 Commission and controversy over the quality of U.S. intelligence analysis indicating the presence of weapons of mass destruction in Iraq prior to the 2003 initiation of Operation Iraqi Freedom. The growth of the Internet and recent declassification initiatives by the United States and other governmental intelligence agencies have increased the amount of literature on intelligence agencies and their activities to scholars and the general public. All of these developments help create a market for works such as the *Encyclopedia of Intelligence and Counterintelligence*.

This two-volume edited work features introductory overviews on a variety of individuals, countries, events, and organizations that have shaped intelligence activities and operations throughout recorded history. It begins with a historical introduction describing how intelligence activity dates from Babylonian civilization and the biblical era. The introduction also provides information on how contributors to this encyclopedia went about compiling this work.

Following a timeline of historically significant intelligence events from the thirteenth century B.C.E. to the present, the heart of this encyclopedia is its descriptions of key intelligence individuals, countries, events, and organizations. Examples of this multifaceted variety of entries include Afghanistan, Aldrich Ames, Cold War, defector, Reinhard Gehlen, human intelligence, KGB, John McCone, Oleg Penkovsky, reconnaissance, scientific and technical intelligence, Six-Day War, George Tenet, Verona, and Markus Wolf. An appendix features excerpts from the 9/11 Commission's 2004 report and a resource guide featuring relevant books, scholarly journals, and intelligence Websites. Encyclopedia entries are written by scholars and former intelligence officers and represent a wide variety of viewpoints. They range in length from one page to several pages and conclude with index cross-references to other encyclopedia entries and brief bibliographic references for additional reading.

Although intelligence scholars may disagree with the interpretations of the significance of given individuals, institutions, and events for various entries, the overall work is fairly evenhanded in tone and represents a generally effective introduction to intelligence and counterintelligence. Areas the work could be strengthened would be including the Websites of congressional and parliamentary intelligence oversight committees and including an entry on William Harvey, a CIA official who was a key architect of the United States' 1950s Berlin Tunnel efforts against the Soviet bloc. Better editing could have prevented the occurrence of errors such as listing incorrect Website addresses for the U.S. Army's Strategic Studies Institute, Defense Department, and Department of Homeland Security in the Al Qaeda entry on page 13, and giving a more detailed Website address on the Library of Congress Website for the Algeria volume in the Area Handbook Series listed on page 15. Despite these flaws, the *Encyclopedia of Intelligence and Counterintelligence* is a highly desirable addition to academic library reference collections. [R: LJ, 1 April 05, p. 123]—**Bert Chapman**

NAVY

Biography

C, P

219.   **United States Marine Corps Medal of Honor Recipients: A Comprehensive Registry, Including U.S. Navy Medical Personnel Honored for Serving Marines in Combat.** George B. Clark, ed. Jefferson, N.C., McFarland, 2005. 202p. illus. index. $45.00. ISBN 0-7864-2271-8.

The Congressional Medal of Honor is the highest award U.S. military personnel can receive for combat action and is generally presented to recipients by the President on behalf of Congress. This work provides listings of U.S. Marine Corps Medal of Honor recipients from the award's creation in 1861 through the Vietnam War in 1973.

This compilation opens with a preface providing historical background on the Medal of Honor and emphasizing that a primary source for its contents is a 1973 U.S. Senate Veterans Affairs Committee publication, *Medal of Honor Recipients 1863-1973*. The book proceeds to list Medal of Honor recipients from 1861-1973 with entries arranged chronologically by major and minor military conflicts such as the Civil War and Second Nicaraguan Campaign, 1927-1932. Within these chronological campaign arrangements, individual recipients are listed alphabetically and their entries describe the actions for which they received the Medal of Honor with a number of recipient photographs being provided to place a visual representation of these individuals.

Appendixes include a chart listing the states or countries of origin for Medal of Honor recipients, the number of awards received by Marine Corps regiments during various campaigns, a chronological and campaign listing of individual award recipients, and a succinct but detailed bibliography featuring government documents and commercially published books. This work will provide an essential reference for those interested in Marine Corps biographical history and information on Medal of Honor Recipients. —**Bert Chapman**

Chronology

C

220.   Rohwer, Jürgen. **Chronology of the War at Sea, 1939-1945: The Naval History of World War Two.** 3d rev. ed. Annapolis, Md., Naval Institute Press, 2005. 530p. index. $59.95. ISBN 1-59114-119-2.

In this highly detailed chronology covering all the major naval powers in the six years of World War II, one can find listings of many kinds of naval activity occurring either daily or monthly in various theaters of war. The vessels engaged encompass the largest battleships, the cruisers, destroyers, troop ships, torpedo and patrol boats, submarines, and even landing craft. A typical daily entry might include a particular U-boat, its commander, the ship(s) it sunk, and the tonnage, as well as the precise location where the action took place. The amount of research gathered from military records and various other sources is noteworthy. A case in point is the detailed account of the attack on Pearl Harbor and the ensuing activities throughout December 1941, in both the Pacific and European theaters. Military libraries, academic libraries with large military collections, historians, novelists, and screen writers will find this extremely well done and reasonably priced chronology a worthwhile purchase.—**Charles R. Andrews**

Handbooks and Yearbooks

P

221.   **The Naval Institute Guide to Combat Fleets of the World 2005-2006: Their Ships, Aircraft, and Systems.** Eric Wertheim, comp. Annapolis, Md., Naval Institute Press, 2005. 1104p. illus. index. $225.00. ISBN 1-59114-934-7.

This is a big book no matter how you look at it. It is 12¼" tall by 9¼" wide and 2¼" thick, and weighs about 5 pounds. But, of course, its importance lies in the 1,104 pages of photographs and the meticulous compilation of data on the ships and aircraft of the world's fighting fleets. The book covers navies from Albania through Zimbabwe, with a postscript on Iraq's seven ship Coastal Defense Force. The navies of the world powers come in for intensive scrutiny—United States (152 pages), France (42 pages), Germany (22 pages), Japan (49 pages), United Kingdom (44 pages), Russia (102 pages), and China (27 pages). The United States entry lists all of the active navy ships plus ships in the ready reserve, the Coast Guard, Army ships, National Oceanic and Atmospheric Administration (NOAA), and the Customs Service. The size and displacement of ships, motive machinery, armaments, electronics, and size of crew are the sort of information available. There are also some clues about naval strategies and tactics. Front matter includes "Sources and Acknowledgements," which is a who's who of active naval researchers and experts, plus a bibliography of information sources. This is followed with a "How to Use this Book" section, and several pages of "Terms and Abbreviations." Back matter has a 19-page "Index by Ships." Finally, there is a portrait and biographical sketch of compiler Eric Wertheim. The plan is to publish future editions every two years. This is a volume that will be used and studied by defense planners, foreign affairs experts, defense contractors, and others. It is a major accomplishment.—**Frank J. Anderson**

P

222.   **The Naval Institute Guide to the Ships and Aircraft of the U.S. Fleet.** 18th ed. By Norman Polmar. Annapolis, Md., Naval Institute Press, 2005. 661p. illus. index. $76.46. ISBN 1-59114-685-2.

The 18th edition of *The Naval Institute Guide to the Ships and Aircraft of the U.S. Fleet* is a must-have for any student of the modern American Navy. The meticulous attention to detail of this guide is typical of the quality of the Naval Institute Press. By drawing on the research of U.S. Navy itself, the Congressional Research Office, the Congressional Budget Office, and several other sources, this work is truly exceptional. Additionally, it offers the reader an insight into the world of the "transformation" that the current Navy is experiencing, while fighting a global war on terrorism in a post-September 11th world.

The entries are arranged by class of ship (e.g., submarines, aircraft carriers, destroyers, command ships). Each entry lasts a page or so, but the individual class of ship may be several pages. The table of contents is helpful. The preface, glossary, ship name and class index, and index are also very useful. The numerous photographs add a rich dimension that many other guides lack. It is a rare page that does not have a black-and-white photograph with a detailed caption. The footnotes on many pages are worthy of attention.

A typical example of an entry is chapter 16, "Frigates" (pp. 160-169). All areas of the frigates past (post-WWII) and future are discussed, including probable scenarios. Seven photographs and one detailed drawing are included, as are six sets of charts or graphs on four separate pages. This work is highly recommended.—**Scott R. DiMarco**

WEAPONS AND EQUIPMENT

Dictionaries and Encyclopedias

C, P, S
223.   **Weapons of Mass Destruction: An Encyclopedia of Worldwide Policy, Technology, and History.** Eric A. Croddy, James J. Wirtz, and Jeffrey A. Larsen, eds. Santa Barbara, Calif., ABC-CLIO, 2005. 2v. illus. index. $185.00/set; $200.00 (e-book). ISBN 1-85109-490-3; 1-85109-495-4 (e-book).

This massive informative set is wisely divided into two volumes—"Chemical and Biological Weapons" and "Nuclear Weapons"— making the work easier to use. Both volumes carry the same index, foreword, preface, and an A-Z list of entries. Each volume, however, has its own introduction, chronology, and specific entries. In the must-read preface, the history of the term "weapons of mass destruction" (WMD) is set forth. Worth noting in the preface is the editors' hope that the encyclopedia will help inform the public debate about the WMD, with the goal of never again seeing such weapons raised in anger.

Among the 500 well-referenced entries, readers will find the familiar napalm, sarin, Agent Orange, and Gulf War Syndrome, as well as the lesser-known fuel air explosive, Livens Projector, yellowcake, and two-man rule. Various key documents are included, such as the Geneva Protocol (1925) on the prohibition of poisonous gas in war and the Atomic Energy Act of 1946. High school, academic, and military libraries will find this attractively designed and superbly indexed set a major purchase that will likely get repeated use.—**Charles R. Andrews**

Handbooks and Yearbooks

C, P
224.   Murphy, Justin D. **Military Aircraft, Origins to 1918: An Illustrated History of Their Impact.** Santa Barbara, Calif., ABC-CLIO, 2005. 319p. illus. index. (Weapons and Warfare Series). $85.00. ISBN 1-85109-488-1.

During its century-long existence, aviation has transformed our world in numerous ways. Its importance in military affairs has become particularly prominent due to the role it has played in a variety of military operations, with the 1999 NATO war against Kosovo being a particularly vivid example. This work encourages students and scholars of aviation and military history to examine the initial historical origin and evolution of military aircraft.

It opens with a historical overview of how humans considered the possibility of flying and of the embryonic efforts to achieve flight prior to the Wright Brothers 1903 triumph. This overview also includes descriptions of the efforts made by U.S. and European militaries to take advantage of this emerging technological capability to benefit their national military objectives. Later chapters address the role played by military aviation during World War I in performing aerial reconnaissance and in conducting combat operations and the activities of reconnaissance, fighter, bomber, and naval aircraft during this conflict from countries such as Austria-Hungary, Britain, France, Germany, Italy, Russia, and the United States.

Appendixes list the names of aircraft by countries; categorize them by their primary combat role; and feature photographs and detailed biographical information such as their manufacturer, crew size, physical dimensions, speed, armament, number produced, and service dates. The work closes with a glossary and selective bibliography.

Murphy has produced a detailed and helpful introduction to the early origins and development of military aviation. A selective bibliography of secondary source literature is also helpful. The bibliography could have been strengthened by including government documents such as the annual reports of the U.S. Secretaries of War and the Navy and other U.S. and British military documents, which are readily available in many research library or archival collections.—**Bert Chapman**

C, P

225.   Sandler, Stanley. **Battleships: An Illustrated History of Their Impact.** Santa Barbara, Calif., ABC-CLIO, 2004. 229p. illus. index. (Weapons and Warfare Series). $85.00; $90.00 (e-book). ISBN 1-85109-410-5; 1-85109-415-6 (e-book).

As so eloquently stated in the preface, "This is one of the few books that chronicle the history of the capital ship from the time of the bronze-beaked galley-rams of ancient times, to the storied multidecked ship-of-the-line of the Age of Fighting Sail, to the squat, grim ironclads, and concluding with the big-gun massive dreadnought." This work is part of ABC-CLIO's Weapons and Warfare Series, which is edited by Spencer C. Tucker. *Battleships* is edited by Stanley Sandler.

This 229-page book has an introduction about the series, a preface, an introduction and overview, six chapters, an appendix area that includes numerous half-page black-and-white photographs, a glossary, a references section, and a complete index. The chapters are chronological—Chapter 1: 2000 B.C. to 1804; Chapter 2: 1800 to 1889; Chapter 3: 1889 to 1905; Chapter 4: 1906 to 1914; Chapter 5: 1918 to 1938; and Chapter 6: 1939 to present. Chapter 6, "Battleships During World War II and After, 1939 to the Present," is an example of a typical chapter. It covers the pages 125 to 152. It starts by stating that the most expensive war tool of World War II was the U.S. Army Air Corp's B-29 Superfortress, not a battleship. In fact, not one battleship was laid down and completed during World War II, yet there were more battleship-to-battleship clashes in World War II than in World War I. A detailed account of World War II battleships and their activities is provided, as is the post-World War II era. This work is recommended for all types and levels of libraries.—**Scott R. DiMarco**

P, C

226.   Westwood, David. **Rifles: An Illustrated History of Their Impact.** Santa Barbara, Calif., ABC-CLIO, 2005. 470p. illus. index. (Weapons and Warfare Series). $85.00; $90.00 (e-book). ISBN 1-85109-401-6; 1-85109-406-7 (e-book).

"Weapons both fascinate and repel," or so goes the first sentence to the introduction to this series, Weapons and Warfare. In our overly sensitive times, the repellent part often gets the headlines to the distraction, dismay, and otherwise dislocation of the rest. For better or for worse, weapons have a most riveting history and only the most weak of heart would want to deny that. Rifles, the subject of this volume, are no different in that regard.

The approach author Westwood (CEO and managing director of Military Library Research Service Ltd, Derbyshire, England) has taken is chronological and it works very well. The birth of firearms, the fourteenth century, commences the study with its evolving definition of the term "firearm" and early renditions of same such as the snaphance and flintlock (actually both are firing mechanisms). From this follows the history of what is termed the propellant and the projectile. There follows, in order, breech-loading rifles (for example, the Braendlin, the Newby, and the Peabody), lever-action rifles (Spencer, Lagatz, and the Berselli system), repeating-bolt actions rifles (such as the Lee, Mauser, and Lebel) and the more familiar and more modern self-loading rifles. Not only are readers treated to a fine history of these ingenious weapons but they also will be regaled by the attending history.

The book is generously peppered with illustrations and photographs, and most chapters have an attending history (as, for example, percussion systems and rifles as a military staple). One appendix includes the most substantial part of the Schön Report, which appeared in Dresden 1855 as part of the Mordecai report on European weapons during the Crimean War. Schön's report is important because it appears as the world moved from muzzle-loaded muskets to the breech-loading bolt rifles of more modern times. This is followed by almost 150 pages of rifles and their makers, arranged by country. A glossary, an extensive bibliography, and a competent index make this a must-have item useful for all libraries.—**Mark Y. Herring**

13 Political Science

GENERAL WORKS

Bibliography

C, S

227.   **Information Sources of Political Science.** 5th ed. Stephen W. Green and Douglas J. Ernest, eds. Santa Barbara, Calif., ABC-CLIO, 2005. 593p. index. $85.00; $90.00 (e-book). ISBN 1-57607-104-9; 1-57607-557-5 (e-book).

The world has experienced vast political upheaval since the 4th edition of this title was published in 1986 (see ARBA 87, entry 679). Since then, information access technology has also fundamentally changed and the amount of information available to researchers has increased exponentially. As a result, the editors of this latest edition have not attempted to include every possible information source of political science. Instead, their goal is to present and describe the most generally helpful and widely available sources at all levels of scholarship.

Information Sources of Political Science is divided into nine chapters, each devoted to a major topic. (In addition to these topics, there is a chapter of biographical information for political figures.) These topics are further divided into specific subtopics and arranged by type of access tool, which includes literature guides, abstracting and indexing services, directories, dictionaries, encyclopedias, guides and handbooks, and atlases. Over 2,000 print and electronic sources are carefully cited and clearly annotated within these categories. Each annotation is usually between 100 and 200 words and describes the "structure, organization, content, and reading level" (p. xix) of the source. When an electronic version is available, a computer icon is placed at the end of the entry. Electronic sources are interspersed throughout the listings, and they include Websites, e-books, CD-ROMs, and electronic versions that are part of subscription databases. Internet addresses are given for Websites; however, specific access instructions for e-books, CD-ROMs, and electronic subscriptions are not provided as access varies among libraries. Detailed author, subject, title, and Website indexes are given and include helpful cross-references.

Information Sources of Political Science has been published since 1971 and is a standard title in many reference collections. In this latest edition, the most obvious change is the addition of electronic sources. A few major features have been eliminated in the interest of simplification, and they include sources covering law and government publications, materials written in a foreign language (unless there is an English translation available), and scholarly information on political science reference theory. Except for some very essential works, sources listed in previous editions are not included in this edition, which will serve to complement them. This work is well organized, clearly written, and comprehensive without being exhaustive. It will be valuable to researchers and students from the secondary school level to graduate level programs.—**Lesley A. Paul**

Dictionaries and Encyclopedias

C, S

228.   Szajkowski, Bogdan. **Political Parties of the World.** 6th ed. London, John Harper; distr., Farmington Hills, Mich., Gale, 2005. 710p. index. $185.00. ISBN 0-9543811-4-9.

When the first editions of *Political Parties of the World* were published in the 1980s and 1990s, numerous political changes, primarily in Eastern Europe, forced the formation of new parties and the dissolution of others. These changes resulted in the need to have a resource that could easily explain and sort out these political transformations. *Political Parties of the World* was the resource to turn to, and even in its 6th edition and at 100 pages longer than the 5th edition (see ARBA 2003, entry 679), it continues to serve as an essential reference item, especially with the recent military and political events that have taken place in the Middle East. The book contains brief descriptions of the numerous parties that presently comprise numerous countries worldwide. It offers concise historical analyses of each country's governmental systems and the political struggles they have faced. Entries are listed alphabetically by country and include Website addresses, telephone numbers, and names of political leaders for each party. All of the book's contributors specialize in or have first-hand knowledge of the country or parties about which they write. A personal name and party index is featured as are two short appendixes on international and Pan-European parties. In terms of physical attributes, the hardcover provides durability and, although it is over 700 pages in length, the book is not the least bit unwieldy. School, academic, and large public libraries will greatly benefit from having this resource in their collections.—**Maris L. Hayashi**

C, S

229.   **Youth Activism: An International Encyclopedia.** Lonnie R. Sherrod, Constance A. Flanagan, Ron Kassimir, and Amy K. Syvertsen, eds. Westport, Conn., Greenwood Press, 2006. 2v. illus. index. $199.95/set. ISBN 0-313-32811-0.

Three introductory chapters written by the editors provide a context for the topics covered in *Youth Activism: An International Encyclopedia* by addressing the three components of youth activism: activism and civic engagement, youth development and activism, and the political nature of activism. This two-volume encyclopedia contains over 160 essay-style entries organized under 18 broad topics related to youth activism. The major topic categories are: Adolescent and Youth Development; Adult Involvement with Youth; Advocacy for Social Causes; Education; Gender and Sexuality; Global and Transnational Issues; Historical Examples, Causes, and Movements; International Examples of Activism and Social Movements; Law and Justice; Media and Internet Influences and Uses; Organizations and Programs; Political Context; Positive Youth Development; Religion; Social Background Factors; Social Relationships and Networks; Voices of Activism; and Youth Culture. The scope of each of the topics is described in the preface. Individual entries cover a variety of concepts and issues and may describe research, programs, organizations, events, or movements; the entry subject may be current or historical, U.S.-centric or international. Each volume of the set begins with an alphabetic list of all 160-plus entries followed by a "Guide to Related Topics" in which the editors have inserted the entry titles under the relevant topic headings; many of the individual entries are relevant to several of the 18 topics and will appear in multiple categories. Each detailed essay, ranging from 1,000 to 4,000 words, is signed and includes a list of recommended readings (and in some cases related Websites). The encyclopedia's contributors come from around the globe and are drawn from many specializations and professions in the private, not-for-profit, and government sectors. Contributors and their affiliations are included with the editor profiles at the end of volume 2. For further information and research an extensive "List of Useful Organizations" (which includes address and contact information as well as a brief description of the organization) and an additional bibliography of books, articles, and Websites precede the index in volume 2.—**Polly D. Boruff-Jones**

Handbooks and Yearbooks

C, S

230.   **Pro/Con 4.** Danbury, Conn., Grolier, 2005. 6v. illus. index. $339.00/set. ISBN 0-7172-5950-1.

Pro/Con 4, the latest addition to the Pro/Con series, consists of six volumes—"World Politics," "Religion and Morality," "U.S. Judiciary," "International Law," "Poverty and Wealth," and "Work and the Workplace." At its heart, *Pro/Con 4* is a collection of debates on complex and controversial subjects collected from newspapers, magazines, surveys, religious tracts, legal opinions, speeches, and other sources. Operating from the premise that it is better for Americans to act on these issues from an informed position rather than from emotion and uninformed opinions, *Pro/Con 4* presents multiple sides of an issue and gives the readers information that will allow them to make up their own mind. Topics are organized under broad categories, and within each category are more specific topic questions with opinions provided on both sides. Each topic question has a summary, with background provided for further reading. For more details, there are margin notes, and at the end of each topic question section there is a key concepts map. The explanations are clearly written, at a level suitable for middle and high school readers.

This set is well written and provides balanced coverage of each issue covered. A glossary is provided for difficult terms, and an index to the entire 24-volume set is provided. Each topic entry refers readers to further articles of interest in the set, as well as other resources for further research. Overall, *Pro/Con 4*, as well as the rest of the Pro/Con set, is an excellent reference resource. Although its cost is rather prohibitive, any middle or high school media center that can afford it should purchase it. It is also useful in academic libraries for lower-level research projects. Large public libraries will also find it useful.—**Mark T. Bay**

POLITICS AND GOVERNMENT

United States

Bibliography

C

231.   Hendrickson, Kenneth E., Jr. **The Life and Presidency of Franklin Delano Roosevelt: An Annotated Bibliography.** Lanham, Md., Scarecrow, 2005. 3v. index. $300.00/set. ISBN 0-8108-5661-1.

This 3-volume set includes nearly 10,000 annotated references to "all books, articles, and dissertations" published to 1994 about President Franklin Delano Roosevelt. References are arranged into nine chapters that highlight a particular aspect of his life. Chapters from the first two volumes cover the following broad subject areas: materials written about his family and early political career; general works about his presidency; a substantial chapter that covers the vice president, cabinet members, agency directors, military officers, and key members of Congress; three chapters devoted to various domestic policy issues; a chapter about pre-war foreign policy; and a chapter that annotates works about the home front and diplomacy and strategy during World War II. A final chapter covers bibliographies, important oral history collections, and major collections within the Roosevelt Library. The third volume contains detailed author and subject indexes.

Each chapter begins with a short introduction that highlights key events and issues noted in the literature and describes the type of material found within the chapter. Although brief, the introductions help to place the literature in historical context. References are arranged alphabetically by author name and subdivided under relevant categories to help the researcher find specific information. For example, the chapter on World War I subdivides the references under subjects, such as transportation, and by country. The breakdown of these categories can be found in the table of contents. Annotations are short but generally remain helpful in determining content and purpose. Front matter includes a list of abbreviations and agency acronyms and a chronology of events that becomes increasingly detailed during the pre-war and war years. Also included is a brief essay highlighting Roosevelt's life and political career.

Considered in total, this work stands out as the definitive bibliography about President Franklin D. Roosevelt. With the exception of literature on military battles, citations to virtually all aspects of Roosevelt's personal and political life can be found here, as represented in the research and historical literature. The comprehensiveness of materials covered makes this an important work about American political history in general and should be considered as such by both student and scholar. This is also an important bibliographic guide to literature about key individuals who participated in the American political arena during the Roosevelt era. For these reasons this bibliography represents a very important contribution to researching the American presidency.—**Robert V. Labaree**

Biography

C, S

232.   Bowling, Lawson. **Shapers of the Great Debate on the Great Society: A Biographical Dictionary.** Westport, Conn., Greenwood Press, 2005. 320p. index. (Shapers of the Great American Debates). $75.00. ISBN 0-313-31434-9.

President Lyndon Johnson's Great Society is the lineal progeny of those other grandiose sounding Progressive political platforms of the twentieth-century: the Square Deal, the New Freedom, the New Era, the New Deal, the Fair Deal, and the New Frontier. Interestingly enough, in some ways it is also the forefather of today's Compassionate Conservatism scheme. All of these programs represented an important transformation in the American polity—a purposeful swing from a relatively laissez-faire economy and minimal state to a governmental leviathan, whereby our personal liberties are encroached upon in the hope of alleviating one form or another of societal malady, individual shortcoming, or cultural injustice. Professor Bowling (Manhattanville College) does an admirable job of dissecting politically the Great Society through biography. This volume examines the life stories and worldviews of 19 individuals who shaped much of the debate of the 1960s. Specifically, the author examines the various fault lines that crisscross such contentious matters as the War on Poverty, the Civil Rights Act of 1964, the Voting Rights Act of 1965, Welfare, Medicare, and federal assistance to precollege education. Biographies include balanced assessments of conservatives like William F. Buckley, Barry Goldwater, Strom Thurmond, and Edward Banfield. Also included are longtime Washington insiders and bureaucrats Sargent Shriver, the creator of the controversial Office of Economic Opportunity, and Wilbur Cohen, who worked tirelessly the corridors of Congress to enact Medicare and Medicaid. New Left radicals and critics of the Great Society include SDS organizer Tom Hayden and the Black Nationalist Stokely Carmichael. Perhaps the most enjoyable part of the book is the last section that examines mainstream, New Deal Democrats like Richard Daley, Edith Green, and Daniel Patrick Moynihan. Each person supported statism, but for varying political reasons was critical of important aspects of the Great Society. This work is well suited for advanced high school and college students and the general public.—**Paul Gerard Connors**

C, P, S

233.   Harris, Bill. **The First Ladies Fact Book: The Stories of the Women of the White House from Martha Washington to Laura Bush.** New York, Black Dog & Leventhal Publishers, 2005. 725p. illus. index. $24.95. ISBN 1-57912-468-2.

This fact book is an engaging volume of essays, suitable for a broad range of audiences, on the 42 First Ladies of the United States. Written by a freelance editor and former New York City tour guide, Harris is the author of *The Presidents Fact Book* (Black Dog & Leventhal, 2004) and 17 books about New

York. Arranged chronologically, the essays range in length from 10 to 25 pages. Each contains quick biographical facts on each first lady, including birth, marriage and death dates, parents' names, and names of children. The very readable essays provide personal insights into the lives of the first ladies, from birth to death. The essays are well balanced, providing an equal amount of coverage on the personal and public lives of the first ladies, but naturally placing their lives into the context of their spouses' presidencies and highlighting their individual contributions as first ladies. The volume is enhanced with over 700 photographs and illustrations. The author provides images of each first lady through the various stages of their lives, their spouses, and children. Other categories of images represented include: birthplaces, family homes, inaugurations and other public events, and candids. The author also provides information on existing presidential libraries, including location, hours, and admission fees. Color inserts focus on fashion and the first lady, highlighting inaugural gowns as well as business and casual attire. While indexed, citations of sources used in the preparation of this volume and photograph credits or a bibliography would have enhanced the overall usefulness of the work for users beyond the casual reader.—**Lisa Kay Speer**

C, P

234.   Knott, Stephen F., and Jeffrey L. Chidester. **The Reagan Years.** New York, Facts on File, 2005. 520p. illus. index. (Presidential Profiles). $85.00. ISBN 0-8160-5343-X.

This is a new volume in the Presidential Profiles series from Facts on File. The book provides a detailed account of the presidency of Ronald Reagan and describes the political history of key domestic and foreign policy initiatives that were implemented during this administration.

The book begins with a comprehensive introduction that traces Reagan's ascension from movie actor to governor of California, his failed 1976 campaign for president, and his eventual nomination and election to the Office of the Presidency in 1980 and his re-election in 1984. The introduction is sufficiently detailed enough to give the reader a clear picture of Reagan's political career and accomplishments. The essay also highlights his political philosophy and the motives behind Reagan's key domestic policy initiatives, which are each treated separately. Some of the policy topics outlined in the introduction include agricultural policy, civil rights, welfare, and various social issues. This is followed by a detailed treatment of the key issues and events that arose during the eight years Reagan was in office. Foreign conflicts (such as with Libya), a review of foreign policy issues (such as addressing terrorism during the Reagan administration), and the relationship with the Soviet Union are among the topics discussed. The chapter concludes by reviewing Reagan's legacy as President. Examining all of these policy issues and world events separately allows the reader to quickly and concisely understands the history of each policy. Following the introduction are profiles of key individuals associated with his administration. Each profile outlines the person's role and political contributions within the administration. Little personal information is provided on each individual; however, the essays help in understanding how specific individuals influenced the policy process. The remainder of the book consists of a set of appendixes, including a chronology of key events and the text of selected primary documents related to Reagan's political life. The primary documents are actually important speeches and addresses the president gave during his political career. The final appendix is a selected bibliography arranged under various policy headings. The list begins with a critical analysis of the current biographical literature devoted to studying Reagan. Although readers would have to use the bibliography to find materials that review his personal life in more detail, this book offers a well-written and thorough examination of Reagan's political career and is highly recommended.—**Robert V. Labaree**

Dictionaries and Encyclopedias

C

235.   **Encyclopedia of Politics: The Left and The Right.** Rodney P. Carlisle, ed. Thousand Oaks, Calif., Sage, 2005. 2v. illus. maps. index. $250.00/set. ISBN 1-4129-0409-9.

The *Encyclopedia of Politics* is a wonderful tool for researching various political topics. It is made up of two volumes. Volume 1 is concerned with politics of the left (liberals) and volume 2 is concerned with politics of the right (conservatives). The introduction describes how right and left came about. The reader's guide in volume 1 has a list of topics and persons listed according to left or right political ideology. This encyclopedia was put together by a group of international scholars. The articles are in the traditional A-to-Z format for each volume. The articles vary in length. They have *see also* references and a bibliography of books, journals, and some Internet sites. They are almost all in English. Some articles are accompanied by maps and black-and-white photographs. The articles cover not just American topics, but also international topics. The glossary is toward the end of volume 2. The definitions for these terms vary in length, with most of them being relatively short. The glossary is appropriately long and extensive. There is a general bibliography that covers books, journals, and Internet sites in English. The index for the set is in volume 2. This set will be a wonderful addition to academic libraries that need reference works on world politics. [R: LJ, July 05, pp. 118-120]—**Benet Steven Exton**

Directories

C, P

236.   **Congressional Yellow Book: Who's Who in Congress, Including Committees and Key Staff.** Summer 2005 ed. New York, Leadership Directories, 2005. 1420p. index. $420.00pa. (annual subscription); $399.00pa. (automatic renewal subscription). ISSN 0191-1422.

In this edition, the *Congressional Yellow Book* continues its fine tradition of providing basic information on members of the U.S. House of Representatives and the Senate. The information for each member includes, among other things, the year they were elected, their date of birth, their educational background, and committee assignments. Additionally, the directory supplies contact information for the members at their Washington, D.C. and state offices—complete with e-mail and Internet addresses. Access to the quarterly updated entries is made easy by the name, subject, and organization indexes.

Despite the presence of a biographical appendix, the biographical information is quite limited. Other sources like the *Biographical Directory of the United States Congress 1774-Present* (http://bioguide.congress.gov/biosearch/biosearch.asp) and *The Almanac of the Unelected* (18th ed.; see ARBA 2006, entry 717) offer fuller information. The directory does excel by making available contact information for key staff aides; composition of Senate, House, and joint committees; detailed state delegation and district maps; and a section on congressional support agencies. The currency of printed directory information is always problematic. *Congressional Yellow Book* handles this by offering The Leadership Library series over the Internet. The Internet version provides access to 13 additional directories and daily changes. Nevertheless, the printed directory is authoritative, easy to read, and complete. It remains an excellent reference tool.—**Shawn W. Nicholson**

C, P

237.   **The United States Government Internet Manual 2004-2005.** Peggy Garvin, ed. Lanham, Md., Bernan Associates, 2004. 754p. index. $59.00pa. ISBN 1-886222-18-5. ISSN 1547-2892.

Originally published in 1997 under the title *Government Information on the Internet* (see ARBA 2003, entry 681; ARBA 2001, entry 710; and ARBA 99, entry 61), the title was changed with the 2003-2004 edition. Arranged by broad subject area (e.g., agriculture, energy, transportation), this annual publication provides an annotated list of 1,552 Websites of the federal government. Each entry includes the site name, URL, sponsors, description (which provides useful comments on content), subject headings assigned as they appear in the master index, and a list of online publications arranged by SUDOC number. Appendixes include a list of re-elected members of the 109th Congress with Web and e-mail addresses and congressional committees of the 108th Congress with Web address and chair and ranking minority member. (A complete list of the 109th Congress will appear in the 2005-2006 edition.) There are three indexes:

sponsor/site name, title, and a master index (which includes subjects, sponsors, and site names). The index by SUDOC number has been eliminated.

The indexes are the strength of this publication and a great improvement over the indexes to the *U.S. Government Manual* (Bernan Press), which this title has been designed to complement. Each annual edition is updated in attempt to provide accurate and current information. This edition contains 125 more entries than the previous edition. Alternative titles such as *U.S Government on the Web* (see ARBA 2002, entry 707) lack the comprehensiveness, indexes, and currency of this title. Web finding tools such as http://www.google.com/unclesam and http://www.firstgov.gov are no cost alternatives but lack the narrative description and subject descriptor access. This work is recommended for all academic and public libraries.—**John J. McCormick**

C, P

238.   **Washington Information Directory 2005-2006. (http://www.cqpress.com).** Washington, D.C., CQ Press, 2005. 1012p. index. $128.00; $140.00 (online edition). ISBN 1-56802-973-X. ISSN 0887-8064.

This directory is a handy roadmap to find the thousands of governmental and nongovernmental organizations operating in Washington, D.C. The information is categorized by public service and advocacy, agriculture, business, communications, culture, education, labor, energy, environment, governmental operations, health, housing, international affairs, justice, the military, national security, science, social services, transportation, and the U.S. Congress. Entries include a brief description of the organization's main activities, address, telephone number, key contact name, and, if available, fax number and e-mail address. So the question is: Why do will users need a hard copy directory when there is Google? The editors have organized the information in a user-friendly format that lets the user get to the right place quickly without surfing through endless Web pages and confusing menus with no assurance of when the information was last updated. The directory's content is also available online, giving users the best of both worlds—current contact information in both print and online format. Users can search the online version by keyword, public policy topic, or organization type. The contact information can be downloaded to electronic address books and users can link directly from the *Directory* to organization Websites. If one is looking for associations that support home schooling, or have a child with a physical disability, resources are listed under these subcategories in the chapter on education. Are you looking for an internship in Washington? Consult the training program pages in the labor and employment chapter. Key features are organization charts to understand how federal departments and Congress are structured and boxes highlighting agency hotlines and public relations contacts. Appendixes include contact information for all members of Congress and Congressional committees; governors and other state officials; and ambassadors, embassies, and foreign offices. There is also a list of U.S. government Websites, plus the text of the Freedom of Information Act and a summary of recent privacy acts. All entries are indexed by name, subject, and organizational name.—**Adrienne Antink Bien**

Handbooks and Yearbooks

C, P

239.   **The American Congress: The Building of Democracy.** Julian E. Zelizer, ed. New York, Houghton Mifflin, 2004. 765p. index. $35.00. ISBN 0-618-17906-2.

For a historian, to edit a one-volume history of Congress is a daunting endeavor. A considerably complex institution, Congress has 535 voting members, who seemingly reflect an infinite number of personal and political agendas, countless committees and subcommittees, and two centuries worth of opaque rules and procedures. Yet, Zelizer has provided an excellent rendering of the subject. No other national legislature has greater power than the United States Congress, yet the elective body remains a "mystery" and its members "ghosts" overshadowed by presidents and social movements. In illuminating Congress, this well-written work has three main strengths. First, it is not a diatribe against partisanship, occasional scandal, or the messy wheeling and dealing endemic to legislative politics. Instead, it is an honest assessment of a venerable institution whose vices and virtues reflect the "diversity and richness of the nation." Moreover, the tome is comprehensive. Zelizer divides the history of Congress into four major eras: the formative era (1790-1829); the partisan era (1830-1909); the committee era (1910-1969); and the contemporary era (1970-today). It consists of 40 chapters, averaging between 10 and 14 pages each, that examine seminal moments when legislators were forced to make critical decisions. Topics range from congressional debates over the meaning of free speech and freedom of the press during the passage of the Sedition Act (1798) to the under-appreciated significance of the Seventeenth and Twentieth Amendments. The book features an array of colorful characters, from William Mahone, a former Confederate General and leader of an interracial, majority-black third party, to Phyllis Schlafly, who led the effort to defeat the Equal Rights Amendment in the 1970s. The book reflects new insights, in part, on slavery, white supremacy, prohibition, and the War Powers Resolution of 1973, which, contrary to conventional wisdom, actually increased the war-making power of the president. Another strength of *The American Congress* is that it will appeal to historians, college students, and the general public alike. It is free of overcomplicated academic jargon and historiographical hair-splitting, but has sufficient intellectual heft to appeal to specialized readers.—**Paul Gerard Connors**

S

240.   Brannen, Daniel E., Jr. **Checks and Balances: The Three Branches of the American Government.** Farmington Hills, Mich., U*X*L/Gale, 2005. 3v. illus. index. $165.00/set. ISBN 0-7876-5409-4.

In *Checks and Balances: The Three Branches of the American Government* Brannen provides an in-depth examination of the American federal government system, from its beginnings to the present. Each of the three volumes focuses on one of the three branches: Executive (v. 1), Legislative (v. 2), and Judicial (v. 3). Each volume begins with a timeline of events relevant to that branch, and then provides a glossary of terms to know. The first chapter of each volume is an identical overview of American government at the national level. The subsequent seven chapters delve deeper into the branch that is the subject of the volume. These include historic roots, Constitutional role, changes through history, key positions, daily operations, and checks and balances with the other two branches (each final chapter therefore appears twice in the set). Each chapter contains its own glossary of important terms, and many illustrations and sidebars are included to help draw out and further explain concepts. The text of the U.S. Constitution and amendments are also included in each volume.

Checks and Balances has a cumulative index in each volume to aid searching, and also provides a bibliography for further reading. The books are high quality, authoritative, and seem to be free from obvious biases. The writing style is readable for high school and above. The price may put the set out of the reach of many libraries, but *Checks and Balances* would be useful in the collections of libraries serving high school students and lower-level undergraduates.—**Mark T. Bay**

S

241.   **Flash Focus: The One-Stop Study Guide to American Politics.** Danbury, Conn., Grolier, 2005. 4v. illus. maps. index. $349.00/set. ISBN 0-7172-5935-8.

Grolier has published a very good reference set on American politics, divided into four volumes. In the first volume, the editor presents a well-researched and highly readable overview of presidential elections from 1788-2000. Typically, each election is divided into the following categorical subheadings: Context, Candidates, Campaign, Issues, and Outcomes, as well as brief presidential bibliographies and related Websites. Although coverage of each election consists of only several pages, each entry is chock-full of information and entertaining anecdotes. For example, in the presidential election of 1852, the reader learns that the Whig nominee General Winfield Scott belittled Democratic candidate Franklin Pierce's lack of war experience by alluding to his penchant for distilled spirits, declaring he was a veteran of "many a well-fought bottle." The reader also learns that Socialist candidate Eugene V. Debs, like a true capitalist, charged people to listen to his 1908 campaign speeches. The second volume examines political parties. After a brief introduction to the roles of political parties, the editor gives an excellent summary of numerous political platforms. Due to their shifting positions over time, the Democratic and Republican Party platforms are re-examined periodically. The editor also discusses well-known minor parties like the Free Soil Party (1840-1848), and lesser-known parties like the Locofocos (1835-1848), Law and Order Party of Rhode Island (1841-1851), and the La Raza Unida Party (1970-1981). Volume 3 contains biographical portraits of U.S. Supreme Court justices and summarizes some of the Court's most important decisions. Both the biographies and cases are grouped chronologically under the name of the era's presiding chief justice. Further, each case is accompanied by a minority opinion extract. The final volume focuses on "Equal Rights Under the Law." The volume is divided into the following seven parts: The Fight Against Slavery, Abolitionism, Reconstruction to 1954, Civil Rights Movement, Black Nationalism, Women's Rights, and Immigrants. Individual entries range from Sojourner Truth to Carrie Chapman Catt and the League of Women Voters. A drawback to the reference set is the editor's occasional ideological drift off the nonpartisan political balance beam. For example, the editor often cites as fact the liberal canard that the Constitution provides for the strict separation of church and state. Nevertheless, it is an impressive reference set that is suitable for high school students and undergraduates. [R: SLJ, Oct 05, pp. 87-88]—**Paul Gerard Connors**

C, P, S

242. **Guide to Political Campaigns in America.** Paul S. Herrnson, Colton Campbell, Marni Ezra, and Stephen K. Medvic, eds. Washington, D.C., CQ Press, 2005. 457p. illus. index. $112.00. ISBN 1-56802-876-8.

Having authored, co-authored, or edited more than 15 titles in this subject area, including *Party Campaigning in the 1980s* (1988) and *Congressional Elections* (2004)), Herrnson, professor of government and politics at the University of Maryland, is well qualified to edit this general overview of political campaigns, covering the history, issues, the people, and the process. The contributors are all political science professors or doctoral students from variety of colleges and universities.

This reference resource is divided into seven parts—overview, laws and regulations, voters and voting, the players, campaigning, specific campaigns, and campaign reform—with each part further divided into an average of four to five chapters. For example, part 2 on laws and regulations contains chapters on suffrage, voting and ballots, primary laws and party rules, and campaign finance. The focus is primarily on presidential elections with some coverage on congressional, gubernatorial, and local campaigns. Photographs, statistical tables, and graphs are interspersed throughout the book, providing excellent support to the text. Suggested readings are listed after each chapter, and a selected bibliography of books and Websites is included in the rear of the book.

This title provides an excellent one-volume introduction to the subject area. The 23-page index is adequate but could be more comprehensive in providing access to the information contained it is pages (i.e., neither Iowa or New Hampshire are listed separately but are found in the index under Primaries). Other titles that cover similar subject matter are *Parties and Elections in America: The Electoral Process* (2005), *American Presidential Campaigns and Elections* (see ARBA 2004, entry 730), and *Encyclopedia of American Parties, Campaigns, and Elections* (see ARBA 2000, entry 360), but none fully duplicate the information provided in this title. The *Guide to Political Campaigns in America* is recommended for high school, public, and academic libraries.—**John J. McCormick**

P, S

243. Matuz, Roger, with Gina Misiroglue and Lawrence W. Baker. **The Handy Presidents Answer Book.** Canton, Mich., Visible Ink Press; distr., Detroit, Omnigraphics, 2004. 545p. illus. index. $46.00. ISBN 0-7808-0773-1.

This book showcases over 800 questions and answers related to the past and present United States' Commanders in Chief. Queries are categorized by topics ranging from the origins of the U.S. presidency to presidential illnesses, deaths, and scandals. It also includes chapters devoted to first ladies and important administrators, such as the vice presidents, presidential advisers, and cabinet members. The question-and-answer format that exists throughout the book allows for quick look-ups and makes it convenient for users to leisurely browse by chapter. Those who prefer to search by a specific topic can use the index that is provided. This resource features black-and-white illustrations of presidential photographs, political cartoons, charts, and drawings. Other highlights include listings of presidential landmarks such as birthplaces, burial sites, and libraries and museums, and basic trivia related to each president laid out in bullet points. Omnigraphics is the exclusive hardcover distributor to libraries and schools of *The Handy Presidents Answer Book*. This informative resource will suit public and school library users, especially those who are writing political science or history term papers. [R: VOYA, Dec 05, p. 433]—**Maris L. Hayashi**

C, P

244.   Maxwell, Bruce. **Homeland Security: A Documentary History.** Washington, D.C., CQ Press, 2004. 522p. index. $99.95. ISBN 1-56802-884-9.

The phrase "homeland security" has become a centerpiece of American political discourse since the September 11th terrorist attacks resulted in the creation of the Department of Homeland Security and other U.S. federal, state, and local government, and private sector efforts to conduct research and initiate policies to prevent further terrorist attacks within the United States. *Homeland Security: A Documentary History* provides historical and contemporary documentation as to how the U.S. government has taken or attempted to take steps throughout U.S. history to protect the security of the American public and governmental institutions from foreign and domestic threats. Maxwell's work opens with an introduction describing the multiple roles the federal government has played and continues to play in formulating and implementing homeland security policy and how numerous federal agencies are responsible for executing homeland security responsibilities.

The primary part of this work is collections of historical and contemporary documents describing proposed or actual federal homeland security policymaking activities. These documents are grouped into broad categories such as "President Lincoln Suspends the Writ of Habeas Corpus," "World War I Laws Limit Speech and Movement," "Aviation Security Before September 11, 2001," "Immigration Agency Reviews and Reforms," "U.S. and Foreign Government Attempts to Cut Off Terrorist Funds," "Federal Actions Aimed at Preserving Continuity of Government," and "Congressional Investigations Fault Intelligence Agencies in Terrorist Attacks." Succinct introductory contextual overviews are provided at the beginning of each of these broad categories.

Within these broad categorical entries are excerpts from documents such as laws, executive orders, speeches, or policy reports representing governmental action taken to cope with or counteract real or perceived threats to homeland security. Examples of these documents include "The Sedition Act, July 14, 1798," "President Wilson's Second Proclamation Regarding Alien Enemies, November 16, 1917," "President Bill Clinton's Remarks at the Oklahoma City Memorial Service, April 23, 1995," "General Accounting Office Congressional Testimony on Security Vulnerabilities in the Aviation System, September 11, 1996," "Congressional Research Service Report on FBI Intelligence Reform April 6, 2004," and "9/11 Commission on First Responder Funding, July 22, 2004." Entries for these excerpted documents include bibliographic citations and Website URLs (when available). Bibliographic citations, annotated descriptions of relevant Websites, and a Department of Homeland Security organizational chart conclude this compendium.

The overall result is a very effective introduction to historical and contemporary documentary sources on U.S. government homeland security policy. The author's use of government reports such as Government Accountability Office reports, commission reports, and Justice Department Office of Inspector General reports is an especially desirable feature of this work and should help students and scholars appreciate the vital importance of reading government documents to properly understand federal policies in homeland security. The only weakness of *Homeland Security: A Documentary History* is failing to cite examples from the growing corpus of reports on this subject being produced by the Department of Homeland Security's Office of Inspector General. This title is highly recommended.—**Bert Chapman**

C, P

245.   Stanley, Harold W., and Richard G. Niemi. **Vital Statistics on American Politics 2005-2006.** Washington, D.C., CQ Press, 2006. 446p. index. $90.00. ISBN 1-56802-976-4.

This work is a compendium of statistical information on American government and politics with more than 225 tables and figures from numerous public and private sources. A general introduction and the introductions for each chapter help users make better use of tables and figures. Its "Guide to References for Political Statistics" refers to more statistical sources. This is a classified listing, including many digital sources.

The book has a broad range of coverage on such topics as election and political parties, campaign finance and PACs, public opinion and voting, the media, three branches of government, federalism and state and local governments, foreign and military policies, and social and economic policies. Two topics, "Election and Political Parties" and "Public Opinion and Voting," have the most tabular information. Some 87 percent of the data are up to 2004. There are data far beyond 2004, including U.S. population (total, urban, and rural) to 2100, hospital insurance fund to 2020, social security (OASDI) to 2080, and U.S. defense spending to 2010. The book would have enhanced its usefulness if statistical information would have been provided in other topics, such as impeachment and international justice. The Iraq war has disappointedly few data.

The book is well compiled with rich statistical information on American government and power politics. It is highly recommended.—**Tze-chung Li**

C, P

246.   **Watergate and the Resignation of Richard Nixon: Impact of a Constitutional Crisis.** Harry P. Jeffrey and Thomas Maxwell-Long, eds. Washington, D.C., CQ Press, 2004. 346p. illus. index. (Landmark Events in U.S. History). $100.00. ISBN 1-56802-910-1.

The Watergate scandal that eventually led to the only resignation by an American president in history represents perhaps the most traumatic period in American politics during the twentieth century, piggybacking on the equally challenging affairs of the Vietnam War. The scandal and resignation, as noted in the foreword written by former White House counsel John Dean, continues to impact the political and cultural landscape of America today. This volume brings these events into clear focus. The 11 essays in this book highlight the transformative effects of the scandal and place them in proper historical context, including describing revisionist attempts to reconstruct the scandal in a new light. The chapters cover the following topics: a biographical profile of Richard Nixon, his influence on American politics, the separation of powers that emerged during the Watergate era, a review of the role of special prosecutors and independent counsels, the issue of executive privilege, a study of Nixon's crisis management style, and the relationship between Nixon and the media. The final three chapters focus on describing the journey leading to the resignation, Nixon's attempts to redefine his place in history, and his legacy as a politician and a private citizen. The authors of each essay assume no knowledge about Nixon, the Watergate scandal, or the events leading to his resignation. Considered collectively, the essays in this book provide clear and accessible insights into this critical moment in history, yet they are not burdened with unnecessary academic rhetoric. The second part of this volume contains a variety of supporting documents, text from key speeches, and transcriptions divided according to Nixon's general relationship to American politics, constitutional and political issues, responses to his resignation, and documents related to post-resignation analysis. These include, for example, early speeches by Nixon, the text of relevant historical documents, the transcript of the "Cancer on the Presidency" conversation between Nixon and Dean, and eulogies given at Nixon's funeral. The volume includes a comprehensive index. However, the hidden gem of this book may be the foreword by John Dean, in which he speculates about how the Watergate scandal may have influenced attempts to impeach Bill Clinton. This work is highly recommended. [R: LJ, 1 April 05, pp. 124-126]—**Robert V. Labaree**

P, S

247.   **The World Book of America's Presidents.** 2005 ed. Chicago, World Book, 2005. 2v. illus. index. $99.00/set. ISBN 0-7166-3698-0.

The World Book of America's Presidents is a two-volume compendium of information relating to the history and unique characteristics of the presidency. The larger of the two volumes opens with a descriptive outline of the periods in United States history with corresponding presidents and a list of the presidents that includes tabular details of their lives and administrations. This introductory material is followed by biographies of the presidents through George W. Bush. Each includes a full-page portrait of the president, a fact box that repeats information found in the introductory presidential list, and copious illustrations that are mostly in color. Each presidential biography closes with another fact box listing key events from the presidency in chronological order. At the conclusion of the biographies, there is a section of presidential quotes and appendixes listing detailed facts about the office of the president, including qualifications outlined in the Constitution, "Modes of Selection," and biographical details of the vice-presidents. The volume concludes with a topical index. The second volume opens with a chapter outlining the origin of the presidency and how the office has developed over time, followed by a chapter describing the duties of the president today. There is a chapter detailing the process of presidential campaigning and another detailing the White House. From a study of the White House, the volume proceeds to a chapter discussing Washington, D.C., a chapter on protecting the president, and a chapter detailing the travels of presidents. The volume closes with a subject index.—**Philip G. Swan**

INTERNATIONAL ORGANIZATIONS

C

248.   Alger, Chadwick F. **The United Nations System: A Reference Handbook.** Santa Barbara, Calif., ABC-CLIO, 2006. 375p. index. (Contemporary World Issues). $50.00; $55.00 (e-book). ISBN 1-85109-805-4; 1-85109-806-2 (e-book).

The United Nations has 191 members and is headquartered in New York City. There are many subsidiary organizations specializing in various areas in cities throughout the world. This system has some 50 subsidiary organizations. Most of the U.S. government departments are in Washington and most countries have their own counterparts in the UN system. The UN system can be considered a laboratory for developing or coping with the new global agendas. This book is divided into chapters that cover background and history, problems, controversies and solutions, ambivalent participation of the Untied States in the UN system, chronologically the emergence and development of the UN system, facts and data, alternative futures of the UN system, directors of organizations, associations and agencies, biographical sketches of present heads of the UN system, selective print and nonprint resources of the United Nations, and an index and information about the author. The binding and printing are acceptable. This book should be in all libraries that need up-to-date information on globalization, the United Nations, and the interrelationship between countries. This would include all university libraries.—**Herbert W. Ockerman**

INTERNATIONAL RELATIONS

Dictionaries and Encyclopedias

C

249.   **Encyclopedia of International Relations and Global Politics.** Martin Griffiths, ed. New York, Routledge/Taylor & Francis Group, 2005. 911p. index. $195.00. ISBN 0-415-31160-8.

This 911-page book is a comprehensive study of international relationships in the twenty-first century. Its alphabetic entries range from diplomatic statecraft and foreign policy analysis to comparative politics, historical sociology, international political economics, international history, strategic studies, military affairs, ethics, and international political theory. This book covers not only global politics but also the dramatic developments that have taken place since the end of the Cold War. The 250 entries are written by 125 contributors from around the world and most are from major universities. The entries are of two types. The first provides critical scholarly introductions to key theoretical approaches, concepts, issues, and international organizations in international relations. The shorter interviews provide an overview of the most important concepts, institutions, and issues in contemporary global politics. These alphabetic listings are followed by a comprehensive index that should be very useful. The book is well written and edited and is readable by the layperson as well as experts in the field. The binding, paper, and font size are adequate for its purposes. This book should be in all libraries that have international relations or a global politics interest.—**Herbert W. Ockerman**

C

250.   Larsen, Jeffrey A., and James M. Smith. **Historical Dictionary of Arms Control and Disarmament.** Lanham, Md., Scarecrow, 2005. 362p. (Historical Dictionaries of War, Revolution, and Civil Unrest, no.28). $85.00. ISBN 0-8108-5060-5.

Although arms control is a concept as old as recorded history, it is only in the last century that it has become an important factor in international diplomacy and national security policy making. The rise of arms control on the international political scene stemmed from the destructive consequences of World War I, which resulted in agreements such as the 1922 Washington Naval Treaty limiting naval armaments. It received further impetus from the growth of nuclear weapons in the aftermath of World War II, which produced the Nonproliferation Treaty and a variety of bilateral and multilateral arms control agreements intended to prevent or diminish the growth of weapons of mass destruction.

Historical Dictionary of Arms Control and Disarmament provides exhaustive coverage of the individuals, concepts, agreements, and weapons systems contributing to the growth of this subject in international political and military discourse. Following the introduction, it opens with a list of acronyms and what these acronyms signify in what is an often esoteric world to those uninitiated into its rhetorical jargon. It proceeds to list historically significant arms control developments for the past three millennia and features an overview of recent arms control and disarmament trends and developments.

This historical dictionary is the main part of this compendium covering over 230 pages. Entries provided here include those describing and analyzing the significance of antisubmarine warfare, the Ballistic Missile Defense Organization, multiple independently targetable reentry vehicle, Paul Nitze, Nuclear Suppliers Group, Sandia National Laboratories Strategic Arms Reduction Talks, and weapons-grade material. These entries feature cross-references highlighted in black to related dictionary entries.

The concluding sections feature a detailed bibliography of relevant books, articles, and government documents on various aspects of arms control and disarmament and specific issues in these fields such as chemical and biological weapons, the Comprehensive Test Ban Treaty, confidence and security building measures, and arms control in regions such as South Asia. A listing of applicable governmental, interest group, and think-tank arms control Websites is also included.

This work is a valuable introduction to those desirous of learning more about arms control and disarmament in international diplomacy and security policy. The introductory historical perspective and bibliographic citations are particularly valuable, although the introduction should also emphasize the difficulties involved in enforcing arms control agreements with totalitarian regimes such as the former Soviet Union and North Korea and that there is significant scholarly literature questioning the utility of arms control agreements. These caveats aside, this work is highly recommended for academic libraries.—**Bert Chapman**

C

251.   Sutter, Robert. **Historical Dictionary of United States—China Relations.** Lanham, Md., Scarecrow, 2006. 239p. (Historical Dictionary of U.S. Diplomacy, no.2). $65.00. ISBN 0-8108-5502-X.

The United States' relationship with China has been a long series of expensive misconceptions, lengthy frustrations, and bitter disappointments for both sides. In the 1990s, with the collapse of Soviet Communism and the growth of China's economic and military power, Beijing replaced Moscow as the most important foreign capital for the U.S. government to take into consideration. The introduction provides the historical sketch of this complicated relationship. The hundreds of entries cover events, locations, theories, and themes, but one should pay close attention to what is said about the individuals involved in this process, for it is people who make the policies and decisions that can have such wide-reaching ramifications. The book is easy to read, and the heavy black type for the entry headings is a big help. There are plenty of *see also* and cross-references scattered throughout the text. Appendix A is list of U.S. Presidents and Secretaries of State, while appendix B lists Chinese Presidents and Prime Ministers; one wonders why the Chinese Foreign Ministers were not listed. The Presidents of the Republic of China on Taiwan are included at the end of this appendix, in small type. There is a list of acronyms and abbreviations, and a chronology (extending from 1784 to March 2005), but no illustrations or index are included. A 32-page bibliography lists the more important works in a large and constantly growing body of scholarly literature on this topic.

Sutter (Georgetown University), a former government official who specialized in international relations with Asia, recently published *China's Rise in Asia: Promises and Perils* (Rowan and Littlefield, 2005). This sturdily bound reference book is probably best suited for academic and large public libraries, along with branches that serve a Chinese-American population, and those specialized institutions that collect in this field. This title is complemented by two earlier related works of a broader nature: David Shavit's *The United States in Asia: A Historical Dictionary* (see ARBA 92, entry 746), which also has a heavy emphasis on important participants, and James Matray's *East Asia and the United States: An Encyclopedia of Relations since 1784* (Greenwood Press, 2002).—**Daniel K. Blewett**

Handbooks and Yearbooks

C

252.   **France and the Americas: Culture, Politics, and History. A Multidisciplinary Encyclopedia.** Bill Marshall, ed. Santa Barbara, Calif., ABC-CLIO, 2005. 3v. illus. index. (Transatlantic Relations). $270.00/set. ISBN 1-85109-411-3; 1-85109-416-4 (e-book).

The title is part of a new series devoted to American and Atlantic/European relations. The focus is on cross-cultural exchange whether that be cultural, political, economic, or social. The area encompassed includes more than simply the United States, but also comprises Canada, the Caribbean, and Latin America. The encyclopedia opens with a set of useful essays on each of the geographic areas, and then is followed by a conventional alphabetic list of figures, events, and concepts. As a directional aid the authors have divided the work into 15 so-called topics ranging from "Art and Culture" to "Theory." The bulk of the entries fall into the category of "Art and Culture." Most of the entries are brief with even briefer bibliographies. Thus, one would not classify the title as a work of high scholarship. On the other hand, the book offers a number of interesting nuggets, and does for the most part attempt to demonstrate in each essay how various individuals or events were influenced or reacted to French and American culture. Browsing the list of entries indicates a preponderance of French subjects, but that is perhaps not surprising for a book published in English. Several of the entries are a bit of a stretch, such as the one on Bob Dylan. One also wonders at the absence of Jean Monnet and Jerry Lewis. However, these are minor quibbles for a work that looks squarely at the often prickly relations between France, and the United States in particular. This work is recommended for undergraduates.—**Jim Millhorn**

C, P

253.   **Encyclopedia of Public Administration and Public Policy. First Updated Supplement.** Jack Rabin, ed. Philadelphia, Taylor & Francis, 2005. 329p. index. $249.95. ISBN 0-8493-3895-6.

This is a supplement to the two-volume set under the same title published in 2003 (see ARBA 2004, entry 765). Containing an additional 70 entries, it follows the same format as the original volumes. Topics covered include Accounting and Reporting for Private Nonprofit Organizations, Capital Purchases, Information Sources and State Policy Making, Pay as You Go Financing, State Enterprise Zones, and Urban Planning and Ethics. There are also six entries on Southeast Asia countries (Cambodia, Indonesia, Laos, Malaysia, Singapore, and Thailand) and six entries on issues in Southeast Asia (e.g., Transparency and Corruption ins Southeast Asia). The bibliographic references included at the end of each entry are one of the volume's strong points. The set may have been more useful if it concentrated on U.S. issues in public administration or international issues and not try to cover both. It is also available in electronic format from the publisher (http://www.dekker.com). This work is recommended to those libraries that found the first two volumes useful.—**John J. McCormick**

14 Psychology, Occultism, and Parapsychology

PSYCHOLOGY

Dictionaries and Encyclopedias

C

254.   **The Concise Corsini Encyclopedia of Psychology and Behavioral Science.** 3d ed. W. Edward Craighead and Charles B. Nemeroff, eds. Hoboken, N.J., John Wiley, 2004. 1112p. index. $150.00. ISBN 0-471-22036-1.

This reference tool meets the expressed goal of providing a concise edition of the highly recommended multivolume set of the 3d edition published in 2001 (see ARBA 2002, entry 770) titled *The Corsini Encyclopedia of Psychology and Behavioral Science.* For those familiar with the earlier edition, the articles found here provide definitions of current topics within the fields of psychology and neuroscience, such as depression, family therapy, or generalized anxiety disorder, to name a few. Topics are diverse in that the reader will find a thorough discussion on the Limbic System, including illustrations, references, and added entries; for the topic of individualism, information includes a common definition, theory behind current connotations, and references to various studies that address this issue. The lengths of the articles vary, with those that deal specifically with the field of psychology receiving a more in-depth treatment than those that have a less direct relationship. All entries have been composed to provide information for both the layperson and the specialist, and are signed with the author's affiliation indicated. Many entries have suggested readings lists and some have cross-references to *see also* subject headings.

Additional valuable features include author biographies, an author index, and a subject index with subheadings that are all located at the back of the book. Physically, this is a quality reference tool in that the binding and paper stock are sturdy, and the font sizes are very legible. Another factor to be considered is that the cost of this title is approximately one-fourth the cost of the original set, making this a much more affordable addition for limited budgets. This work is recommended for all academic libraries and larger public libraries where there is a need for this subject matter.—**Marianne B. Eimer**

C, P

255.   Cordón, Luis A. **Popular Psychology: An Encyclopedia.** Westport, Conn., Greenwood Press, 2005. 274p. illus. index. $75.00. ISBN 0-313-32457-3.

Popular Psychology: An Encyclopedia discusses important concepts and figures in pop psychology and the science of psychology. The author's goal is to provide basic information about scientific psychology and to counteract common misinformation in pop psychology. Topics range from Memory to Alien Abduction. The author assumes no previous knowledge of psychology or the scientific method. The writing level is appropriate for the average high school student through college undergraduate. The entries provide an uncritical explanation of mainstream psychology topics and a critique of pop psychology topics using scientific analysis. This double standard of evaluation can be jarring to the reader with sufficient background in psychology to question the scientific rigor of some mainstream entries. However, it will probably not bother the audience for which it is intended. Each entry is followed by a section labeled further reading that contains references to recommended books, articles, and Websites providing additional information. An alphabetic list of entries and a list of entries grouped by major topics are located at the beginning of the book. An annotated bibliography of resources consulted by the author and a combined subject/topic index follow the entries. The annotated bibliography is the weakest section of the book. Not all of the citations are annotated. Citations are arranged in sections that are based partly on topic and partly on format. Fortunately this section is short enough that users should be able to navigate through the citations. This work is recommended for public and school libraries.—**Cynthia Crosser**

C, S

256.   **Encyclopedia of School Psychology.** Steven W. Lee, ed. Thousand Oaks, Calif., Sage, 2005. 656p. index. $150.00. ISBN 0-7619-3080-9.

Sage's *Encyclopedia of School Psychology* is a comprehensive work dealing with all aspects of school psychology. The book is written on an introductory level and is intended for a wide range of users. The foreword suggests that the book will be useful for educators, psychologists, and specialists in vocational guidance.

The strength of this resource is in the content of the articles. The book contains over 250 signed entries written by 175 scholars in school psychology. The content is accessible to lay readers and is scholarly enough for graduate students and faculty to use for background information. All entries contain a section with references and a list for further reading. The number of references listed ranges from 21 for the large entry of "Behavior" to only 1 for the specialized entry of "Goal Attainment Scaling." Topics dealing with controversial areas, such as "Learning Styles", contain "Point Versus Counterpoint" sections comprised of information bullets outlining the general arguments. Tables and/or figures are used in some of the entries. For example, "Norm-Referenced Tests" contains an illustration of a normal curve. Related entries are noted with a *see also* section.

The weakness of the book is in its finding aids. There is no real table of contents. The contents page notes that entries are on pages 1-600. The "List of Entries" is an alphabetic listing, but no page numbers are given. The "Reader's Guide," which also does not include page numbers, is an attempt to organize the entries by topic. However, each topic is listed under only one heading. This means that the entry "Reading Interventions and Strategies" is listed under the topic of "Interventions" but not under the topic of "Reading." Users wishing to locate the pages of specific topics should use the index. Overall, this is a good resource and is recommended for academic, public, and high school libraries.—**Cynthia Crosser**

Handbooks and Yearbooks

P

257.   **Mental Health Disorders Sourcebook.** 3d ed. Karen Bellenir, ed. Detroit, Omnigraphics, 2005. 636p. index. (Health Reference Series). $78.00. ISBN 0-7808-0747-2.

This is the 3d edition of *Mental Health Disorders Sourcebook*, which is part of Omnigraphics' extensive Health Reference Series. The 2d edition was reviewed in ARBA 2001 (see ARBA 2001, entry 769). The book is designed to provide basic consumer mental health information. The content is taken from relevant government agencies, professional associations, and journals. This work is divided into eight parts and includes basic mental health facts, information on specific disorders, and practical advice for people seeking help. The last chapter includes reference information, including a dictionary of mental health terms, a directory of mental health resources, a list of programs that provide free medication, suggested readings, and an alphabetic index. The main differences between this edition and the 2d are a reduction in the number of suggested readings in the final chapter, the inclusion of the Web address of the source used at the beginning of (almost) each informational section, a larger section on the role of genetics in mental illness, and the addition of a section on mental health issues for children and adolescents. This edition acknowledges an audience that is turning increasingly to the Web and provides a well-organized and well-written print resource that adds value to what can be found online. *Mental Health Disorders Sourcebook* is recommended for public libraries and academic libraries with an undergraduate program in psychology.—**Cynthia Crosser**

C

258.   Mook, Douglas. **Classic Experiments in Psychology.** Westport, Conn., Greenwood Press, 2004. 362p. illus. index. $69.95. ISBN 0-313-31821-2.

Most of the experiments discussed in *Classic Experiments in Psychology* will be familiar to anyone who has taken an undergraduate survey course in psychology. This is intentional; Mook's criteria for inclusion as a "classic experiment" requires that the study be published prior to the 1980s and preferably be cited in introductory psychology texts. Beyond these criteria, selection was based on creating a good balance of topics. Thorndike, Helmholtz, Mischel, Skinner, and Fechner are a sample of the authors that are included. Readers familiar with psychology will find a few authors missing (e.g., Piaget, Lorenz, Zimbardo), but those authors who are included provide an excellent representation of important research in experimental psychology. These discipline areas consist of psychobiology, motivation and emotion, learning, memory, cognition, perception, and social psychology. The writing style is clear and informal. The introductory chapter includes a wonderful discussion of the experimental method in psychology. Students new to psychology will benefit from interesting and clear descriptions of dependent and independent variables, control groups, confounding variables, and the ability (or limitations) to generalize from animal experiments to human behavior.

The author's nontechnical style is consistent throughout the text. Each description of a classic experiment includes four to seven pages of discussion and a brief bibliography. Descriptions may include information about the background and training of the author, along with a discussion on the influence that the study has had on our understanding of behavior. Mook does an excellent job of describing the experimental setup and findings in a way that is both understandable to the general audience and interesting. Examples are often similar to what one would read in a general psychology textbook, with examples from everyday life used to explain the technical jargon of psychology. He often relates experimental findings back to our own lives or observations, and as a result gives these classics a new and interesting light. This book will be an excellent introduction to experimental psychology for the general reader and the high school or college student.—**Lorraine Evans**

OCCULTISM

P

259.   Buckland, Raymond. **The Spirit Book: The Encyclopedia of Clairvoyance, Channeling, and Spirit Communication.** Canton, Mich., Visible Ink Press; distr., Detroit, Omnigraphics, 2006. 500p. illus. index. $52.00. ISBN 0-7808-0922-X.

The Spirit Book: The Encyclopedia of Clairvoyance, Channeling, and Spirit Communication is an interesting reference resource. While most libraries will never have a need for it, sometimes there are reference questions that would be difficult to answer without it. *The Spirit Book* is written by Raymond Buckland, a well-known author of books on the occult, as well as a practicing spiritualist for over 50 years. *The Spirit Book* is a storehouse of information on everything Spiritualism and its related subjects, such as divination and channeling. It contains more than 500 entries on just about anything or anyone connected with Spiritualism. Most fascinating are the full biographies of the major figures related to the Spiritualist movement. People well known in the field, such as Edgar Cayce, are profiled, but even more interestingly, so are Winston Churchill (who was intrigued with the occult for most of his life) and actress Mary Pickford.

The book is well researched, well written, and the author is obviously well versed in the subject. It is also free from bias, excepting the fundamental bias of assuming that Spiritualism has some basis in fact. The black-and-white photographs are mostly of high quality, and enhance the biographies provided. Each entry lists its sources, there are plenty of *see* and *see also* references, and terms used in an entry that are described in depth elsewhere in the book are in boldface. A bibliography of print sources consulted is included at the end, along with a long and useful list of Web resources for further study. An extremely well-constructed index makes it easy to locate specific information quickly. *The Spirit Book* is a high-quality resource in an area that may never be of interest in some libraries. It is recommended for public libraries that field questions of this nature, and academic libraries with folklore, anthropology, or comparative religion programs. [R: LJ, 15 Nov 05, pp. 93-94; BL, 1 & 15 Jan 06, pp. 153-154]—**Mark T. Bay**

PARAPSYCHOLOGY

P

260.   Clark, Jerome. **Unnatural Phenomena: A Guide to the Bizarre Wonders of North America.** Illustrated by John Clark. Santa Barbara, Calif., ABC-CLIO, 2005. 369p. illus. index. $85.00; $90.00 (e-book). ISBN 1-57607-430-7; 1-57607-431-5 (e-book).

This latest volume by the author of *Extraordinary Encounters: An Encyclopedia of Extraterrestrials and Otherworldly Beings* (see ARBA 2001, entry 775) and *Strange and Unexplained Happenings: When Nature Breaks the Rules of Science* (see ARBA 97, entry 638) extends his documentation of paranormal phenomena to the area of anomalies, which he describes as strange experiences that have the "resonance of reality" but may not always manifest on an "event level." Examples of anomalies include reports by eyewitnesses of armies in the sky, lake and river monsters, ghost trains, creatures falling from the sky, poltergeists, men in black, and other oddities.

Anomalies are also known as "Fortean phenomena" after Charles Fort (1874-1932), the author of four books on the topic, and Clark's inspiration for this work. Clark conducted a comprehensive examination of Fort's sources and what could have been his sources, he says, in newspaper archives and on the Internet. Of the material contained here, however, little actually derives from Fort, and at least 90 percent has never been published, Clark says.

All reports come from North America, including 49 American states (Hawaii is the exception). The book's organization is geographic, and includes a detailed introduction that discusses the folkloric background of the stories and the social milieu at the time, a good index, and 50 original black-and-white illustrations. Most entries are transcriptions of the original eyewitness and journalistic accounts, and all entries conclude with a citation for the original source. This work is recommended for libraries and individuals with interest in collecting this topic.—**Madeleine Nash**

15 Recreation and Sports

GENERAL WORKS

Bibliography

C, P

261.   Allen, Mary Beth. **Sports, Exercise, and Fitness: A Guide to Reference and Information Sources.** Westport, Conn., Libraries Unlimited/Greenwood Publishing Group, 2005. 287p. index. (Reference Sources in the Social Sciences). $68.00. ISBN 1-56308-819-3.

Mary Beth Allen's *Sports, Exercise, and Fitness: A Guide to Reference and Information Sources* indexes English-language sports reference sources published between 1990 and May 2004. The chapters are organized initially by chapter headings that provide general categories of activities, such as "Small-Ball Sports." Within these chapters, the sports that fall into these categories are then arranged alphabetically. For example, within the chapter "Small-Ball Sports" the first sports category is baseball. Allen then breaks the sport or activity down by three types of information sources, established reference sources, instructional sources, and Websites.

Each information source includes a well-written and concise description of the sport or activity. These brief annotations provide the reader with thorough explanations of each activity and make browsing through each chapter very easy. The organizational scheme of this book makes it a very valuable resource for researchers and librarians. The guide also includes an author, title, and subject index that helps the reader to navigate easily through the many different types of sports, exercise, and fitness categories.

This guide contains over 1,000 informational sources that can be used by researchers from high school to the post-graduate level. The sources listed in the book also contain bibliographies to provide for further research on the activity. The Websites that are listed contain URLs as well as the date the page was accessed for indexing in this guide. Some of the sports and actives covered include swimming, canoeing, kayaking, badminton, croquet, curling, martial arts, motor sports, walking, and extreme sports, to name a few.

Librarians and researchers will find this guide useful for collection development as well as general reference and research assistance. This work will provide librarians and researchers with a tool to gain quick access to information about sports exercise and fitness that is concise and easy to use. Allen's background as an applied life studies librarian is evidenced by the quality of resources collected for this guide.—**Manuel Frank Santos**

Dictionaries and Encyclopedias

C, P

262.   Duncan, Joyce D. **Sport in American Culture: From Ali to X-Games.** Santa Barbara, Calif., ABC-CLIO, 2004. 479p. illus. index. $95.00; $100.00 (e-book). ISBN 1-57607-024-7; 1-85109-559-4 (e-book).

Sports in America is a multi-billion dollar enterprise that broadly influences and interacts with our culture in such areas as literature, film, civil rights, gender issues, children's concerns, advertising, and business. The editorial board of this book attempted to select topics that "reflect the unbreakable tie between our cultural world and the world of sport" (p. xi). However, for a one-volume work, the selection criteria should have been more precisely defined because the reader quickly focuses on what is left out. There is an entry on Italian Americans in Sport, but not ones on Jewish or Irish Americans; there is an entry on Bill Russell but not Wilt Chamberlain; there is an entry on Alex Karras but not Red Grange or George Halas; there is an entry on Joyce Carol Oates but not A. J. Liebling; there is an entry on Jesse Ventura but not Arnold Schwarzenegger; there are entries on the Basketball Hall of Fame and the Women's Basketball Hall of Fame but not on the Pro Football Hall of Fame; there is an entry on Tom Landry but not on the much more influential Vince Lombardi after whom the Super Bowl Championship trophy is named. For that matter, there is no entry on the Super Bowl despite the fact that Super Bowl Sunday has practically become an American holiday.

Many topics have a clearly academic angle such as "Athletes as Symbolic Heroes," "Audience Rituals," "Children in Sport: Necessity of Play," "Fetishes in Sport," and "Academic Skepticism in Sports." While offbeat, these are interesting and worthwhile topics. In fact, the strength of this book is mostly in its offbeat entries, including "White Hope," "Title IX," "Carnivals," "Sneakers," "Outdoor Clubs," "Parental Involvement," "Dueling," "Bear Baiting," and "Cock Fighting."

The 400-plus entries in this alphabetically arranged volume were written by roughly 150 scholarly contributors who cover significant people, sports, events, and topics in articles ranging from a couple of paragraphs to a couple of pages. Some of the entries should have been updated. For example, the Michael Jordan entry does not mention his second comeback in 2003, and the Mike Tyson entry does not go beyond 1998. Each entry features further readings, many list *see also* references, and some have *see* references as well. A bibliography and an index complete the work. The index is helpful in finding an entry like NASCAR, which is listed under National Association of Stock Car Automobile Racing, but is no help in finding the Baseball Hall of Fame, which is listed under its official name of the National Baseball Hall of Fame. What is included in this reference work is useful and well done, but there is so much unused material that the subject would be better suited to a two-volume work. This title is recommended for academic libraries. [R: SLJ, June 05, pp. 88-90; LJ, 1 Mar 05, p. 116]—**John Maxymuk**

Directories

C, P

263.   **Sports Market Place Directory, 2005.** Millerton, N.Y., Grey House Publishing, 2005. 1888p. index. $225.00pa.; $479.00 (CD-ROM); $479.00 (online database). ISBN 1-59237-077-2.

C, P

264.   **Sports Market Place Directory Online. http://www.sportsmarketplace.com.** [Website]. Millerton, N.Y., Grey House Publishing. $479.00 (online database). Date reviewed: May 05.

If doubts persist that sports is a major industry, this exhaustive reference volume will erase any such premise. In 10 chapters, the business of sports is documented in detail; from professional to college sports, trade shows and facilities, and agents and manufacturers, the 13,000-plus listings provide access to the contact information on any aspect of sports information. The 10 chapters represent single sports, multiple sports, college sports, events, meetings and trade shows, media, sponsors, professional services, facilities, manufacturers and retailers, and a brief final section on statistics. The statistics chapter provides attendance figures, consumer purchase data, and sports participation information. There are entity, name, and geographical indexes.

The information presented here can also be found in an online format. Users can search by keyword, state or country, or categories (with subcategories) that are found in convenient drop-down menus.

In its second year of publication, Grey House has improved on a useful yet expensive comprehensive sports directory. For the professional involved in any aspect of the sports business, this is an essential source. For the academic or public library supporting business research and activity, the directory will prove useful.—**Boyd Childress**

Handbooks and Yearbooks

P, S

265.   **Chambers Sports Factfinder.** New York, Houghton Mifflin, 2005. 663p. index. $13.95pa. ISBN 0-550-10161-6.

Chambers Sports Factfinder features many types of sports from all parts of the world. The book includes origin, rules, a brief description, and other highlights for each sport examined. Also included for most sports covered in book is a biography section highlighting athletes, past and present.

The information in this 663-page book is current through the early part of 2005 and is organized by sports in alphabetic order. Diagrams and pictures are used as good tools to help the reader get a better understanding of the particular sport. For example, in the section on darts, the authors show a picture of the dartboard, including the dimensions of the board and an explanation of key scoring areas on the board (e.g., the double and treble rings). This is very helpful for a person learning about the sport. One of the most useful features in this book is the A-Z section that explains key terms and slang for the particular sport. The index in the back of book is also a nice tool for quick reference when looking up the names of sports and key terms from the A-Z section and the athletes. The index makes looking up quick references very easy.

Chambers Sports Factfinder is a good introduction and quick reference tool for many types of sports. The information is very reliable. However, this publication lacks in-depth coverage of certain sports. This publication is ideal for sports novices and fanatics of all ages.—**Manuel Frank Santos**

BASEBALL

Dictionaries and Encyclopedias

P

266.   Bjarkman, Peter C. **Diamonds Around the Globe: The Encyclopedia of International Baseball.** Westport, Conn., Greenwood Press, 2005. 607p. illus. index. $75.00. ISBN 0-313-32268-6.

Bjarkman has written extensively about international baseball topics over the years—particularly concerning Latin America—and is uniquely qualified to produce an encyclopedia for baseball played outside the United States. In this compact volume, he has delivered an original and valuable reference work that is useful not only to baseball fans but to those interested in other cultures as well.

Individual chapters are devoted to Cuba, Canada, Japan, the Dominican Republic, Venezuela, Puerto Rico, Mexico, and the Caribbean Basin (i.e., the remaining Latin American countries). There is also a catchall chapter on Europe, Africa and the Pacific Rim, one on the Olympics and other international competitions, and a final one on the Winter Leagues in Latin America. The longest chapters are those on Cuba and Mexico, with Japan getting perhaps less ink than it deserves, but that is a minor quibble. Each chapter provides a narrative history of organized baseball in that country with extended profiles of its top players. Every chapter also includes a statistics and records section that lists all players who played in the U.S. Major Leagues with basic statistics and a rundown of league champions and leaders. The Japanese chapter also includes the statistics of major leaguers who played in Japan and the career Japanese League statistics of Japanese stars. When a country has its own baseball Hall of Fame, inductees are listed as well. A bibliography concludes each chapter.

The appendixes include the membership roster of the International Baseball Federation and a 35-page timeline of international baseball. The book also features an annotated overall bibliography and an index. This skillfully executed, indispensable resource is highly recommended for all collections. [R: BL, June 05, p. 1845; LJ, 1 June 05, p. 174]—**John Maxymuk**

P
267. Light, Jonathan Fraser. **The Cultural Encyclopedia of Baseball.** 2d ed. Jefferson, N.C., McFarland, 2005. 1105p. index. $75.00. ISBN 0-7876-2087-1.

While many books explore baseball history and trivia, Light's monumental collection of facts and anecdotes may well have the best balance between the two. Updating his 1997 volume (see ARBA 98, entry 733), Light offers histories of each present and past team and short biographies of prominent players, including all those in the Baseball Hall of Fame, managers, owners, umpires, sportswriters, and broadcasters, with brief bibliographies at the end of most. There are entries devoted to agents, bats, injuries and illness, Jewish players, Little League, stadiums, ugly players, and baseball in countries other than the United States. Although Light, an attorney, never explains what he means by culture, there are sections about advertising, baseball cards, marriage, movies, music, politics, radio, television, and sex.

Light's readers learn that the Braves were the first team to make its highlight film in color, carriages and automobiles were parked in outfields as late as 1900, Harpo Marx played "Take Me Out to the Ballgame" on his harp in an episode of *I Love Lucy*, and some people think alkaline batteries were named for Detroit Tiger star Al Kaline. There are many black-and-white photographs and an index. Light commits a few errors, as when, in a caption, he identifies Pat Corrales, an Atlanta Braves coach, as Bobby Cox, the team's manager. Despite such occasional mistakes, this exhaustive study provides much useful and amusing information, making it both a valuable reference tool and an entertaining read.—**Michael Adams**

Handbooks and Yearbooks

P
268. **The Official Major League Baseball Fact Book.** 2005 ed. St. Louis, Mo., Sporting News Publishing, 2005. 423p. illus. $19.95pa. ISBN 0-89204-771-2.

In 1997, this new Sporting News publication joined a host of annual and periodically revised handbooks designed to meet the insatiable demand for information on this national pastime. *Total Baseball* (7th ed.; see ARBA 2002, entry 799) remains the standard statistical and biographical source, but the low price, attractive format, and current coverage of the 2005 *Fact Book* make it a fine choice for either smaller public and academic libraries with limited budgets or for larger libraries needing a circulating book with recent data to complement the standard baseball reference volumes.

The *Fact Book* opens with a preview of 2005 season teams and rosters followed by a thorough review of the entire 2004 season. Team day-by-day game tables showing opponents, pitchers, and results will be of special interest to avid fans. A who's who section covers Hall of Fame players (1936-2005), major award winners (1931-2004), and prominent faces for 2005.

The remarkably detailed history section, a season-by-season (1876-2003) review, runs to almost 200 pages and is distinguished by noteworthy annual "Significant Events" and "Memorable Moments" features. The franchise histories yield such nuggets as ballpark chronologies, retired uniform numbers, and no-hit pitchers. The "For the Record" section cites all-time individual and team records, spotlights selected "classic seasons," and provides box scores for "classic games." Interesting black-and-white field and dugout photographs enliven all five sections of this well-designed book.—**Julienne L. Wood**

BASKETBALL

P

269.   **Basketball: A Biographical Dictionary.** David L. Porter, ed. Westport, Conn., Greenwood Press, 2005. 589p. index. $89.95. ISBN 0-313-30952-3.

Simple, straightforward, and concise best describe this one-volume basketball biographical encyclopedia. In alphabetic order users will find the usual suspects, from Larry, Michael, and Magic to Pete Maravich, Oscar Robertson, and Jerry West. From the basketball archives are names like George Mikan, Doggie Julian, and Walter Kennedy. Individuals such as C. M. Newton, Ed Diddle, and Sue Gunter may not be so easily recognized but all are included in an impressive array of 575 men and women (over 60) in the history of roundball. Editor Porter (William Penn University professor and notable author of numerous sports books) and 76 contributors write clear biographical sketches concluding with current information on the lives of those past their game (very current as evidenced by the dates for the recently deceased Mikan and legendary coach Bighouse Gaines). Each entry includes appropriate nicknames, a brief bibliography, and the book concludes with an excellent index. Contributors do not avoid controversial off-court issues such as the legal problems of Allen Iverson. In summary, although a tad expensive, libraries wanting a single volume on basketball through the ages need look no further than this highly successful reference work.—**Boyd Childress**

FOOTBALL

P

270.   Maxymuk, John. **Uniform Numbers of the NFL: All-Time Rosters, Facts and Figures.** Jefferson, N.C., McFarland, 2005. 429p. $39.95pa. ISBN 0-7864-2057-X.

Numbers are a vital part of any game, and football is no exception—first downs, rushing yards, yards gained passing, and punting average are just a few examples. Yet there are other numbers, in the case of this exciting new book, jersey numbers. Joe Willie Namath wore #12, Walter Payton #34, and Jim Brown #32. But what numbers did New York Jet Johnny Sample, or all-time Packer great Fuzzy Thurston, Redskin fan favorite turned announcer Sonny Jurgensen, or Pittsburgh all-star Mike Webster wear? The answer to these questions and endless listings of other uniform numbers are available in this one-volume reference work. Divided by NFL team, the player rosters by uniform/jersey number represent the main section of each team entry. Other fascinating facts (3-5 pages) include most and least popular numbers, retired uniform numbers, numbers worn by the greatest players, uniform numbers of greatest draft busts, players who wore the most numbers on one team, numbers with the most catches or passes or rushing yards, players who wore #13, and numerous other fun and intriguing features. There is a player listing indicating team(s) and number(s) that serves as an index. Two more brief sections list players from defunct teams of the NFL and the old AAFC. The usual statistical suspects are now rather easily available with the Internet, but this book offers a unique look at football by the numbers. [R: LJ, July 05, p. 124]—**Boyd Childress**

P

271.　Schatz, Aaron, with others. **Pro Football Prospectus 2005.** New York, Workman Publishing, 2005. 440p. $18.95pa. ISBN 0-7611-4019-0.

Elias Sports Bureau has always had the lock on football statistics—until now. *Pro Football Prospectus 2005* by Aaron Schatz, the brainchild behind *FootballOutsiders.com* (http://www. footballoutsiders.com/), offers a statistical approach to professional football that is creative, in-depth, and actually useful. The book is more than columns of numbers and rankings of teams and players. The predictions for each team in 2005 are based on a detailed analysis of every play of every game played in 2004, weighted according to the context of the situation on the field at the time of the play. This is a model than can actually explain why teams win and lose, and why players perform the way they do.

If you are a stat freak, this book will have you drooling. The first section describes the author's own statistical approach and refreshingly different statistical categories, such as Defense-Adjusted Value Over Average, Defense-Adjusted Points Above Replacement, Pythagorean Projection, Adjusted Line Yards, Success Rate, Similarity Score, Stop Rate, and many others. Each of the 32 teams has a 6- to 8-page analysis of its 2004 season and its projected 2005 performance, including its odds of making it to the Super Bowl. This section is followed by chapters that evaluate the skill positions of quarterback, running back, wide receiver, tight end, and kicker. There is also a section predicting Fantasy Football player success for 2005. And don't miss the interesting chapter on the best quarterback season ever played, based on the unique statistical analysis by Schatz.

This book is fairly priced at $18.95 and easy on the eyes with large pages and generous white space. Anyone who is serious about football (or picking the best Fantasy Football players possible) needs to read this book.—**Mark J. Crawford**

GOLF

P

272.　*Golf Digest*'s **Golf Weekends: The Best Places to Play and Stay Near the Nation's Biggest Cities.** New York, Fodor's Travel Publications/Random House, 2004. 454p. illus. maps. index. $19.95pa. ISBN 1-4000-1368-2. ISSN 1551-6415.

Golf Digest's Golf Weekends lists the best places to play, stay, and eat near large cities. The areas covered are Atlanta, Boston, Chicago, Dallas, Denver, Detroit, Houston, Los Angeles, Minneapolis and St. Paul, New York, Orlando, Philadelphia, San Francisco, Seattle, and Washington, D.C. More than 650 great courses within a day's drive of those cities are listed.

The course listings were taken from the 2005 edition of *Golf Digest's Places to Play* (see ARBA 2005, entry 773), and include contact information, statistics, ratings from the magazine's readers, and comments written by the experienced staff writers Matthew Rudy and Ron Kaspriske. Data provided for each entry include the course design, yardage, green fee, walking policy, season, tee times, credit cards accepted, and other notes. Listings are in alphabetic order in each chapter an a overview of the region is provided at the beginning of each chapter. Course charts and maps are helpful in deciding courses quickly. The hotel and restaurant listings are based on recommendations from staff writers and freelancers who live in the area they cover. Each entry in the "Where to Stay" and "Where to Eat" sections include contact information, price range, and brief descriptions written by those local writers. The "Essentials" at the end of each chapter includes details about transportation and other resources. There is a comprehensive index in the back of the publication.

This guide will be helpful for anyone who wants to plan golf weekends near the large cities. The ratings and comments by editors and local writers seem particularly useful. This guide is recommended for large public libraries.—**Mihoko Hosoi**

HIKING

C, P

273.   Hartemann, Frederic V., and Robert Hauptman. **The Mountain Encyclopedia: An A-Z Compendium of More Than 2,300 Terms, Concepts, Ideas, and People.** Lanham, Md., Scarecrow, 2005. 291p. illus. index. $60.00. ISBN 0-8108-5056-7.

Mountains have been loved and feared by humans forever. They deserve their own up-to-date encyclopedia. A physicist and a reference librarian who are avid mountaineers have compiled this excellent broad, yet fundamental, encyclopedia on mountains. The A-Z listings cover everything connected to mountains, yet are brief, basic, and easy to use. The book has 400 color photographs and schematics of mountains, plants, animals, and climbing equipment in the center of the book, as well as black-and-white historical photographs and line drawings throughout the book. In addition, sidebars highlight interesting lists, such as the 10 Best Mountain Movies, 20 Great Modern Mountaineers, 10 Best Female Mountaineers, and 10 Great Mountain Adventure Books.

The foreword is written by Jamling Tenzing Norgay, son of Tenzing Norgay, who summited Mt. Everest with Edmund Hillary. The appendixes offer hours of enjoyment for those who love lists: the world's 1,000 highest peaks; 4,000 meter peaks in the Alps; 6,000 meter peaks in the Andes; North America's 14ers; unclimbed peaks above 7,000 meters; highpoints in U.S. and Canada; and a lengthy list of mountain Websites. A bibliography and index complete this useful, fun, and handy reference for high school, public, and academic libraries. Even so, climbers may find important details missing; for example, "The Mountaineers" is listed as a club and prolific publisher of mountaineering books, but the listing does not include it's Washington state location or 1906 origin. Thus, this reviewer looks forward to the next edition with expanded and even more detailed entries, larger pictures, and information about equipment from producers other than Black Diamond. This book is highly recommended for both public and academic libraries. [R: BL, 1 & 15 Jan 06, p. 152]—**Georgia Briscoe**

SOCCER

P, S

274.   **DK Soccer Yearbook 2004-2005: The Complete Guide to the World Game.** By David Goldblatt. New York, DK Publishing, 2004. 528p. illus. maps. index. $30.00pa. ISBN 0-7566-0426-5.

This gorgeous and informative soccer annual from DK Publishing will delight soccer fans of the worldwide professional game. This London-based work manages to encompass soccer everywhere, with sections on the UEFA (European), CONMEBOL (South American), CAF (African), AFC (Asian), OFC (Oceanian), and CONCACAF (North and Central American) nation groups, with each group's pages color-coded for easier ready reference.

Each nation and major city with professional soccer gets a lavish treatment of the 2003/04 season in review (essays, photographs, and results); colorful detailed maps indicating home stadium location and jersey for each team; history of soccer in that nation; analysis of players, fans, and owners; and historical records of major tournaments. On a global level, sections include a global history of soccer and the federations, rules of the game, and an analysis of the different playing styles. The major world and regional tournaments are well covered and include history and results of each with descriptions of important matches, including diagrams of some of the goals.

Fans of United States soccer or women's soccer need to look to another reference; U.S. soccer gets four pages and women's soccer gets only two (college soccer receives no coverage at all). However, the majority of soccer fans these days are interested in the world game and will be well served by this excellent work. The *DK Soccer Yearbook* is recommended as an annual purchase for all public libraries.—**Christina L. Hennessey**

16 Sociology

GENERAL WORKS

C

275.   **A Dictionary of Sociology.** 3d ed. John Scott and Gordon Marshall, eds. New York, Oxford University Press, 2005. 709p. $45.00. ISBN 0-19-860986-8.

Arranged like a dictionary but encyclopedic in scope, this volume is clearly written and easy to read. *A Dictionary of Sociology* lists over 2,500 entries, in all aspects of sociology, including international terms, methods, and concepts, and related terms from the fields of psychology, economics, anthropology, political science, and philosophy. With more than 70 new entries, this volume is considerably longer in length and varying in depth than its predecessor. Entries in this new volume are fully revised and updated and others completely rewritten. This 3d edition also lists new material on a wide range of topics, including biographical coverage of prominent figures of living sociologists. For example, new entries will be found on Anthony Giddens and Jurgen Habermas. Also notable in this edition is its inclusion of Web links that are useful for further reading and research.

A problem with this volume is its excessive use of asterisks for related references, some of which are not real entries. This title otherwise is the most comprehensive, authoritative, and up-to-date dictionary of sociology available in a single volume. The scope, caliber, quality of writing, and the authority of the editors establish this volume as an essential resource and a must-have title for academic and public libraries. Libraries that own the previous edition should consider purchasing this as it is expanded and is reasonably priced. The book's treatment of the subject makes it an invaluable introduction to those new to the subject and an essential reference tool for advanced students and professionals.—**Njoki W. Kinyatti**

C

276.   Stolley, Kathy S. **The Basics of Sociology.** Westport, Conn., Greenwood Press, 2005. 302p. index. (Basics of the Social Sciences). $75.00. ISBN 0-313-32387-9.

This book contains 11 chapters preceded by a "Sociology Timeline of Selected Events and Influential Publications," from the 1200s to 1998. At the end are a glossary, references, and an index. Its coverage is extensive on such topics as theory; culture and society; socialization and social interaction; social groups and organizations; deviance and social control; stratification; population structure, movement, and concentration; social change, behavior, and movements; research methods; and being a sociologist and career opportunities.

Each chapter consists of four parts: topic discussion; biographies; careers in sociology (except in the chapter on career opportunities); and additional resources. The topic discussion provides an introduction to the topic. The chapters on career opportunities provides interesting data such as the number of sociology degrees awarded, percentage of doctorate degrees earned by women in selected disciplines, recipients of sociology doctorates by race, and average sociology faculty salaries.

There are 73 sociologists profiled, from 5 to 8 in each chapter. The number is quite limited, thus omitting some noted sociologists, including Ellsworth Faris and William F. Ogburn. Career opportunities are listed under each topic. Some of them, such as administrator, consultant, executive director, recruiter, and researcher, are too general to be meaningful. They could be for any discipline. "Additional Resources" lists both books and Websites. The 28 pages of reference are a useful bibliography for further studies in sociology.

The book is both an introduction to and reference source on sociology. Sociology as a discipline is well presented here.—**Tze-chung Li**

COMMUNITY LIFE

C

277.   **The Cambridge Encyclopedia of Hunters and Gatherers.** paperback ed. Richard B. Lee and Richard Daly, eds. New York, Cambridge University Press, 2004. 511p. illus. maps. index. $34.99pa. ISBN 0-521-60919-4.

Originally published in 1999, this work has recently been reprinted in a paperback edition, making it much more affordable to smaller reference collection. Members of hunting-gathering societies are those that depend on killing wild animals, fishing, and collecting edible plants and grains for their food. These activities constitute the two oldest forms of organized activities in human history, but there are contemporary groups that still rely on this method of subsistence. Richard Lee, a professor of anthropology at the University of Toronto; Richard Daly, a freelance anthropologist; and nearly 100 other scholars have produced the first encyclopedic work to survey modern hunters and gatherers.

The volume is in three parts. The first, and longest, provides case studies of 53 communities divided into 7 world regions. For each region, there is an introductory essay and an essay analyzing the archaeology of the hunter-gatherers in that region. The second part consists of topical chapters on such themes as health, art, music, mythology, gender, and social life. The final section examines how these societies have fared under colonial and modern governments and highlights their ongoing struggles for survival. The volume concludes with a list of indigenous peoples' organizations and a subject index.

This is an important and fascinating work. The numerous black-and-white photographs, drawings, and maps are excellent and well placed. The bibliographies at the end of each chapter, along with filmographies of the various native groups, are convenient springboards for further research. Recommended for undergraduate, graduate, and specialized collections.—**Hope Yelich**

DEATH

C, P

278.   Cassell, Dana K., Robert C. Salinas, and Peter A. S. Winn. **The Encyclopedia of Death and Dying.** New York, Facts on File, 2005. 369p. index. (Facts on File Library of Health and Living). $75.00. ISBN 0-8160-5376-6.

Death has become a popular topic. This is the third major encyclopedia or handbook on death in the last two years. Both the *Macmillan Encyclopedia of Death and Dying* (see ARBA 2003, entry 816) and the *Handbook of Death and Dying* (see ARBA 2004, entry 822) are two-volume works with fewer, but longer, articles. This one-volume work has over 500 entries that cover all aspects of dying, including customs, beliefs, cultural, legal, moral, emotional, and social issues surrounding the end of life. The articles are concise, well written, and many have bibliographic references included. Several articles include references to Websites that will also give further information. Within the entries are references to other entries in this volume that appear in all capital letters. There are *see also* references included. There is a very good introductory essay that looks at death and death customs from prehistory to the present.

The last one-third of the book consists of several appendixes with useful information such as an advanced care plan document, death statistics, where to write for death certificates, a checklist for end-of-life planning, and more. There is a good bibliography that is divided into articles, books, and videos that provides further references. Most of the articles, books, and videos were published within the last eight years. A very good index is also included. This will be a useful volume for most libraries.—**Robert L. Turner Jr.**

DISABLED

P
279.   **The Complete Directory for People with Disabilities, 2005: A Comprehensive Source Book for Individuals and Professionals.** 13th ed. Millerton, N.Y., Grey House Publishing, 2004. 986p. index. $165.00pa.; $215.00 (online database); $300.00 (print edition and online database). ISBN 1-59237-054-3. ISSN 1063-0023.

P
280.   **Complete Directory of Disabilities. http://www.greyhouse.com.** [Website]. Millerton, N.Y., Grey House Publishing. $165.00pa.; $215.00 (online database); $300.00 (print edition and online database). Date reviewed: May 05.

The 13th edition of this directory of resources for the disabled is not much changed from the 2003/2004 edition (see ARBA 2005, entry 798). The one new feature is an essay for parents and caregivers discussing the value of estate planning and supplemental trusts. Other than that there are once again almost 10,000 entries covering resources, products, and services organized into 27 chapters and 100 subchapters. Major chapters cover national and state agencies, numerous associations and organizations, assistive devices, travel, sports and camps, education, media (print, audiovisual, and electronic), assistive computer devices, and rehabilitation centers. Subchapters further divide the topics into specific areas by type of resource and disability.

There are sections covering visual and hearing aids, kitchen and bath aids, and four types of wheelchairs. The media and print section has 17 subdivisions covering periodicals, books, and audiovisual material. Bibliographic information includes ISBN number, publisher, and publication date. All entries are numbered sequentially and contain as many as 14 fields. Contact information is provided and includes e-mail, fax number, and Websites.

The information provided in this *Directory* is also available in an online format from the publisher (http://www.greyhouse.com). Users can search the information by entry name, major category (e.g., Camps, Education, Independent Living Centers), minor category (e.g., Aging, Aids for Classroom), keyword, executive last name, or state.

The most extensive sections deal with state departments of aging and education, veterans' hospitals, camps, and learning disabilities. Often hard-to-find information on ADA compliant construction and architecture is included, although the agencies and organizations listed are primarily for the professional. The disabled and their caregivers seeking advice on adapting a home will have to look elsewhere since useful organizations such as the National Resource Center on Supportive Housing and Home Modification and the federal government's Eldercare.org (www.eldercare.org) are not included. These omissions point out the problem of a directory created from survey responses. Valuable agencies not contacted or not returning the survey do not appear. Some of the many useful entries that are included are difficult to find despite the table of contents and three indexes (geographical, entry name, and disability/subject). A general alphabetic index would facilitate locating information. A search for entries on service dogs required going through the list of entries to find appropriate organizations. The same is true for services for amputees. Even though there are frustrations for directory users those must be weighed against the comprehensive coverage of disability resources. Public librarians at busy information desks may find an Internet search provides quicker access when looking for specific information. Hospitals, rehab centers, and social workers will want to have this directory to use when assisting clients. Another comparable source is the two-volume *Resources for People with Disabilities* (Ferguson, 2001) It contains fewer entries but covers similar subject matter. Alas, that title also suffers from the lack of a general index.—**Marlene M. Kuhl**

FAMILY, MARRIAGE, AND DIVORCE

C

281.   **The Blackwell Companion to the Sociology of Families.** Jacqueline Scott, Judith Treas, and Martin Richards, eds. Malden, Mass., Blackwell, 2004. 596p. index. (Blackwell Companions to Sociology). $124.95. ISBN 0-631-22158-1.

This title is an important addition to the Blackwell Companions to Sociology series. The contributors represent various perspectives within the discipline of sociology, both domestic and international. The scholars discuss the changing family within the contexts of courtship, divorce, and remarriage; family composition (e.g., gay and lesbian families, blended families); demographic and economic factors; and law and public policy modifications.

The book is divided into 5 sections, for a total of 28 chapters: "Families in a Global World," "Life-Course Perspectives on the Family," "Inequality and Diversity," "Changing Family Forms and Relationships," and "Changing Social Contexts." Each section is comprised of a preface followed by chapters relating to that section's theme. Each chapter includes ideas for future research and extensive references.

The volume includes an extremely useful cumulative bibliography and comprehensive index, complete with cross-references. Aimed at a scholarly audience, upper-level undergraduates and graduate students alike will benefit from this title. This companion is highly recommended for all academic libraries supporting programs in sociology and family studies. [R: LJ, 1 April 04, p. 85]—**Leanne M. VandeCreek**

C, P

282.   **Children and Youth in Adoption, Orphanages, and Foster Care: A Historical Handbook and Guide.** Lori Askeland, ed. Westport, Conn., Greenwood Press, 2006. 222p. index. (Children and Youth: History and Culture). $59.95. ISBN 0-313-33183-9.

Children and Youth in Adoption, Orphanages, and Foster Care is divided into three parts. Part 1 consists of six, short, original essays, based primarily on secondary sources, that provide a historical and multicultural view of the major issues in U.S. adoption and foster care from pre-Colonial days to the present. Editor Lori Askeland makes an important contribution to the historical literature in chapter 1, "Informal Adoption, Apprentices, and Indentured Children in the Colonial Era and New Republic, 1606-1850," with her discussion of the Native American tradition of adoption and African traditions of kinship and the black community, topics usually neglected in monographic literature on adoption history. In chapter 2, "Adoption Reform, Orphan Trains, and Child Saving," the foremost authority on the orphan trains, Marilyn Irvin Holt, provides a sophisticated overview of the history of New York's Children's Aid Society, which transported and placed some 200,000 children and teenagers in homes by trains across the country between 1854 and 1929. Inviting further research for validation, she tosses off the provocative remark that state laws enacted to curb orphan train placements in the late nineteenth century shaped state adoption laws. The third chapter, "Science, Social Work, and Bureaucracy: Cautious Developments in Adoption and Foster Care, 1930-1969," by Diane Creagh, skillfully focuses on the growth of adoption by bureaucratized adoption agencies and professional social workers, and the concomitant emergence of confidentiality and secrecy surrounding adoption procedures. Chapter 4 by Martha Satz and Lori Askeland, "Civil Rights, Adoption Rights: Domestic Adoption and Foster Care, 1970 to the Present," expertly synthesizes the history and controversies surrounding the adoption search movement; the effort by adopted adults to reunite with members of their original families and to gain access to their adoption records that have been sealed by state law; open adoption; and transracial adoption. Chapter 5, "International Adoption," by Elizabeth Bartholet, is a cogent and insightful overview of the history of and recent legal developments within international adoption, and presents a balanced view of the politics and ethics of this controversial practice. The sixth chapter, by Claudia Nelson, "The Orphan in American Children's Literature," surveys children's literature in America, across many cultures and centuries, and deftly notes the similarities and differences in the way orphans have been treated and how they have changed over time. Part 2 contains six hard-to-find primary sources that match up with the chapters, illustrating their main themes. Part 3 contains an extensive bibliography of secondary sources, easily one of the best in print.

One of the stated goals of *Children and Youth in Adoption, Orphanages, and Foster Care* is to be a starting point for students and researchers. It has succeeded admirably in this goal. This work is recommended for all libraries.—**E. Wayne Carp**

C, P

283.   Monger, George P. **Marriage Customs of the World: From Henna to Honeymoons.** Santa Barbara, Calif., ABC-CLIO, 2004. 327p. illus. index. $85.00; $90.00 (e-book). ISBN 1-57607-987-2; 1-57607-988-0 (e-book).

The author of this book is a "freelance museum conservator, consultant, and folklorist based in East Anglia, United Kingdom, and he has a special particular interest in marriage traditions. He has published papers and reviews in folklore and ethnological journals." He is also a good writer who has thoroughly documented his articles.

The book is set up like an encyclopedia with articles under the entries that are listed in the table of contents. Citations to other works follow each article. The articles are from two to three pages in length and the text is liberally sprinkled with black-and-white photographs. Within the columns of articles there are cross-references to other topics that are related to the current one.

The content is fascinating. It covers most of the world, including places like the Middle East, South East Asia, Russia, Tibet, and Niger. Topics are different kinds of ceremonies, special objects related to marriage (e.g., ribbons, rice, favors, henna), people important to the marriage, and particular styles of wedding dress. It also covers the special topics related only to marriage, such as wife-selling, dowries, common-law marriage, same-sex marriage, or marriage by capture. His style is reminiscent of an academic text, but the language is very clear and uncomplicated.

Access to the content is especially good, which makes this a good book for reference collections. There is access through the table of contents (which is a listing of the article headings), but everyone should use the index because it is especially good. It was obviously done by a professional because it brings out all of the richness of the text. The table of contents alone does not do the book justice. There is a very good *see* and *see also* structure and there are no long strings of locators to chase down. The indexer did a good job of using subheadings to keep the searching easy.

The readability of the book makes it appropriate for all ages above middle school. As a reference book it would be very good in academic and public libraries. It could also be used as a text for comparative marriage customs.—**Lillian R. Mesner**

GAY AND LESBIAN STUDIES

C, P

284.   Kranz, Rachel, and Tim Cusick. **Gay Rights.** rev. ed. New York, Facts on File, 2005. 362p. index. (Library in a Book). $45.00. ISBN 0-8160-5810-5.

This two-part, information-rich volume provides a great deal of information about gay rights in the United States. Part 1, a 200-plus page overview of the topic, starts with an introductory chapter surveying a variety of issues of concern to gays and lesbians: marriage, domestic partnership, recognition of gay families, employment rights, response to violence, religious recognition, participation in society, cultural expression, political power, and sexual freedom. Subsequent chapters address legislation and legal battles (in which the background, salient legal issues, and the impact of key cases are discussed), gay rights and culture (focusing on education and religion), and then provide a chronology (a timeline starting in 1869 when the word homosexual was coined until April 2005, when Kansans approved an amendment to their state constitution banning gay marriage and civil unions), a biographical listing (1-3 sentence descriptions of key people), and a glossary (50-plus important terms). More subheadings would make the information in the opening chapters more easily accessible, but there is definitely a wealth of information to be mined here. Part 2, a 100-page "Guide to Further Research," enables readers to gather information elsewhere thanks to an outstanding annotated bibliography of books, articles (organized topically), and Websites as well as a list of organizations and agencies. The book concludes with two appendixes: the first provides excerpts from important court decisions and the second provides excerpts from statements of government policy and legislation. Since this book contains so much information about so many topics of relevance to gay rights in the United States, it is fortunate that its index is finely detailed. Because of the importance of the subject and the currency of the information, the revised edition of *Gay Rights* is recommended for any public or academic library's reference collection.—**G. Douglas Meyers**

PHILANTHROPY

C

285.   **Directory of Research Grants 2006.** Jeremy T. Miner and Lynn E. Miner, eds. Westport, Conn., Oryx Press/Greenwood Publishing Group, 2006. 952p. index. $145.00pa. ISBN 1-57356-619-5.

The updated *Directory of Research Grants* is fundamental to any collection serving, either directly or indirectly, the research community working in the areas of "medicine, the physical and social sciences, the arts and humanities, and education." This work gathers together information on funding for nearly 6,000 "research-related programs and projects, scholarships, fellowships, conferences, and internships."

Entries are listed in the main body of the text in alphabetic order; four indexes provide cross-referencing by subject, sponsoring organization, program type, and state. Many helpful features make for user-friendliness, such as the diamond-shaped icons indicating grants that have geographic restrictions and the simple diagrams explaining how to read each grant program entry. When available, Web addresses are included. Anyone who has ever attempted to plow through the *Catalog of Federal Domestic Assistance* will also appreciate the fact that this directory has simplified that unwieldy source, supplying each program's numbers, along with its basic requirements, deadlines, and so forth. Finally, diagrams instruct users on how to navigate each index, translation of acronyms is provided, and there is even a mini-lesson in proposal writing.

Given the rapidly changing nature of information, the directory acknowledges the changing nature of its contents. Having said that, using hard copy these days for absolutely current information is always best backed up by supplemental research. Nevertheless, this unique book has successfully collocated a wide variety of resources geared toward a specific audience, and that audience should be delighted with the way it simplifies their search for funding.—**Wendy Miller**

SEX STUDIES

C

286.   **Encyclopedia of Sex and Gender: Men and Women in the World's Cultures.** Carol R. Ember and Melvin Ember, eds. New York, Springer Publishing, 2003. 2v. index. $475.00/set. ISBN 0-306-47770-X.

The purpose of this work is to present a comparative perspective on gender, gender differences, gender roles, and the relationship between gender and sexuality in many cultures throughout the world. The work is divided into two main sections. The first section, which takes up nearly 250 pages, is a topical overview that is divided into four main topics dealing with the cultural conceptions of gender, the observed differences between males and females in behavior and personality, the institutionalized aspects of gender and sexuality, and male-female interactions. These essays include observations on many cultures. The second part of the work consists of a detailed look at 82 widely diverse cultures. Some essays address a country, others a very small group. In this section each culture is presented in an almost identical outline giving the alternate names of the culture; the location and linguistic affiliation; a cultural overview; a cultural construction of gender; gender over the life cycle; the socialization of boys and girls; puberty and adolescence; attainment of adulthood; middle age and old age; personality differences by gender; gender-related social groups; gender roles in economics; parental and other caretaker roles; leadership in public arenas; gender and religion, leisure, recreation, and the arts; relative status of men and women; sexuality, courtship, and marriage; husband-wife relationships; other cross-sex relationships; changes in attitudes, beliefs, and practices regarding gender; and references. Each essay is written by an anthropologist or other social scientist that has lived with the culture that is being written about. The references are extensive.

There is a glossary of terms in the front of the work and there is a culture name index and a subject index in the back of the work. This resource will be useful for those studying cross-cultural variations in sex and gender.—**Robert L. Turner Jr.**

C, P, S

287.   **Youth, Education, and Sexualities: An International Encyclopedia.** James T. Sears, ed. Westport, Conn., Greenwood Press, 2005. 2v. illus. index. $175.00/set. ISBN 0-313-32748-3.

This outstanding two-volume international encyclopedia belongs in every reference collection. With its multidisciplinary presentation of knowledge on research, policy, and practice on gay, bisexual, and transgender (LGBT) sexualities as they relate to educational curriculum, policies, and teaching approaches around the world, this work is comprised of nearly 250 individually authored signed entries. Each entry, written by a respected scholar in language accessible to a general audience, includes a 1,000- to 2,500-word discussion of the topic, an up-to-date bibliography, references, and at least one Website. Cross-referencing of topics is accomplished through the effective use of bold font within each entry and a well-detailed index at the end of volume 2. The volumes' visual appeal is enhanced by the occasional use of black-and-white photographs, illustrations, and figures, and its scholarly value is enriched by a general bibliography of key books and reports, book chapters and journal articles, and electronic resources. This excellent reference work would have special relevance to school administrators, teachers, counselors, and youth workers, while at the same time functioning as a superb sourcebook for parents, students, and professionals in a wide variety of disciplines addressing human sexuality.—**G. Douglas Meyers**

SOCIAL WELFARE AND SOCIAL WORK

P

288. Dumouchel, J. Robert. **Government Assistance Almanac 2005-2006.** 19th ed. Detroit, Omnigraphics, 2005. 1033p. index. $275.00. ISBN 0-7808-0700-6. ISSN 0883-8690.

Guides to government programs that provide assistance to its citizens have been a traditional form of serving citizens attempting to make sense of their bewildering number. The 19th annual edition of the *Government Assistance Almanac* (GAA) presents updated information on all 1,613 federal programs described in the U.S. General Services Administration's massive (1,967 pages) Catalog of Federal Domestic Service (CFDA). These programs represent $1.7 trillion worth of federal assistance that is available to civic and organizational leaders, scholars, parents and students, veterans, local governments, businesses, and other organizations.

A comparison of the GAA with the CFDA reveals several distinct advantages of the former. The GAA contains an extensive master index, sections on program funding levels and field office contacts, and a simplified listing of all U.S. programs. Nevertheless, where the CFDA is superior is its comprehensive detail of programs, the variety of indexes (including functional, applicant eligibility, and deadlines), and appendixes on the mechanics of developing and writing of grant proposals. Moreover, any advantages the GAA may have over the CFDA are seriously compromised by the availability of the Catalog of Federal Domestic Service, which is free and online (http://12.46.245.173/cfda/cfda.html). The online version's 10 separate search categories (by function area, agency, sub-agency, program title, applicant eligibility, beneficiary, program deadline, type of assistance, programs requiring Executive Order 12372 Review, and Budget Function Code [App. III]) add to its superiority. Also, extremely advantageous are the CFDA's bi-weekly updates compared to the annual updating of the GAA.

The *Government Assistance Almanac* is well organized and provides an excellent introduction to the Catalog of Federal Domestic Service, but it is clearly no substitute for it. An applicant would still have to consult the CFDA if serious about applying to one of its programs. In light of the cost of the GAA and the fact that the CFDA is free online, it is hard to justify the purchase of the GAA. [R: LJ, Aug 05, p. 120]—**E. Wayne Carp**

C

289. **Encyclopedia of Social Welfare History in North America.** John M. Herrick and Paul H. Stuart, eds. Thousand Oaks, Calif., Sage, 2005. 534p. index. $125.00. ISBN 0-7619-2584-8.

Social science reference books in general have either a nationalistic or international approach. The editors of the *Encyclopedia of Social Welfare History in North America* have decided to avoid this trend and have taken a "continental, tri-national approach" to their subject matter.

With 180 articles written on various issues and policies of the social welfare movements of Canada, Mexico, and the United States, the editors give the user the opportunity to compare the unique policy approaches of each country. Most of the major topics are discussed in three separate articles, each dedicated to one of the three North American countries. Over 30 of the articles are biographical entries on important figures of the various movements. Included with the articles are a "List of Entries" for quick reference, and a "Reader's Guide," which is a subject listing of all articles on individual topics. The appendixes include research guides, chronologies of each nation's social welfare movements, and an excellent master bibliography.

The strength of this title is in its uniqueness. Including Canada and Mexico on an equal footing with the United States makes the book not only a great comparison tool, but also a source for a trinational approach to topics—something no one else has ever attempted. The contributors are from all three nations, and brought their national perspectives to the issues.

Where the editors of the *Encyclopedia* stumble is when they do not follow their own format. For example, there are entries for "Multiculturalism (Canada)" and "Race and Ethnic Relations (Canada)" but the editors did not have articles highlighting these issues for either Mexico or the United States. On the topics of homelessness and voluntarism, Mexico and Canada lacked articles. These omissions weakened this generally solid tool.

Overall, despite the flaws, this reviewer would still highly recommend this original and unique title for academic and research libraries. I hope later editions of this title will be further expanded to include more entries and continue the trinational balance. [R: BL, June 05, p. 1852]—**Rob Laurich**

C, P

290.   Padró, Fernando F. **Statistical Handbook on the Social Safety Net.** Westport, Conn., Greenwood Press, 2004. 582p. index. (Oryx Statistical Handbooks). $99.95. ISBN 1-57356-516-4.

The *Statistical Handbook on the Social Safety Net* is organized into three sections. The first three chapters provide background and context for the entire volume. Chapter 1 explicates the definition of a social safety net in an international comparative framework; chapter 2 discusses the economic and budgetary health of nations, principally the United States; and chapter 3 defines poverty and how nations, and again mainly the United States, use that definition to provide services to clients. The second section (chapters 4-8) is focused on ideas about safety net programs and insurance that are available in the United States and other countries. Chapter 4, which centers on Social Security programs such as old age, survivors, and disability insurance (OASI and DI, or OASDI), also offers comparisons with how selected countries provide similar benefits. Chapter 5 discusses two other aspects of the U.S. Social Security Act of 1935, unemployment insurance and worker compensation, with some international comparative data. Chapter 6 presents information on the U.S. Medicare and Medicaid programs, set in an international comparative framework in order to illustrate resources allocated to public health. Chapter 7 reviews the Clinton administration's Temporary Assistance for Needy Family Act (TANF), known as workfare, which provided a new paradigm for the U.S. welfare system by replacing the paradigm of public welfare first enacted as part of the Social Security Act of 1935, the Aid to Dependent Children (ADC). Chapter 8 looks at "supplemental income programs based on the concept of the negative tax and other benefit programs such as housing" (p. xxi). The last section (chapters 9-10) focuses on the public safety net for women and children. Each of these chapters begins with a detailed, edifying synopsis of the subject, which are little gems in themselves, followed by 23 to 31 meticulous tables (except for chapter 10, which contains only 10 tables) and concluding with extensive bibliographies at the end of every chapter including numerous, invaluable Websites.

Padró wrote the *Statistical Handbook on the Social Safety Net* with two principal purposes in mind: to provide readers with a statistical background for doing basic research on the subject of a national social safety net and to provide individuals with socioeconomic data on key indicators to write grant proposals on the topic. On both counts, Padró's highly informative, well-researched labor of love is an unqualified success. It belongs in all research libraries.—**E. Wayne Carp**

SUBSTANCE ABUSE

C, P, S

291.   **Drugs and Society.** Tarrytown, N.Y., Marshall Cavendish, 2006. 3v. illus. index. $249.95/set. ISBN 0-7614-7597-4.

Aimed at students, this multivolume encyclopedia focuses on legal and illegal drugs of abuse. The entries, which are arranged alphabetically across the three volumes, fall into one of three categories: substances, substance abuse, and society. An introductory table of "thematic contents" lists all of the entries that fall within each of these three categories. Entries on drugs or substances usually include their chemical name and formula, origin, physical and psychological effects, drug classification, short- and long-term effects, street names, and signs of abuse. The substance abuse category includes articles on the behavioral, psychological, and physiological aspects of abuse. Entries falling within the society category focus more on the social context of drug use and abuse. The signed entries, written by experts in the field, run anywhere from one to six pages in length and generally include diagrams, charts, photographs, or key facts. They are also accompanied by *see also* references to related entries found elsewhere in the volumes. The contents of entries on substance abuse topics, such as binge drinking, are necessarily idiosyncratic, reflecting the topic and the sorts of social and contextual issues that are unique to it. Entries within the society category, such as music, movies, advertising, rave culture, organized crime, poverty, and sports, are also dealt with in a manner that is unique to their social context. There is an index and small glossary in the back of each volume. The final volume in the set includes a comprehensive glossary as well as subject and comprehensive indexes. The appended list of resources for further study includes Websites, books, research studies, organizations, journals, fiction, government agencies, and treatment centers. Overall, this is a nicely produced set that would be suitable for public, school, and academic libraries.—**Stephen H. Aby**

YOUTH AND CHILD DEVELOPMENT

C, P

292.   **The Cambridge Encyclopedia of Child Development.** Brian Hopkins, Ronald G. Barr, George F. Michel, and Philippe Rochat, eds. New York, Cambridge University Press, 2005. 670p. index. $120.00. ISBN 0-521-65117-4.

This interdisciplinary reference work pursues and largely realizes the ambitious objective of surveying the leading topics in contemporary academic and applied child development. Authoritatively written from culturally diverse orientations, this bulky single volume covers, in a jargonless manner, a number of topical areas sure to be of interest to a wide-ranging readership, including social workers, education specialists, health care workers, and social scientists. Major areas covered include leading theories, the history of child development, psychopathology, and sociologically based development. Readers may struggle, however, with a pronounced natural science and medical treatment of several entries on such topics as pediatrics and child development research techniques (e.g., magnetic resource imaging).

Graduate students, academicians, and applied researchers will appreciate the many entries devoted to research methods in child development, ranging from data collection techniques, cross-cultural comparisons, and index development to parent and teacher rating skills and even cross-species comparison. The theory section is composed of a fairly even representation of discipline perspectives from both the hard and social scientists. While social scientists will benefit from quality in-depth treatment of theory, methods, childhood domains from infancy, and numerous selected topics such as aggression and other behavioral problems, as well as prosocial behaviors, coverage of epidemiological and psychoanalytical topics is a particularly thick and advanced read. The role and nature of play, child depression, and a number of disorders and syndromes other than aggression are also covered and serve as excellent points of departure for further research. Attention to historical issues is limited to one entry. A pronounced theme of the work is interdisciplinary relevance from the introduction to the final section on "crossing the borders." This encyclopedia is successful in this regard and, accordingly, serves as a ready source for initial exploration of various childhood development topics, which, is, after all, why encyclopedias are compiled.—**James Mitchell Miller**

17 Statistics, Demography, and Urban Studies

DEMOGRAPHY

General Works

C, S

293.   Powell, John. **Encyclopedia of North American Immigration.** New York, Facts on File, 2005. 464p. illus. index. (Facts on File Library of American History). $75.00. ISBN 0-8160-4658-1.

The history of immigration to North America is as diverse as it is important. John Powell, professor of history at Oklahoma Baptist University, has provided an informative and comprehensive resource in his timely new addition to the Facts on File Library of American History series. Considering the significance migration has had in shaping this continent's history, and more recently, the attention immigration has received after the events of September 11th, this first-rate effort will make a valuable addition to any library collection serving students, researchers, or interested general readers.

Consisting of over 300 alphabetically arranged entries, the *Encyclopedia of North American Immigration* provides a wealth of information about events, peoples, themes, biographies, significant movements, and legislation relating to North American immigration over the past 500 years. Articles are informative, end with bibliographies to aid researchers, and are supported by a generous collection of historical photographs, maps, graphs, and tables. An important addition to the volume is the inclusion of several appendixes that provide more useful statistical information; excerpts from primary source documents; maps, graphs, and tables; a comprehensive general bibliography; a glossary of terms; a subject guide; and a solid index with main entries in boldface type. Powell's engaging description of so many distinctive experiences and interesting tales in one, easy-to-use reference volume is certain to contribute to more tolerance and a better understanding of our unique heritages, making this particular addition to the Facts on File series a pleasure to recommend. [R: SLJ, Aug 05, p. 76; BL, 1 & 15 Jan 06, p. 19]—**Vincent P. Tinerella**

United States

C, P

294.   **American Generations: Who They Are and How They Live.** 5th ed. Edited by the Editors of New Strategist Publications. Ithaca, N.Y., New Strategist, 2005. 501p. index. $89.95. ISBN 0-885070-69-1.

As we age, we change. But persons of the same age, for example 60, differ over generations. A person of that age in today's society is likely to differ from a 60 year old of, say, 50 years ago. Thus, age in itself is unable to explain changes in a maturing society over time. In *American Generations: Who They Are and How They Live*, the editors group all living Americans into five generations (e.g., Baby Boomers). While each group, or generation, can be roughly defined by age, differences between generations develop, as well, from environmental and socioeconomic influences. Utilizing data collected by various bureaus and departments of the federal government, the editors characterize each generation by education, health, housing, income, labor force, living arrangements, population, spending, time use, and wealth. *American Generations* brings life, meaning, and usefulness to otherwise basic, raw data. Presentation is basically in the form of tables and charts, accompanied by text that highlights significant points, particularly similarities and differences among generations. The book makes available, in readily accessible form, much pertinent information to those who need to understand differences among generations and who must tailor their messages accordingly (e.g., marketers, public officials, educators). In broader terms, anyone interested in generational differences in the United States would find this book of interest.—**William C. Struning**

C, P

295.   **American Marketplace: Demographics and Spending Patterns.** 7th ed. Edited by the Editors of New Strategist Publications. Ithaca, N.Y., New Strategist, 2005. 524p. index. $89.95. ISBN 1-885070-60-8.

First published in 1992, *American Marketplace* describes demographic and spending data in a user-friendly format. It includes nine chapters: "Education," "Health," "Housing," "Income," "Labor Force," "Living Arrangements," "Population," "Spending," and "Wealth." Each chapter starts with the overview of key trends related to the chapter.

New to the 7th edition is the latest housing market data based on the Census Bureau's American Housing Survey, findings from the Bureau of Labor Statistics' American Time Use Survey, and the spending of households with incomes of $100,000 or more from the new Consumer Expenditure Survey. Each table includes the original source of the data at the bottom, and researchers who need more details can go back to the source if needed. At the back of the book, there is a comprehensive index and a glossary that defines the commonly used terms.

Although most of the tables are based on data collected by the federal government and can be accessed via various Websites, this title organizes the information into easily comprehensive tables for average readers. Thus, users who might spend hours searching for information through various sources such as the Census Bureau and the Bureau of Labor Statistics can identify key consumer trends more easily through this book. This work is recommended to all libraries.—**Mihoko Hosoi**

C, P

296.   **Immigration and Asylum: From 1900 to the Present.** Matthew J. Gibney and Randall Hansen, eds. Santa Barbara, Calif., ABC-CLIO, 2005. 3v. illus. index. $285.00/set; $310.00 (e-book). ISBN 1-57607-796-9; 1-57607-797-7 (e-book).

The twentieth century, as the editors point out, was a time of tremendous upheaval and continuous movement of peoples worldwide. With wars and disasters populations around the globe participated in mass involuntary migrations at the same time as smaller groups and individuals migrated in search of a better life. Matthew J. Gibney and Randall Hansen's *Immigration and Asylum: From 1900 to the Present* examines all aspects of immigration during this period with a truly international perspective.

The first two volumes of the set contain signed articles on four general themes, discussed in detail in the preface: the distinction between (forced) asylum and (voluntary) immigration; émigré groups in diaspora; historical trends; and the politics of migration. This last theme is examined largely, although not exclusively, from a United States perspective. Many of these themes overlap in the same entry.

Articles are generally four to five pages in length, although some are a single page. Topics range broadly from "Afghanistan and Refugees" to "Border Controls," "Crime and Migration," "Ethnic Cleansing," "Humanitarian Intervention," "Ius Sanguinus," "Mariel Boatlift," "Postnationalism," "Schengen Agreement," "U.S. Nativism," and "Zaire/Democratic Republic of Congo and Refugees." Articles focus on specific legislation, broad concepts, peoples, and places that help provide an understanding of the issues surrounding migration. The articles are well written and have good bibliographies. The *see also* references and the strong index provide useful help in navigating the text.

The third volume consists of legal documents on immigration from national governments and international organizations. Although the collection is useful, it lacks any references to or from the articles in the earlier volumes. Further, it lacks newspaper articles, speeches, or other sources that could give a good sense of general perceptions about immigration.

Although the set's focus is obviously the twentieth century, earlier historical context is often provided. The article on the "Irish Diaspora," for instance, has a section on "Historical Patterns," which traces migration back to before 1700. With its international focus, the set complements nicely James Ciment's *Encyclopedia of American Immigration* (see ARBA 2002, entry 874). *Encyclopedia of Diasporas* (Kluwer, 2004), while a useful set, focuses on groups and does not provide much insight into cross-ethnic trends. *Immigration and Asylum: From 1900 to the Present* would make a useful addition to any reference collection.—**Michael Levine-Clark**

STATISTICS

International

C

297.   **Statistics Sources 2006: A Subject Guide to Data on Industrial, Business, Social, Educational, Financial, and Other Topics ....** 29th ed. Farmington Hills, Mich., Gale, 2006. 2v. index. $575.00/set. ISBN 0-7876-8859-2. ISSN 0585-198X.

As many librarians are painfully aware, there are few reference queries more difficult to satisfy than those involving statistics. While some statistical questions can be answered using the old standard, "tried-and-true" resources like *Statistical Abstracts of the United States* (123d ed.; see ARBA 2005, entry 850), U.S. Census Bureau publications, agency Websites, and so forth, occasionally patrons need relatively obscure data from international sources or from agencies that are not readily identifiable. Other than often fruitless and tedious Web searches or turning to expensive online statistical products, there are very few places to look that will point the patron to the correct place to search. One of the few resources, and possibly the best, is *Statistical Sources*. Now in its 29th edition, this 2-volume set is a lifesaver for reference librarians seeking statistical sources.

The first volume begins with an extensive bibliography of key sources—both foreign and domestic—for finding statistical information. Materials in several formats are cited, along with contact information for personnel who can assist in a data search at the listed agencies. The bulk of the two volumes is taken up with a subject list, arranged alphabetically, with publications or Websites that provide statistical information for the subject or subheading. The subject classification makes sense and is relatively easy to use, although patrons may need a bit of professional expertise to utilize the resource fully. The appendixes list the published and unpublished resources used by the editor to compile the two volumes. While the price is high for many smaller libraries, any academic library that can afford *Statistical Sources* should consider adding this to its collections.—**Mark T. Bay**

United States

P

298.   **State Rankings 2005: A Statistical View of the 50 United States.** 16th ed. Kathleen O'Leary Morgan and Scott Morgan, eds. Lawrence, Kans., Morgan Quitno Press, 2005. index. $56.95pa. ISBN 0-7401-0938-3. ISSN 1057-3623.

Now in its 16th edition, this series continues to provide a wealth of data from a wide variety of sources focused entirely on the individual states. As the editors state, the mission of the work "is to translate complicated and often convoluted statistics into meaningful, easy-to-understand state comparisons" (p. iii). This they have done in an admirable fashion.

The organization of the 2005 edition remains the same as in previous editions, although most of the statistics have been updated to reflect newer data. The work is organized into 15 sections: agriculture; crime and law enforcement; defense; economy; education; employment and labor; energy and environment; geography; government finance: federal; government finance: state and local; health; households and housing; population; social welfare; and transportation. Each section contains a variety of related topics with each one presented using two different tables. The first table gives the states in alphabetic order and the other gives the states in rank order on that particular topic. Full source information is given for each chart. The work also includes a listing of additional sources of information along with relevant Websites and a sparse but useful index.

For libraries that seek to provide current statistical comparisons for the states, this is a useful purchase. The main advantage of this work compared to standard reference sources such as the *Statistical Abstract of the United States* (123d library ed.; see ARBA 2005, entry 850) is its presentation of data at the state level, especially of comparative information. No other work provides such a wide variety of information in such a straightforward manner.—**Gregory A. Crawford**

P

299.   **State Trends: Measuring Change in the 50 United States.** 2d ed. Kathleen O'Leary Morgan and Scott Morgan, eds. Lawrence, Kans., Morgan Quitno Press, 2005. 463p. index. $59.95pa. ISBN 0-7401-0947-2. ISSN 1549-1315.

State Trends is the 2d edition of a statistical compilation that replaces a monthly journal, *The State Statistical Trends*. It is similar to *State Rankings* also published by Morgan Quitno (see entry 843). Both are designed to monitor important changes in the social, political, and economic climate of the United States by measuring the rate of change over a period of time. They are invaluable for measuring the comparative performance of states in various sectors.

The 2d edition of *State Trends* features an entirely new set of state data. The six new areas of focus for the 2d edition are employment, federal government finance, healthcare finance and insurance, higher education, social welfare, and state and local government finance. One advantage with the format is that rankings are presented in both alphabetic order and in rank order on the same page. Source information and footnotes are shown at the bottom of each page and national totals, rates, and percentages at the top of each page. A roster of sources with addresses, telephone numbers, and Websites is found at the back of the book. In all, *State Trends* provides over 370 tables comparing key quality of life indicators.

For data-hungry public policy analysts, the book is a boon. Raw data are among the hardest things in the world to analyze, and this book helps even lay readers to gain an understanding of the changes taking place at the state level in the most important sectors of national life.—**George Thomas Kurian**

URBAN STUDIES

Dictionaries and Encyclopedias

C, P, S

300.   Marley, David F. **Historic Cities of the Americas: An Illustrated Encyclopedia.** Santa Barbara, Calif., ABC-CLIO, 2005. 2v. illus. maps. index. $185.00/set; $200.00 (e-book). ISBN 1-57607-027-1; 1-57607-574-5 (e-book).

Urbanography is the branch of urban studies that deals with urban history. It has been overshadowed for many decades by country studies and national history. The focus is now shifting and a number of new books on cities attest to a growing interest in urban history as a discrete branch of history. One example is *Historic Cities of the Americas*, whose two volumes profile the birth of 70 of the most famous cities in the New World, their early colonial development, and their modern growth. These profiles provide a commentary on the growth of the New World under the European powers. When Columbus reached the New World in 1491 there were only a handful of places that could be called towns in the two continents. Columbus himself in one of his letters complained of the lack of villages and towns in the places where he landed. The early colonists tended to congregate in urban settlements so that the New World soon became more urban than Europe or Asia. With a historian's eye for detail Marley sketches the progression of primitive settlements beset by natural disasters, sieges, diseases, and pirates and buccaneers into sprawling metropolises in the space of three centuries.

The text is meticulously documented and enriched by a matchless collection of antique photographs and maps from rare collections. The narrative is accompanied by an extensive bibliography that cites sources in both Spanish and English dating back to over 300 years. The bibliography is a major resource that makes this work even more valuable to students of urban history. The books are well produced and are designed to be useful for not only scholars but also students in high schools and colleges. This set is highly recommended. [R: BL, 1 & 15 Jan 06, p. 152]—**George Thomas Kurian**

Directories

P

301.   **Moving & Relocation Directory 2005-2006.** 5th ed. Nancy V. Kniskern, ed. Detroit, Omnigraphics, 2005. 1279p. index. $235.00. ISBN 1-7808-0802-9.

This latest edition of the *Moving & Relocation Directory* includes several added features for each city profiled, including detailed state and local tax information, percent change employment figures, and the percent change rate in the median price of homes. New front matter also includes listings of employment agencies and national real estate companies. Other special features are a map of time zones, a mileage table illustrating the distance by automobile and airline from one city to another, a table of telephone area codes as well as listings of city and state chambers of commerce, national moving companies, national real estate firms, and state realtors associations. Each city profiled continues to include basic data on climate and population and a brief history of the community is provided. Each entry then provides comprehensive information under the following categories: government, important telephone numbers, on-ground and online information sources (such as libraries and tourism Websites), area communities, economic information, principle industries, quality of living indicators, education, hospitals, transportation, utilities, telecommunications, banking institutions, media, local attractions, sports teams and facilities, and annual events. Arranged alphabetically by city name, this directory continues to be a rich source of information about 121 cities and "popular relocation destinations" (p. 7) in the United States. A strength of this resource is that the information found herein is not gleaned from secondary sources, but acquired directly from real estate firms, chamber of commerce, and local government sources. All contact information is also independently verified. There is no statement about how cities were determined to be included or excluded from the directory (for example, Anchorage, Alaska is profiled but not Fairbanks). In addition, the list of attractions combines all forms of cultural and institutional organizations into one alphabetic listing. In future editions, subdividing this list under the type of attraction, such as museums, would enhance this section. Overall, however, this work continues to be an invaluable resource, both to individuals seeking information on relocating to another city and as a basic information guide on cities in the United States.—**Robert V. Labaree**

Handbooks and Yearbooks

P

302.   **America's Top-Rated Cities, 2005: A Statistical Handbook.** 12th ed. Millerton, N.Y., Grey House Publishing, 2005. 4v. $59.95/vol.; $195.00/set. ISBN 1-59237-076-4. ISSN 1082-7102.

This edition updates information for over 75 percent of the statistics in the previous edition (see ARBA 2005, entry 852) and expands ranking and topical statistical tables. The format and organization of previous editions is retained. Four volumes provide statistics for 100 cities in total. Cities selected for inclusion have a population over 100,000 and have ranked well in surveys and site visits for their business and living conditions. Supplementary material includes maps and appendixes with lists of historical and current geographic areas.

Statistics are first presented for each individual city, with statistics most often provided for the named city. In some cases statistics for other geographic areas such as Metropolitan Statistical Areas (MSAs), the new Core Based Statistical Area (CBSA) geographic type, or the entire United States are provided in addition or in place of statistics for the city itself. Users searching for statistics for a single type of geographic area may be disappointed, but the multiplicity of sources used makes this inevitable. Statistics are drawn from a wide array of magazine surveys and rankings, government agencies, nonprofit groups, and private sources. Statistics provided are standard across all cities, ranging from business to demographic to social. Each volume includes tables of comparative statistics for all cities for most of the topics included in each city's profile, facilitating comparison. Rankings are provided in bulleted paragraphs, and while there is much overlap between sources used for each city, the format and lack of standardized content across cities makes comparison more difficult in this area. This set is recommended for libraries with a need for a wide-ranging array of statistics for large cities.—**Hui Hua Chua**

C, P

303.   **County and City Extra, 2005: Annual Metro, City, and County Data Book.** 13th ed. Deirdre A. Gaquin and Katherine A. DeBrandt, eds. Lanham, Md., Bernan Associates, 2005. 1191p. maps. $120.00. ISBN 1-886222-17-7. ISSN 1059-9096.

Because the *County and City Data Book* from the U. S. Bureau of the Census is on a five- to six-year publication cycle, Bernan Associates continues to fill in the gaps with this very useful series. Now in its 13th edition (see ARBA 2005, entry 854 and ARBA 2000, entry 778, for recent reviews), this volume follows the format established by the Census Bureau. New material in this edition includes data from the 2002 Economic Census, the 2002 Census of Governments, the 2002 Census of Agriculture, and recent immigration statistics. A series of large color maps highlight major population shifts in the United States—migration, ethnic populations, age distribution, population density, educational attainment, unemployment, land use, and the 2004 presidential election. As with most Census Bureau compilations (most notably the *Statistical Abstract of the United States* [see ARBA 2005, entry 850]), the currency of information varies from table to table. Some categories still only provide data from 1997 or 1999, but there is much more from 2002 and 2003 in this edition.

Depending on budgets and need, this is a title that might not have to be purchased every year. However, all editions are highly recommended for public and academic libraries where it will be used heavily as a ready-reference resource.—**Thomas A. Karel**

18 Women's Studies

BIBLIOGRAPHY

C

304. **Feminist Theory Website. http://www.cddc.vt.edu/feminism/.** [Website]. Kristin Switala, comp. Free. Date reviewed: Oct 05.

This Website features mainly bibliographies of feminist theory and biographical sketches of feminist theorists. Feminist philosophy is well represented along with other strains of feminist theory, particularly within two of the site's major categories: fields within feminism and individual feminists. (The third major category is national and ethnic feminisms.) "Fields within Feminism" include, besides philosophy, several narrower categories as well as related fields with philosophical import, notably aesthetics, critical theory, epistemology, essentialism, ethics, liberal feminism, Marxism, and postmodernism.—**Hans E. Bynagle**

BIOGRAPHY

C, P

305. **Notable American Women: A Biographical Dictionary Completing the Twentieth Century.** Susan Ware and Stacy Braukman, eds. Cambridge, Mass., Harvard University Press, 2004. 729p. index. $45.00. ISBN 0-674-01488-X.

The appearance of the first three volumes of *Notable American Women* in 1971 (see ARBA 72, entry 221) was a truly groundbreaking publishing event because biographical information of any kind about notable women was otherwise very difficult to find. Volume 4, published as a supplement in 1980 (see ARBA 82, entry 771), profiled women who died between 1951 and 1975. This 5th volume includes biographical profiles of 483 women who died during the last quarter of the twentieth century. The five volumes in the set now include profiles of 2,284 women. Even today, with a plethora of print and online sources readily available, librarians should turn to this set first for information about notable American women.

The new editorial team refined the already rigorous selection process of the previous volumes. They made a special effort to avoid a Northeastern bias, and roughly one-fourth of the entries are about non-white women. Although this reviewer expected considerable overlap with comparable sources, more than half of the women who are profiled in this volume are not covered in *American National Biography Online* (see ARBA 2004, entry 19).

The entries are well written, and substantial enough to give readers a strong sense of why a woman is considered notable. Even the articles about women scientists convey complex topics in a manner that is accessible to a general audience. Fortunately, the bibliography that accompanies each entry includes both primary (if applicable) and secondary sources.

The Index to Biographies by Field facilitates access to information about women who may not be known to many readers. Although Georgia O'Keeffe is of course listed among the artists covered, we are also directed to the entry for Estelle Ishigo, whose art captured the hardships that internment camp detainees faced during World War II. Readers impressed by Helen Taussig's determination to obtain a medical degree can quickly learn how Martha May Eliot, Edith Jackson, and others also overcame bias against women doctors.

As Susan Ware notes in her fascinating introduction, this volume also provides multiple perspectives on the issues and events that marked the twentieth century, particularly during the period between 1920 and the mid-1970s. Thus, the volume stands on its own quite well. All academic and public libraries should purchase this very reasonably priced volume.—**Ken Middleton**

DICTIONARIES AND ENCYCLOPEDIAS

C
306. **Encyclopedia of Women & Islamic Cultures. Volume II: Family, Law and Politics.** Joseph Suad and others, eds. Boston, Brill Academic, 2005. 837p. index. $296.00. ISBN 90-04-12818-2.

C
307. **Encyclopedia of Women & Islamic Cultures. Volume III: Family, Body, Sexuality, and Health.** Suad Joseph, ed. Boston, Brill Academic, 2006. 564p. index. $296.00. ISBN 90-04-13247-3.

The second volume in this 6 volume series, with volume 6 serving as the cumulative index, focuses on family, law, and politics (see ARBA 2005, entry 870, for a review of volume 1). "Family, Law, and Politics" serves to "bring together the core materials of state functioning, especially through law, in relation to family" (p. xxvii). The volume is arranged topically. The 11 sections focus on law-related subheadings, including law enforcement, articulation of Islamic and non-Islamic systems, and access to the legal system. The nine sections focus on political social movements subheadings. The volume also includes a section on women's studies programs in Muslim countries, which includes three entries. Most sections offer an overview followed by entries by geographic region for that topic. The general editor acknowledges the geographic gaps and inconsistencies across the sections. While representative scholarship is not available for all regions, this volume does a great job of facilitating access and understanding on the subject in a useful way. Each of the 360 entries are signed and followed by a bibliography. The international contributors and scholarship they cite provides balance to the entries. A name index and subject index are also included, adding to its ease of use.

The third volume focuses on family, body, sexuality, and health. This volume presents 196 articles that discuss such issues as aging, breastfeeding, celibacy, courtship, genital cutting, HIV and AIDS, reproduction, incest, sexual harassment, suicide, and virginity. The editors admit that this appears to be a disparate grouping of topics; however, they pull together the topics by defining the body as "at once a biological entity and a product of cultures, of specific context, and of the genealogies of knowledge which constitute local understandings of the body, its capacities, purposes, possibilities, regulations, and limitations" (p. xxi). The entries are well written and accessible for all levels of users. This series is recommended for all collections.—**Courtney L. Young**

C, P, S

308. **Encyclopedia of Women's Autobiography.** Victoria Boynton and Jo Malin, eds. Westport, Conn., Greenwood Press, 2005. 2v. index. $249.95/set. ISBN 0-313-32737-8.

A valuable tool for women's studies, Boynton and Malin's scholarly collection of 200 essays by 142 specialists investigates the range and motivation of women's self-analysis. The text covers authors, classic titles, and humanistic and literary themes. Commentary on voice, memory, patriarchy, feminism, race, and sexuality clarifies the female perspective on issues that define and constrain women. Coverage of global and cultural trends expands the scope to views on situational focus, genre selection, and individual style. Enhancing the applicability of the work to research, lesson planning, and library reference are an appendix of authors and works by culture and nation and a chronological listing of authors from Hildegard von Bingen to Donna Williams. In addition to ample entry bibliographies, a general bibliography suggests research on autobiography as a genre. Meticulous indexing directs the user to such subtopics as pioneers, otherness, the Jewish diaspora, lesbianism, and domestic abuse. Weaknesses are few. The editors overlook the bi-cultural adventurism of Welsh governess Anna Leonowens, the naïve female narrator in Laura Ingalls Wilder's Little House series, and the advocacy of suffragist Helen Keller for handicapped women. These two volumes should fill a niche in public, high school, and college libraries. [R: LJ, 15 Oct 05, p. 82; BL, 1 & 15 Jan 06, p. 150]—**Mary Ellen Snodgrass**

C, S

309. Mays, Dorothy A. **Women in Early America: Struggle, Survival, and Freedom in a New World.** Santa Barbara, Calif., ABC-CLIO, 2004. 495p. illus. index. $95.00; $100.00 (e-book). ISBN 1-85109-429-6; 1-85109-434-2 (e-book).

An encyclopedic treatment of women in early America from the founding of Jamestown in 1607 to the outbreak of the War of 1812, this volume seeks to redress the idea that women did not play an important role in the founding of the American colonies. As the author contends, while women may not have played a direct role in landmark events, the survival of the colonies, in part, depended on them. In her 175 alphabetically arranged entries, the author highlights scholarship of the last several decades that illuminates the contributions of women to early American life, focusing specifically on women of European ancestry (primary English, French, German, Dutch, and Spanish) as well as Native American, Africans, and African Americans. Geographically, the volume is limited to the territory that later became part of the United States, and primarily the east coast and the eighteenth-century frontier, an area defined as "rarely west of Ohio and Alabama" (p. xvi). Intended for a pre-college and college-level audience, each essay provides suggestions for further reading, representing the leading scholarship in the field. While the volume is indexed, a topic finder also provides subject-level access to the entries on 67 topics spanning the public and private spheres, and inclusive of race, class, gender, religion, and sexual orientation. Additional useful features include appendixes on "Household Chores Common to Early American Women," and a selection of primary documents. An excellent topically arranged annotated bibliography provides access to the best literature in the field as current as 2004, and includes sections on primary source readers, historical fiction, and online resources. This work will be an excellent addition to any high school or college library. [R: SLJ, April 05, p. 84]—**Lisa Kay Speer**

C

310. **The Women's Movement Today: An Encyclopedia of Third-Wave Feminism.** Leslie L. Heywood, ed. Westport, Conn., Greenwood Press, 2006. 2v. index. $199.95/set. ISBN 0-313-33133-2.

The topic of this new, two-volume encyclopedia is "the third wave of feminism," sometimes also referred to as "post-feminism," which is considered to have begun in the early 1990s. The first volume consists of more than 200 encyclopedic entries, while the second volume is made up of 65 primary documents (i.e., previously published articles, from books and periodicals, written mostly by women). The scope of the work is "multidisciplinary, multicultural, inclusive of diverse gender orientations and sexualities." The focus of the encyclopedia is almost exclusively on women's movement in the United States, although some other English-speaking countries are also included. The length of the entries varies from one paragraph to several pages. Each entry includes a note on further reading. Apart from an introduction and the encyclopedia section itself, volume 1 consists of a chronology, starting from 1991, an alphabetic and a topical index to the entries, a selected bibliography with dozens of relevant Websites and films, and a list of contributors. Although the chronology starts with Anita Hill, also referred to several times in a number of entries, there is no entry for her; however, there are entries for many lesser-known women. And while an entry has been assigned to "sex tourism/sex work," there is no entry for "sex trafficking," a crime industry that is currently the second most profitable after drug trafficking and whose victims are almost exclusively women. Articles in volume 2 are arranged under 4 main headings: "Third-wave Feminism: Definitions and Debates"; "Consumerism, Globalization, and Third-wave Lives"; "Resisting Culture"; and "Producing Third-wave Identities." Altogether *The Women's Movement Today* is an interesting and informative reference work and an indispensable tool for anyone doing research on any feminist issue since 1990, or for anyone who simply wants to know about recent developments in feminism.—**Leena Siegelbaum**

HANDBOOKS AND YEARBOOKS

C, S

311.   Frost-Knappman, Elizabeth. Cullen-DuPont, Kathryn, ed. **Women's Suffrage in America.** updated ed. New York, Facts on File, 2005. 496p. illus. index. (Eyewitness History). $75.00. ISBN 0-8160-5693-5.

There are very few people left who might remember firsthand any aspect of the trials and tribulations of the three-quarters of a century it took, roughly 1848 to 1920, for women to achieve the right to vote in the United States of America. This updated work may tweak our collective unconscious and give us a feel for the perseverance and strength of will necessary to accomplish enfranchisement for women. It documents, by way of hundreds of historical resources such as letters, diaries, speeches, sermon excerpts, photographs, flyers, and legal petitions, the long, emotional, even violent history of women's struggles for the right to vote. The editors of this work have published widely in the area of women's studies. Kathryn Cullen-DuPont wrote or edited such books as the *Encyclopedia of Women's History in America*, winner of the New York Public Library's "Outstanding Reference Book of 1997" (2d ed., see ARBA 2001, entry 899; and ARBA 97, entry 736) as well as books about Elizabeth Cady Stanton and Margaret Sanger. Elizabeth Frost-Knappman, editor and literary agent, is president and founder of New England Publishing Associates (NEPA), which specializes in nonfiction books, including four on women's studies. This book, part of the 19-volume Facts on File "Eyewitness Series," is bound to be a favorite of history and women's studies professors, who are more and more requesting that students venture into the primary source literature to retrieve actual documentation that may represent an era, a movement, a historical construct. Each of the 13 chapters covers a chronological period (e.g., "What Do Women Want? 1800-1834"). Chapters are consistently arranged: historical context, chronicle of events, and eyewitness testimony. Photographs and drawings supplement the narrative text. Near the book's end are appendixes containing documents, biographies of major personalities, and U.S. maps charting 19th Amendment ratification, state by state. This well-edited and substantially updated title (over 50 new pages and 800 new dates) is recommended for 9th grade students and up. It will be equally at home on the shelves of public and undergraduate college libraries, alongside such titles as *International Encyclopedia of Women's Suffrage* from ABC-CLIO (see ARBA 2001, entry 901). [R: SLJ, Oct 05, p. 88]—**Linda D. Tietjen**

C

312.   Sheffield, Suzanne Le-May. **Women and Science: Social Impact and Interaction.** Santa Barbara, Calif., ABC-CLIO, 2004. 409p. illus. index. (Science and Society). $75.00; $80.00 (e-book). ISBN 1-85109-460-1; 1-85109-465-2 (e-book).

Women and Science is a monograph in the Science and Society series edited by Mark A. Largent. It is bound and sized to look like a textbook, but it would serve equally well as a popular nonfiction book for middle school and above audiences interested in the history of science, the history of women, or who need more information on one of the women profiled in the book.

The book consists of chapters on various aspects of women and science, including sections on women as science writers, women as assistants, educating women in science, and feminine/feminist science. The second half of the book is devoted to supporting materials such as a glossary, chronology, extensive bibliography, primary documents, and the index. *Women and Science* is recommended for academic institutions with women's studies or history of science collections.—**Christina K. Pikas**

Part III
HUMANITIES

19 Humanities in General

GENERAL WORKS

Dictionaries and Encyclopedias

C, P

313.   **Encyclopedia of the Harlem Renaissance.** Cary D. Wintz and Paul Finkelman, eds. New York, Routledge/Taylor & Francis Group, 2004. 2v. illus. index. $225.00/set. ISBN 1-57958-389-X.

As the preface to these two volumes points out, the exact dates, success, and even whether the ultimate effect of the Harlem Renaissance was positive or negative are subject to debate, and the 260 different contributors reflect these differences. The influence of Harlem on the arts was strongest between World War I and the late 1930s and geographically extended far beyond New York City as blues and jazz migrated north from New Orleans, Memphis, and St. Louis. The famed Cotton Club with its black performers and white patrons typified the ambiguities as it extended appreciation for black music and culture without promoting integration.

The *Encyclopedia of the Harlem Renaissance* is organized for easy use. An alphabetic list of entries is followed by a thematic list divided by persons (from actors to writers), works, topics (ideologies to politics), organizations (businesses to theater companies), and periodicals. A map of Harlem is shaded to show its size in three distinct phases between 1913 and 1930.

The 640 major entries include both black writers such as W. E. B. Du Bois and James Weldon Johnson who recognized the movement as a new identity rather than an artistic rebirth, and white writers like Carl Van Vechten and Sherwood Anderson who were influenced by it. The topical essays are especially informative. Many of the entries have illustrations and all are followed by brief bibliographies for further reading. A 44-page index makes it easy to find or cross reference material. The two-volume encyclopedia is an invaluable resource that extensively documents the events, people, and importance of the Harlem Renaissance. [R: LJ, 1 Nov 04, pp. 122-124]—**Charlotte Lindgren**

C, P

314.   **Oxford Dictionary of Phrase and Fable.** 2d ed. Elizabeth Knowles, ed. New York, Oxford University Press, 2005. 805p. $40.00. ISBN 0-19-860981-7.

This 2d edition, revised and updated from its first appearance in 2000 (see ARBA 2001, entry 913), includes the origins of hundreds of phrases in the English language. Familiar and obscure names and sayings, from ancient times up to the present, are available in this book that draw's from Oxford's bank of reference and language online resources. Areas such as popular culture, folk customs, science and technology, history, mythology, philosophy, religion, and superstitions are some of the topics from which word origins, sayings, maxims, proverbs, and adages are drawn. If a user wants to find out what "dark matter" is, what "elephant in the room" means, or what the origin of "women and children first" is, then this is where to find out. The *Oxford Dictionary of Phrase and Fable* will make a worthwhile addition to any library's reference collection.—**Bradford Lee Eden**

Directories

C, P

315. **Directory of Grants in the Humanities 2005/2006.** 19th ed. Jeremy T. Miner and Lynn E. Miner, eds. Westport, Conn., Oryx Press/Greenwood Press, 2005. 876p. index. $89.95pa. ISBN 1-57356-616-0.

The format of this annual guide to grant-funding opportunities in the arts and humanities has remained unchanged in recent years. As with earlier editions an alphabetic list of public and private funding programs continues to make up the majority of the volume. Although the focus is on programs in the United States, a small portion of the list refers to programs in Canada and several other countries. Each entry includes: name and description of the grant; requirements and restrictions for application; examples of previous awards; typical funding amounts; application deadline; contact telephone number, fax number, and e-mail address; Internet address (if available); and sponsor contact information. The program number entry for grants that are also listed in the *Catalog of Federal Domestic Assistance* is provided. Four indexes offer useful access points—a subject index, a sponsoring organization index, a program type index (which arranges grants into 37 broad categories), and a geographic index for grants that focus on a particular locale. Useful introductory sections provide guidance on efficient use of the volume, helpful information on grant writing, and a directory of sponsors with Internet sites (URLs are included). While even more up-to-date information can be obtained for a fee through the *GRANTS Database*, this annual volume remains a valuable resource for both academic and public libraries of all sizes.—**Janet Dagenais Brown**

20 Communication and Mass Media

GENERAL WORKS

Dictionaries and Encyclopedias

C

316. **American Voices: An Encyclopedia of Contemporary Orators.** Bernard K. Duffy and Richard W. Leeman, eds. Westport, Conn., Greenwood Press, 2005. 486p. index. $125.00. ISBN 0-313-32790-4.

This volume could be considered to be volume 3 in an unnumbered set, with the two previous works being *American Orators of the Twentieth Century* and *American Orators Before 1900*. The current work covers recent orators, with politicians, activists, and jurists the primary subjects. American presidents and "recognized speakers" from the 1960s have been included. Some 61 editors and contributors worked on the project, which took 4 years to complete. There are 58 entries, 41 of which cover male orators, with 17 female orators (even though the book cover art shows one male and two females).

The editors indicate that they tried to use a " broad net for inclusion," and to some degree that effort has been successful. African American men and women have been included, as well as a person of Hispanic origin and an American Indian, but no entry for an Asian American person can be found. To most readers who have been tuned into the mass media during the recent past, the names of the overwhelming majority of the entries will be quite familiar. There may be a few names that do not immediately come to mind, but as soon as you read the entries and recognize the contexts, the inclusions will make eminent sense.

Each entry includes some biographical details before launching into a consideration of the oratorical record. The entries close with locations of research collections and collected speeches, some selected critical studies, and a chronology of major speeches. The contributors to this work are, with three exceptions, all college and university professors. Some 52 of the 61 are in speech communication or communication studies, or communications departments (2 are in mass communication and political communication). The uses for this volume include: general reference for the biographical information, and as a textbook for communication and political science classes. *American Voices: An Encyclopedia of Contemporary Orators* is recommended. [R: LJ, 15 Nov 05, p. 93; SLJ, Dec 05, p. 90]—**Graham R. Walden**

Handbooks and Yearbooks

C, S

317. Signorielli, Nancy. **Violence in the Media: A Reference Handbook.** Santa Barbara, Calif., ABC-CLIO, 2005. 263p. index. (Contemporary World Issues). $50.00; $55.00 (e-book). ISBN 1-85109-604-3; 1-85109-6009-4 (e-book).

Although much has been written about mass media and the portrayal of violence, the most current entry in the Contemporary World Issues series from ABC-CLIO offers an effective mix of narrative discussion with traditional reference format. By combining an overview of basic theoretical concepts with practical resources for further research, it provides a good starting point for readers unfamiliar with the subject

The first three chapters focus on the history of violence and the mass media; an overview of scholarly research covering media content and its effects; and problems, current controversies, and possible solutions. These chapters also provide useful bibliographies. The remaining chapters of the book provide information for additional research, including: an annotated bibliography of print, film, and video resources; a facts and figures section; and a list of organizations and Websites. Less useful sections include a compilation of biographical sketches and a chronology that includes a number of entries with little apparent relevance to the central topic.

Curiously, this is presented as a 1st edition by the publisher despite the fact there was an earlier publication in the series titled *Violence and the Media: A Reference Handbook* that closely resembles this book (see ARBA 97, entry 748). Notwithstanding the similarities between the two, the changes in the legal/regulatory environment and the amount of scholarly research completed in the interim provide an appreciable amount of unique content. The author, a University of Delaware communications professor, has researched and published extensively in areas related to mass media effect and portrayal. This work is recommended for academic libraries serving undergraduates and public libraries.—**Patrick J. Reakes**

AUTHORSHIP

General Works

Directories

P
318.   **Children's Writer's & Illustrator's Market, 2006.** 18th ed. Alice Pope, ed. Cincinnati, Ohio, Writer's Digest Books/F & W Publications, 2006. 448p. index. $24.99pa. ISBN 1-58297-402-0.

The 18th edition of this annual directory is more than just a "how to" source for creating plots, characters, or illustrations for children's books. It also includes such business principles as promotion and marketing. Experts in children's literature offer advice on such varied topics as creating Websites, creating promotional materials, converting books to film, co-editing anthologies, and more. The "Markets" section of the book includes insider reports from editors, authors, and illustrators. Markets highlighted are for U.S. book publishers; international book publishers; publishers of greeting cards, puzzles, and games; play publishers and producers; and young writer's and illustrator's markets.

The "Resources" section contains not just a helpful list of books and publications, but also information about agents and representatives; clubs; regional and national conferences and workshops; contests, awards, and grants; and online resources. A glossary and five indexes complete the work. The indexes are by age-level, subject, poetry, photography, and a general index. The authors suggest beginning with the indexes to determine which companies buy the type of manuscript one might be interested in submitting for publication. Listings are very concise; many of them begin with one or more symbols to avoid repetition and to save space. This is a must-have resource for those who wish to specialize in writing or illustrating for the children's market. The price makes it affordable for individuals and the smallest of public and academic libraries.—**Lois Gilmer**

Handbooks and Yearbooks

P

319.   Feiertag, Joe, Mary Carmen Cupito, and the Editors of Writer's Digest Books. **Writer's Market Companion.** 2d ed. Cincinnati, Ohio, Writer's Digest Books/F & W Publications, 2004. 344p. index. $19.99pa. ISBN 1-58297-291-5.

The *Writer's Market Companion* provides a wealth of information on the process of writing and publishing. The readable text offers sound advice, presents topics in a logical order, and lists a wide variety of resources for completing each step of the process. The content and organization of the 2d edition are comparable to those of the 1st edition (see ARBA 2001, entry 926). The beginning writer can consult the volume for information about topics such as current trends in the publishing industry; investigating and generating topics; research tools and strategies for writing; selling, promoting, and submitting work to publishers and media outlets; legal, financial, and tax issues; finding a community of writers; and financial support (including fellowships, grants, and prizes). The authors have also addressed timely technology issues. Information is presented on writing e-books and other content for the Web, formatting and submitting e-mail inquiries, and legal rights in the world of electronic writing and publishing. The appendixes include guidelines and resources for setting and negotiating fees and rates, and managing expenses; additional lists of reference resources for writers (including books, Websites, magazines, and newsletters); lists of publishers and their imprints; and a glossary of publishing terms. The index is rather limited (under six pages), but straightforward. *Writer's Market, 2005* (see ARBA 2005, entry 892) includes some information presented in the *Writer's Market Companion* (such as lists of publishers and their imprints, and guidelines for crafting a query letter). On the other hand, the *Writer's Market Companion* provides a more extensive overview of the entire process of writing and publishing. Public and academic libraries that purchase the long-standing *Writer's Market* should also consider adding the *Writer's Market Companion* to their collections.—**Sharon Ladenson**

Style Manuals

C, P

320.   **The Cambridge Guide to English Usage.** By Pam Peters. New York, Cambridge University Press, 2004. 608p. $35.00. ISBN 0-521-62181-X.

The Cambridge Guide to English Usage is a comprehensive guide to style and usage intended for writers, editors, teachers, and students. In an alphabetic format, these entries address easily confused terms, alternate spellings, grammar, political correctness issues, diacritics, punctuation, commonly used foreign terms, and myriad other language questions. The "international" scope indicated on the cover means that the "English" here includes American, British, Canadian, and Australian conventions, based on corpus data as well as language reference books used in these countries. As noted in the front matter, this guide is "descriptive" rather than "prescriptive," and thus the user can make an informed choice. This reviewer found the explanations for that old bugbear "that or which?" both thorough and enlightening. With more than 4,000 entries, *The Cambridge Guide to English Usage* offers a wealth of information for all English users. [R: LJ, 15 June 04, p. 96; BL, 15 Oct 04, p. 436]—**Lori D. Kranz**

P

321.   Einsohn, Amy. **The Copyeditor's Handbook: A Guide for Book Publishing and Corporate Communications.** 2d ed. Berkeley, Calif., University of California Press, 2006. 560p. index. $19.95pa. ISBN 0-520-24688-8.

This 2d edition of *The Copyeditor's Handbook* by Amy Einsohn, a veteran editor with 25 years of experience in trade and scholarly publishing, provides up-to-date information on copyediting in the book publishing and corporate fields. This book has been updated with the latest information from the new editions of *The Chicago Manual of Style* (15th ed.; University of Chicago Press, 2003), the *Publication Manual of the American Psychological Association* (5th ed.; see ARBA 2003, entry 891), and *Merriam-Webster's Collegiate Dictionary* (11th ed.; see ARBA 2004, entry 29). No other new material appears to have been added from the 1st edition (see ARBA 2001, entry 932).

The book discusses in depth the "ABC's of Copyediting," including what copyeditor's do, basic procedures of hard copy and on-screen editing, and essential reference books and resources. Einsohn then goes on to discuss editorial style topics, such as punctuation, spelling and hyphenation, capitalization, numbers and numerals, handling quotations, abbreviations and acronyms, references, tables and art, front and back matter, and typecoding (codes used in the typesetting process). The final section discusses language editing to make the writing clearer in meaning as well as grammatically correct. The final chapter discusses bias-free language as well as publishing law. The work concludes with a sample checklist of editorial preferences, a glossary of copyediting terms, a glossary of grammar terms, a selected bibliography, and an index.

This handbook remains a valuable guide for those just entering the copyediting and publishing business as well as for those veterans that need to keep up with the new rules. Libraries owning the 1st edition of this volume may not want to invest in the 2d edition since very little new information has been added or updated. However, those that missed out on the 1st edition may want to offer the 2d edition of this worthwhile copyediting guide to their patrons.—**Shannon Graff Hysell**

RADIO, TELEVISION, AUDIO, AND VIDEO

Biography

C, P

322.   Cox, Jim. **Music Radio: The Great Performers and Programs of the 1920s Through Early 1960s.** Jefferson, N.C., McFarland, 2005. 369p. illus. index. $55.00. ISBN 0-7864-2047-2.

Much of the history of radio during the "Golden Age" (the period from the 1920s through approximately the early 1960s) has been well documented. Ironically, the resources covering details of the radio music of the era are scarce. Author Jim Cox, an avowed fan of Old Time Radio (OTR) as well as a knowledgeable radio historian, recognized the lack of a comprehensive source and attempts to fill that gap with this book. Cox, well known by OTR enthusiasts, has written six previous books on topics related to radio history. His appreciation of early music radio is apparent, and he provides insightful narrative giving the book a unique feel that qualifies it as more than simply a reference source. Cox supplies context by providing the reader with valuable background information and mixing well-informed discussion with reference entries. The book consists of 19 sections, 9 of which cover specific programs. The 10 remaining entries cover groups of performers (e.g., Big Bands, Disc Jockeys, Horse Operas). Chapter notes, a bibliography, illustrations, and an extensive index are provided, adding value as a research source. One minor drawback is the disconcerting organization of the book. Although the sections are in alphabetic order, the sections covering performers and programs are interspersed together. Separating the performer entries and the program entries may have been more effective and the combined entries may be confusing to the reader.

The length of the entries, along with the narrative format, make this the type of book that many patrons may want to sit and read. Despite the seemingly specialized topic of the book, the nature of the subject and Cox's writing style could give it broader appeal. *Music Radio* is recommended for both public libraries and academic libraries, particularly those supporting music and/or mass communication programs. —**Patrick J. Reakes**

Chronology

C, P

323.   Sampson, Henry T. **Swingin' on the Ether Waves: A Chronological History of African Americans in Radio and Television Programming, 1925-1955.** Lanham, Md., Scarecrow, 2005. 2v. illus. index. $395.95/set. ISBN 0-8108-4087-1.

This large, two-volume chronological history attempts to document the contributions of African Americans to broadcasting in the United States, from the birth of commercial radio broadcasting to 1955. While a number of other books on commercial broadcasting have covered the African American contribution, this is the first attempt at a comprehensive, year-by-year chronology. Much of the information has been gleaned from radio and television trade publications, and African American newspapers. In many cases the primary sources have been reproduced directly into this the chronology, which is arranged by date beginning with an entry for October 24, 1924. In addition to the chronology are a number of useful appendixes, including a list of African American Radio and Television Programs, Miller and Lyles Radio Script, Amoe's Wedding Radio Script, Cab Calloway's Quizzical Script, and others. The work also includes a name index. The great value of *Swingin' on the Ether Waves* is that it provides original reviews, articles, and other materials from the sources consulted, providing a wealth of research materials for students and scholars. The work is highly recommended for all public and academic libraries, and is a must for all dedicated African American collections. [R: LJ, 15 Nov 05, p. 98]—**Robert L. Wick**

Directories

P

324.   **Video Source Book: A Guide to Programs Currently Available on Video ....** 34th ed. Farmington Hills, Mich., Gale, 2005. 3v. index. $510.00/set. ISBN 0-7876-8970-X. ISSN 0748-0881.

Now in its 34th edition, this *Video Source Book* (VSB; see ARBA 2004, entry 895, for a review of the 30th edition), is universally recognized as one of the two standard reference sources for locating in-print video programs. The other, *Bowker's Complete Video Directory* (see ARBA 96, entry 986), is the direct competitor of VSB. The VSB provides access to over 126,000 complete programs, encompassing over 165,000 videos (8mm, DVD). All subject areas are covered (movies, entertainment, education, how-to) in a single alphabetic listing. A typical entry includes year of release, a plot synopsis, credits, target audience, ratings, producer, and purchase/rental information. Reviews for theatrical releases are taken from a sister publication, *VideoHound's Golden Movie Retriever* (see entry 418). Access to the main group of listings is provided by seven indexes: alternate title, subject, credits, awards, special formats, and program distributors. As noted in the past review of VSB, while Bowker's is very similar to this source, there are potentially important differences. Bowker's, a four-volume set compared to VSB's three volumes, separates "Entertainment" from "Education/Special Interest" unlike the VSB, which lists all programs in a single alphabetic list. Compiled from the *Books in Print* database (see ARBA 2002, entry 10), Bowker's includes ISBN numbers that many libraries use in ordering material for its collections. Also, for entertainment listings, Bowker's provides a separate entry for each release of the film. For instance, the movie *Fatal Attraction* has an extra entry (plus detailed information) for the "Director's Cut," while VSB merely notes the new offering in its single entry for the film. The reviews for theatrical releases are "hipper" in VSB and patrons may not care if complete ordering information is not provided. For in-house library use, however, *Bowker's* at $405 for four volumes compared with VSB at $510 for three volumes would seem to be the better choice. This work is recommended for public and university libraries.—**David K. Frasier**

21 Decorative Arts

COLLECTING

General Work

P

325. **Made in the Twentieth Century: A Guide to Contemporary Collectibles.** Paul, Larry. Lanham, Md., Scarecrow, 2005. 334p. index. $34.95pa. ISBN 0-8108-4563-6.

This book is designed to help lay people and antique dealers quickly establish the approximate production date of most twentieth-century manufactured items. The author has been a collector and antiques dealer for over 35 years. The book is basically divided into two parts: basic information related to all items produced in the twentieth century, and specialized information related to various areas of research or collecting. Caution notes are constantly provided by the author to keep the reader from misinterpreting information. While probably not a reference book for academic libraries, some public libraries would probably want to have this in their reference collection. This is an interesting and helpful resource for anyone trying to determine whether their "antiques" are really worth something or not.—**Bradford Lee Eden**

Antiques

P

326. **Antique Trader Antiques & Collectibles 2006 Price Guide.** Kyle Husfloen, ed. Iola, Wis., Krause Publications, 2005. 1072p. illus. index. $19.99pa. ISBN 0-87349-989-1.

The *Antique Trader Antiques & Collectibles Price Guide* traces its roots back to 1970 where it was first published as a monthly newsletter entitled *The Antique Trader Price Guide to Antiques and Collectors' Items*. The annual guides started coming out 20 years ago in 1984 and this is the 21st anniversary edition. The main competitor to this guide is the *Official Price Guide to Antiques and Collectibles* by the House of Collectibles, which started in 1979. There is a little bit of rivalry between these two publications with the *Official Guide* claiming to have 60,000 prices listed, while the *Antique Trader Guide* lists 12,500 prices. The main difference between the two guides, however, is that the *Official Guide* only has one-line entries for each item, while the *Antique Trader Guide* a has some 11 or more lines of descriptive information with each illustration.

The arrangement of the price guide is by type: glass, toys, ceramics, furniture, firearms, kitchenware, rugs, and more. Almost 400 pages of the 1,072-page volume is devoted to various types of glass and ceramic collectables. In some cases the condition of the item is noted; for example, a doll might be listed as having repair to left arm, but prices are assumed to be for items that are in the best possible condition. The book is illustrated with over 5,800 color photographs. The author has written a number of specialty antique monographs including ones on Black Americana, clocks, lamps, and tools. The volume has a table of contents to the types categories and an index that also contains *see also* references for a number of terms. Overall, the work is well done and very attractive. The additional descriptive entries help the reader to better identify the item at hand. Prices stated seem fair for items in mint condition. Like many readers this reviewer is always disappointed with the limited number of items that can be covered in general guide compendiums such as this, but nonetheless it is a handy one-volume guide that will be useful in most reference collections.—**Ralph Lee Scott**

P

327.   Kovel, Ralph, and Terry Kovel. **Kovels' American Antiques 1750-1900.** New York, Random House, 2004. 384p. illus. index. $24.95pa. ISBN 0-609-80892-3.

Ralph and Terry Kovel have written a very readable guide that covers 23 basic areas of antique collecting. Typical topics covered are: dolls, clocks, tools, silver, jewelry, textiles, lighting fixtures, furniture, glass, and bottles. Special sections at the end cover nineteenth-century jewelry and metalwork marks and a bibliography of additional recommended readings. The topics are covered in a general, basic way. For example the "Tools" section consists of three pages of general information on woodworking tools, a brief history the Stanley tool brand, and a page on antique fire fighting equipment.

Readers who are familiar with the Kovel's television show on Home and Garden Television's *Flea Market Finds with the Kovels*, will recognize the format in which the authors describe antique items. The work is heavily illustrated and attractive to read and view. Many pages are accompanied by sidebars with topics like "Is it flint glass?" and "Materials used for wicker furniture." Readers will find basic information on American antiques and if they can look past the authors' chatty television writing style, some highly valuable information for beginning collectors. If you want advice on the family antique Stradivarius your aunt has that was passed down through the generations, then this is the place to start. Advanced dealers and collectors will find the work a useful refresher in areas they are not familiar with. *Kovels' American Antiques 1750-1900* is recommended for general reference collections as a basic antique reference tool.—**Ralph Lee Scott**

Coins (and Paper Money)

P

328.   **U.S. Coin Digest 2006: A Guide to Average Retail Prices from the Market Experts.** Joel Edler and Dave Harper, eds. Iola, Wis., Krause Publications, 2005. 262. illus. index. $12.99 spiralbound. ISBN 0-87349-165-8.

The *U.S. Coin Digest* is a guide to United States coinage and valuations. The first 60-plus pages are packed with information on the history of American coinage, mechanics of coin production, grading, and so on. Following these initial chapters, coins are listed by denomination starting with the smallest, the half-cent, then within a denomination, coins are listed by year of production. Each denomination or type of coin is shown with a half-tone photograph, both obverse and reverse, and in some cases sections may be shown magnified to highlight a special feature. A short paragraph describing the coin and any interesting historical bit of information is included in the entry.

The primary use of a guidebook like this is the assignment of market valuations. What distinguishes this guide from others is the number of grades listed for each coin, typically 4 to 6 grades. Other guides may give 3 or 4. A grade is the code numismatists use to reflect the condition of the coin. Although the code is a standard, applying it is still a subjective process. The advantage to having more grades gives the collector an improved chance of accurately evaluating a specimen in hand, which translates to improved valuation accuracy. Grading and valuations are not linear. Therefore, trying to estimate grades and valuations between those listed can be problematic.

The main section of this guide is allotted to the standard United States Mint issues. There are additional sections, however, covering U.S. commemoratives, colonial coinage, territorial gold, and a small section on Hawaii, Philippines, and Puerto Rico coinage. These fringe coinages seldom get extensive treatment in other guides. An article-like chapter, appearing as an appendix, discusses a hoard of Carson City silver dollars. The index is adequate for a guide like this. This guide is suitable for public library reference collections.—**Margaret F. Dominy**

Firearms

P

329.   Schwing, Ned. **Standard Catalog of Firearms, 2005: The Collector's Price & Reference Guide.** 15th ed. Iola, Wis., Krause Publications, 2005. 1504p. illus. index. $34.99pa. ISBN 0-87349-900-X. ISSN 1520-4928.

This ready-reference guide to firearms provides pricing information for new and used civilian firearms and comes from a recognized subject authority. (Purely military firearms have their own separate volume, although "civilianized" variants of military weapons are covered here.) Coverage is thorough and comprehensive, with over 25,000 different weapon models (ranging from palm-sized derringers to the 35-pound Barrett Model 82 sniper rifle) being treated in a clear, accurate presentation of the salient facts. Such relative rarities as the Dardick and Glock pistols are represented, although the Gyrojet series is not, perhaps because, being a rocket weapon, it is not considered a "firearm." Most of the illustrations are in monochrome, with a small color insert displaying some particularly noteworthy specimens; all of the illustrations are clear and enable easy recognition of significant detail. In addition to the carefully categorized pricing information, introductory essays provide an illuminating summary of the collecting environment, and the main text is interspersed with collector advice and individual reminiscences concerning particularly popular examples of the gun maker's art. A table of contents, running heads, and an index make finding any specific item fast and easy. A high standard of accuracy is maintained throughout.

This volume is sturdily perfect-bound in a lay-flat binding, and clearly printed on good-quality newsprint, deserving consideration from any library serving a firearms collection clientele. Worth noting is the capacity of this book to serve as a reasonably effective tool for firearms identification in addition to its primary function as a pricing guide.—**John Howard Oxley**

Toys

P

330.   **Schroeder's Collectible Toys, 2006: Antique to Modern Price Guide.** 10th ed. Sharon Huxford and Bob Huxford, eds. Paducah, Ky., Collector Books, 2006. 499p. illus. index. $17.95pa. ISBN 1-57432-479-9.

Toys have become one of the hottest collectibles in the last decade. This guide provides current price and identification information for more than 20,000 toys. Entries are divided into several categories, such as battery-operated toys; character, TV, and movie collectibles; Disney; dolls and accessories; guns; Star Trek; and many more. Each entry is very brief with only a simple description of the item, a dealer code that corresponds to a guide in the back of the book, and a price.

Several black-and-white photographs help users identify items, but the brief descriptions will make it difficult for some users to locate the information they are looking for. The editors point out in their introduction that due to obvious space constraints there are numerous collectibles not included in this edition. Thus, while this work is fun to browse, users will need to consult more specialized price guide to find items not listed in this work.—**Shannon Graff Hysell**

INTERIOR DESIGN

Dictionaries and Encyclopedias

C, P

331.   Woodham, Jonathan M. **A Dictionary of Modern Design.** New York, Oxford University Press, 2004. 520p. index. $45.00. ISBN 0-19-280097-3.

This dictionary covers the last 150 years of international modern designing lexicon. By design, the author does not just mean fashion (although that is included), but instead the whole panoply of design from cars to buildings and furniture to brands. Within these pages are references to Volkswagen, Coco Chanel, Coca-Cola, Frank Lloyd Wright, Charles Rennie Mackintosh, Apple Computer Macintosh, Laura Ashley, Ikea, Mercedes-Benz, and Olivetti. The dictionary includes brief articles that focus on the major movements and key concepts of the age (such as the differences between Moderne and Modernism) as well as entries on key figures, events, and companies. The dictionary includes selected iconic black-and-white illustrations of modern zeitgeist designs such as Lego people, Mary Quant clothes, and Fiskars scissors, along with an index, timelines, and a bibliography. While much of this information is available scattered elsewhere, this new dictionary makes a useful selection for academic libraries and larger public libraries. [R: LJ, 15 April 05, p. 124]—**Neal Wyatt**

Handbooks and Yearbooks

C, P

332.   Bowers, Helen. **Interior Materials & Surfaces: The Complete Guide.** New York, Firefly Books, 2004. 256p. illus. index. $35.00. ISBN 1-55297-967-9.

This specification guide to the array of materials useful in interior decorating covers 11 different categories of materials: wood, metal, glass, fabric, paper, leather, paint, ceramic, concrete, plaster, and a range of plastics. For each material type Bowers, a trained architect, describes the material's properties, use, maintenance, safety, environmental issues, specifications, availability, and cost. While each two-page section includes a full-page picture of the material, it is a close-up shot of a selection of material types or colors and not a picture of the material used in a design concept. While homeowners may find answers to some hard-to-find questions here (such as the use of fleece can reduce the level of chemical contaminates in a home), the lack of visual design ideas will limit the practical applications of the book. The real use of this book will be by professionals who want a quick ready-reference resource to general material issues. The work is recommended for academic libraries supporting programs in interior decorating and for public libraries.—**Neal Wyatt**

C, P

333.   Habegger, Jerryll, and Joseph H. Osman. **Sourcebook of Modern Furniture.** 3d ed. New York, W. W. Norton, 2005. 788p. index. $89.95. ISBN 0-393-73170-7.

The 3d edition of this essential guide to modern furniture now offers 2,000 entries (almost 800 more than the previous edition). Entries are organized by furniture type and include the date, designer, manufacturer, materials, and dimensions for each piece. The images that accompany the entries largely come from furniture manufacturers. Image quality is generally good, but there are occasional inconsistencies. A notable and welcome improvement is the inclusion of many color images. A chronology of specific furniture pieces with brief descriptions introduces the dictionary. Indexes of designers, model names, and manufacturers provide a choice of access points. The list of suppliers is also helpful, but could be improved by the inclusion of more Internet addresses. The breadth of this work and its ease of use make it an indispensable source for students, designers, and the general public.—**John Schlinke**

22 Fine Arts

GENERAL WORKS

Biography

C, P

334.   **Biographical Encyclopedia of Artists.** Sir Lawrence Gowing, ed. New York, Facts on File, 2005. 4v. illus. index. $260.00/set. ISBN 0-8160-5803-2.

Considered as a companion to the *Facts on File Encyclopedia of Art* (2005) , this four-volume set contains biographies of artists working in a wide range of media in the visual arts. The set includes not only artists in the canon of Western art but also artists of the late twentieth and early twenty-first centuries and from under-represented groups, including women. The authors claim that "no major Western artist is missing" (p. vii), a valid claim based on checking a small random sample of entries from a current history of Western art against the source's coverage. The book includes artists from other cultures only if the contributors/editors had an "impression personal enough to compare with those of our own" (p. vii). Each entry contains basic biographical data, descriptive characteristics of artist's creative output, significance of work, career milestones, locations where artist's work is displayed, and sometimes bibliographies for additional reading. The size of entry ranges from one paragraph to several pages. More significant artists merit more in-depth treatment and longer entries. The entries are not signed, but a list of contributors and their affiliations, but not their article responsibility, is included separately. Black-and-white and colored reproductions illustrate the volumes; captions indicate the artist, title of work, medium, size, creation date, and current location/owner. Besides the individual entries, the books also contain a 25-page glossary of art terms, some illustrated by black-and-white drawings, and a chronology of artists grouped by nationality with nationalities covered varying over time periods. The chronology does not cover all artists included in the volumes, and there is no table of contents listing all artists in the book. Arranged alphabetically by artist, the set also has a single index to all entries, which appears only in volume 4. The index, printed in minuscule, almost unreadable print, covers subjects of entries, including glossary terms, major locations, and concepts. The index is sporadic in including access to illustrations, with access to some titles through a subdivision under the artist, but does not does not include access by title of art work for paintings mentioned in the biographies, a significant lack. Brief picture acknowledgments are noted alphabetically by source in volume 1.

Gowing was Slade Professor of Fine Art, University College, London, and has published research on several major British and European artists; his team of editors are all distinguished art scholars from Great Britain. The approximately 88 contributors are mainly from the British Isles. The book is adapted, with updates, from Encyclopaedia Britannica's *Encyclopedia of Visual Art* (Prentice Hall, 1983). Well written, the volumes are understandable by readers in the ninth grade or older. Supplementary access arrangements, such as the index and a table of contents, need improving. The publication's orientation, indicated in the preface but not in the title, is clearly to Western art. [R: LJ, Dec 05, pp. 170-174; BL, 1 & 15 Jan 06, p. 149]—**Marilyn Domas White**

Dictionaries and Encyclopedias

P

335. Chaplik, Dorothy. **Defining Latin American Art. Hacia una Definición del Arte Latinoamericano.** Jefferson, N.C., McFarland, 2005. 129p. illus. index. $45.00. ISBN 0-7864-1728-5.

Defining Latin American Art is a brief, bilingual history of its art and artists with stunning reproductions. It includes a table of contents and acknowledgments followed by a foreword. The foreword is a very critical review of the art establishment of Manhattan and the Latin American countries' apathy to support their own art and artists. The writer, Angel Hurtado, a former chief of the Audio Visual Unit, Art Museum of the Americas, Washington, D.C., is very positive about the author and her influence on viewing Latin American art. A preface, written by Chaplik, explains that "the book sets out to illustrate how Latin American art was influenced by the early twentieth century modernist movement in Europe, as well as by the muralist movement in Mexico" (p. 5).

Chapter 1, "Latin America: The Land and Its People," describes these factors and how they often create barriers, but also how they are linked by their proximity to each other and by their common history. Chapter 2, "Latin American Art," offers a brief description of various styles utilized by Latin American artists and describes how they use more than one style with a universal theme. Illustrations provide a brief description of numerous art works and a just as brief biography of the many artists, in an unknown order. There are both black-and-white and beautiful color reproductions of the same works. Confusion reigns when repetitive illustration numbers are used. To complete this small volume there is a selected bibliography that includes recorded interviews, books, and articles, as well as an index—the only listing in alphabetic order. This volume is recommended for public libraries with a bilingual community interested in a brief history of Latin American art.—**Nadine Salmons**

C, P

336. **The Complete Dictionary of Symbols.** Jack Tresidder, ed. San Francisco, Calif., Chronicle Books, 2004. 544p. illus. index. $22.95pa. ISBN 0-8118-4767-5.

This new resource on symbols is set apart from earlier works in that it aims to be more "worldwide" in its approach. The majority of entries, over 2,000, are related to Classical or Christian themes, but there are some examples of symbolism from other areas, such as Africa, North and South America, and Asia. The book is well constructed visually, with the main text offset by notes and cross-references in the margin printed in a light purple font, making them more noticeable and presumably more useful. Entries are alphabetical and range in length from a couple of sentences to an entire page. A few illustrations are included, perhaps fewer that other similar publications, but this allows the author to include a larger number of entries. The limited number of illustrations makes this book more useful to look up terms rather than pictorial symbols. Two useful finding aids include an index of themes and an index of supplementary words, which highlights terms used in the texts that are not main entries themselves. Some of the themes included in the index are "agriculture and food," "animals," and "hunters and hunting." A useful addition would have been themes by country, continent, or culture (such as "Africa" or "Incan") . The bibliography, however, does categorize books by region. *The Complete Dictionary of Symbols* is easy to use, provides concise but relevant information, and even supplies alternate versions of popular myths. It will be useful as a reference across many disciplines and is highly recommended. [R: SLJ, Aug 05, p. 78; LJ, 15 Mar 05, p. 116]—**Terrie L. Wilson**

C, P

337. **Facts on File Encyclopedia of Art.** Sir Lawrence Gowing, ed. New York, Facts on File, 2005. 5v. illus. index. $325.00/set. ISBN 0-8160-5797-4.

The *Facts on File Encyclopedia of Art* is a thoughtful study of the visual arts from the Paleolithic Age to the contemporary art world. Broken down into five volumes that are arranged chronologically, the

Encyclopedia addresses art in a wide variety of formats, from paintings and sculpture to architecture and ceramics. Roughly half of the illustrations are in full color, and the reproductions are generally excellent. The text is replete with maps imparting a variety of information, from the distribution of Neolithic sites to the location of Gothic cathedrals in Europe. The writing is academic in nature, and would be most suited to a college and even graduate-level audience. That being said, the text is extremely well written and impressive in its breadth of discussion, seamlessly intertwining the painting, decorative arts, and architecture of a given culture and time, with most major world civilizations represented. Given that each article is written by a different author, the consistency of tone and quality is also remarkable. Each article also includes a "Close Study" section set within the main text that discusses a particular topic within the larger discussion in greater detail, such as a discussion of Cortona's "Barberini Ceiling" in the Baroque chapter. Each "Close Study" section includes suggestions for further reading, as does each chapter. The first volume includes a timeline, and the last volume includes an illustrated glossary and a subject index. Despite the plethora of similar titles, this one is highly recommended for all college and public libraries. [R: LJ, Dec 05, pp. 168-174; BL, 1 & 15 Jan 06, p. 149]—**Philip G. Swan**

Directories

P

338.   **Artist's & Graphic Designer's Market, 2005.** Mary Cox and Lauren Mosko, eds. Cincinnati, Ohio, Writer's Digest Books/F & W Publications, 2004. 617p. index. $24.99pa. ISBN 1-58297-278-8. ISSN 1075-0894.

This is an invaluable guide for anyone launching into a career as a freelance artist or designer. The helpful how-to sections and featured interviews provide a good balance of reality and encouragement while the core of the book, the listings of possible sales venues, is a treasure trove of information. The listings, categorized by broad market categories, include contact information as well as details on how and what the outlets buy. Instructions for how to prepare submissions, possible terms, and pricing are also of great help. Within each category the listings are arranged by state. Both a niche marketing index and a general index make the listings easy to use. Experienced artists and designers may find this volume of less value—they will surely have developed strategies that work for them—but anyone looking for a foot in the door will find this book a way to start narrowing their search for success. Although the listings are broad, they are not comprehensive for a given area and are obviously biased toward more commercial endeavors. But, *Artist & Graphic Designer's Market, 2005* is still valuable as an objective education in the ways and means of commercial art sales.—**R. K. Dickson**

Handbooks and Yearbooks

C, P, S

339.   Harrison, Lorraine. **Artist's Materials: All the Materials You Will Ever Need to Make Art.** Edited by Curtis Tappenden. New York, Firefly Books, 2005. 288p. illus. index. $35.00. ISBN 1-55297-995-4.

What artist or would-be artist has not had the desire to learn and understand more fully the materials that comprise their artwork? Those interested individuals will find a solid, well-illustrated, and well-thought-out work in *Artist's Materials*. Covering a wide variety of materials used in creating two-dimensional art, the work provides a thorough understanding of the properties, working methods, and expected results of papers, paint, pastels, charcoals, ink, and many other items used by the artist. The work is profusely illustrated with images of materials, diagrams of techniques, and images of existing art pieces using the materials and techniques described for inspiration purposes. The work closes with a section discussing the care, handling, and storage of materials and finished works. It also gives some council on the establishment of a studio space for the creation of art and options for the display of art in studios, galleries, exhibitions, and the Internet. A subject index wraps up the work. One minor complaint of the index is the typeface used. It is an interesting typeface visually, but makes consulting the index somewhat more laborious than is needed when looking up a subject. This is a minor criticism to make in an otherwise worthwhile and useful work on a subject basic to the needs of the creative process.

This work will be of special interest to libraries attached to art schools or to libraries supporting art programs at the high school level and above. It will also find use in general libraries as a reference tool for those self-starting artists who want to learn more about the materials they work with in creating drawings, watercolors, or paintings. The reasonable price and the solid binding are also attractive assets of the volume.
—**Gregory Curtis**

ARCHITECTURE

Dictionaries and Encyclopedias

P
340.   **The Elements of Style: An Encyclopedia of Domestic Architectural Detail.** new ed. New York, Firefly Books, 2005. 592p. illus. index. $75.00. ISBN 1-55407-079-1.

Described as a visual survey of domestic architecture, *The Elements of Style* focuses on details, particularly interior details, of key architectural styles through history. It begins with the Tudor and Jacobean periods and continues chronologically to the present day, dividing each period or style into a set of design features, including doors, windows, walls, floors, and ceilings. Readers familiar with previous editions will immediately feel comfortable with this revised and expanded work. Revisions are minimal, and expansion is limited to 50 additional pages in the "Beyond Modern" and "Contemporary Era" chapters. Ironically, the eclectic nature of the two periods prevents them from being understood as coherent visual styles, and they are the least successful aspects of the work. Overall, however, the design and format make the book an excellent ready reference, and for the interior designer or homeowner the updated "Directories of Suppliers" (North American and British) continue to be particularly useful resources.—**John Schlinke**

PAINTING

P
341.   **National Gallery of Art: Master Paintings from the Collection.** John Oliver Hand, comp. New York, Henry N. Abrams, 2004. 474p. illus. index. $60.00. ISBN 0-8109-5619-5.

The selected paintings presented here represent the high points of art history from the thirteenth to the twentieth centuries, reflecting the techniques of artists from various regions and schools of expression. The entries highlight many of the additions that have been made to the gallery's holdings since the 1984 edition of John Walker's *National Gallery of Art, Washington*. The listings are basically in chronological order with several color plates, some of which show minute detail in order to focus on certain techniques. Interspersed throughout are discussions of particular works and the techniques used by artists, along with biographical information on the artists and background information on the subject presented in each painting. Each illustration includes the artist's name (or name by which they were known), their place of origin and dates of birth and death, the title of the painting and the date it was completed, the type of material and technique used, the size of the painting in both centimeters and inches, the donor or collection name, and the date upon which it was received by the gallery. At the beginning are some preliminary sections offering interesting and concise background information on the gallery and its collections. At the end are indexes for

the artists and their works and for the various donors. The plates are beautiful and the text is well written, informative, and easy to read. Although not a comprehensive representation of everything housed at the gallery, this work is an excellent overview of some of the most important and significant works available.
—**Martha Lawler**

PHOTOGRAPHY

P

342. Palmquist, Peter E., and Thomas R. Kailbourn. **Pioneer Photographers from the Mississippi to the Continental Divide: A Biographical Dictionary 1839-1865.** Stanford, Calif., Stanford University Press, 2005. 742p. illus. $150.00. ISBN 0-8047-4057-7.

This biographical dictionary covers some 3,000 photographers who were active in the area from the Mississippi River to the Continental Divide during the period 1839-1865. It is a companion volume to the authors' 2000 work *Pioneer Photographers of the Far West: A Biographical Dictionary, 1840-1865* (see ARBA 2002, entry 1002).

The volume begins with a 60-page essay "Photography Goes West," which chronicles the introduction of photography into the Plains and the Rockies. This excellent essay provides an overview of the makeup of the photographers, their education, equipment, and exhibitions. It is a fascinating look into the introduction of a new technology into a largely sparsely settled area. The authors note that "the subjects of this book were honest, hard-working people, but there also was a scattering of rascals, charlatans, and felons." The photographers traveled not only within what is now the United States, but also into the prairies of central Canada and portions of Mexico as well. There is a section and the end of the main alphabetic photographer sequence that covers and shows some photographs made by anonymous workers. Appendixes include: a partnership, company, and gallery names cross-reference index; a panorama, stereo, magic lantern, and public performance cross-reference index; a list of "women workers"; a list of workers know only as "artist"; a geographic listing of photographers by area they worked in; and a bibliography. The bibliography contains a wide range of sources, including manuscript and census records as well as current books and journal articles.

The volume is lavishly illustrated with many photographs and line drawings. Historians of the Plains and the Rockies will find this work an interesting look into the social history of the area. Photographers not only made images for individuals, but they also conducted shows and performances of their wares. These shows provided relief from what at times was a lonely, isolated existence for many. Libraries with clients interested in photography and the history of the West will want to purchase this volume and its earlier companion.—**Ralph Lee Scott**

P

343. **Photographer's Market 2006.** 29th ed. Donna Poehner, ed. Cincinnati, Ohio, Writer's Digest Books/F & W Publications, 2006. 640p. index. $24.99pa. ISBN 1-58297-395-4.

This is the 29th edition of an essential reference book that began publication with the 1st edition coming out in 1978. The volume is divided into a number of resource intensive sections: "Just Getting Started"; "Getting Down to Business"; "Portfolio Review Events"; "Making It in Niche Stock Photography"; "The Markets" (publications, consumer publications, newspapers and newsletters, trade publications, book publishers, greeting cards, posters and related products, stock photo agencies, advertising, design and related markets, and galleries and contests). At the end of the volume there are a series of appendixes (called "Resources") : "Photo Representatives"; "Workshops & Photo Tours"; "Professional Organizations"; "Publications"; "Websites"; "Portfolio Review Events"; "Glossary"; and geographic, international, subject, and general indexes.

A typical entry in "The Markets" section includes the name of the publication or agency, contact person (including postal and e-mail address), and a brief description of the publication including circulation numbers. Next is a section that describes the needs of the publication in terms of photographs. This is followed by a "Specs" section and a "Making Contact & Terms" section. The entries conclude with a "Tips" section. The most frequent tip is to read the publication and become familiar with the type of photographs the company uses.

Photographers wanting to enter the professional market will find this volume hard to beat. It is a comprehensive introductory review of the field, yet it is also a timely update for current professionals. It is on the bookshelf of all professional photographers. It is paperbound, has a few black-and-white photographs, and costs only $24.99. Most libraries will want to add this volume to their general reference collections.—**Ralph Lee Scott**

23 Language and Linguistics

GENERAL WORKS

P

344. Davies, Christopher. **Divided by a Common Language: A Guide to British and American English.** New York, Houghton Mifflin, 2005. 248p. index. $14.95. ISBN 0-618-00275-8.

In *Divided by a Common Language: A Guide to British and American English*, Christopher Davies provides an enjoyable glimpse of the English language from both sides of the Atlantic. He feels that most English-speakers are unaware of the differences between British and American English. Considering the global effect of media and the Internet, most would assume that differences would be waning. Davies successfully reveals that regardless of globalization significant differences still exist.

Davies has the personal experience to author this work. He was born and raised in England, lived in Australia, and has resided in the United States for the past 25 years. Davies uses this experience to provide a personal touch in his narrations of everyday expressions and helpful explanations. Many of the chapters, including "Tourist Tips," "Transportation," and "Differences in Customs & Etiquette," read like a travel guidebook. Most chapters contain lists comparing U.S. and UK words and phrases. Unfortunately, not all of these words are included in the main Lexicons; for example, 79 percent of the transportation list is not included. Chapters "What Not to Say" and "Idioms and Expressions" are interesting and enlightening, even for the armchair traveler.

This title was originally published in 1997; minor formatting changes are apparent, as are the removal of the humorous cartoons. The strength of this book lies in Davies' genuine humor and accurate portrayals revealed in his personal observations of American and British societies. The 1997 publication was purchased mostly by public libraries. This version is recommended for public libraries, too.—**Alice Crosetto**

C

345. **Encyclopedia of Linguistics.** Philipp Strazny, ed. New York, Routledge/Taylor & Francis Group, 2005. 2v. index. $275.00/set. ISBN 1-57958-391-1.

The editor of this encyclopedia has created a highly effective structure of the entries. For instance, there is an entry "Modern Linguistics" (p. 696), which offers a bird's eye view of the developments that have taken place in the nineteenth and twentieth centuries; individual schools of thought are discussed in separate entries. In the same way, the entry "History of Linguistics: Overview" (p. 464) is accompanied, among others, by "European Tradition: Grammar" (p. 307) and "Grammar, Traditional" (p. 395). There is also an entry on "Grammar: Theories" (p. 397) and many other related topics, such as "Arabic Traditional Grammar" (p. 78). This is a sample of the author's system of entries and of their coherence; they can offer quite detailed but well-distributed information. For instance, not only sign languages like American Sign Language are covered, but also Indo-Pakistani Sign Language (p. 524) and Japanese Sign Language (p. 555). Traditional notions like "Word" (p. 484) are treated in the same manner; that is, the whole variety of definitional and other difficulties appear in a survey, and then the various modern and new, but often delightfully contradictory, approaches are given. This system of survey and detailed entries is presented in the alphabetical and topical indexes, printed in both volumes. Also, each entry, whether of the survey in general or dealing with a single school of thought, a single language, or a sound law is located in the alphabetic sequence of entries.

No encyclopedia can be exhaustive, so each reviewer will have his or her own list of desiderata. My list contains a few topics, such as the inclusion of "Decipherment of Scripts and Languages", since there is a good entry on "Philology" (p. 824). Since many founders of some modern schools of thought are included, I think that "Korzybski" would fit well. On the whole, the editor of the *Encyclopedia* does his best to supply the reader with as much useful information as possible; there even is an entry on "Professions for Linguistics" (p. 874).

On the whole, one can say that this is one of the rather rare books that are highly professional, or specialized, but can be read for pleasure, preferably but not necessarily by a linguist. With entries such as "Personalities and Language" (p. 821), one always finds something interesting. [R: LJ, 1 Feb 05, p. 114]—**L. Zgusta**

ENGLISH-LANGUAGE DICTIONARIES

General Usage

C, P, S
346. **Cambridge Advanced Learner's Dictionary.** 2d ed. New York, Cambridge University Press, 2005. 1572p. illus. $39.00; $28.00pa. ISBN 0-521-84378-2; 0-521-60498-7pa.

This new international dictionary of the English language is based on the Cambridge International Corpus and the Cambridge Learner Corpus. It is aimed at persons learning English as a second language. A major feature of this edition is the inclusion of a guide to the most important words and meanings to learn. This edition also includes boxes with concise collation information for common words, in addition to sample sentences showing the word in context. Another important advantage of the dictionary is that it is available in CD-ROM format. The accompanying CD-ROM includes spoken pronunciation, extra example sentences, interactive exercises, and a thesaurus. There is a clearly marked, useful description of how to use the dictionary. A center section includes 16 pages of color pictures as well as an additional 20 study sections giving extra help with vocabulary and grammar in particular areas of English. Valuable supplementary information includes an idiom finder, a table of word families, a listing of geographical names, irregular verbs, symbols, units of measurement, and a pronunciation guide. The use of two columns, two colors, and words in boldface improve ease of reading and use of the dictionary. Blue letter tabs on each page are another useful feature. It is important to keep in mind that although the dictionary distinguishes between British and American English, in terms of spelling and usage it is a British based tool. However, because of its many useful features, good physical format, and ease of use, it is a valuable addition to reference collections in American high school, college, or university libraries supporting English as a Second Language programs.—**Susan J. Freiband**

C, P, S
347. **Webster's New Explorer Dictionary and Thesaurus.** new ed. Darien, Conn., Federal Street Press, 2005. 1366p. maps. $19.98. ISBN 1-892859-78-5.

This is a revised edition of a book first published in 1999. It has the advantage of combining (in separate sections) both an up-to-date abridged but comprehensive dictionary of current American English with a thesaurus. Additional features making this book a useful purchase for home reference include lists of frequently used foreign words and phrases, prominent biographical names, geographical names, a concise handbook of style, basic English grammar rules, some help in identifying English word roots, irregular English words, and a list of some confused and misused words. The thesaurus has approximately 30,000 entries. Unlike many other thesauri, this one includes a brief definition of the word (although the preface recommends, correctly, that the discriminating reader should always check a separate dictionary entry to be sure of the context of a word chosen as a synonym), which is followed, in most cases, not only by synonyms (words that mean close to the same as the head word), but with separate lists of related words, antonyms, and near antonyms.

Because this book was published in 2005 it includes numerous new words not found in older dictionaries, such as *webcast* and *fuzzy logic*. But since it is an abridged and therefore necessarily selective resource it does not include other new words one might hope to find, such as *blog* or *weblog*. Definitions include pronunciation, part of speech, numbered definitions (when there is more than one sense of meaning), cross-references, and a few synonyms (despite the separate section of synonyms. The work makes good use of boldface type to set off main entries and related words.

Readers who want other up-to-date abridged dictionaries that include not only more words but also more detailed definitions, should consider the *American Heritage Dictionary of the English Language* (4th ed.; see ARBA 2001, entry 1011) or *The New Oxford American Dictionary* (see ARBA 2002, entry 3004.). *Webster's New Explorer Dictionary and Thesaurus* is a very useful purchase for an undiscriminating user at home, who does not want to spend a lot of money, and who wants a lot of condensed language information in one handy reference book.—**David Isaacson**

C, P, S

348.   **Webster's II New College Dictionary.** 3d ed. New York, Houghton Mifflin, 2005. 1518p. $25.95. ISBN 0-618-39601-2.

Webster's II New College Dictionary was last published in 1995 (see ARBA 96, entry 1079) and the editors have since added thousands of new words in areas such as politics, science, computers, and pharmacology that are relevant to the twenty-first century. Examples include *WiFi*, *SARS*, *blog*, and *Amber Alert*.

In the introductory pages the editors provide sample entries and dissect each part by pointing out where the explanations for pronunciation, variants, etymology, and regional labels are located. This is followed by seven pages of notes that provide detailed analyses of the dictionary's scope and contents. Abbreviations and pronunciations that are commonly found in the resource are also listed. The dictionary is thumb-indexed and includes illustrations for select words.

One of the dictionary's nice features is the appendix, which includes a longer listing of abbreviations, biographical and geographical entries, foreign words and phrases, listings of four- and two-year colleges and universities, a brief guide to punctuation, tables of measurement, forms of address, the periodic table of elements, and signs and symbols. The biographical entries feature names of politicians, athletes, writers, historians, scientists, and entertainers. The geographical entries list cities, countries, lakes, islands, and mountains worldwide. Current populations of cities and countries are also provided. The colleges and universities section lists alphabetically the names of higher education institutions in the United States and includes enrollment figures and whether or not an institution is private or public. It would have been nice if the editors included World Wide Web addresses for each of the colleges and universities. Nonetheless, this resource is recommended for school, public, academic, and special libraries.—**Maris L. Hayashi**

Etymology

C, P, S

349.   Liberman, Anatoly. **Word Origins . . . And How We Know Them: Etymology for Everyone.**
New York, Oxford University Press, 2005. 312p. index. $25.00. ISBN 0-19-516147-5.

There are many books that discuss the problems of word origins. The present book is written on the
same topic by an outstanding linguist, Anatoly Liberman. The book is highly interesting and original because it offers in single chapters the main types of word creation and, to some degree, modifications, deri-
vations, and more. This is a successful scheme of topic distribution, because individual principles of the
origin, change, and loss of words are related and overlapping. For example, with Chapter 3, "Sound Imita-
tive Words" and chapter 4, "Sound Symbolism" one can admire how the overlapping topics are organized.
In addition, the author does not avoid difficult topics; for example, chapter 2, "The Thing and the Sign"
and chapter 10, "Words and Names". It is also important to note that while the book is an excellent example of erudition, it is written in a style of its own. The selection of the illustrative examples is rich and well
clarified by the author's discussion. Many examples discussed are original—this is an advantage gained
by the author being a first-class etymologist and being in the process of preparing his own etymological
dictionary.

This certainly is not an easy book for the interested layperson. However, the discussion is as accessible as possible. The author has an attractive style, so his texts are not only reliable as to correctness of his
explanation, but offer a combination of accuracy, clarity, and last but not least, wit. The only thing that
should be improved in the next edition (there will be one, no doubt) is the plethora of misprints in the
Greek words, printed in the Greek script.—**L. Zgusta**

Grammar

P, S

350.   **The American Heritage Guide to Contemporary Usage and Style.** New York, Houghton
Mifflin, 2005. 512p. $19.95. ISBN 0-618-60499-5.

Like *The American Heritage Dictionary of the English Language* (4th ed.; see ARBA 2001, entry
1011), this eponymous guide to contemporary usage and style is based on surveys of a panel of about 200
authors, journalists, educators, and other experts. Its alphabetically arranged entries include points of
grammar, spelling, word choice, pronunciation, parts of words, punctuation, capitalization and italics, and
treatment of numbers. The guide also makes distinctions between formal and informal, and standard and
nonstandard, English. In the event of more contentious issues, such as the acceptability of split infinitives
or using convince and persuade synonymously, the percentages of panel experts for and against are
provided.

Being a 1st edition, it is probably not surprising that the guide has a few omissions. *Since* receives an
entry regarding its temporal and its causal sense, but *while*, also a temporal word and sometimes used as a
synonym for *though*, does not. The commonly confused terms *premiere/premier* and *instants/instance* are
not here. Nor is the distinction *earth/Earth*. One hopes these will be added to a future edition.

The design of the guide makes items easy to find: entry heads are presented in white type on a black
band across the page; examples are set in italics; and cross-references are in boldface type. Furthermore,
the explanations are clear and well written. Although *The American Heritage Guide to Contemporary Usage and Style* does not have the academic rigor and thoroughness of, say, *The Cambridge Guide to English
Usage* (see ARBA 2006, entry 883), it will still appeal to a general audience.—**Lori D. Kranz**

Idioms, Colloquialisms, Special Usage

C, P, S

351.   Makkai, Adam, M. T. Boatner, and J. E. Gates. **A Dictionary of American Idioms.** Hauppauge, N.Y., Barron's Educational Series, 2004. 395p. $14.95pa. ISBN 0-7641-1982-6.

Alphabetically arranged, the 4th edition of this excellent, popular guide contains more than 8,000 idiomatic words, phrases, regionalisms, and informal English expressions. Each entry lists the part of speech, the definition, and the use of the idiom in a sentence. One needs only to look at the word hit, with such idioms as "hit the books," "hit the deck," "hit the dirt," "hit the fan," "hit the jackpot," and "hit the nail on the head," or at another choice, full, with idioms like "full blast," "full-bodied," "full of oneself," and "full tilt" to understand and appreciate the difficulty faced by students, workers, and immigrants for whom English is a second language when new to this country. A helpful, must-read introduction includes an easily remembered, concise definition of an idiom as "a new meaning to a group of words which already have their own meaning." The introduction is also printed in Arabic, Chinese, French, German, Hebrew, Italian, Japanese, Russian, and Spanish.

High school libraries, continuing education classes, and centers where the Teaching Of English as a Foreign Language (TOEFL) is offered will find this inexpensive, easy-to-use, and attractively formatted guide a purchase well chosen. Neighborhood public libraries may want multiple copies.—**Charles R. Andrews**

C, P, S

352.   **The Oxford Dictionary of Idioms.** 2d ed. Judith Siefring, ed. New York, Oxford University Press, 2004. 340p. index. $28.00. ISBN 0-19-852711-X.

This handy guide serves two purposes: to offer clear definitions of phrases and sayings that most of us use in our everyday writing and speaking, and to provide in many instances interesting facts about the origins of the phrases and examples of their use. In the more than 5,000 entries there are 350 new terms added since the 1999 first edition. A nice balance has been achieved between British and American idioms. Many writers who turn again and again to the term "sweetness and light" may be surprised to learn that the term was used by Jonathan Swift in *The Battle of the Books* (1704) and later by Matthew Arnold in *Culture and Anarchy* (1869). On the one hand, most late 20th -century readers will doubtlessly be aware that the expression "hit the ground running" seems likely to refer to military personnel disembarking quickly from a helicopter. On the other hand, "sail close to the wind" (behave or operate in a risky way) may lack familiarity. We may be amused to learn that the over-used and well-known term "Murphy's Law" had its origin in the world of aviation when a Captain Edward Murphy said that if an aircraft part can be installed incorrectly, someone will install it that way. Public, high school, academic, and special libraries should find this a very worthwhile and affordable addition. [R: LJ, 15 April 05, pp. 120-124]—**Charles R. Andrews**

Juvenile

P, S

353.   **DK Merriam-Webster Children's Dictionary.** rev. ed. New York, DK Publishing, 2005. 911p. illus. $19.99. ISBN 0-7566-1143-1.

This inviting dictionary is written for elementary school children. Its bright colors, plentiful illustrations, and concise definitions open young eyes to our language and will quickly expand a student's vocabulary. This reference is more than definitions. The child learns homographs, synonyms, origins of words, and the pronunciation of words. The introductory essay describes how to use a dictionary, setting a good foundation for future research skills. The entries use appropriate vocabulary for this age group without talking down to the reader or frustrating the younger user. At the end of the alphabetic entries there is a reference section that gives a geographic overview of each continent with maps, pictures of the flags of the American states and world nations, a listing of the capitals of U.S. states and Canadian provinces, a chronology of U.S. presidents and presidents elect, commonly used abbreviations and symbols, and phonetic tips for pronouncing the names of the world's major cities. While browsing through the volume, we learn that berries are defined as soft fruit with seeds. Therefore, red peppers, eggplants, melons, tomatoes, and avocados are berries. The word *surly* comes from the word *sir*. Because English sirs were usually arrogant and high-handed, surly has come to mean an individual who is rude, angry, and difficult to get along with. This resource starts the elementary school student on a life-long journey of discovery about our language. It is a reference that children will return to over and over as their curiosity about words grows.—**Adrienne Antink Bien**

P, S

354.   **The Facts on File Student's Thesaurus.** 3d ed. By Marc McCutcheon. New York, Facts on File, 2006. 586p. (Facts on File Library of Language and Literature). $60.00. ISBN 0-8160-6038-X.

With over 9,000 entries (some new, some updated), the 3d edition of *The Facts on File Student's Thesaurus* is a useful and indispensable tool for the student writer. A brief introduction explains what a thesaurus is and how to use it to improve one's writing. After that, it is as straightforward as one would expect a thesaurus to be; alphabetic listings of synonyms (and antonyms) for commonly used words are provided. Each entry also contains an example sentence, which is handy for establishing usage and context.

The Facts on File Student's Thesaurus also contains a feature called "Word Search." "Word Search" can be used as a vocabulary building resource, as well as for guiding the student writer to related words he or she can use to infuse their writing with more detail and variety. It should be noted that the thesaurus is marketed for junior and senior high school students, aiming to be more for students than adult-intended reference resources. It achieves this goal without being simplistic and sacrificing the idea of vocabulary building, which is admirable.

Describing itself as concise and easy to use, *The Facts on File Student's Thesaurus* is just that. It is a compact, user-friendly resource that belongs in every middle, junior, and senior high school, as well as public libraries with strong young adult literature programs.—**Megan W. Lowe**

P, S

355.   **Merriam-Webster's Primary Dictionary.** Illustrated by Ruth Heller. Springfield, Mass., Merriam-Webster, 2005. 436p. illus. $16.95. ISBN 0-87779-174-4.

This children's dictionary is designed with kindergarten through second grade students in mind. The publisher acknowledges that many of the intended users will not be able to read, but believes that the work is designed and formatted so that it will help them learn new words and their meanings. Plus it will give even the youngest students a head start on how to use reference materials. The publisher provides a detailed explanation of how the words for this work were chose in the introduction. They began by selecting 3,300 words from *Merriam-Webster's Elementary Dictionary* and then reducing the number selected to 2,000—a number that would provide "rich content" but would keep the book to a manageable size.

As in all dictionaries the words are listed alphabetically. Here they also provide a two- to three-sentence description, an example sentence, part of speech, a list of related words, "bonus" words (which are often related words with a short description), and an illustration. The work is filled with other tidbits of information, such as how certain words got their names, or jokes and poems to help users remember certain words. The work concludes with some tips for spelling, word functions, and a short language timeline.

This work is word intensive for a dictionary designed for this age group. The publishers designed it this way, however, so that users can use this work with a parent or teacher and also so that they can continue to learn from it for years. This work is recommended for public and elementary school libraries. [R: SLJ, Oct 05, p. 90]—**Shannon Graff Hysell**

Terms and Phrases

C, P

356.   Davidson, Mark. **Right, Wrong, and Risky: A Dictionary of Today's American English Usage.** New York, W. W. Norton, 2006. 570p. $29.95. ISBN 0-393-06119-1.

Why is the term *Caucasian* applied to what are generally called "white" people? As it turns out, not for a good reason, because all white people do not, in fact, originate in the Caucasus mountain region, as the nineteenth-century German anthropologist who originated this usage believed. The use of this term in reference to whites is ignorant, and therefore is "risky" in this book's terminology: "Recommendation: Unless you are referring to people of the Caucasus mountain range, forget *Caucasian*."

This book is filled with such nuggets of knowledge, and its 2,500 definitions, in dictionary form, constitute a delightful treasure trove of knowledge about culture and language for any intellectually curious person. The author covers not only the obvious problems that people have, such as *affect* vs. *effect*, or *there/their/they're*, but also many terms that the average person would never worry about, such as *cavalier* (one should be careful using it to mean "carefree, casual, indifferent," because some might interpret it in its other sense of "*arrogantly* indifferent") .

In addition to words and phrases, the author worked in grammar lessons on punctuation (commas, semicolons, dashes) and parts of speech as dictionary entries also, and provides good common-sense explanations for how to use the mechanics of English well. There are so many questions that are answered in this book, and answered well, not only by having consulted with many earlier guides to usage and standard dictionaries (listed in the bibliography), but also through the author's own knowledge, and common sense, supported by frequent quotations for respected newspapers.

This book was apparently created for the author's own students, to answer questions that the author could not find clear answers for in other sources. Davidson is not afraid to pronounce what is right and wrong, and any student would benefit greatly from spending time with this book. It is doubtful, however, that the average student today would take the trouble to consult a work such as this. The book makes great reading, and provides excellent guidance to many questions that would naturally occur to any serious writer. Anyone with a serious interest in language should ideally have this book in a personal collection, and certainly all libraries should have it. A plus is that the type is large and very readable. [R: LJ, 15 Oct 05, pp. 81-82]—**Bill Miller**

Visual

P, S

357.   Corbeil, Jean-Claude, and Ariane Archambault. **The Firefly Five Language Visual Dictionary.** New York, Firefly Books, 2004. 1092p. illus. index. $49.95. ISBN 1-55297-778-1.

This beautiful dictionary is full of information in English, French, German, Italian, and Spanish. It contains more than 6,000 color illustrations that demonstrate the meanings of 35,000 words. The dictionary has 17 color-coded chapters representing subject areas: astronomy, the animal kingdom, food and kitchen, society, and more. Each of these is divided into sections and subsections representing increasing degrees of detail. The animal kingdom section begins with a chart of evolution and a diagram of the cell and progresses to the primates. Each picture is clearly labeled in all five languages, including gender designation for non-English nouns. The entry for honeybee includes the morphology and anatomy, the types of bees, a beehive, and a honeycomb on three pages. The entry for lighting in the house section has pictures every type of light bulb as well as the parts of a lamp socket.

This is a wonderful tool for students learning languages because they can use it to find the word to express an idea or find the exact meaning of a word. Since this dictionary only contains nouns, they will need to use it in conjunction with more complete sources to construct full sentences. It is, however, extremely useful for anyone looking for the name of an object and as a communication tool when working with those who speak other languages. It is highly recommended for all reference collections. [R: LJ, 15 Feb 05, p. 158]—**Barbara M. Bibel**

NON-ENGLISH-LANGUAGE DICTIONARIES

French

C, P

358.   **Webster's French-English Dictionary.** Darien, Conn., Federal Street Press, 2004. 374p. $9.98pa. ISBN 1-892859-79-3.

This work enters the competitive market for small, concise bilingual dictionaries. It carries into this market several positive aspects. First, its size is slightly larger than most small pocket dictionaries making it easier to view and to use, but still a convenient size for backpack, briefcase, or purse. Secondly, the dictionary covers Canadian terms and expressions, a useful inclusion for someone traveling or doing business in Canada. A final attribute is that this dictionary is produced under the Merriam-Webster banner, a known quantity for quality dictionaries of this type. The dictionary includes 40,000 entries and 50,000 translations both from English to French and French to English. It also includes the conjugation of French verbs, common French abbreviations, French numbers, and pronunciation symbols.

This volume should find favor with students, teachers, tourists, and business travelers because of the size, convenience of use, and price. For libraries, multiple copies might be in order to fulfill the needs of patrons.—**Gregory Curtis**

German

C, P

359.   **Oxford-Duden German Dictionary: German-English, English-German.** 3d ed. Edited by the Dudenredaktion and the German Section of the Oxford University Press Dictionary Department. New York, Oxford University Press, 2005. 1752p. $55.00 (w/CD-ROM). ISBN 0-19-860974-4.

Though it has only been a few years since the publication of the 2d edition of this work, the 3d edition of the *Oxford-Duden German Dictionary* has implemented some noteworthy changes. It includes over 3,000 new up-to-date words, especially from technology and pop culture, such as *blogger* and *reality TV*. Headwords are now in blue bold type. It incorporates both the old and the new 1996 reform spellings, cross-referencing the old to the new. A supplemental CD-ROM provides instruction on how to pronounce the language. The special correspondence guide includes traditional guidelines as well as a section on text messaging. A calendar of traditions, festivals, and holidays describes the German ones in English and vice versa; likewise call-outs on the respective cultures of the two countries are described using terminology of the opposite language. This policy makes sense in light of the bilingual nature of the work, but if Americans are looking for a counterpart definition of the Ku Klux Klan in English, they will not find it here.

With a total of over 320,000 words, the *Oxford-Duden German Dictionary* is now one of the largest bilingual dictionaries on the market. In terms of size and comprehensiveness, its closest competitor is the *Collins German-English Dictionary* (see ARBA 99, entry 928). Its currency and readability make it a paragon of modern lexicography, and the Oxford-Duden publishing combination is simply tops.—**Lawrence Olszewski**

Spanish

C, P

360.   Butt, John, and Carmen Benjamin. **A New Reference Grammar of Modern Spanish.** New York, McGraw-Hill, 2004. 605p. index. $32.95pa. ISBN 0-07-144049-6.

The 4th edition of this excellent reference grammar mimics the earlier editions in terms of layout. The very comprehensive contents have been updated. The stated aim of the authors is to collect and organize "most of what English-speaking students can reasonably be expected to know about the syntax and morphology of the Spanish of Spain and Latin America as it is spoken and written at the beginning of the 21st century" (p. v). This book hits its target efficiently and elegantly.

Spanish is the exclusive language of 21 countries worldwide. Each place where Spanish is spoken has its own variations and local rules. This diversity makes it difficult to say what is "correct" in terms of usage. To account for a variety of possibilities, this book includes examples that illustrate both global and national usage. This book is not written for beginners, although an adult beginner could make use of it. The authors assume the reader has some knowledge of the English language as well as knowledge of Spanish pronunciation.

The preface contains a clear explanation of the philosophy behind the book. In the following section conventions, spelling, and abbreviations used in the book are explained. The chapters are divided by parts of speech and types of usage, moving from basic to more complex concepts. For example, the first chapter covers the gender of nouns. This is followed by chapters on plural nouns, articles, adjectives, pronouns, and verbs in their various forms. The later chapters of the book cover special verbs, existential sentences, expressions of time, conjunctions, and relative clauses. The final chapter covers spelling, accents, and word division. There is a glossary of grammatical terms as well as an index of English words and an index of Spanish words and grammatical points.

This book will be a valuable addition to any academic reference collection, and will be especially useful for collections supporting foreign-language education. It is highly recommended.—**Joanna M. Burkhardt**

24 Literature

GENERAL WORKS

Bio-bibliography

C, P, S

361. **Popular Contemporary Writers.** Michael D. Sharp, ed. Tarrytown, N.Y., Marshall Cavendish, 2006. 11v. illus. index. $495.95/set. ISBN 0-7614-7601-6.

In his introduction to this well-crafted and beautifully designed encyclopedia, editor Michael D. Sharp notes that in a literary context the term "popular" has always been a double-edged sword. While it should seem positive for an author's work to be embraced by a wide audience, popularity may also carry a connotation of commonness or catering to the lowest possible denominator. Recently, however, many teachers and experts have begun questioning the validity of a supposed dichotomy between popularity and literary value, and this work, which is aimed at young readers, registers the importance of this trend.

For writers to be included in this 11-volume set, they had to be not only well regarded by youth but also judged valuable by a "significant number" of librarians and other educators, says Sharp, an assistant professor of English at Binghamton University. The 96 chosen are diverse and a number of selections surprising. Some are youthful idols in their prime, like J. K. Rowling; others, like John Updike and David McCullough, have been read by people of all ages for many years. Young new writers with tremendous talent like Zadie Smith are also represented. Diversity is also evident in types and genres of writing, encompassing not only poetry (e.g., Rita Dove, James Dickey) and conventional fiction (e.g., Dorothy Allison, Jane Smiley), but also mystery and crime (e.g., Patricia Cornwell, Patricia Highsmith), science fiction (e.g., Octavia Butler, Arthur C. Clarke), plays and film scripts (e.g., Laura Esquivel, August Wilson), journalism (e.g., Jon Krakauer, Jorge Ramos), and cartoons (e.g., Matt Groening, Lynda Barry).

There are 10 volumes of profiles, averaging about 15 pages of text and illustration, and an index volume. All profiles are signed and follow a consistent format, including a photograph and a one-page summary on the author and his or her significance, biographical essay with detailed chronology of important events, a section of accessible literary criticism and background, a reader's guide to major works, and a section on less representative works. Critical sections contain short bibliographies, and articles end with a list of resources such as archives and Websites. Profiles are comprehensive, filled with new and surprising information, and beautifully illustrated with items ranging from an author's own photographs to reproductions of thematically linked works of art. All 10 volumes end with a 2-page author/title index. The 11th volume contains a glossary and 11 different indexes, including a comprehensive index of writers; literary characters; people, places, movements, and events; visual arts, and genres. This outstanding reference source should be highly enjoyed by youth and is recommended for public, school, and community college libraries.—**Madeleine Nash**

Dictionaries and Encyclopedias

C, S

362.   Cook, James Wyatt. **Encyclopedia of Renaissance Literature.** New York, Facts on File, 2006. 598p. index. (Facts on File Library of World Literature). $70.00. ISBN 0-8160-5624-2.

The distinguishing feature of this helpful volume is its wide-ranging coverage of literatures including Europe and beyond during the period 1500-1700. Cook presents over 600 entries on works of literature from 40 languages, from Arabic to Urdu. Russian and Byzantine Greek literatures are omitted because they seem to have been "in a period of literary stasis." The principle for inclusion is thus literatures that offer "parallels" to the creative changes typical of the European Renaissance. Most entries have short bibliographies, but one misses them for such broad topics as "Puritanism," "Scholasticism," and "Satire." Absent among English authors are Robert Herrick, Emilia Lanier, and the literary sermonizers Lancelot Andrewes and Jeremy Taylor. There is no general entry on the "Sonnet": sub-entries in the index must be consulted first; the entry on "Ficino" is cross-referenced to "Plato" but not vice-versa; and the selected bibliography lists three titles in seventeenth-century editions not likely available to most readers. Shortcomings such as these, however, do not greatly diminish the book's usefulness for its intended audience of students and general readers, who will find the concise summaries of unfamiliar non-European works and genres especially handy. All entries and the introductory overview are written in a clear, accessible style. The book includes a list of writers covered, authors' timeline, select bibliography, and index. —**Christopher Baker**

C, S

363.   Ruud, Jay. **Encyclopedia of Medieval Literature.** New York, Facts on File, 2006. 734p. index. (Facts on File Library of World Literature). $75.00. ISBN 0-8160-5497-5.

Written by various contributors, each article focuses on key authors, characters, titles, and aspects of works that exemplify the importance of the Middle Ages. The selections are from Europe and Asia and represent various cultural backgrounds. The articles are very well written and informative and each is followed by a brief bibliography of sources. A full bibliography of sources on the historical and cultural development of the Middle Ages is found at the end of the book with a list of contributors and an index. An introduction outlines the layout of the book and examines the development of medieval literature. It is followed by an authors' timeline and a listing of the authors arranged by native language. There are no illustrations but there is a wealth of information in the form of concise biographies of authors and characters, excellent plot summaries that are developed logically and clearly, and descriptions of various techniques that are enhanced by excerpts from the original works. There are also discussions of certain aspects of literature and writing, such as Ogham (the ancient Celtic alphabet), the razos and vidas found with troubadour poetry, and the seven forms of liberal arts. Individuals interested in a source of basic information from which to begin a study of the Middle Ages will find this volume to be especially useful.—**Martha Lawler**

C, P, S

364.   Whitson, Kathy J. **Encyclopedia of Feminist Literature.** Westport, Conn., Greenwood Press, 2004. 300p. index. $65.00. ISBN 0-313-32731-9.

Whitson, a professor from Eureka College has selected 69 female writers from the past 640 years whose works have influenced the field of feminist studies. Over one-half of the authors chosen are from North America, but writers from Europe, Asia, Africa, Australia/Oceania, and South America are also included. While there are many other reference books that provide plot summaries or biographical information about women authors, some of whom deny they are feminists, this volume is unique in defining a feminist author as one who whose work explores themes about the oppression of women and whose characters "challenge traditional gender roles" and "critique the patriarchy and advocate for the social, political, and economic equality of women" (p. xi). The life and at least one major work of each author are discussed in a way that relates to this definition. The arrangement is alphabetical and essays vary from one to eight pages in length. Novels are frequently analyzed, but other genres are also represented. Twenty additional topical entries have been contributed by Lisa R. Williams (e.g., "Silence and Voice," "True Woman," "New Woman"). Short bibliographies and cross-references follow every entry. The cross-references would be more useful if they led from an author to the topic, instead of just from the topic to one of the authors. This one-volume encyclopedia will be useful for high school teachers and students, undergraduates in women's studies and literature courses, and for readers' advisory librarians. [R: LJ, Jan 05, p. 158]—**Patricia Rothermich**

Handbooks and Yearbooks

C, S

365.   Wilson, Charles E., Jr. **Race and Racism in Literature.** Westport, Conn., Greenwood Press, 2005. 154p. index. (Exploring Social Issues Through Literature). $49.95. ISBN 0-313-32820-X.

This is a kind of *Masterplots* volume intended for high school students, but usable by anyone, that focuses on racism in literature. It is part of a continuing series entitled Exploring Social Issues Through Literature, which apparently has three other volume in print: *Literature and the Environment* (see ARBA 2005, entry 1008), *Youth Gangs in Literature* (see ARBA 2005, entry 1030), and *Bioethics and Medical Issues in Literature.* Most of the dozen novels treated in *Race and Racism in Literature* are American in setting, although Arlene J. Chai's *The Last Time I Saw Mother* (1995) takes place in Australia and the Philippines, and Amy Wilentz's *Martyr's Crossing* takes place in the area of the Israeli-Palestinian conflict.

The novels discussed here were chosen to represent various racial and ethnic identities (e.g., black, Asian, Hispanic, Jewish, Italian, Native American). Each novel, such as *The Adventures of Huckleberry Finn* or *The House on Mango Street*, is summarized, discussed in terms of its historical and social significance, and then discussed again as a work of literature. The focus of all these discussions, obviously, is the racial nature of the work. A short bibliography accompanies each of the 12 sections. The book also includes an introductory essay on race and racism.

Charles E. Wilson Jr.'s plot summaries and commentaries are thoughtful and mature, and anyone could learn from reading them. One has to wonder if students will attempt to use this volume's summaries and discussions as a substitute for reading the primary works themselves, and many undoubtedly would, but the author cannot be held responsible for that. He is to be commended for drawing together a dozen novels that focus on race, and treating these works in a thoughtful and focused way.—**Bill Miller**

CHILDREN'S AND YOUNG ADULT LITERATURE

Bibliography

P, S

366.   Barancik, Sue. **Guide to Collective Biographies for Children and Young Adults.** Lanham, Md., Scarecrow, 2005. 447p. index. $44.95pa. ISBN 0-8108-5033-8.

This book was written out of the experience of a youth services librarian. It includes biographies of over 5,000 subjects/people from many aspects of life that students engaged in writing projects about as well as people of which special commemorative displays have been done. Like a true librarian, Barancik has arranged the text to include several different points of access to the books analyzed in this work.

Part 1 provides an alphabetic list by author of the 721 collective biographies, written between 1988 and 2002, that are included in this compilation. Codes were devised to identify each of the titles and are included along with the bibliographic information about each title. The biographees are arranged in part 2. A brief statement identifies the subject listed (in alphabetic order). Codes representing titles found in part 1 lead the reader to the appropriate title(s) to access for information about the biographees. Part 3, titled "List of Subject Headings," ranges from abolitionists to zoologists, and is used as a guide to career, nationality, or ethnic group of the biographees. Part 4, the 275-page "Subject Guide to Biographees," arranges the biographees into the subject headings listed in part 3.

Decisions about inclusion in this guide were apparently made on the basis of collective biographies available, as coverage is uneven among subjects. Some subject headings, as might be expected, have only one entry (e.g., arachnologists, bobsledders, Incas, mineralogists, volleyball players), while other subject headings have pages of entries. Many *see* and *see also* reference are also included.

Auto racers and automakers receive equal treatment (15 to 16 entries each), as do educators, explorers, and inventors, with approximately 3 pages of entries each. However, there are more than twice as many entries for presidential Medal of Freedom recipients as there are for presidents of the United States. There is heavy emphasis on the military and on African Americans, arranged in several different subject categories. The heaviest emphasis appears to be on women.

From the brief description given of the contents of this work, any teacher or librarian who has worked with young people seeking biographical information can readily see its value as a guide to the literature in the field. It can also be an invaluable reference book for library collection development. [R: SLJ, July 05, p. 135; BL, June 05, pp. 1864-1866]—**Lois Gilmer**

P, S

367.   Lynn, Ruth Nadelman. **Fantasy Literature for Children and Young Adults: A Comprehensive Guide.** 5th ed. Westport, Conn., Libraries Unlimited/Greenwood Publishing Group, 2005. 1128p. index. $65.00. ISBN 1-59158-050-1.

In the 5th edition of a guide originally published as *Fantasy for Children: An Annotated Checklist* in 1979, there are annotations for 7,600 titles, 4,500 of which are main entries. This is a 62 percent increase since the previous edition in 1995. The author states in the introduction that fantasy literature, defined here as containing both magic and impossible events, is one of the hottest genres in publishing, and she proceeds to discuss its appeal and history. Titles are situated within one of twelve subgenres and themes, including the following types of fantasy literature: allegorical, animal, ghost, high, humorous, magic adventure, time travel, and witchcraft. There are cross-references to titles that could fall within multiple categories. The titles are all fantasy novels and short story collections published between 1900-2004 in English in the United States, except for the occasional "classic" included despite an earlier publication date. To be included, a title must be recommended by at least 2 sources from 20 professional review sources used, and titles recommended by at least 4 sources are starred. Science fiction and horror titles are excluded, but out-of-print titles are included and noted as such. Generally, the titles are aimed at grades 3-12, but there are some crossover adult fantasy titles denoted by grades 10 and up.

Each entry contains bibliographic information, including the author name, title, original country of publication, the translator or illustrator, original publication information and information on the most recent edition, where applicable. Also included is the appropriate grade level, a brief summary of the plot, citations to reviews, and if appropriate sequels, related works, or important awards won. Supplementing the entries is a list of outstanding titles, an author and illustrator index, a title index, a series index, and an "award winners" list and subject index that have been expanded since the previous edition. Unfortunately, gone in this edition is the bibliography section that cited 10,500 sources on fantasy authors in the previous edition, making the applications of the book a little narrower. Nonetheless, libraries with the previous edition need to update it with the current one.—**Susan J. Gardner**

S

368.   **Middle and Junior High School Library Catalog.** 9th ed. Anne Price, ed. Bronx, N.Y., H. W. Wilson, 2005. 1237p. index. $275.00. ISBN 0-8242-1053-0.

An upgrade of a respected reference work, Anne Price's compendium is an essential, but pricey addition to the school and public library, junior high school, and curriculum planner's professional shelf. As a check on the core collection, on maintenance of young adult fiction and nonfiction materials, and as a guide to expansion or discarding, this Dewey-based text offers a number of useful helps. A compilation of some 600 outstanding works, it provides author, title, subject, and analytical indexes and notes some out-of-print titles. As a readers' advisory, entries offer brief overviews plus grade level and publishing data. Coverage aids librarians, curriculum supervisors, and teachers in choosing classics and new works in an array of genres, including world cultures, technology, ethics and values, social and political issues, the environment and ecology, and the protection of endangered species. The key to this work's staying power among library reference is its selectivity. Editor Anne Price understands publishing trends and appreciates the best of print works for readers in grades 5-9. In addition, a balance of interests and intellectual levels assures users that library shelves will answer a variety of users' needs. This work is highly recommended, especially in budget-conscious institutions that want the most for their money.—**Mary Ellen Snodgrass**

P, S

369.   Schon, Isabel. **Recommended Books in Spanish for Children and Young Adults: 2000 Through 2004.** Lanham, Md., Scarecrow, 2004. 415p. index. $45.00. ISBN 0-8108-5196-2.

Isabel Schon, the doyen of Spanish-language literature for children and young adults, has again produced a valuable, selective bibliography of recommended books in Spanish for readers from preschool through senior high. For many years the volumes in this series were called *Books in Spanish for Children and Young Adults* and appeared in four-year intervals. The change in title to the present volume came with the seventh volume in 1997. This included books published from 1991 through 1995 (see ARBA 98, entry 1079). A further continuation covered 1996 through 1999 (see ARBA 2001, entry 1077). The present volume lists books published from 2001 through 2004. Like the books contained in the earlier volumes, the 1,300 books in the current volume are arranged by a combination of subjects and genres. The beginning section on the reference books (e.g., dictionaries, atlases), is followed by a lengthy section on nonfiction works organized under such subjects as science, the arts, geography, history, and biography. This is followed by material on publishers' series and an extensive fiction section subdivided into "Easy Books" and "General Fiction." In addition to extensive bibliographic information, each entry contains an indication of grade level suitability, and a concise 5- to 15-line annotation that supplies a description of the book's contents and critical comments on its merit. The book ends with an appendix that lists dealers of books in Spanish for children and young adults, and extensive author, title, and subject indexes. As expected from this highly respected source, this is another thoroughly edited, well-written, and very useful bibliography that will be an essential selection aid where materials in Spanish are being purchased for children and young adults.—**John T. Gillespie**

P, S

370.   Thomas, Rebecca L., and Catherine Barr. **Popular Series Fiction for K-6 Readers: A Reading and Selection Guide.** Westport, Conn., Libraries Unlimited/Greenwood Publishing Group, 2004. 799p. index. (Children's and Young Adult Literature Reference Series). $60.00. ISBN 1-59158-203-2.

In 1999, Bowker published *Reading in Series* by Barbara Barstow. That work forms the basis of this new series by Libraries Unlimited. This new and richly updated set has been redesigned into two volumes (the volume reviewed here and a work for older readers entitled *Popular Series Fiction for Middle School and Teen Readers: A Reading and Selection Guide*). This useful readers' advisory work is primarily designed for librarians serving elementary readers. The work includes 1,200 series and is arranged in alphabetical order by title of the series. Each entry contains the series title, author (when a series has multiple authors each author is listed with his or her respective title), publisher, grade level, genre, accelerated reader indication, annotation, and a list of titles in the series listed in chronological order by publication date (given) or in the case of numbered series, by number order. Prequels and alternative reading orders are indicated within the annotation. Annotations are very brief but serve to give the user a general sense of the overall series and include some specific individual book examples. Occasionally appeal elements will be included as well as indications of added elements such as fan clubs, movies, and related items. The book is augmented by several indexes—author, title, and genre/subject—as well as a listing of books for boys, books for girls, and books for reluctant readers/ESL students. Regrettably, there is no separate listing for accelerated reader series. Since it is difficult to quickly and accurately track down all the titles in a series in their proper order and because books in series are so deeply enjoyable, this book should be a boon to a whole range of librarians and readers and it is recommended for all public libraries and academic libraries supporting an education curriculum.—**Neal Wyatt**

P, S

371.   Thomas, Rebecca L., and Catherine Barr. **Popular Series Fiction for Middle School and Teen Readers: A Reading and Selection Guide.** Westport, Conn., Libraries Unlimited/Greenwood Publishing Group, 2005. 514p. index. (Children's and Young Adult Literature Reference Series). $50.00. ISBN 1-59158-202-4.

A savvy overview of some 800 teen works, this reference book offers the student, parent, teacher, and librarian a quick survey of fiction series by author, grade level, type, and number. Each entry lists the titles of a series in order of publication. Beautifully laid out in logical, easy-to-read style, the text covers a wide range, from the classic T. H. White Once and Future King series to the six Harry Potter fantasy novels of J. K. Rowling. An author index names some of the most respected writers for the young adult audience—Caroline Cooney, Virginia Hamilton, Lois Lowry, Richard Peck, J. R. R. Tolkien, Cynthia Voigt, and Lawrence Yep. Contributing to usability are a title index and suggestions of books appealing to boys or girls. A valuable listing for teachers and homeschoolers is the genre/subject index, which suggests books on such specific topics as the Amish, football, robots, history, hospitals and illness, dieting, and horses. This is a superb source at a reasonable price. School and public libraries should not miss this one. —**Mary Ellen Snodgrass**

Bio-bibliography

P, S

372.   **Ninth Book of Junior Authors and Illustrators.** Connie C. Rockman, ed. Bronx, N.Y., H. W. Wilson, 2004. 583p. illus. index. $105.00. ISBN 0-8242-1043-3.

The growth of children's book publishing in recent decades has required an equally proliferate stream of authoritative, evaluative tools. Fewer offer insight into the souls of the creators. This 9th edition of the junior author book series begun in 1934 serves such a purpose. Expanded and revised several editions ago, it is now among the only concise biographical dictionaries to offer personal views into the best of both authors and illustrators of English-language children's nonfiction and fiction—poetry, picture books, and novels alike.

Clear in its scope and closely following the layout of its predecessor (see ARBA 2001, entry 1079), this edition comprises 173 entries gathered from awards lists and confirmed by a voting process. Each entry consists of an autobiographical essay (complete with photograph and autograph), followed by a biography, a representative list of works, and in some cases, further suggested reading. Expanding a practice begun in the 8th edition, Rockman now includes a representative jacket illustration for every entry. Although the focus is on new contributors, she continues her practice of updating previously profiled distinguished creators (now neatly asterisked in the table of contents, and totaling no more than 10 percent of the entries) to include new awards of biographical updates. So long-standing award-winners such as Marcia

Brown and Robert McCloskey share pages with relative newcomers Ian Falconer and "Lemony Snicket." A descriptive appendix lists the 45 awards and honors cited (up from 26 referenced in 2000). Unlike earlier editions, this volume features a cover designed by one of the illustrators represented (a practice also begun by Rockman). The handy index adds value to the entire series by referencing previously profiled authors and illustrators to their respective editions. Interestingly, the number of profiles has decreased steadily for the last three editions (down from 235 in the seventh).

Although there are numerous reference resources with similar aims, such as *Something About the Author, Autobiography Series* (see ARBA 99, entry 988) and most notably Lee Bennett Hopkins' 1995 compilation, *Pauses: Autobiographical Reflections of 101 Creators of Children's Books*, few can rival this book for both its comprehensive coverage and its compact, attractively designed format.

This series should continue to prove practical for teachers, parents, and children's librarians; but more importantly, since it offers a view into the creators themselves it also promises to be illuminating for young people and aspiring writers. It is now also available in a cumulative electronic edition.—**Lucy Duhon**

Dictionaries and Encyclopedias

P, S

373. **Cyclopedia of Young Adult Authors.** Hackensack, N.J., Salem Press, 2005. 3v. illus. index. $225.00/set. ISBN 1-58765-206-4.

The 251 authors covered in this 3-volume set are major figures in young adult literature who were initially chosen for the database *NoveList*. Each author entry (about three pages) includes birth date and place, Website address, principle young adult fiction titles, and a discussion of the author's life and work. Sidebars give brief explanations for terms or topics that appear in the body of the entry. The layout is attractive and colorful, with an easy-to-read font and illustrations, including photographs of the authors and adaptations of their works. The subject index in the third volume lists the authors and their works, and the sidebar topics. The intended audience, young adults themselves, are sure to find this an attractive resource for author information. Unfortunately, the focus on major authors means that the information provided is easily found in other sources such as Gale's Something About the Author series and Authors and Artists for Young Adults. This set is recommended for middle school and high school libraries, and public library collections that need updated young adult author information. [R: SLJ, Oct 05, p. 87]—**Rosanne M. Cordell**

Directories

S

374. York, Sherry. **Ethnic Book Awards: A Directory of Multicultural Literature for Young Readers.** Worthington, Ohio, Linworth, 2005. 157p. index. $36.95pa. ISBN 1-58683-187-9.

Multicultural literature for the K-12 student continues to be a high priority for librarians and educators. Identifying such literature continues to be a challenge. In this current title, librarian Sherry York, author of *Picture Books by Latino Writers* (see ARBA 2003, entry 1013), *Children's and Young Adult Literature by Latino Writers* (see ARBA 2003, entry 1019), and *Children's and Young Adult Literature by Native Americans* (see ARBA 2005, entry 1021), continues her mission of providing the resources that address this need.

York spotlights seven ethnic book awards in this handy directory, including all of their winners and honor books. A brief history of each award is provided at the beginning as is a subject index at the end. The major portion of the book is the combined alphabetic listing of the award-winning titles. York lists the reading and the interest levels and grade levels for each title, including a caveat of current purchasing availability (i.e., out of print). This information alone is a valuable asset to both librarian and educator. However, the one sentence synopsis is too brief to appreciate the title's contents, evaluate its usefulness, or project potential curricular use.

One disheartening and challenging factor is discovered—of the over 600 titles listed, more than 26 percent are currently out of print. This unfortunate reflection on the state of publishing in the area of children literature and especially in multicultural titles creates yet a deeper chasm in an area already so woefully underrepresented.

By basing this directory on established book awards, York needs to be commended for applauding their significant contribution to the world of publishing and librarianship. Many of the awards were established by librarians who understood the need and value of book awards for children's literature and the subsequent value such awards would have for multicultural literature. York's directory is a convenient resource. As a good starting point for locating quality multicultural literature, this title belongs on the K-12 library shelf. [R: SLJ, Jan 06, p. 176; TL, Dec 05, pp. 46-47]—**Alice Crosetto**

DRAMA

Dictionaries and Encyclopedias

C, P, S

375.   **The Facts on File Companion to Classical Drama.** By John E. Thorburn, Jr. New York, Facts on File, 2005. 680p. index. (Facts on File Library of World Literature). $71.50. ISBN 0-8160-5202-6.

John Thorburn, a classics professor at Baylor University, has produced a fine resource for high school and undergraduate students studying classical drama, its mythology, and history. His guide is written in clear and easily understood language with the intent of explaining and putting into context plays, playwrights, myths, and history. The work is a great resource for students and life-long learners who want to understand the world of classical drama and to discover the rich interconnectedness of the classical world. The companion is arranged in alphabetic order and includes entries on people, events, myths, mythical figures, characters, plays, and playwrights. Entries on characters who are featured in more than one play contain contextual comparisons between treatments of the character. Individual play entries include a detailed summary of the play, its history, major themes, explanations of key characters, and a commentary that puts the action and meaning of the play into context with both the times and other classical plays. Other entries explain the importance of an event on classical drama (such as the Peloponnesian War), provide biographical data on writers, and explain common dramatic terms. Each entry provides both explanation and context, elevating it above the more typical dictionary-type companions common to reference publishing. Multiple appendixes and a lengthy bibliography round out this well-conceived resource that should be useful in large public and academic libraries. [R: LJ, 15 Sept 05, p. 94; SLJ, Oct 05, p. 92]—**Neal Wyatt**

FICTION

General Works

Handbooks and Yearbooks

P

376. Pearl, Nancy. **More Book Lust: Recommended Reading for Every Mood, Moment, and Reason.** Seattle, Wash., Sasquatch Books, 2005. 286p. index. $16.95pa. ISBN 1-57061-435-0.

Nancy Pearl, National Public Radio book commentator, has cooked up a tempting buffet for the avid reader who feels reading is as necessary to living as eating. This volume is a sequel to her first publication, *Book Lust*, and tempts us with books on a broad range of topics, from the serious to lighter fare. All the selections are works that Pearl has personally enjoyed and wants to share with other compulsive readers. Her philosophy is that reading should be fun. Her advice is: If the author has not grabbed your attention in the first 50 pages, do not waste your time. Go on to another book. She gives readers plenty to sample. For example, you will find novels about adopting children, the Beat Generation, codes and encryption, books that take place in libraries, mysteries with a Hong Kong flavor, Queen Victoria and her times, Krakatau, stories that take place in West Virginia, and many more. Entries include fiction and nonfiction—even cookbooks. For each title, Pearl gives a brief description, just enough to whet the appetite. Her chatty style and obvious love for books engages your attention and provides an array of new and tasty treats. It is also fun to find your own favorites included in her recommendations. This book will cause users to rush to their nearest library or bookstore with a long list of new authors to try.—**Adrienne Antink Bien**

Horror

P

377. Frank, Frederick S. **Guide to the Gothic III: An Annotated Bibliography of Criticism, 1994-2003.** Lanham, Md., Scarecrow, 2005. 2v. index. $200.00/set. ISBN 0-8108-5101-6.

This two-volume reference guide is meant to update *Guide to the Gothic* I (1984) and *Guide to the Gothic II* (1995). It adds 1,651 new annotated entries to the previous two editions. The year 2003 was chosen as the terminal publication point for this edition, with some exceptions. There are new individual author sections on Angela Carter and Anne Rice, a number of new special subject areas such as "Classical English Authors and the Gothic," and a new section on "Teaching Gothic Fiction" because of the rise of undergraduate and graduate classes on this topic. In the introduction, the author defines the term "Gothic" for this work, and goes into some detail on his viewpoint regarding various interpretations and approaches to the topic. Volume 1 focuses on British gothic writers, both overall and individually. Volume 2 focuses on special subject topics in gothic literature, national gothics, American gothic fiction and authors, and a miscellaneous section on related topics. This volume is an excellent and definitive reference work on this topic.—**Bradford Lee Eden**

Science Fiction and Fantasy

Bibliography

P

378.   Barron, Neil. **Anatomy of Wonder: A Critical Guide to Science Fiction.** 5th ed. Westport, Conn., Libraries Unlimited/Greenwood Publishing Group, 2004. 995p. index. $80.00. ISBN 1-59158-171-0.

The newly revised *Anatomy of Wonder: A Critical Guide to Science Fiction* contains annotated bibliographies, well-rounded synopses, and critical discussions of a myriad assortment of science fiction materials. More than 1,400 science fiction novels, short story anthologies, and collections are included, organized by two broad timeframes and genres, including cyberpunk. Young adult materials are integrated into the material, rather than segregated. Websites and author e-mails are included, as well as sections on research library collections and teaching science fiction. Information on history and criticism, film and television, illustration and "fandom" round out the book's focus. In its 5th edition this title remains a critical and authoritative guide to the genre, and an asset for scholars, readers, and librarians alike. [R: VOYA, Dec 05, p. 433]—**Denise A. Garofalo**

P

379.   **Science Fiction and Fantasy Research Database. http://lib-oldweb.tamu.edu/cushing/ SFFRD/.** [Website]. Free. Date reviewed: 2004.

Originally published in book form as *Science Fiction and Fantasy Reference Index, 1878-1985: An International Author and Subject Index to History and Criticism*, the citations were computerized and now are part of easily the largest such database, with more than 65,000 entries as of summer 2004. New entries are added quarterly. Approximately 90 percent are in English. Particularly valuable is the indexing of the principal fan news magazines (fanzines) from the 1940s on. Fanzines have for decades served as an informal and unrefereed, yet valuable, forum. A major achievement is the indexes that provide scholars a comprehensive index to the secondary literature. A template permits users to submit additional citations. This site is linked to the large science fiction collection at Texas A&M. Compiler, H. W. Hall, received the Pilgrim award from the Science Fiction Research Association in 2000 for his bibliographic efforts.—**Neil Barron**

P

380.   **Science Fiction Studies. http://www.depauw.edu/sfs/.** [Website]. Free. Date reviewed: 2004.

This is one of the best sites for scholars of science fiction. The home page has links to a search engine for the site, contents pages of recent issues of *Science Fiction Studies*, and full-text featured essays. There is also a list of special issues with links to contents pages, contents pages of all past issues (1973-date), a reviews index by author and issue, abstracts of all articles by author and issue, a major bibliography of science fiction criticism (http://www. depauw.edu/sfs/biblio.htm), documents in science fiction history appearing in earlier issues, and a carefully compiled list of links, amusingly called wormholes, to other useful sites (http://www.depauw.edu/sfs/links.htm), including scholarly journals and organizations, library collections, a list of universities offering degrees in science fiction, 29 recommended Internet sites, groups whose focus is science fiction, topical resources, science fiction magazines and e-zines of critical interest, "interesting" author sites, science fiction in film and television, mainstream and "edge" science, and five sites "in the zone" (i.e., focusing on pseudoscience such as alien abductions). Some of these sites are annotated in this guide. Superior design, excellent internal and external linkages, and free advertisements are featured. This is an essential site for the serious reader or scholar of science fiction. —**Neil Barron**

Dictionaries and Encyclopedias

C, P

381.   **The Greenwood Encyclopedia of Science Fiction and Fantasy: Themes, Works, and Wonders.** Gary Westfahl, ed. Westport, Conn., Greenwood Press, 2005. 3v. index. $349.00/set. ISBN 0-313-32950-8.

The Greenwood Encyclopedia of Science Fiction and Fantasy covers literature, film, television, and both canonical and contemporary works. The entries define and discuss the themes relating them to works of science fiction and fantasy, and cite numerous resources. Entries provide critical information and discuss central themes. The encyclopedia offers a selected, general bibliography of major studies, and contains quotations from classic works highlighting themes in science fiction and fantasy. This reference work's three volumes are organized as follow: volume 1 treats themes from A-Z, (e.g., Androids, Black Holes, Curses, Dinosaurs, Dragons); volume 2 treats themes L-Z (e.g., Lost Worlds, Mad Scientists, Monsters, Politics); volume 3 treats 200 classic works from A-Z (e.g., *Alice's Adventures in Wonderland*, *Brave New World, Buffy the Vampire Slayer*).

There is an "Alphabetical List of Themes" in volumes 1 and 2 listing over 400 thematic subjects. The "Alphabetical List of Classic Works" offers about 200 titles, from *Alice's Adventures in Wonderland* to *Xena: Warrior Princess*. The "Guide to Related Topics" lists themes by categories: abstract concepts and qualities, animals, characters, disciplines and professions, events and actions, games and leisure activities, horror, literary concepts, love and sexuality, magical beings, magical places, objects and substances, religions and religious concepts, social and political concepts, science and scientific concepts, settings, subgenus and narrative patterns, and time. The "Classic Works By Categories" index lists book and film titles discussed in this reference work. All entries contain themes and book titles in bold type, referring the reader to discussions of these key entries in the three volumes.

The Greenwood Encyclopedia of Science Fiction and Fantasy is edited by Gary Westfahl, a member of the faculty at the University of California, Riverside. A leader in the science fiction field, he has written or edited seven books. Advisory editors of this reference work are equally talented. The entire list of over 100 contributors includes more than 60 university professors from the United States, Europe, and Asia; more than 40 individual contributors from numerous countries; 9 doctoral students; and 5 academic librarians.

This encyclopedia is scholarly and simultaneously easy for the layperson to read. It is an extremely comprehensive work, written by experts in the field from several continents. It is highly recommended for undergraduate collections and graduate research collections. Although the price is a bit steep, these three volumes are well worth it.—**Mark Padnos**

NATIONAL LITERATURE

American Literature

General Works

Bibliography

P

382.   **African American Literature: A Guide to Reading Interests.** Alma Dawson and Connie Van Fleet, eds. Westport, Conn., Libraries Unlimited/Greenwood Publishing Group, 2004. 470p. index. (Genreflecting Advisory Series). $65.00. ISBN 1-56308-931-9.

The title of this book is somewhat of a misnomer: it is not a comprehensive guide to all African American literature. Its purpose is considerably narrower: it is an annotated guide primarily for readers' advisory librarians to genre fiction written by African Americans between 1990 and 2003. Some teachers and general readers interested in recent African American fiction will also find this book useful, but the major audience is librarians seeking to build a collection of genre literature and/or to provide readers' advisory assistance to individual readers. The book seems to more focused on public librarians, although some academic librarians interested in popular rather than literary fiction will also want to consult this book. Because the focus is popular literature, readers interested in the established canon of literary novels by major writers such as James Baldwin and Toni Morrison should consult other guides.

This reviewer is somewhat confused by the selection criteria for this book. On the one hand, the editors do not seem to agree completely with the standard definition of genre fiction as that which is written to a formula or pattern. On the other hand, they also say they do not intend this to be a list of best books (page xiv), or a critical guide, but rather a widely diverse list of books in categories of popular fiction. Apparently, then, since the editors do not want to go out on a limb to recommend the best books, the books selected (since not all novels and short stories by African American authors between 1990 and 2003 are included) constitute a representative sample. Annotations are both descriptive and evaluative, providing considerable guidance to readers' advisory librarians, with special attention to award-winning books. Annotations also include a few sentences selected from the recommended book, the better to give the reader a flavor of the author's style.

The first part of the book devotes three chapters to discussing broad issues: readers' advisory services; trends in African American publishing, and collection development. The second part has nine chapters, each devoted to a different kind of genre fiction: detective and crime fiction; frontier literature; historical fiction; inspirational literature; life stories (some nonfiction is included in this section); mainstream fiction; romance fiction; speculative fiction; and resources. Since some fiction obviously fits into more than one of these categories individual works are listed under keywords as well, which, in turn, are listed in an indispensable subject index. There is also an author-title index to the works cited in the bibliography.—**David Isaacson**

P

383.   Reisner, Rosalind. **Jewish American Literature: A Guide to Reading Interests.** Westport, Conn., Libraries Unlimited/Greenwood Publishing Group, 2004. 339p. index. (Genreflecting Advisory Series). $55.00]. ISBN 1-56308-984-X.

Readers' advisory service is an important part of library work. Readers who enjoy certain authors or certain types of books often want to find more of them. Those interested in Jewish literature produced in the United States now have a new source to help them. *Jewish American Literature: A Guide to Reading Interests*, winner of the Association of Jewish Libraries 2004 Judaica Reference and Bibliography Award, offers advice about books by authors whose works illuminate and reflect the Jewish experience. The work focuses on books that depict the diversity within the contemporary Jewish community. All of the books listed are either award winners, listed in bibliographies of recommended titles, or favorably reviewed and published between 1980 and 2003. These titles are likely to be in public libraries. A few titles with earlier publication dates or by non-Jewish authors (e.g., Thomas Keneally's *Schindler's List*) are included because they are relevant. The emphasis is on authors from the United States, but some Canadian and Latin American works are included if their work is published in English. Authors such as Elie Wiesel and I. B. Singer, whose works are translated and who live or are widely read in the United States are also represented. Although the emphasis is on literary and genre fiction, biographies, autobiographies, and memoirs also appear.

The first chapter contains collection development information: publishers, review sources, lists of award winners, organizations, and special collections. The rest of the book is a series of annotated bibliographies by genre. The entries include the author's name as it appears in the book with the real name if he or she uses a pseudonym, bibliographic information for the U.S. or Canadian edition, reprint information (if available), and annotations describing the style and themes of the work without revealing crucial plot elements. Symbols denoting suitability for young adult readers and awards and lists of related titles also appear. A chapter with a bibliography of reader' advisory materials and resources for book discussion groups is very useful. Author/title and subject indexes complete the work. Reisner, program coordinator at the Central Jersey Regional Library Cooperative in Freehold, New Jersey, has created a resource that will help librarians working in public, school, and synagogue libraries find books that readers will enjoy. [R: LJ, 15 April 05, p. 128]—**Barbara M. Bibel**

Dictionaries and Encyclopedias

C, S
384.   **Beat Culture: Icons, Lifestyles, and Impact.** William T. Lawlor, ed. Santa Barbara, Calif., ABC-CLIO, 2005. 392p. illus. index. $85.00; $90.00 (e-book). ISBN 1-85109-400-8.

The Beats, or "Beat Generation," flourished in the 1950s and early 1960s but the influence of the writers, artists, and musicians has been felt ever since. The movement produced a thriving academic industry of books, articles, and dissertations, as well as biographical and critical studies of its major figures (e.g., Allen Ginsberg, Jack Kerouac, William Burroughs, Gary Snyder, Gregory Corso, Lawrence Ferlinghetti, Diane Di Prima). It also spawned a mini-industry of reference books devoted to the Beats, to which this title is a worthy addition. Earlier reference guides of note include: the three-volume *The Beat Generation: A Gale Critical Companion* (see ARBA 2004, entry 1036); *The Beats: Literary Bohemians in America* (see ARBA 84, entry 1162); and *The Beats: A Documentary Volume* (Gale Group, 2001).

The editor, William T. Lawlor, is interested in the impact of the Beats as much as in the personalities themselves, and this emphasis is evident in the list of 262 entries. Major cultural figures who were influenced by the Beats are profiled—Andy Warhol, Bob Dylan, Norman Mailer, Jackson Pollack, Philip Glass, Thomas Merton, and Hunter S. Thompson, among others. Editors, mentors, wives, and lovers are also well represented. Lesser-known Beat writers are covered (e.g., Jack Micheline, Joanne Kyger, Philip Whalen), which gives this volume a comprehensiveness not found in other compilations.

The treatment of the major writers is impressive, although not as consistent as the entries found in the three-volume *The Beat Generation: A Gale Critical Companion*. Ginsberg receives 20 pages, including a 4-page detailed chronology of his life. Burroughs gets 14 pages and Kerouac 12, but Ferlinghetti only has a 3-page entry (perhaps because he is still alive and actively writing). There are entries for significant places (e.g., Big Sur, Denver, Black Mountain, New York City), events, conferences, exhibitions, and themes (e.g., memory, eastern culture, sexual freedom, spontaneity). Among the more interesting entries are "The Beat Pad," "Travel: The Beats as Globetrotters," "Beats as Teachers," and "Library Holdings" (which identifies major archival collections). Photographs are sprinkled liberally throughout the book, although bibliographic references are rather sparse. Most entries contain a list of the person's principal works and a brief critical bibliography. There is a three-page "Survey of Scholarship and Critical Appreciation," which is also disappointingly selective.

Lawlor provides a five-page introductory essay with a full-page bibliography, but the volume lacks a separate comprehensive bibliography of all works cited. Another weakness of this book is that although every entry is signed, there is no further information given about the contributors. On the plus side, a valuable 35-page chronology traces the genealogy and lives of the Beats from 1905 to the present and links them to writings, events, and culture. The contents section organizes the entries by categories: people, places, events, forms and movements, themes, and contexts. However, the main arrangement of the book is strictly alphabetical. The index is excellent.

Beat Culture is highly recommended for those academic and large public libraries that do not own *The Beat Generation: A Gale Critical Companion*. It is most suitable for a high school through undergraduate audience. [R: LJ, 1 Nov 05, p. 112; SLJ, Dec 05, pp. 90-92]—**Thomas A. Karel**

British Literature

General Works

Dictionaries and Encyclopedias

P, S

385. **Encyclopedia of British Writers.** Alan Hager, ed. New York, Facts on File, 2005. 2v. index. (Facts on File Library of World Literature). $150.00/set. ISBN 0-8160-5132-1.

The *Encyclopedia of British Writers* is part of Facts on File's four-volume set covering British Writers of the sixteenth to twentieth centuries. These two volumes cover the sixteenth through eighteenth centuries and are a good resource for young students to use for a background in the literature of the time period. The books are aimed at a high school audience, and the writing is clear and appropriate for the age level. The introduction should be useful to students who are new to the material, and gives a broad outline of major movements and writers of Renaissance and early modern literature.

There are alphabetic entries in each for major literary figures of the eras, and short bibliographies at the end of each entry will help students research other sources. The entries give biographical information and outline the author's major works. A bit of critical analysis is offered for some of the larger entries, but for more in-depth criticism students should use the bibliographies and consult other works. More advanced students, or those who are interested in more than just the basics on these writers, would be advised to check into such reference works as the Literature Criticism from 1400 to 1800 series (Gale). These volumes are recommended for public or high school libraries. [R: SLJ, June 05, p. 90]—**Chris Tuthill**

C, P

386. **The Facts on File Companion to the British Novel.** By Virginia Brackett and Victoria Gaydosik. New York, Facts on File, 2006. 2v. index. (Facts on File Library of World Literature). $130.00/set. ISBN 0-8160-6377-X.

Marketed by Facts on File as part of a five-title Companion to Literature "set" that also includes volumes on Classical drama, the American short story, twentieth-century American poetry, and American drama, *The Facts on File Companion to the British Novel* is intended to be a guide to the authors and works most frequently studied in high school and lower-division undergraduate courses. Volume 1, authored by Virginia Brackett, covers the genre from its beginnings in the late seventeenth century through the nineteenth century, and volume 2, by Victoria Gaydosik, is devoted entirely to the twentieth century. Both volumes utilize an alphabetic arrangement for the main sequence of entries and include a general index, a glossary of basic literary terms related to fiction, and a selected bibliography. Volume 2 also provides lists of the British and Commonwealth winners of various literary prizes for fiction. Individual entries, about 500 in each volume, consist of brief essays mainly on major authors and novels, although some attention is also given to worthy lesser writers and works and to critical concepts, influential periodicals, literary subgenres and movements, and pertinent historical events and social trends. Most of the essays end with a very brief bibliography. The authors, particularly Brackett, attempt to counteract the inherent inadequacies of the alphabetic arrangement by the extensive use of cross-references. While both authors are clearly competent and knowledgeable, their efforts to provide basic introductory information as well as a broader picture are necessarily constrained by the physical format: each volume is only about 500 pages long, including the indexes and other supporting materials. Thus, the *Companion* succeeds very well as a basic guide for students of the British novel, but given the fact that much of its content is already available from other sources, smaller collections seeking to remedy deficiencies in this area would be the most likely to consider purchasing it.—**Gregory M. Toth**

Individual Authors

Jane Austen

C, S

387. Olsen, Kirstin. **All Things Austen: An Encyclopedia of Austen's World.** Westport, Conn., Greenwood Press, 2005. 2v. illus. index. $149.95/set. ISBN 0-313-33032-8.

Written by independent scholar Kirstin Olsen, author of *All Things Shakespeare* (see ARBA 2003, entry 1085), this work is not quite "all things Austen" in that it does not include information about her writings. What it does include is a wealth of information about the context in which she wrote. Some 200 alphabetic entries in 800 pages cover background material ranging from the chapter-length general to the paragraph-length particular, from architecture to umbrellas. Additional features help the reader make use of all this detail: a listing of the entries grouped by general topics such as "Education and Intellectual Life"; references to relevant passages in Austen's works embedded in each entry; annotated illustrations, many of them from Yale University's Lewis Walpole Library for research in eighteenth-century studies; an index; and a 1731-1872 timeline with columns covering events related to the Austen family, politics/military, religion/culture, and medicine/technology/science. Scholars of the late eighteenth and early nineteenth century will not learn anything new here and may criticize some errors of fact or interpretation, but they might find the extensive, thematically arranged bibliography of print materials and Websites useful. In any case, they are not the intended audience. General readers and beginning researchers in Austen and her context can gain a deeper appreciation of her work with these explanations of what she took for granted as understood by her contemporaneous readers. Attractively bound and written in clear, unstuffy prose, this set is a recommended purchase for public and undergraduate academic libraries. [R: LJ, 15 Sept 05, pp. 92-93; SLJ, Oct 05, p. 92]—**Helene Androski**

William Shakespeare

C, S

388. Boyce, Charles. **Critical Companion to William Shakespeare: A Literary Reference to His Life and Work.** New York, Facts on File, 2005. 2v. illus. index. $104.50/set. ISBN 0-8160-5373-1.

There are many Shakespeare handbooks in print, such as the recent *Essential Shakespeare Handbook* by Leslie Dunton-Downer and Alan Riding (see ARBA 2005, entry 1080). These handbooks are a genre all to themselves and generally consist of background essays, detailed plot summaries of the plays, and explanatory entries for each character, no matter how minor. The latest entry is Charles Boyce's *William Shakespeare: A Literary Reference to His Life and Work*, a new, two-volume edition of Boyce's own 1990 one-volume work in larger format, also published by Facts on File, and titled *Shakespeare A to Z* (see ARBA 92, entry 1209). *Shakespeare A to Z*, which cost $45 when first published, was arranged in a simple alphabetic arrangement, as its title would indicate. This new work, however, as part of the Facts on File Critical Companion Series, follows a different format: "The first part of the book consists of a brief biography of the writer. The second part contains entries on the writer's works, including the characters in each work, crucial historical and thematic information, and critical discussion. The third part contains entries on related people, places, themes, topics, and influences, and the fourth part consists of a bibliography of the writer's work, a bibliography of secondary sources, and a chronology of the writers life." The practical effect of this re-organization is profound. In *Shakespeare A to Z* the first entry is "Aaron," a character in *Titus Andronicus*. All one needs to have in order to find out about this character, therefore, is a knowledge of the alphabet. On the other hand, the only real way to find "Aaron" in the new edition, unless one knows in advance in which play he occurs, is to use the index at the end of volume 2. This index does not indicate the play, or in which volume the entry occurs, but gives a page reference (the two volumes are continuously paginated). At the first of several page references, Aaron is there, and one discovers that his entry is within the material on *Titus Andronicus*, in the section on "Characters," which occurs after the synopsis, the commentary, sources of the play, text of the play, and theatrical history of the play. The text of the entry for "Aaron," however, is identical in both editions except for an insignificant wording change in the last few words.

When one looks up the title of a play in *Shakespeare A to Z*, one finds the same sections as mentioned above for each play: synopsis, commentary, sources, notes about the text, and theatrical history. This is the material that makes up "Works," which is the second part of this new edition. The entries for each play are essentially identical, with minimal updating. For instance, the extensive entry on *Othello*, which runs for nine pages, has not been changed, except that the very end of it regarding performance history has been updated with several additional sentences.

The bulk of volume 1 and a bit of volume 2 consists of the entries for the plays and major poems ("Works") ; the bulk of volume 2 of this work, entitled "Related Entries," contains all of the old entries not covered in the new volume under either "Biography" or "Works." This includes articles on people, places, things, and concepts (such as "Fanny Kemble" or "academic drama") .

The earlier edition has a list of suggested readings and a series of short appendixes listing things like names of "actors and other theatre professionals, composers, and musicians," and "places," all of which can be found alphabetically in the entries. The newer edition updates the bibliography of suggested readings, and also includes the same "contents by category" information, but one would have to use the index to find these things, and indeed almost anything in this new edition; it therefore includes a 55-page index that was not necessary in the earlier edition but is crucial now. It also includes "a collection of quotations from Shakespeare's works"; 20 pages of quotations organized by play but with no explanation of how or why they were chosen; and a "Shakespearian time line" citing historical events from 1200 B.C.E. to 2004 in terms of their relevance to one or another of the plays—a most interesting and valuable idea.

The first element in the newer edition, in a separate "Biography" section, was simply a dictionary entry for William Shakespeare in the original. It is only seven pages long, and thus could have appeared in section 3 of the new work without having been broken out as a separate section the beginning of volume 1. It is identical in both editions, and as such illustrates the conundrum of this book. Shakespeare's life has not changed much, nor have the plots of his plays. Interpretations have changed, of course, but this new edition does not deal with these changes, and indeed disavows any scholarly intent. The preface declares that "this book is not meant as scholarship; my intention has been to assemble conveniently a body of lore for the information and entertainment of the student and general readers," which is almost identical to what the first edition said in the preface.

In summary, this new edition of *Shakespeare A to Z* represents a repackaging of the information found in the earlier edition, with next to nothing in the way of revision. The 60 black-and-white photographs and drawings remain identical. The new formatting, implemented in conformity with a predetermined formula, makes information, if anything, harder to find than it was before. There would be little reason, therefore, to acquire this volume should a library have the earlier edition. For libraries without the 1st edition, however, this is a worthwhile acquisition for those who would find a basic overview of Shakespeare's plays and characters useful. [R: LJ, 1 June 05, p. 174]—**Bill Miller**

African Literature

C

389.   Killam, Douglas. **Literature of Africa.** Westport, Conn., Greenwood Press, 2004. 204p. index. (Literature as Windows to World Cultures). $49.95. ISBN 0-313-31901-4.

It would take more than one guide to help one understand, in depth, the richness of African literature, in any language or from any country. This title, *Literature of Africa*, is a small window into the world of African literature in English, and adds to all those others that attempt to make the job easier.

The author of this book has put together a few well-known African writers, such as Chinua Achebe, Miriama Ba, and Sembene Ousmane. African literature courses are fast becoming part of the reading lists for both undergraduate and graduate students across the United States and in some other parts of the world. This title is meant to help those students who show an interest in African writings and to give them an understanding of the issues raised by African writers. It is also meant to give the students an appreciation of the African culture.

The book is divided into four geographical parts: a selected history of West African literature; a selected history of East African literature; a selected history of South-Central African literature; and a selected of history of South African literature and politics. A part of south eastern Africa is not represented, such as Zambia, Malawi, and Zimbabwe, because the writers from these particular countries have not achieved much prominence. The introduction to this book is worth reading as it explains the choices and selections made by the author. The brief biographies of each author in the selection are divided geographically. A list of further and additional readings is a plus for the readers. *Literature of Africa* will be a worthy addition to other undergraduate guides to African literature.—**Valentine K. Muyumba**

Latin American Literature

C, P

390.   **Notable Latino Writers.** Edited by the Editors of Salem Press. Hackensack, N.J., Salem Press, 2006. 3v. illus. index. $207.00/set. ISBN 1-58765-243-1.

Notable Latino Writers compiles 115 essays on great novelists, poets, playwrights, and short story writers, plus 7 supplementary overview essays on genres. The definition of Latino is very broad here, as it encompasses those who speak or whose family speaks any romance language, as well as those of Latin American descent living in the United States. Although obviously the use of the term eliminates those born in Spain, it allows for the unexpected inclusion of Alejandro Casona, a Spaniard who spent many years in exile in Argentina, and W. H. Hudson, an English-language writer who left his native Argentina at the age of 28.

Each entry begins with birth and date dates; the mention of the 2005 deaths of Roa Bastos and Cabrera Infante reflects the editors' commitment to currency. The chronological listings of the author's works by genre contain English translations, although occasionally comprehensiveness has not been maintained; the most notorious example is the omission of all three volumes of the monumental translation of selections of Borges' fiction and nonfiction (Viking, 1998-1999). The accompanying portraits, although interesting, are unnecessary and take up space. An additional benefit to this work, a key to author's pronunciation, was well-intended but poorly executed, since so many of them have errors that they must be used with extreme caution. The write up for each author is generally equally split between biography and criticism and written most appropriately for school and public library patrons. Thus, the bibliographies, although very current, are likely too advanced for that user group. Each essay also includes a sidebar called "What to Read," a guide to one of the author's most famous works available in English. A listing of 401 additional writers, an annotated bibliography of print and electronic resources, a listing of authors by birth year, and five indexes round out these three volumes.

The contributors all hail from academia, although about 10 percent are called "independent scholar." A final word of caution: most of the essays are reprints (occasionally updated), mostly from the 4th revised edition of the *Cyclopedia of World Authors* (see ARBA 2005, entry 984), with only those for Nicolás Guillén and José Martí written expressly for this volume. Thus, if libraries already own the master set, they may be more than adequately set for coverage in this area. [R: LJ, Jan 06, p. 160]—**Lawrence Olszewski**

Spanish Literature

C, P

391.   **The Cambridge History of Spanish Literature.** David T. Gies, ed. New York, Cambridge University Press, 2004. 863p. index. $130.00. ISBN 0-521-80618-6.

David T. Gies, Commonwealth Professor of Spanish at the University of Virginia and editor of *The Cambridge Companion to Modern Spanish Culture* (Cambridge University Press, 1999), has joined with 46 other distinguished scholars to produce a seminal work on Spain's rich literary history. This work is comprised of 56 authoritative essays. The essays are divided under 10 headings, such as "History and Canonicity," "Early Modern Spain: Renaissance and Baroque," and "In and Out of Franco Spain." Complementary materials include an 11-page chronology that contextualizes Spain's literary history by including political and cultural events that would have influenced the writing of the day. There is also a 44-page comprehensive bibliography that alone is worth the price of this volume. The work concludes with an index that allows researchers to find nuggets of information that would otherwise be difficult to find within the pithy essays. This outstanding reference tool is an essential purchase for all academic libraries supporting literature programs and should also be strongly considered by public libraries.—**John R. Burch Jr.**

POETRY

Dictionaries and Encyclopedias

C, S

392.   **The Facts on File Companion to 20th-Century American Poetry.** Burt Kimmelman, ed. New York, Facts on File, 2005. 572p. index. (Facts on File Library of American Literature). $65.00. ISBN 0-8160-4698-0.

Over 400 contemporary American poets are featured in this authoritative guide that should prove useful to a multitude of students and readers. Major figures such as Eliot, Pound, Frost, Robinson, and Williams have been allotted over 1,000 words. Less popular poets are covered in shorter entries running 500-800 words. Written by some 200 or so American literature specialists at leading colleges and universities, the alphabetically arranged entries are biographical, analytical, and comparative. Taken together, they record representative poetic articulations of twentieth-century American life and thought.

On the whole, the editor has done a good job in the selection of figures featured. Space limitations have forced the omission of several deserving poets, but much to his credit, the editor has a representative number of women, African American, Native American, Hispanic, and other ethnic poets. Especially commendable are his inclusion of individual entries on leading poems; among them, for example, are Crane's "The Bridge," Lowell's "For the Union Dead," Plath's "Daddy," and Ginsberg's "Howl." Dozens of additional essays cover such worthwhile topics as cyberpoetry, imagism, objective poetry, poetry anthologies, poetry presses, and poetry prizes.

Two appendixes add to the usefulness of the volume: the first defines and exemplifies a host of poetic terms; the second is a bibliography for those desirous of further study. Finally, there is a detailed index for quick retrieval of the vast amount of information in this praiseworthy companion to twentieth-century American poetry. [R: SLJ, Aug 05, p. 76]—**G. A. Cevasco**

Indexes

C, P

393. **Index of American Periodical Verse 2003.** Rafael Catalá and James D. Anderson, comps. Lanham, Md., Scarecrow, 2005. 649p. $100.00. ISBN 0-8108-5197-0. ISSN 0090-9130.

The primary purpose of this *Index* is to provide an important resource for research to more than 6,500 contemporary poets whose work has graced the pages of some 260 periodicals published in the United States, Canada, and the Caribbean during 2003. A concomitant inference indicates that poetry is flourishing through North America.

Selection of periodicals was a responsibility of the editors based on recommendations from literary scholars and critics, librarians, and publishers. Chief among the editors' criteria for inclusion were the reputations of the poets and the quality of their recent poems. Within these broad and subjective guidelines, the editors have come up with more than 18,500 poems, the listing of which reveals trends and influences.

Poets are arranged alphabetically by surname, and under each entrant's name poems are set up alphanumerically by title, or if lacking a title, by first line. An appended index provides access to poems by title or first line. Being that this *Index* is the only reference tool of its kind, it deserves a place in large literature collections, especially in those that have reason to believe that the 15 annually published volumes that preceded this latest addition to the series have been put to use.—**G. A. Cevasco**

25 Music

GENERAL WORKS

Dictionaries and Encyclopedias

P
394.   Perone, James E. **Woodstock: An Encyclopedia of the Music and Art Fair.** Westport, Conn., Greenwood Press, 2005. 230p. illus. index. $69.95. ISBN 0-313-33057-3.

Woodstock: An Encyclopedia of the Music and Art Fair explores the original concert of 1969 in the context of festivals both before and long after. The text opens with an exploration of the rock music festivals immediately preceding and following Woodstock, from the famous Monterey Festival of 1967 to the infamous Altamont of 1969. This is followed by chapters discussing the Woodstock of 1969, 1994, and 1999, with some black-and-white photographs illustrating each. The chapters are straightforward historical narrative, with works cited listed at the end of each. A final chapter, titled "A-Z of Woodstock," is the first section of the book that can be considered a reference resource, and consists of brief articles about the people and organizations associated with the original concert of 1969. There is an appendix that includes a list of the musicians who appeared in 1969, along with their set lists. A second appendix lists the various audio and visual records of all three Woodstocks. The text closes with an extensive annotated bibliography and an alphabetic index. The text is well written and seems aimed at a high school or college level audience. Given the amount of material written about Woodstock, it is not clear what this particular work adds to the canon. The "A-Z of Woodstock" is helpful, but the information cited can be found in any number of works on the history of rock music, making this a sincere but negligible contribution to the field of popular music history. [R: LJ, Dec 04, p. 166; LJ, 15 April 05, p. 124]—**Philip G. Swan**

INDIVIDUAL COMPOSERS AND MUSICIANS

Dictionaries and Encyclopedias

C, P
395.   Butterworth, Neil. **Dictionary of American Classical Composers.** 2d ed. New York, Routledge/Taylor & Francis Group, 2005. 548p. illus. index. $150.00. ISBN 0-415-93848-1.

The 2d edition of the Dictionary of American Classical Composers is an updated version of the edition first published in 1984 by Garland. When Taylor & Francis acquired Garland in 1997, their Routledge press set out to update and re-format many of Garland's larger works. This new edition of the Dictionary of

American Classical Composers adds many more American composers. The author's criteria for the selection of American composers to be included in the volume are that the persons must have their music performed widely, and must be citizens (naturalized or by birth) of the United States. Not included are composers of light music, jazz, and popular song unless they have produced works in other media. There are some 850 composers represented in this 2d edition. An appendix, subtitled "Legacy: American Composers and Their Students," lists 35 composers from the volume along with some of their eminent students. From this list one might ascertain the possible influences these teachers had on their pupils' works. The volume also includes a bibliography arranged by composers, and a general index.

The volume centers around composers of the nineteenth century and the early twentieth century. A few of the earliest composers represented are: Jeremiah Denke (b.1725), William Billings (b.1746), and Supply Belcher (b.1752). Some of the youngest composers, and there are not many, are Tod Machover (b.1953), Tobias Picker (b.1954), and Michael Torke (b.1961). Here lies the age gap, for out of 650 composers listed in the volume there are only a very few younger composers mentioned. Is it because young composers need to prove themselves before being included, or is it because not enough promising composers have been researched? True, young composers need wide exposure for the ultimate test, but there is talent out there to be examined, and a few more contemporary composers should have been included.

Regardless, the volume is a vital reference source, as it includes ready information such as biographical data (often submitted by the composer), educational background, analysis of the composer's major works and typical style of composition, and much more. The *Dictionary of American Classical Composers* is highly recommended for inclusion in reference divisions of university and public libraries.—**Robert Palmieri**

P

396.   **The Cambridge Mozart Encyclopedia.** Cliff Eisen and Simon P. Keefe, eds. New York, Cambridge University Press, 2006. 662p. index. $175.00. ISBN 0-521-85659-0.

The first celebratory offering to the extravaganza of the 250th anniversary of Mozart's birth arrives early in the year, *The Cambridge Mozart Encyclopedia*. It may well be impossible for any even modestly literate person to miss this celebration, and who would want to? Among the world's composers it is hard to think of a more competent, more versatile, more widely known, or widely loved, musician than Mozart. What we know of him is so inextricably mixed with myth and legend that sorting everything out may well be impossible for mere hobbyists. It is hard enough for the aficionados who live and breathe his music, his fame, his riotous living.

To many of us, Mozart is that impish enfant terrible of the 1984 file, *Amadeus*. This first of what is sure to be many gifts to the Maestro will go a long way to help us unravel fact from fiction. *The Cambridge Mozart Encyclopedia* attempts to update and bridge the differences between two great classics, Landon and Mitchell's *Mozart Companion* (1953) on the one hand, and Landon's *Mozart Compendium* (1990) on the other. While the *Companion* proffered essays organized by genre but little on his life, the *Compendium* focused on the prodigy's life but not as much on his music. *The Cambridge Mozart Encyclopedia*, however, does both, allowing wary readers to pick and choose, or indefatigable ones to read cover-to-cover. Entries are beautifully and entertainingly written by some of the best Mozart scholars in the world.

Not every person, place, or thing will be found as an individual entry, but by using the volume's very extensive cross-references and index, all are covered. Following the encyclopedia are a series of excellent appendixes. One covers Mozart's known works by type; another, key movies and/or theatrical releases as well as a listing of his operas on DVD or video; and one of worldwide Mozart organizations, Websites, and finally his works by Köechel number. If all such gifts come as brilliantly packaged as this one, it will indeed give all Mozart lovers something to sing about. [R: LJ, 15 Nov 05, p. 94]—**Mark Y. Herring**

MUSICAL FORMS

Operatic

P

397.   **The Billboard Illustrated Encyclopedia of Opera.** Stanley Sadie, ed. New York, Watson-Guptill, 2004. 320p. illus. index. $45.00. ISBN 0-8230-7721-7.

This rich and splendidly illustrated volume is an opulent visual and intellectual tour of the world of opera. Included in its gorgeous pages are history, music, staging, story lines, composers, librettists, and more. Eight chapters cover opera from its earliest beginnings to its most fashionable stagings. Chapters on the baroque period and the early and high romantic periods provide even the most naVve novice with enough background to enjoy some of opera's most difficult and involved settings. Arranged chronologically, each section provides a historical, social, and cultural background. Synopses of over 200 operas—in full and rich detail—are given. Brief phrases of music delight the eye of the avid opera lover. All of this comes in a colorful guide that makes of this volume one of the truly art-like coffee-table books or serious reference tools.

This is not surprising. Stanley Sadie, the volume's general editor, would not oversee any slipshod thing into being. His introduction breathes just the right life into this wonderful work. A glossary provides enough vocabulary to navigate, while indexes to the operas and a general index make this useable at the most general level, to its most complex. Brief biographical sketches of composers, from the most familiar to the more obscure, will delight all levels of sophistication. Purists will be delighted to see Puccini and Verdi held up as the rightful standard-bearers, while the more modern-minded will be tickled over the faddish, such as Adams' *Nixon in China* or Berg's *Lulu*. Pictures, illustrations, diagrams, and sidebars of every conceivable aspect of opera make this cornucopia of coloratura and the perfect ticket to an enjoyable night at the opera. [R: LJ, 15 Nov 04, p. 86]—**Mark Y. Herring**

Popular

General Works

Handbooks and Yearbooks

P, S

398.   **Hit Singles: Top 20 Charts from 1954 to the Present Day.** 5th ed. Dave McAleer, comp. San Francisco, Calif., Backbeat Books, 2004. 505p. illus. index. $24.95pa. ISBN 0-87930-808-7.

Hit Singles: Top 20 Charts from 1954 to the Present Day features lists from Billboard in the United States and NME/Music Week in the United Kingdom, with U.S. and UK top 20 charts side by side and month by month, listing the hits from 1954 through 2003. *Hit Singles* includes an introduction showing the reader how to use the book; a list of the top 100 Singles for 1954-2000 for both the United States and United Kingdom; the chart file, listing by artist, and listing by title; artist's name and nationality; current and previous months' chart positions; record label; weeks on the chart; and position in the United Kingdom (if available). As the author states, "the aim of the book is to try and put the 12,500 most successful records of the rock era into some kind of perspective," letting users see and compare the "tastes of American and Britain, the most important and influential countries in the world of music." The book includes many pictures of artists at the time of their hits, along with facts and trivia such as deaths of notable musicians, announcements of acts splitting up, information about a song first appearing on the charts, and the subsequent artists that had hits with the same song over the years. *Hit Singles* is fun reading, is chock full of fun facts and trivia, and would be a nice addition to a high school or public library collection.—**Linda W. Hacker**

Country

P

399.   **Joel Whitburn's Top Country Songs 1944 to 2005.** Menomonee Falls, Wis., Record Research, 2005. 621p. illus. $59.95. ISBN 0-89820-165-9.

This 6th edition of *Joel Whitburn's Top Country Songs* provides information on the country artists and their songs that have reached the top 100 songs based on airplay and sales. The book is arranged alphabetically by artist or band name and provides the following information: a one-line biography of the artist, week the song debuted on the charts, peak number on the charts, weeks in the top 100, title of the song, songwriter, and the label the song was recorded under. New to this edition is information about the songwriter, titles of songs that were hits for artists before 1944, and award winners of Country Music Awards and Grammy Awards. The work concludes with a listing of entries by song title, lists of top artists (by decade, by achievement, and the top 300 artists of all time), a list of number one hits, and chart facts (top number one hits by decade, top country songwriters, and singles with longevity). For those libraries that have clientele researching popular music, and country music in particular, this volume will answer many questions and provide a quick source of reference.—**Shannon Graff Hysell**

Folk

C, P

400.   Cohen, Norm. **Folk Music: A Regional Exploration.** Westport, Conn., Greenwood Press, 2005. 335p. illus. index. (Greenwood Guides to American Roots Music). $75.00. ISBN 0-313-32872-2.

This book is a welcome overview to American folk music from a leading authority on the subject. Its regional organization is appropriate to folk music, which is often tied to locality and is characterized by regional styles. Within broad categories of the Northeast, Southeast, Midwest and Great lakes Region, and Far West, Cohen gives attention to the ethnic and geographic influences that shaped the styles of the music. The emphasis, however, is less on the many strains of immigrant folk song in various languages brought to this country, rightfully deserving a separate volume, and more on the English-language ballads and songs, and especially the textual rather than musicological aspects. To Cohen's credit, his narrative provides abundant contextual information linking the music to regional cultures. Another praiseworthy feature is the sidebars with lists concerning popular distribution or collection. Examples are "Most Widespread Broadside Ballads and Their Themes" and "Most Collected Indigenous Ballads." The volume's illustrations are stellar, especially the inclusion of broadsides that influenced the spread of folk music. Also useful is the number of song texts reproduced in the entirety with recording information. Of special interest is the chapter on urban centers, often neglected in folk music surveys. It has handy useful appendixes with biographical sketches, plot synopses of traditional ballads most commonly found in the United States and Canada, and a glossary. Although the volume is priced and packaged like a reference work, it may also have value as a course text in surveys of folk music to expand beyond the more ethnically organized *Introducing American Folk Music* by Kip Lornell (McGraw-Hill, 1993).—**Simon J. Bronner**

Jazz

C, P

401.   Yanow, Scott. **Jazz: A Regional Exploration.** Westport, Conn., Greenwood Press, 2005. 287p. illus. index. (Greenwood Guides to American Roots Music). $75.00. ISBN 0-313-32871-4.

Jazz, often considered underground music, has a number of varied styles and influences, including rock, fusion, and Latin. This book differs from others in that it emphasizes regional aspects, noting the present as well as the past. A chronology (pp. xiii-xxi) traces major events from Buddy Bolden in 1895 to the Newport Jazz Festival's 50th anniversary in 2004. Along the way it chronicles births, compositions, and performances of Scott Joplin, Louis Armstrong, Count Basie, Benny Goodman, Duke Ellington, and others.

After defining jazz as a combination of improvisation and the blues, and a brief pre-history of jazz, Yanow journeys through several regions that had distinct jazz styles prior to the age of worldwide mass communications. We tour Sedalia and St. Louis for ragtime, New Orleans for Dixieland, then Chicago, New York, and Kansas City for classic and swing eras; to this point Yanow is basically in the past. After exploring New York for bebop and Latin styles, and Los Angeles for West Coast jazz, we return to New York and Chicago for hard bop, soul jazz, free jazz, and the avant-garde. Yanow addresses the recent past as he describes young lions of New Orleans, and moves beyond regionalism to fusion and smooth jazz.

Each chapter is written in easy-to-read language, citing several titles of music, and ending with a list of recommended recordings. Black-and-white pictures are laced through the volume, but there are neither musical examples (in notation) nor footnotes.

Yanow presents a concise biographical dictionary of over 200 jazz leaders and legends (pp. 247-276). The general index that follows lists people (e.g., Gillespie, Dizzy) and styles (e.g., Swing era, Third Stream). The book succeeds in highlighting the regional variations in jazz up to the present day, and may serve as a text for secondary education or non-major courses at college.—**Ralph Hartsock**

Sacred

P

402.   **Encyclopedia of American Gospel Music.** W. K. McNeil, ed. New York, Routledge/Taylor & Francis Group, 2005. 489p. illus. index. $150.00. ISBN 0-415-94179-2.

Recent years have seen a revival of interest in gospel music. McNeil has compiled an encyclopedia using a multicultural approach. He sought to cover "every important aspect" of gospel music (p. xviii), while admittedly being subjective in some of the selection. The format is alphabetical, with an index.

Components include biographical profiles of performers (e.g., Roy Rogers), composers (e.g., William Bradbury), and writers (e.g., Isaac Watts); important events in the history of gospel (e.g., Azusa Street Revival); broadcasting outlets, such as radio stations and record labels; and publications (e.g., *Singing News*), publishers (e.g., Stamps-Baxter), and societies (e.g., Gospel Music Association). Topical thematic entries include instruments (e.g., banjo, trumpet, piano), types of ensembles (e.g., Barbershop quartets), and forms and styles of music (e.g., Bluegrass, Gospel Boogie, Soul Gospel, shape note singing). Various denominations' attitudes or use of gospel is also included.

Biographical entries in the volume, including those who influenced gospel, such as Richard Allen (1760-1831), contain dates and places of birth and death, significance, a brief biography, and references for further reading. Some include a discography. Ensembles identify the individuals of the group, with each member's birth and death dates. It includes illustrations of some ensembles, such as the Fisk Jubilee Singers. Others have fewer details available, such as Smith's Sacred Singers (pp. 354-355) and Soul Stirrers (pp. 356-358). Certain articles list references to entries about individual members, types of ensembles with broader coverage, and record companies.

Illustrations dot the book. Writing is objective, as in the case of evangelist Jimmy Swaggart (pp. 384-385). Naturally, with a volume of several contributors, the length of bibliographies varies. Data exceeds that of the *Gospel Music Encyclopedia*, by Robert Anderson and Gail North (Sterling, 1979); McNeil's source lists birth and death dates of most ensemble members, while more extensive sources for further reading include Websites and discographies. The late W. K. McNeil successfully led a team that has addressed the dearth of reference materials on gospel music, providing much more detail on performers, historical persons, ensembles, and styles. The index lists associations between people, titles of documentaries, and reference sources. [R: LJ, 15 Nov 05, p. 96]—**Ralph Hartsock**

26 Mythology, Folklore, and Popular Culture

FOLKLORE

Dictionaries and Encyclopedias

C, P, S

403.   **The Greenwood Encyclopedia of World Folklore and Folklife.** William M. Clements, ed. Westport, Conn., Greenwood Press, 2006. 4v. illus. maps. index. $449.95/set. ISBN 0-313-32847-1.

This four-volume reference work is an excellent compilation on the topic of world folklife and folklore, divided into geographic areas of the world. Volume 1 is a listing of topics and themes, from Antiquarianism to Worldview, along with general essays on folklore in Africa, Australia, and Oceania. Volume 2 focuses on Southeast Asia, India, Central and East Asia, and the Middle East. Volume 3 has essays related to countries in Europe, and volume 4 centers on North and South America. Over 200 specialists have been recruited to write the essays, detailing over 170 cultural groups. Every entry includes a bibliography, and there are many illustrations, maps, and photographs. The following template for contributors was provided by the editors, to guide them in their writing: geographical setting, sociocultural features, ethnohistorical information, belief system, verbal art, musical art, sports and games, graphic and plastic arts, effects of modernization and globalization, and references and bibliographic essay. This set is a well-constructed and illuminating addition for all reference collections.—**Bradford Lee Eden**

Handbooks and Yearbooks

C, P

404.   **Archetypes and Motifs in Folklore and Literature: A Handbook.** Jane Garry and Hasan El-Shamy, eds. Armonk, N.Y., M. E. Sharpe, 2005. 515p. illus. index. $110.00. ISBN 0-7656-1260-7.

The Motif-Index of Folk Literature has been a standard reference tool for folk narrative research since the 1930s, and continues to be examined as an artifact of folkloristic thinking as well as an ongoing indexing project. The grand goal of the six volumes, found in most academic libraries, is to systematically classify the "stuff of which tales are made," according to its compiler Stith Thompson, such as objects, events, and characters that draw attention to themselves in traditional narratives around the world. This work is an essential guide to navigate through the Motif-Index as well as understand its limitations. More than merely an introductory handbook to summarize key motifs, such as "fairies and elves" or "magic invisibility," in comparative perspective, the 66 essays in the volume frequently expound on the Jungian concept of "archetypes" related to "motifs," but not articulated in Thompson's work. Broad archetypes such as "shadow," "child," and "mother" are viewed as persistent cultural symbols passed down through generations through folklore. The handbook also adds discussion of new motifs, especially those introduced in the monumental *Types of the Folktale in the Arab World* (2004) compiled by one of the handbook's editors, Hasan El-Shamy. The handbook is divided into two sections devoted to selected motifs discussed under Thompson's alphabetic organization, such as A for Mythological Motifs, B for Mythical Animals, C for Tabu, and D for Magic. Some sections such as A and D understandably have a larger amount of essays devoted to them, reflecting the considerable scholarship on myth and märchen, than E (the Dead) and G (Ogres), and no essays under V for Religion, W for Traits of Character, and X for Humor are included. A general index at the end offers an opportunity for cross-referencing of subjects, although it might have been useful to have an index by tale type and Grimm Brothers' tale numbers discussed in the text. Still, the handbook is an essential supplement to the Motif-Index that admirably plows new ground for an "old" folkloristic analysis.—**Simon J. Bronner**

MYTHOLOGY

POPULAR CULTURE

Dictionaries and Encyclopedias

P

405.   **The DC Comics Encyclopedia.** By Phil Jimenez, Scott Beatty, Robert Greenberger, and Dan Wallace. New York, DK Publishing, 2004. 351p. illus. index. $40.00. ISBN 0-7566-0592-X.

More than 1,000 characters of the DC Universe make up this beautifully designed coffee-table encyclopedia, obviously created in collaboration with DC Comics. If not, the legal procedures and financial demands for reprint rights that are part of DC's policy would be prohibitively staggering. Nevertheless, the oversized volume is a fascinating mix of character profiles—of legendary superheroes, such as Superman, Wonder Woman, Batman, and Captain Marvel, and lesser-known weirdoes, such as Bad Samaritan, Folded Man, the ugly Gorgeous Gilly, Lump, Murmer, and others—and two page features about their "amazing" vehicles, weapons, and bases, "great team-ups and battles, and alien races and worlds, romantic moments, and strange times and places. Each profile provides basic data, such as first appearance, real name, status, and special powers, as well as information only fan boys would care about (e.g., color of eyes and hair, weight and height).

From the encyclopedia, one can get a feel not just for the characters, but for the times in which they were created (Uncle Sam in wartime 1940s, Karate Kid of 1966, or The Hacker Files in the computer age) and for the ways in which their creators conceived them. Concerning the latter, women were usually shown as scantily clad, whether heroine or villainess; certain character traits were duplicated (Joker, Trickster, Prankster; Elongated Man, Plastic Man, Folded Man); and playing with language was important in naming characters (T. O Morrow, Mister Mxyzptlk, Mister Zsasz, Roulette Scorch, and even one called Onomatopoeia). Some prefixes to names were very popular; there were 17 Blacks (although very few were black characters), 15 Doctors, and 13 each Captains (including Captain Nazi) and Misters.

Once curious aspect of the book was that the creators were not mentioned, but his might be explained by DC's corporate thinking that the company nurtured and owned the characters. [R: SLJ, Feb 05, p. 84]—**John A. Lent**

P

406. Henderson, Helene. **Patriotic Holidays of the United States: An Introduction to the History, Symbols, and Traditions Behind the Major Holidays and Days of Observance.** Detroit, Omnigraphics, 2006. 408p. illus. index. $56.00pa. ISBN 0-7808-0733-2.

The scope of this book is about holidays that are central to the identity of the United States as a nation. Both legal public holidays and patriotic days of remembrance are included. The work is geared toward a general audience, and begins with an extended essay and history of patriotic holidays in the United States. Fifteen holidays are then listed in alphabetic order, describing various items associated with each, including history, various states and a sample of observances, Websites, and sources for further reading. The appendix provides excerpts and examples of a number of primary sources associated with the various patriotic holidays detailed within the book. An extended bibliography and list of Websites, with an index, concludes the book. Because it is geared toward a general audience, this book is a good reference work for both public and academic libraries, providing some detail on the history, traditions, and symbols behind the major patriotic holidays and days of observance in the United States.—**Bradford Lee Eden**

P

407. **Holidays, Festivals, and Celebrations of the World Dictionary.** 3d ed. Helene Henderson, ed. Detroit, Omnigraphics, 2005. 906p. index. $110.00. ISBN 0-7808-0422-8.

This is the 3d edition of the classic reference source on holy days, festivals, fasts, feasts, commemorations, and holidays, as well as other observances from all over the world. There are nearly 500 new entries, a perpetual calendar, and an expanded section on calendar systems. More Website and e-mail addresses are also available for contact information regarding specific events detailed in the book. Alphabetically arranged, the entries cover religious, regional, national, local, international, popular, and ethnic events related to the topic.

Each entry provides the observance's name, variant names, and the date or month of the celebration. One or two paragraphs follow each entry, detailing the origins and background of the event along with any special rituals associated with the festival. Sponsoring or related organization contact information is included. A number of appendixes are included, such as admission days and facts about the states and territories, United States presidents, domestic tourism information sources, international tourism information sources, bibliography, legal holidays by state, and legal holidays by country. In addition, three indexes—general, chronological, and special subject—are included as well. [R: SLJ, Aug 05, p. 74]—**Bradford Lee Eden**

C, P

408. Roy, Christian. **Traditional Festivals: A Multicultural Encyclopedia.** Santa Barbara, Calif., ABC-CLIO, 2005. 2v. illus. index. $185.00/set; $200.00. ISBN 1-57607-089-1; 1-85109-689-2 (e-book).

This work defines traditional festivals as "regularly occurring sets of actions aimed at making present and effective a certain dimension of human beings belonging to a sacred cosmic order as reflected in ever-recurring cycles of time." The scholarly definition sets the tone for the 150 descriptive essays on the festivals of the major world religions, including both ancient and modern civilizations.

Entries are approached from a variety of perspectives, such as traditional theology, cultural anthropology, folklore studies, and social theory. Whatever the approach, each essay gives a description of the festival's content and its context in the culture. Historical development, geographic variations, and how it reflects a culture's spiritual principles complete the entry. The spiritual principles are identified as being of the utmost importance since they express "a society's beliefs, fears, hopes, founding myths and redemptive visions." They also explain why the festival has become a tradition.

One of the most fascinating revelations to be found in the encyclopedia is the commonality of spiritual principles across cultures. These relationships are discussed within the text and are identified by cross-references. Thus, the reader can follow the references to discover patterns, connections, and variations across time and cultures. The encyclopedia devotes most space to festivals of Ancient Greece and

Rome and to the many traditions of the Far East. Native American, African, and Indian festivals are less represented because the author felt there were other current resources covering those traditions. References, including audiovisual, print and electronic sources, are given at the end of each entry. There are several appendixes: festival dates by religion for the years 2001 to 2010, festivals organized by culture and season of the year, and a list of entries by cultural area. The latter provides a quick way to locate all the entries for a specific tradition. The table of contents lists the festivals alphabetically with the country or religion in parentheses.

This is a serious work designed for the advanced student or researcher. It is not the type of encyclopedia to go to for a quick synopsis of a festival. It requires attention and concentration to fully appreciate the contents. It will find its best audience in college or university libraries and large, research-oriented public libraries. [R: LJ, 15 Oct 05, pp. 82-84; SLJ, Dec 05, p. 94]—**Marlene M. Kuhl**

27 Performing Arts

GENERAL WORKS

Directories

P

409. **Hollywood Creative Directory, Spring 2006.** 56th ed. Hollywood, Calif., Hollywood Creative Directory, 2006. 435p. index. $64.95pa.

The *Hollywood Creative Directory*, also known as "the phone book to Hollywood," was originally created in 1987 by an aspiring screenwriter as the "Who's What and Where in Motion Picture/Television/Cable Development and Production." Updated three times a year, the directory provides executive and staff contact information for more than 1,750 film production companies, television shows, studios, and networks, plus state and country film commissions and professional associations. Additionally, the company entries list current projects in development and in pre- and post-production as well as completed credits. All entries are indexed by "Type" (e.g., Animation, Features, Made-for-TV, Syndication) and by "Name." "The Concierge" section includes telephone numbers and addresses of essential businesses for entertainment industry professionals in Los Angeles and New York: restaurants and catering, personal shoppers, travel and transportation, office supplies and services, and much more. This directory is a fascinating browse even for those of us who are not in the "the business."

The *Hollywood Creative Directory* may be ordered as a single issue or a three-issue subscription; it is also available online in a four directory subscription package with the *Hollywood Representation Directory* (30th ed.; see ARBA 2006, entry 1132), the *Hollywood Music Industry Directory* (3d ed.; see ARBA 2006, entry 1076), and the *Hollywood Distributors Directory* (16th ed.; see ARBA 2006, entry 1131). See the publisher's Website (http://www.hcdonline.com) for more information.—**Polly D. Boruff-Jones**

FILM, TELEVISION, AND VIDEO

Bibliography

P

410. **Cinema Review. http://www.cinemareview.com/.** [Website]. Free. Date reviewed: 2005.

Cinema Review evaluates films in theaters, on videos and DVDs, and on television for quality and appropriateness for children. They do so by citing prominent critics and polling approximately 100 viewers for each film to find out what age and gender enjoyed the movie. Browsers may look at all or recent films alphabetically or by genre or see them by MPAA rating, fan rating, teen favorites, or movies suitable for children. Records for individual films summarize the story and the genre; list cast and crew credits; explicitly describe the film's content in terms of profanity, violence, sex, drugs, and alcohol; and offer reviews from leading critics with links to the full article. Cast and crew names link to detailed biographies. This site will be of interest not only to parents, but to fans deciding what movie to watch.—**Mark Emmons**

Biography

C, P

411.   Terrace, Vincent. **Television Characters: 1,485 Profiles, 1947-2004.** Jefferson, N.C., McFarland, 2006. 442p. index. $65.00. ISBN 0-7864-2191-6.

The author of this volume, Vincent Terrace, has written over 25 books, most of which deal with television history, trivia, and folklore. From this wealth of knowledge he has compiled a fascinating biographical dictionary of fictional television characters. Included are 1,173 numbered entries covering 1,485 characters (some siblings and husbands and wives double up) from about 500 mainstream series first shown on television from 1949 through 2004. An alphabetic list of the series, from *The A-Team* to *Zorro*, with the characters covered from each, is found in an appendix. The body of the work is arranged alphabetically by the first name of the character (e.g., the Mertz's of *I Love Lucy* are found under Fred and Ethel Mertz); there is a useful last name index if, for example, one has forgotten the first names of the characters in *The Brady Bunch*. The decision to include a specific series seems arbitrary and no criteria for inclusion are given. Thus, there are many unexplained omissions. For example, Howdy Doody is present but no Kukla, Fran, or Ollie; *The Beverly Hillbillies* is covered but no *Petticoat Junction*; and Phil Silvers, in any of his recurring television roles, including Sergeant Bilko, is absent. The average number of characters highlighted per series is two or three, but some, such as *MASH*, have as many as nine. An average entry is about 250 to 300 words and begins with the names of the character, the actor playing the role, and the dates he or she played the character. There follows a biographical sketch that gives material on the character's background, occupation, family, likes and dislikes, interests, important incidents in the series involving the character, his or her development, and significance of the role in the series. As well as the previously mentioned appendixes, there is an index by actor with references to entry number. This is an entertaining, very browsable book that will have some research value in large collections that need material on popular media.—**John T. Gillespie**

Catalogs

P

412.   **All Movie Guide. http://www.allmovie.com/.** [Website]. Free. Date reviewed: 2005.

With over 270,000 films and nonfiction titles and over 25,000 biographies, the *All Movie Guide* (AMG) is one of the premier international film databases available anywhere. The opening page offers feature articles, lists of new movies, miscellaneous facts, and daily birthdays, but the real value lies in the database. The simple search box on the main page searches by title or name. Film entries include a one- to five-star rating, director, parental guidance and MPAA rating, box office figures, major awards, production company, and purchase information. Two-thirds of the films receive synopses and 1 in 20 include an in-depth review. Most list cast and production credits. Of particular value are the lists of genres, keywords, themes, and the unique categories of tones and moods. Because the database is completely relational, these are used to offer lists of similar and related movies and movies with the same personnel. Biographical entries include date and place of birth and death, occupation, years active, a career biography, a filmography, and awards won. AMG also lists the filmmakers and actors with whom they have worked. The advanced search lets users search two people who have films in common, by author or title of an adapted work, by location, by technical process, or by creator. The browser lets users peruse lists by genre, country, or time period. AMG also provides a glossary of 1,400 film terms organized into 18 broad categories. While best know for its *All Music Guide*, the *All Movie Guide* is every bit as worthy of attention.—**Mark Emmons**

C, P

413.   Welsch, Janice R., and J. Q. Adams. **Multicultural Films: A Reference Guide.** Westport, Conn., Greenwood Press, 2005. 231p. index. $49.95. ISBN 0-313-31975-8.

Multicultural Films: A Reference Guide provides an overview of nearly 200 films arranged by ethnic groups predominant in the United States: African Americans, Arab Americans, Asian Americans, European Americans, Hispanic Americans, and Native Americans. Each chapter opens with an introduction discussing how an ethnic group has been depicted cinematically over time. For example, films reviewed in this volume that relate to slavery range chronologically from *Birth of a Nation* to *Roots* to *Amistad*. This long-range examination of changing views of ethnicity in popular culture is especially helpful pedagogically. After a general introduction, the plots of the films relating to a specific ethnicity are summarized. The audience seems to be primarily teachers who may want to use one of these films as an instructional aid in the classroom. Each film summary is followed by a brief bibliography for further study. The final chapter explores films that illustrate a marked interplay of characters from a variety of ethnic backgrounds. The main text closes with an index of films arranged by themes, such as "Coming of Age" and "Intergenerational Relationships." This is followed by a Webliography of film distributors, a selected bibliography, and a general subject index. While the rationale for choosing certain films is sometimes murky, the book is a unique resource for teachers and is especially recommended for faculty libraries. [R: LJ, 15 May 05, p. 150]—**Philip G. Swan**

Dictionaries and Encyclopedias

C

414.   **Encyclopedia of Early Cinema.** Richard Abel, ed. New York, Routledge/Taylor & Francis Group, 2005. 791p. illus. index. $225.00. ISBN 0-415-23440-9.

Richard Abel, a professor of film studies at the University of Michigan, and a team of about 150 international contributors (chiefly academics) have produced a thorough and important reference work on film history. The "early cinema" of the title refers to roughly the first two decades of film history, from 1895 through 1915. Although entries cover the entire world, the concentration of material is, as expected, on the two most important centers of film development, Europe and the United States. The more than 950 alphabetically arranged articles cover a wide range of topics but focus on film production, filmmakers, kinds of films, and important individual films (with material on changing patterns of distribution), as well as the evolving nature of audiences, the general culture of the times, and its relation to the film industry (e.g., there is an entry for the social worker Jane Addams because she was a vociferous critic of the moral content of early films). A random sampling of topical entries include several on different kinds of cameras, film genres, editing and lighting technology, and various film studios. The biographical entries concentrate on actors, exhibitors, producers, directors, scriptwriters, and editors, and average 15 lines each. Once again, coverage ends about 1915 (the Chaplin biography stops with his move from the Max Sennett to the Essanay Company in 1915 with no mention of later contributions). Particularly notable are the extensive overviews on individual countries—the one on France, for example, covers 10 double-columned pages. Longer entries end with brief bibliographies of books and articles for further reading and bold type within articles is used to indicate related articles. Other important features include an introductory list of the entries grouped under such broad subjects as key figures and film companies (both arranged by country), a list of contributors with credentials, and about 150 illustrations (mainly photographs) within the text. The book ends with a general bibliography and an excellent, thorough subject index. Although this book's price and specialized subject matter will restrict its purchase somewhat, libraries with film studies programs should welcome this excellent reference tool. [R: BL, June 05, p. 1848; LJ, 15 April 05, p. 117]—**John T. Gillespie**

C, P

415.   Fearn-Banks, Kathleen. **Historical Dictionary of African-American Television.** Lanham, Md., Scarecrow, 2006. 526p. (Historical Dictionaries of Literature and the Arts, no.7). $85.00. ISBN 0-8108-5335-3.

Communications professor Fearn-Banks (University of Washington—Seattle) strives in her new work to list African American actors and performers with starring, regular, or key roles in nationally aired television series, made-for-television movies, and miniseries from the early days of national television through early 2005. However, included with the biographical entries are such topics as skin color of actors, boxing matches, biopics, domestic workers, and individual shows of note (although entries in the latter category need not be "black shows" per se). Production teams (e.g., directors, producers, writers) are excluded. Entries are arranged alphabetically and vary in length from a single line to one page, but unfortunately information is often sketchy and occasionally missing. For example, the entry on Pearl Bailey makes no mention of her variety series (ABC, 1971) or her regular appearances on *Toast of the Town* (1949-1966), and the entry on "Petula" does not note that it was a representative of show sponsor Plymouth Motors who complained about the arm-touching incident. Fearn-Banks does include a chronology of Emmy winners and ratings, in addition to a good secondary bibliography. Given those caveats, the *Historical Dictionary of African-American Television* is still a handy guide for beginning researchers in the field, in conjunction with Bogle's *Blacks in American Film and Television: An Encyclopedia* (Garland, 1988) and the excellent TV Acres Website (http://www.tvacres.com/ethnic_afro_a.htm), which offers a more comprehensive listing of shows. This work is recommended for all media and black studies collections. —**Anthony J. Adam**

Filmography

C, P

416.   Mitchell, Charles P. **Filmography of Social Issues: A Reference Guide.** Westport, Conn., Greenwood Press, 2004. 318p. index. $49.95. ISBN 0-313-32037-3.

Films tackling social issues work best, states Charles P. Mitchell, when they avoid preaching and camouflage their messages. Mitchell demonstrates his point through examining how 20 social topics are treated in 100 mostly American theatrical and made-for-television films. He looks at abortion in *Blue Denim*, addiction in *The Man with the Golden Arm*, aging in *The Straight Story*, AIDS in *Philadelphia*, capital punishment in *I Want to Live*, censorship in *Lenny*, civil rights in *Conrack*, divorce in *The War of the Roses*, hate groups in *American History X*, homelessness in *Modern Times*, homosexuality in *Gods and Monsters*, immigration in *Border Incident*, poverty in *The Grapes of Wrath*, suicide in *Slender Thread*, and women's rights in *Sleeping with the Enemy*. In most cases, Mitchell considers more than one issue per film, as with child abuse, education, poverty, and violence in *Good Will Hunting*. In addition to the films he analyzes, Mitchell mentions many more addressing social issues in his lengthy introduction.

Each entry, usually two or three pages, consists of a list of the issues dealt with by the film, the film's credits, a brief overview of the film, a plot synopsis, and a critique of how the film handles its topics. Mitchell, a former library director whose previous books include *A Guide to Charlie Chaplin Films* (1999), discusses not only themes but the strengths and weaknesses of the films in his concise but insightful analyses. He occasionally includes information about the making of a film, includes warnings about how some elements may disturb some viewers, and explains how the mores of the times hindered the realism of some films. While he looks at films since 1930, slightly more than half were made after 1980. There is a lengthy index of names, titles, and topics.—**Michael Adams**

Videography

P

417.   **Leonard Maltin's Movie Guide.** 2006 ed. Leonard Maltin, ed. New York, Penguin Books, 2005. 1535p. $20.00pa. ISBN 0-452-28699-9.

The selective listing of films represented in the 2006 edition covers the years from 1910 to the first decade of the twenty-first century. Included are over 16,000 reviews, among them 8,000 DVDs, and 14,000 video listings. There are over 300 new entries, and hundreds of changes and amendments made to existing ones.

A directory of mail-order sources for home video precedes listings, arranged alphabetically, letter-by-letter. Each capsule review has title, year of release, running time, rating, director, cast, color or black-and-white, plot summary, MPAA designation, and availability in other formats (e.g., DVD, laserdisc). An index of stars, with leading performers, and an index of directors complete the volume. Both refer to only the films appearing in this book.

After 36 years, Maltin states that this *Guide* remains a work in progress. We hope so. It is comprehensive, and each entry is limited to about a paragraph. The readers is, however, referred to his many other books and newsletters for further information.—**Anita Zutis**

P

418.   **VideoHound's Golden Movie Retriever, 2006.** Jim Craddock, ed. Farmington Hills, Mich., Gale, 2005. 1692p. index. $24.95pa. ISBN 0-7876-8979-3. ISSN 1095-371X.

VideoHound's Golden Movie Retriever, now in its 15th edition, has carved out a unique place on the cinema reference shelf as one of the most reliable, economical, opinionated, and just plain fun guides to theatrical movies available on videocassette and DVD. In keeping with the canine motif, over 27,000 films are rated on the infamous four bones (excellent) to "woof" (bomb) system. Unlike many reviewing sources, *VideoHound* employs a comparative ratings system; the editors understand that an entertainingly good science fiction/horror flick cannot be judged using *Citizen Kane* as the ultimate cinematic yardstick. Horror films are assessed against other horror films and rated accordingly. In addition to the rating, each film title entry contains a wealth of compressed information: alternate title, year released, MPAA rating, description/review, length, format, country of origin, cast, director, writer(s), cinematographer(s), composer, narrator, AND awards. The reviews are opinionated, informed, and may be too flip for some readers.

As noted in an earlier review of this resource (see ARBA 2004, entry 1169), a major *VideoHound* plus is the inclusion of several indexes that provide imaginative access to the 27,000-plus entries. The "Category" index groups films under subject/genre listings like "Femme Fatale," "Loner Cops," "Organized Crime," "Mystery & Suspense," "Period Piece" (decade-by-decade), and several others. Additional indexes include alternate title, awards, cast/director, writer, cinematographer, and more. A "Web Site Guide" offers URLs of top entertainment pages categorized under headings like "Film Festivals," "Film Reviews," and "Video Outlets." This work is a steal at $24.95 for any public or academic library.—**David K. Frasier**

THEATER

Dictionaries and Encyclopedias

C, P

419.   **The Oxford Dictionary of Plays.** By Michael Patterson. New York, Oxford University Press, 2005. 523p. index. $45.00. ISBN 0-19-860417-3.

Oxford University Press has published what it describes as a concise and useful reference to the most important 1,000 plays of the western world. They are presented in alphabetic order, starting with *Abie's Irish Rose* and concluding with *The Zoo Story*. Each entry is composed of the title (and/or alternative title), author(s), date of composition, date of first performance, genre, setting, cast size, a brief synopsis, and a brief commentary. Although there are occasional minor errors, the entries are usually informative and well written. Certain plays that are felt by the author to be particularly important are dealt with in greater detail than the other entries.

The author supplied an index of characters and the plays in which they appear, which allows the reader to follow the path of those characters that have appeared in multiple works. An index of playwrights also appears, which gives the title and dates of their creations. For those fans of Shakespeare, a useful family tree of characters in the historical plays is presented by the author. These are preceded by a listing of the elected works according to country of origin, period, and genre. The plays selected for special attention appear in bold face. A somewhat modest selected bibliography is also provided.

Readers may disagree about the selection of the "Best 1,000." No criteria for selection are given. The selection procedure seems to be an intuitive process coupled with consultation with others. No criteria, such as "number of world performances," was used. However, if one wants good information about a play or its characters, they will probably find it in this volume. Academics, professionals, and lovers of the theater will want to have access to this reference work. [R: LJ, 1 Oct 05, pp. 112-114]—**Charles Neuringer**

C, P

420.   Stewart, John. **Broadway Musicals, 1943-2004.** Jefferson, N.C., McFarland, 2006. 1039p. index. $195.00. ISBN 0-7864-2244-0.

When seeing this title, users may ask why we need another work listing Broadway musicals. After all, we recently have had Richard C. Norton's monumental three-volume *Chronology of American Musical Theater* (see ARBA 2003, entry 1201), Gerald Bordman's *American Musical Theater: A Chronicle* (see ARBA 2002, entry 1242), and Kurt Gänzl's *The Encyclopedia of the Musical Theatre* (2d ed.; see ARBA 2002, entry 1243). But after examining this title users will fine it complements and supplements the earlier volumes. Stewart, a seeming polymath, has prepared other reference works for the publisher, on such disparate subjects as the solar system (see ARBA 93, entry 1707), Antarctica (see ARBA 92, entry 92), the British Empire (see ARBA 97, entry 44), and Africa (see ARBA 2000, entry 430). One only, however, is on the performing arts—*Italian Film: A Who's Who* (see ARBA 95, entry 1365).

In this new work Stewart lists 772 musicals that have appeared in New York. He begins with a chronology of Broadway openings for each year 1943 through 2004. Next the shows are listed in alphabetic order by title, including cross-references when a title has changed (e.g., *Drood*). For each show he gives a brief plot summary, its pre-Broadway history, and its Broadway run. He lists the creative staff, the production staff, and the performers. For performers he indicates who received above-the-title billing as well as replacements, standbys, and understudies. There follows a list of the scenes and songs. For many of the shows he gives a short summary of their post-Broadway history, tours, and revivals. The information for each show is tightly packed on the page. Even though there are two columns to the page, the type is small enough that users might need a straight edge to guide them along each line. Good running heads at the top

of each page make the volume easy to use. There is so much anecdotal information, including a summary of critics' assessments, that this tome becomes more than just a standard reference work. A lengthy appendix follows, with another 2,076 entries (three columns to the page), listing shows that did not run on Broadway. Here we have off- and off-off Broadway productions as well as some English shows, including the new English musicals that have yet to reach Broadway, *Billy Elliot* and *Mary Poppins*. In this section the entries are briefer but even so of great value because these shows are often not included in works listing Broadway musicals (e.g., *Little Mary Sunshine*). There are also some cross-references; for example, the entry for *Jollyanna*, which had a short run in California, refers back to the Broadway show on which it was based, *Flahooley*. Thus, if users do not find a title in the main section, they should try the appendix. Stewart selected 1943 as the starting point for his volume, because in his estimation the "first modern musical" was produced that year, *Oklahoma!* Happily, if a pre-1943 musical was revived, Stewart does list the revival with notes on the original production. For example, *The Desert Song*, which dates from 1926, was revived in 1973, and so it is listed along with substantial information about its original production, earlier revivals, and film history. The volume concludes with a brief bibliography and two lengthy indexes. The personnel index lists in one alphabet all individuals involved with the shows, giving entry numbers (not page numbers). The song index complements similar indexes in Ruth Benjamin and Arthur Rosenblatt's *Who Sang What on Broadway* (see ARBA 2006, entry 1171) and Ken Bloom's *American Song: The Complete Musical Theatre Companion* (see ARBA 2002, entry 1171, and ARBA 97, entry 1077). Because of the length of the entries under some headings in the indexes, one consults them with considerable patience. This excellent work merits a place on the reference shelves in all performing arts collections as well as larger academic and public libraries.—**Richard D. Johnson**

Directories

C, P

421.   **Summer Theatre Directory 2005: A National Guide to Summer Employment ....** 22d ed. P. J. Tumielewicz and Peg Lyons, eds. Dorset, Vt., Theatre Directories, 2004. 152p. index. $29.50pa. ISBN 0-933919-59-X.

This 22d annual volume is a compendium of available summer jobs for prospective theater workers. It covers 350 summer theaters, and 80 summer training programs, as well as theme parks, cruises, tours, Renaissance fairs, outdoor dramas, and festivals in the United States and Canada.

The citations are listed alphabetically by state. Each employment entry is laid out in the following format: name and address of company, union status, season information, facilities, hiring information (including number, type of position, and salary), housing and transportation, application procedure, apprenticeship and internship (if available), and descriptive information about the company. The summer training program entries follow the same format but add information for prospective faculty applicants and classes to be taught. Students interested in the programs will find information about classes, fees, and housing.

Several appendixes are supplied. They include tips on finding summer employment, tips on preparing for interviews and auditions, union regulations, and an alphabetic index of theaters cited in the book. A nationwide overview of combined summer theater auditions (and their dates) is also included.

There is no question that this annual listing of summer training and employment opportunities is (as it has been in the past) a must-have reference work for anybody seeking summer opportunities in the theater. It would also be an excellent idea for theater training programs to have a copy of this volume on hand for their students.—**Charles Neuringer**

28 Philosophy and Religion

PHILOSOPHY

Bibliography

C

422.   **EpistemeLinks.com: Philosophy Resources on the Internet. http://www.epistemelinks.com.** [Website]. By Thomas Ryan Stone. Free. Date reviewed: Oct 05.

This is arguably the most widely useful guide at present to philosophy-related Web resources. Among its several virtues is that it is often not content to simply list and link to significant sites in their totality, but will burrow into a site to link to specific information on individual pages. For example, its online encyclopedia section does not simply offer a directory of titles, but provides a consolidated index to several key online encyclopedias both philosophical (e.g., *Stanford Encyclopedia of Philosophy*) and general (e.g., *Wikipedia, Columbia Encyclopedia*), linking directly from a specific topic to the relevant articles in one or more encyclopedias. Similarly, its e-text section does not simply list sites where one can find a directory or collection of e-texts, but permits searching by author across many such sites to locate online books or other texts.

Labeled "Main Sections" on the *EpistemeLinks* site are the twin categories "Philosophers" and "Topics." The former offers pages on individual philosopher, some 450 at this writing, searchable alphabetically, by historical periods, or by subject categories, such as ethics or Eastern philosophy. The "Topics" section classifies Websites by historical periods, by philosophical subdisciplines (e.g., applied ethics, metaphysics, political philosophy), by schools and traditions (e.g., analytic philosophy, postmodernism), and by aspects of the practice of philosophy. Other substantial categories on this site include a journal directory, which accommodates searching by title, topic, or publisher for either online journals or print-journal home pages or both; a comprehensive directory of college/university philosophy department pages; a directory of organizations searchable by name or topic; a calendar of events searchable by date, topic, and location; and a directory of classroom teaching resources, with both general and subject-specific resources.

As a commercial site, this has non-obtrusive advertisements sprinkled throughout, and there is a list of "affiliate links" including *Amazon, eBay, Alibris,* and *HotJobs.* The Webmaster seems committed to keeping this aspect low-key.—**Hans E. Bynagle**

C, P

423.   **The Internet Encyclopedia of Philosophy. http://www.iep.utm.edu.** [Website]. James Fieser and Bradley Dowden, comps. Free. Date reviewed: Oct 05.

The Internet Encyclopedia of Philosophy (IEP) is the product of "a non-profit organization run by the editors" that "receives no funding, and operates through the volunteer work of the editors, authors, and technical advisors." Around two dozen subject area editors are listed, affiliated mainly with universities in the United States but also a few abroad. Articles are divided at this point between signed "original contributions by specialized philosophers around the internet" and "proto-articles," adapted by the editors mainly from public domain sources and intended to be replaced eventually, identified by the initials IEP. While the contributors are indeed specialists on their topics, they are less likely to be top experts than is the case for the *Stanford Encyclopedia of Philosophy* (http://plato.stanford.edu/). An ongoing project, the IEP by now has entries for most of the principal topics and names in Western philosophy, and a modest but growing number in non-Western philosophy; but it still has some significant gaps and maintains an extensive list of desired articles by areas as well as a list of "100 most desired articles." Existing articles (even some of the "proto-articles") are typically quite substantial, running from the several pages to several dozen pages if printed. They usually include substantial bibliographies. Avenues of access to entries include alphabetic lists, a keyword list with cross-references to related entries, and a timeline of Western philosophy with links to pertinent entries.—**Hans E. Bynagle**

C, P

424.   **The Oxford Companion to Philosophy.** 2d ed. Ted Honderich, ed. New York, Oxford University Press, 2005. 1056p. illus. index. $60.00. ISBN 0-19-926479-1.

Originally published in 1995, *The Oxford Companion to Philosophy* has been updated and expanded, and the present 2005 edition contains over 300 new articles. Entries are arranged alphabetically in dictionary style and range from the history of aesthetics to an entry about women and philosophy. Included are biographies of the great thinkers of western civilization, such as Aristotle, Plato, Augustine, Descartes, and Kant and also entries on non-western philosophers, such as Confucius. Written by 249 contributing philosophers under the editorial guidance of University College London philosopher Ted Honderich, the present 2d edition also contains a chronological table of philosophy and many entries on national philosophies. There are gaps and omissions in this edition. For example, while there are biographical profiles of several thinkers from the political left, there is no mention of Russell Kirk, who was one of the most important conservative thinkers in twentieth-century America. Not all entries are dispassionate or unbiased. For example, the entry on animals is really an article on the importance of animal rights and makes many references to the importance of the works of philosopher Peter Singer to the animal rights movement. It comes as no surprise then that the author of this particular entry is none other than Peter Singer. Interestingly, although there are entries for Buddhist philosophy, Hindu philosophy, and Islamic philosophy, there is no corresponding entry on Christian philosophy. Despite these shortcomings, *The Oxford Companion to Philosophy* remains a valuable compendium for philosophic inquiry and reference. [R: LJ, 15 Sept 05, p. 94; SLJ, Oct 05, p. 90]—**Alan Asher**

C

425.   **Routledge Encyclopedia of Philosophy. http://www.rep.routledge.com/index.html.** [Website]. Edward Craig, ed. New York, Routledge/Taylor & Francis Group. Price negotiated by site. Date reviewed: Oct 05.

The online *Routledge Encyclopedia of Philosophy* (REP) has as its basis the text of the print version (1998), but incorporates ongoing revisions and additions that, if its promise and its record to date are maintained, will make this format increasingly advantageous—quite aside from the usual benefits of online resources, such as multiple search capabilities and the ability to offer access to students and faculty in their dorm rooms and offices. The "REP Online Updates" page on the Website often lists more than 100 new or revised articles, the great majority new, broken down by a combination of subject categories (e.g., nineteenth-century philosophy, Russian philosophy) and dates of implementation. The articles themselves also include a notice of their new or revised status.

Access options include a basic keyword search that searches not only entry headings but subheadings within articles; advanced search options including full-text searching with a variety of strategies for limiting, Boolean searching, and "concept" and "pattern" (basically wildcard and truncated term) searching; browsing an alphabetic list of entries; and a "subject themes" search via a classification of articles under the broad subject categories represented also by "signpost" articles. The signpost articles, which can also be accessed quickly via a special tab, themselves serve as a kind of subject guide to related articles. A "Help" function is provided.

It should be emphasized that this is not a free Website but a subscription resource. However, the site's home page and a limited selection of REP content, notably 28 "signpost" articles, together with various pages of information about the REP Online, are publicly accessible at this time.—**Hans E. Bynagle**

C

426.   Taylor, Rodney L., with Howard Y. F. Choy. **The Illustrated Encyclopedia of Confucianism.** New York, Rosen Publishing, 2005. 2v. illus. maps. index. $212.95/set. ISBN 0-8239-4079-9.

K'ung Fu-tzu was a Chinese philosopher and educator whose teachings came to have a lasting influence on the cultures of several Asian nations, including China, Japan, Korea, and parts of southeast Asia. More readily known in the West by his Latinized name, Confucius left a philosophical legacy that has lasted from the sixth-century B.C.E. to the present day. The traditions of Confucianism touch on philosophy, religion, politics, literature, and art. This two-volume reference work touches on all of these areas. The work contains a lengthy preface that contains an overview of the religious aspects of Confucianism, Confucian thought on the human condition, and neo-Confucianism. Although Confucianism was influential throughout Southeast Asia, this work is focused on Chinese Confucianism. The encyclopedia is arranged alphabetically. Some, but not all, of the individual entries conclude with short bibliographies. One of the strengths of the work is the extensive English-language bibliography that is found at the end of the second volume. For quick reference, the work contains a timeline of Chinese dynasties and a glossary of terms and their corresponding Chinese characters. The glossary also contains a list of terms and their transliterations into English using both the Pinyin and the Wade-Giles systems. A particular virtue of this work is the cross-referencing of entries. For instance, in the entry for "asceticism", there are cross-references highlighted in bold typeface for "soul," "the absolute," "self-denial," and "Principle of Heaven." Using this cross-referencing system, the reader can follow a single theme through a variety of related topics. *The Illustrated Encyclopedia of Confucianism* will be a valuable resource for scholars and students of comparative religions, philosophy, and Chinese cultural history. [R: LJ, 1 Sept 05, p. 182]—**Alan Asher**

RELIGION

General Works

Dictionaries and Encyclopedias

C, P

427.   **Worldmark Encyclopedia of Religious Practices.** Thomas Riggs, ed. Farmington Hills, Mich., Gale, 2006. 3v. illus. maps. index. $350.00/set. ISBN 0-7876-6611-4.

This ambitious endeavor attempts nothing less than to survey religion in every country in the world, from the large (e.g., China, India, Brazil, Russia) to the small (e.g., Togo, Tuvalu, Haiti, Saint Kitts). Of course, not everything about a particular country's religious development could be covered. Choices had to be made, and that task fell to an advisory board of 10 scholars (8 from the United States) that chose for special emphasis 13 major groups—traditional African religions, Christianity, Confucianism, Hinduism, Islam, Jainism, Judaism, Shinto, Sikhism, Taoism, and Zoroastrianism. Some 28 subgroups, such as

Coptic Christianity, Pentecostalism, Sunnism, and Reform Judaism, were also included. In all, 245 scholars from around the globe participated in the project, either writing essays or reviewing the submissions of others. Comprising volume 1 are essays on the major religions and subgroups. Each essay uses identical subject headings, such "Central Doctrines," "Sacred Books," "Rituals," and "Controversial Issues," thus allowing for an easy comparison of one group to another. Volumes 2 and 3, which together makeup 193 essays, deal with contemporary religious practices in specific countries. Again, the essays adhere to a common pattern: statistical data on the population and major religions; a historical overview of the country; a section on religious tolerance touching on matters of church and state, freedom of worship, ecumenical movements, and religious discrimination; a discussion of the major religions (those comprising 25 percent or more of the country's population); some mention of other faiths; and a bibliography. Some deviation was permitted, as in the case of China. Buddhism and Christianity represented only 8 percent and 6.5 percent of the Chinese population, respectively, but nonetheless were considered major religions. The justification was that 8 percent of China's enormous population translated into almost 108 million Buddhists.

Enhancing this study's overall appeal are several additional features: a timeline running from 1800 B.C.E. (the birth of Zarathustra, founder of Zoroastrianism) to 2003 C.E. (the consecration of the first openly gay, noncelibate bishop of the Anglican Communion); a list of holy days; quotations from various faiths on God (gods), prayer, duty, wealth and poverty, women, and death; an extensive glossary; a thorough index; and numerous photographs throughout the three volumes. Without a doubt, university libraries should consider adding this to their reference collections, for it would be immensely useful to anyone interested in religion, scholars as well as students.—**John W. Storey**

Handbooks and Yearbooks

P, S

428.   Breuilly, Elizabeth, Joanne O'Brien, and Martin Palmer. **Religions of the World: The Illustrated Guide to Origins, Beliefs, Traditions & Festivals.** rev. ed. New York, Facts on File, 2005. 160p. illus. index. $29.95. ISBN 0-8160-6258-7.

Religions of the World is a beautiful, informative, and outstanding introduction to today's living religions. The "history, basic beliefs, scriptures, places of worship, lifestyles, festivals and modern developments" (p. 6) of each are presented in an eye-catching, content-rich format. The three sections—Abrahamic faiths (Judaism, Christianity, and Islam), Vedic faiths (Hinduism, Buddhism, and Jainism), and other major traditions (Shinto, Taoism, Sikhism, and Baha'i)—are arranged clearly and sympathetically. Discussing indigenous religion in the introduction is greatly appreciated—underscoring the fact that there are significant pockets around the globe that, regardless of cultural contact, decline to be yoked to any "organized" religion.

Combining many diverse faiths into the last section creates a whiff of ethnocentrism the authors surely did not intend. Japan and China are seen as marginal, and Confucius is largely overlooked. Mentioned just twice in the text, Confucians are portrayed as "bureaucratic" and "imperialistic," "hat(ing)" the spontaneous, ecstatic ways of the shamans, forc(ing) them out of power" and creating the "rigid hierarchical system" that "shaped China for over two thousand years."

Lush full-color pictures, informative sidebars, maps, graphs, and charts serve to succinctly break down what can at times be complex doctrine into bite-size pieces for the younger reader. The introduction contains a reproducible chart that provides a concise side-by-side comparison that condenses the content without a "bullet point" feel. The updated final section continues to provide direction for further study. This is an exceptional reference text, essential for both school and public libraries.—**Stephen J. Shaw**

P, S

429.   **Introduction to the World's Major Religions.** Lee W. Bailey, ed. Westport, Conn., Greenwood Press, 2006. 6v. illus. maps. index. $325.00/set. ISBN 0-313-33634-2.

This is a superb reference set of the world's religions, covering Judaism, Confucianism and Taoism (both in one volume), Buddhism, Christianity, Islam, and Hinduism. The volumes are small enough not to be intimidating, and have an identical structure, making comparative studies substantially easier. A timeline is provided for each religion, followed by six chapters: "History of Foundation," "Texts and Major Tenets," "Branches," "Practice Worldwide," "Rituals and Holidays," and "Major Figures." Several black-and-white illustrations break up the text (color would have been nice). Charts, tables, maps, as well as a glossary and bibliography are included. A set index is incorporated in each volume; an incredibly useful tool for the high school target audience. What is most impressive is that these chapter divisions are appropriate for all volumes—absent is the impression that a volume "struggles" to fill the chapter. The volume on Confucianism and Taoism, especially, does a good job of weaving the history of China into the elucidation of the religions. However, the author of this volume relies on an archaic electronic representation of the Chinese pictographs, with a result that looks dated and detracts slightly from the overall aesthetics of the book. This set is essential for all high schools, select middle schools, and community colleges.—**Stephen J. Shaw**

C

430.   **Religions of the Ancient World: A Guide.** Sarah Iles Johnston, ed. Cambridge, Mass., Harvard University Press, 2004. 697p. illus. index. $49.95. ISBN 0-674-01517-7.

To survey the religious landscape of contemporary America is to become aware of the nation's remarkable diversity and multiplicity of sacred traditions. Pluralism prevails, the preponderance of certain groups in specific areas notwithstanding. And so it was in the ancient Mediterranean world, spanning timewise the years from approximately 3000 B.C.E. to 400 C.E. and extending geographically from roughly Etruria to Persia and from Mesopotamia to Egypt. Edited by Sarah Iles Johnston, a professor of Greek and Latin at Ohio State University, this outstanding reference, based upon recent scholarship, documents that diversity. "No ancient culture was left untouched by its neighbors," Johnston asserts, as "itinerant charismatic practitioners journeyed from place to place, selling their skills as leaders, purifiers, cursers, and initiators" (p. x), and as merchants and conquerors criss-crossed the terrain, encountering new gods, creation myths, and rituals, adopting or adapting that which was useful.

This volume, to which some 140 scholars contributed, examines side-by-side 10 Mediterranean cultures, showing how religious beliefs, practices, and gods migrated back and forth, so to speak, between Egypt, the Levant, Mesopotamia, Anatolia, Iran, Greece, and Rome. Discussed in the process are such topics as cosmology, mythology, rituals, law and ethics, magic, divination, sacred spaces, and religious personnel. The volume's unifying theme is that the ancient world, time and space notwithstanding, exemplified a state of mind, one in which religion played a unique role and occupied a central position. It was a world in which one would as readily attribute religious significance to a toothache as look to the gods for some sign of favor before engaging in combat. According to this study, this frame of mind dissolved very slowly, ending with the ascendancy of Christianity, Judaism, and Islam. Enhanced by numerous illustrations, many in color, a thorough index, and brief bibliographies at the end of each essay, this would be a worthy addition to the reference collections of high school and university libraries. Anyone interested in religion, even contemporary religion, would find this work illuminating. [R: LJ, Jan 05, p. 156]—**John W. Storey**

Indexes

C

431.   **American Religion Data Archive. http://www.thearda.com.** [Website]. Free. Date reviewed: Mar 05.

Funded by the Lilly Endowment, the *American Religion Data Archive* (ARDA) archives and facilitates access to electronic data on religion as a sociological phenomenon, not as a set of beliefs. The archive contains about 300 data files on churches, church membership, religious professionals, and religious groups in the United States, with individuals, congregations, denominations, and geographical units as units of analysis. The data coverage ranges from 1890 to 2004. Data sources are varied, including, for example, the U.S. Bureau of the Census, Educational Testing Service, and ABC News/Washington Post. The archive collects no primary data itself; it serves as a repository for data collected by other organizations and researchers.

For a particular data set, the file contains a description of the study (e.g., number of cases, variables, collection date, funder, sampling procedures, principal investigator, related publications, notes), the codebook (including survey procedures), and the data for downloading or manipulation. For a specific data file, the search and analyze function allows the user to search for a specific variable and create tables and charts (pie, bar, and cumulative bar) for responses on that variable. The custom tables feature allows cross-tabulations of data with some variable-related constraints. Only numbers and percentages are provided in the codebook and on tables. Users wishing more sophisticated statistics need to download the data to use with statistical software; data can be downloaded in ASCII, SPSS, and Microcase formats and, for files with few variables, Microsoft Excel. The user can generate maps for the United States or individual states and reports for state, county, groups of counties, and metropolitan area from demographic, congregational, and congregational membership data and reports.

The site has both search and browsing capabilities. The search engine allows for natural language access to abstracts, individual researchers, or questions on individual surveys. The default requires specifying a file; advanced search allows for searching all files with greater variation in specifying search terms. Users can browse the file directory, arranged by broad population category. In addition, the site instructs users: it includes a "getting started" tutorial and five learning modules on specific topics, such as the religious landscape in the United States, allowing a user to explore data in many files.

ARDA is maintained by the Department of Sociology, Pennsylvania State University. ARDA maintains no bibliography of publications using the data series as the *Interuniversity Consortium for Political and Social Research* (see ARBA 2004, entry 60) does for some data files. The archive has no religious affiliation, and its scope is limited only by the availability of reliable data. More data files are available on prominent, mainstream denominations. It is an excellent example of a user-oriented social science data archive.—**Marilyn Domas White**

Bible Studies

Dictionaries and Encyclopedias

C, P

432.   **Expository Dictionary of Bible Words: Word Studies for Key English Bible Words Based on the Hebrew and Greek Texts.** Stephen D. Renn, ed. Peabody, Mass., Hendrickson, 2005. 1171p. index. $29.95 (w/CD-ROM). ISBN 1-56563-938-3.

In this work key biblical words are listed alphabetically in English followed immediately by the equivalent Old Testament words, first in English script, followed by the Hebrew or Aramaic, and then the New Testament equivalent words in Greek. For many words there is a third division entitled "Additional

Notes" discussing the relationship between the Old and New Testament words. An "Analytical Concordance to the Revised Standard Version of the New Testament" by Clinton Morrison (published in 1979) had some similar uses, but dealt only with the New Testament and did not have the in-depth study of the vocabulary found in the present work. This book can be particularly helpful to pastors and other serious Bible readers with limited or no knowledge of the biblical languages. For example, a pastor working with the concept of "Blessing" can look up the alphabetical listing of the word and find the several equivalent words in both Hebrew and Greek with a scholarly discussion of their meaning. The discussions are based on competent use of standard Hebrew and Greek lexicons. There is an index for both Greek and Hebrew words. In each case, echoing the form of the main text, a transliteration of the word in English script is followed by the word in Hebrew or Greek script. All words are coded to the numbering system used in the Revised Strong's system. A CD-ROM is included.—**Robert T. Anderson**

Christianity

Dictionaries and Encyclopedias

C, P

433.   **Encyclopedia of Christianity.** John Bowden, ed. New York, Oxford University Press, 2005. 1364p. illus. index. $125.00. ISBN 0-19-522393-4.

While there are several one-volume reference books pertaining to Christianity, the *Encyclopedia of Christianity* offers its audience many advantages. Bowden organized the work well through an overall table of contents, a listing of boxes (highlighted subtopics), and a substantial index. While varying in overall length, scholarly experts wrote the articles, signing them and offering further reading in most cases. Cross-references to other pages and topics discussed in this volume abound in the articles. In addition to trends and themes within Christianity, the work offers insight into Christian relations with other religions and trains of thought. (The articles on Christian-Islamic relations, evolution, and science merit consideration as initial orientation points for students in this regard.) A "Who's Who" section in the back summarizes important Christian figures for the reader. A timeline divided by centuries orients the user to Christian historical events. The glossary explains important terms. Maps, color plates, and pictures enhance the articles' quality.

As with any volume of this nature, certain people and topics were relegated to general articles rather than receiving their own entry. In all fairness, however, space and expertise issues make that inevitable in these projects. Bowden's work is a first-rate reference text and merits inclusion in any collection pertaining to Christian studies. This text is recommended for public, academic, and special libraries. [R: LJ, Dec 05, p. 170]—**David J. Duncan**

C, P

434.   Melton, J. Gordon. **Encyclopedia of Protestantism.** New York, Facts on File, 2005. 628p. illus. index. (Encyclopedias of World Religions). $75.00. ISBN 0-8160-5456-8.

Here is a useful research tool in the study of Protestantism. It is part of Facts on File's Encyclopedia of World Religions series. It covers a lot of material with around 800 entries. These entries are biographical, historical events, theological topics, groups, and other topics connected with Protestantism. It tries to cover material from before the Protestant Reformation started, during the Reformation, and afterwards up to today. Special effort has been made to include women and non-Westerners as much as possible. This makes this book very extensive and succeeds in that goal. This book is in the traditional A-to-Z format. The introduction gives the history of Protestantism. There is a chronology followed by the entries, which vary in length. Each entry has a further reading list. There are *see also* references and black-and-white illustrations. There is a short bibliography at the end of the book followed by an index. The book is good for academic and public library reference sections. It is a good source since it covers a lot of material and is quite inclusive. [R: LJ, 1 Sept 05, p. 180; SLJ, Dec 05, p. 92]—**Benet Steven Exton**

C, P

435.   **The Oxford Dictionary of the Christian Church.** 3d ed. F. L. Cross and E. A. Livingstone, eds. New York, Oxford University Press, 2005. 1800p. $150.00. ISBN 0-19-280290-9.

With over 480 contributors, the 3d edition of *The Oxford Dictionary of the Christian Church* provides the reader with the most distinguished volume of academic perspectives on the Christian Church to be found in a single volume. The contributors are leading scholars, from various religious bodies and academic settings, from Europe, the United States, Australia, and elsewhere around the globe. Their entries are written in an unbiased and authoritative manner, reflecting the latest academic research on the subject. This A-Z dictionary of 1,800 pages is an ideal desk reference for the religious or church scholar, professor, or minister, which provides information on the obscure (e.g., Mit brenender Sorge) and the commonplace (e.g., mixed chalice) as well as the ethical (e.g., mixed marriage) and theologically significant (e.g., Logos). With over 6,000 entries on theology, the Bible, Patristic scholarship, churches and denominations, the church calendar and organization, and biographies of significant (and historical) church leaders and contributors to the Christian legacy, the challenges of updating this volume are staggering. First published in 1957, new entries and rewritten older entries with fresh evidence and understanding provide a priceless work of immense quality to the reader. The updated and new entries make this an important volume for university, college, and seminary libraries. Its coverage of the Christian Church and Christianity remains unrivalled today.—**Joseph P. Hester**

Islam

Dictionaries and Encyclopedias

C, P

436.   Renard, John. **Historical Dictionary of Sufism.** Lanham, Md., Scarecrow, 2005. 351p. (Historical Dictionaries of Religions, Philosophies, and Movements, no.58). $70.00. ISBN 0-8108-5342-6.

The *Historical Dictionary of Sufism* stands as a testament to Scarecrow Press's continuing commitment to address current topics of global importance. As number 58 in the series Historical Dictionaries of Religions, Philosophies, and Movements, it complements the *Historical Dictionary of Islam* (see ARBA 2002, entry 1299). This resource is one of the first in English dedicated to Sufism, a relatively unknown sect of Islam.

Nationally recognized scholar and author John Renard (Saint Louis University) employs his extensive knowledge of both Western and Eastern spirituality and mysticism in each section. The extensive chronology spans the pan-Muslim world. Renard establishes a familiar framework for the reader by including both Western and Islamic dates and a sprinkling of notable Christian mystics. The concise introduction traces Sufism from its beginning to modern times. The dictionary's boldface entries and keywords represent the strength of this work. In addition, there are abundant cross-references of people, places, and concepts. The much-appreciated and useful glossary lists Arabic terms with brief explanations. As further proof of Renard's comprehensive treatment, Berber, Chinese, Persian, and Turkish terms are also included. The 71-page bibliography, divided into manageable topics (e.g.< primary sources, individual figures), is the final jewel.

Although the black-and-white plates fall short of doing justice to the vitality of mysticism and spirituality within the Sufi world, Renard uses his words to illuminate this elusive topic. This is an absolute must for Islamic, philosophy, and religious studies collections in all libraries, especially academic. Destined to become a definitive resource, the *Historical Dictionary of Sufism* is highly recommended.—**Alice Crosetto**

Handbooks and Yearbooks

C, P, S

437. Gordon, Matthew S. **The Rise of Islam.** Westport, Conn., Greenwood Press, 2005. 180p. illus. index. (Greenwood Guides to Historic Events of the Medieval World). $45.00. ISBN 0-313-32522-7.

As with the rest of this series, Matthew Gordon's *The Rise of Islam* provides readers with a timely introduction to this religion. As with the other texts in this series, the work contains a historical overview, discussion of key parts of the religion and Islamic society, pertinent biographical sketches, a glossary of important terms, a timeline, maps and suggested additional readings. Gordon's historical overview covers the first 400 years of Islamic history. From an introductory sketch of the political and societal landscape in the Near East and Arabian peninsula before Islam through the founding and expansion of the religion and the establishment of Islamic legal traditions, the text provides facts and details in a concise manner. The Abbasid and Ummayad dynasties receive attention in their own respective sections. In addition, the text covers social, political, and economic topics. The accompanying primary source selections include sections from the Qur'an, biographies, chronicles, descriptions of cities and palace courts, and anecdotal pieces taken from longer tales. Gordon's treatment justly defines the contrasts between the different parts of the Islamic world as one can tell from reading about the Arabian accounts as opposed to those from Egypt or al-Andalus. The selections also include Shi'i as well as Sunni viewpoints. The biographical sketches touch upon important figures from Muhammad's lifetime in addition to those who played an important role in developing Islamic societal, legal, and religious traditions in the following centuries. This work is recommended for public, high school, and college and university libraries.—**David J. Duncan**

Judaism

C, P

438. **A Dictionary of Jewish-Christian Relations.** Edward Kessler and Neil Wenborn, eds. New York, Cambridge University Press, 2005. 507p. index. $195.00. ISBN 0-521-82692-6.

This dictionary is a comprehensive collection of over 700 articles on Jewish and Christian relations. These articles have been produced by over 100 international scholars. The entries vary in length according to their importance. The dictionary is in A-Z format with an introduction and a section on how to use the book in the front. There are *see also* references and cross-references indicated by bold print in the text of the articles. The book also features seven black-and-white maps, but no illustrations. Bibliographic information is in the back of the book and divided according to the subjects of Bible, theology, history, institutional documents, journals, and dictionaries. The citations include non-English sources. Academic libraries with a religious studies collection and large public libraries will find *A Dictionary of Jewish-Christian Relations* useful. [R: LJ, Dec 05, pp. 168-170]—**Benet Steven Exton**

C, P, S

439. Karesh, Sara E., and Mitchell M. Hurvitz. **Encyclopedia of Judaism.** New York, Facts on File, 2006. 602p. illus. index. (Encyclopedia of World Religions). $75.00. ISBN 0-8160-5457-6.

With the *Encyclopedia of Judaism*, part of Facts on File's Encyclopedia of World Religions series, authors Karesh and Hurvitz have provided an excellent resource of information about Judaism throughout history and around the world. The encyclopedia covers over 2,000 years of recorded history, and explores a religious belief system that has found its way into nearly every culture on earth. It explores Jewish belief, practices, and culture from the Temple period, through the Exile and Diaspora, to the state of Israel and expansion of Jewish sects and denominations in America, Asia, Europe, and the rest of the world. It has entries on historic events, Jewish theology, biographies of important Jewish figures, and the modern development of Judaism today.

The entries are well written, concise, accurate, and authoritative. The authors, a teacher of Jewish history and a rabbi, have delivered a resource that is objective and free from obvious bias. Terms that are entries elsewhere in the encyclopedia are highlighted, and *see also* references are provided. Users are directed to further readings to explore a topic in more depth. A complete index is provided in order to aid the user in locating needed information quickly. The only weakness might be a need for more illustrations. Overall, the *Encyclopedia of Judaism* is an outstanding reference resource that is appropriate for academic, school, and public libraries.—**Mark T. Bay**

Part IV

SCIENCE AND TECHNOLOGY

29 Science and Technology in General

BIOGRAPHY

P, S

440.   Carey, Charles W., Jr. **American Scientists.** New York, Facts on File, 2006. 434p. illus. index. (American Biographies). $65.00. ISBN 0-8160-5499-1.

American Scientists contains nearly 300 biographical entries of historic and contemporary American scientists. The volume begins with a name list of the scientists included, followed by an introductory essay giving an overview of the major science disciplines and highlighting selected scientists within each discipline. After the individual biographies, there is a bibliography of additional biographical sources, a list of biographical names by scientific discipline, a list of entries by year of birth, and a name and topic index.

Most individual entries are one to two pages long, and give information on the scientist's professional career and accomplishments within their area of expertise, as well as family information (marital status, for example). References to other scientists within a specific entry are presented in capital letters, to indicate an entry to that scientist is included in the volume. There are occasional photographs accompanying the biographies; entries conclude with brief further readings lists.

American Scientists offers brief biographies in a single volume. Academic libraries should have additional biographical sources that would be more comprehensive. This work is most appropriate for school and public libraries.—**Caroline L. Gilson**

S

441.   **Women's Adventures in Science Series.** Danbury, Conn., Franklin Watts/Scholastic Library Publishing, 2005. 10v. illus. index. $310.00/set; $31.00/vol. ISBN 0-531-16824-7.

This series of 10 books from Franklin Watts focuses on the careers and achievements of 10 women scientists. The series has been assisted by the National Academy of Sciences and one woman in particular, Sara Lee Schupf. The goal of the series can be summed up in one sentence from the series preface: "The challenges of a scientific career are great but the rewards can be even greater."

Each volume in the series focuses on one woman scientist and include: Inez Fung (climate scientist), Mimi Koehl (biochemist), Marta Tienda (sociologist), Shirley Ann Jackson (physicist), Adriana Ocampo (geologist), Cynthia Breazeal (robot designer), Nancy Wexler (neuropsychologist), Diane France (forensic anthropologist), Amy Vedder (wildlife biologist), and Heidi Hammel (planetary astronomer). Each volumes goes into the scientists' career achievements, research goals, new areas of study in the science, and background on how the scientist became interested in their study and how they motivate young scientists. Each volume concludes with a timeline of the scientist's life, a glossary, books and Websites to consult for further research, a bibliography, and an index. The books are full of color photographs, quotes, and sidebars, which will appeal to young students.

The obvious use for these books are for students doing research on either specific areas of science or for those researching one of the women featured in the series. They could also be used, however, as motivation and inspiration to young women looking to go into the scientific field. This set is recommended for middle and high school libraries.—**Shannon Graff Hysell**

DICTIONARIES AND ENCYCLOPEDIAS

C, P, S

442.   Hamblin, Jacob Darwin. **Science in the Early Twentieth Century: An Encyclopedia.** Santa Barbara, Calif., ABC-CLIO, 2005. 399p. illus. index. (ABC-CLIO's History of Science Series). $85.00; $90.00 (e-book). ISBN 1-85109-665-5; 1-85109-670-1 (e-book).

A companion to *Science in the Ancient World: An Encyclopedia* (see ARBA 2006, entry 1258), *The Scientific Revolution: An Encyclopedia* (see ARBA 2003, entry 1280), *Science in the Enlightenment: An Encyclopedia* (see ARBA 2004, entry 1237), and *Science in the Contemporary World: An Encyclopedia* (see entry 444), this work consists of alphabetically arranged articles on concepts and fields/disciplines, inventions/innovations, phenomena, science and society, institutions/organizations, and individuals, with references to print (but not Web) resources and *see also* references. A chronology from 1895-1950, and a selected bibliography, form an appendix. There is a thorough index.

The author is a professional historian of science. The articles are clearly written, accessible to a general audience, and, making allowances for simplifications imposed by brevity, generally accurate. Noteworthy is the emphasis on science and society, reflected in choice of topics and inclusion of social context of the science. Different individuals might have been chosen to treat in full articles but most key people are at least mentioned; some, such as Pauling, are included instead in *Science in the Contemporary World*, although R. B. Woodward appears in neither book, and chemistry in general is somewhat neglected. In a short book it is impossible to be comprehensive. This is a useful, instructive, and entertaining reference for libraries serving high school through university audiences, and for public libraries.—**Robert Michaelson**

C, P

443.   **McGraw-Hill Concise Encyclopedia of Science & Technology.** 5th ed. New York, McGraw-Hill, 2005. 2651p. illus. index. $185.00. ISBN 0-07-142957-3.

This condensed work covers all the major disciplines of science and technology. The essential information has been extracted from its parent multivolume work and made more appropriate for those users that want a source that provides concise yet authoritative information. This edition includes 7,300 alphabetically arranged entries with illustrations, diagrams, and cross-references included. The entries provide a good introduction and a jumping point for further research on a topic. If one cannot find what they are looking for, the extensive 30,000-item index can also be used. The appendixes are also informative in that they provide a bibliography arranged by subject areas, a listing of measurement systems (including mathematical and scientific notations), and a biographical and contributors listing.

This work is recommended for most libraries. The concise format offers an alternative and affordable option to the larger work. Earlier editions of this resource are probably already present in many academic and public libraries.—**Julia Perez**

C, P, S

444.   Swedin, Eric G. **Science in the Contemporary World: An Encyclopedia.** Santa Barbara, Calif., ABC-CLIO, 2005. 382p. illus. index. (ABC-CLIO's History of Science Series). $85.00; $90.00 (e-book). ISBN 1-85109-524-1; 1-85109-529-2 (e-book).

Science in the Contemporary World is one title in ABC-CLIO's History of Science Series. It is an introductory, alphabetic resource containing over 200 entries, with approximately 96 of the articles being biographies of contemporary individuals important to science. The encyclopedia details the scientific achievements of the contemporary world, after the end of World War II, 1950-2004. Topics cover a breadth of scientific disciplines and presents important scientific trends and discoveries. The introduction provides the foundation for the work, introducing readers to the context in which science plays a large part in our contemporary world.

The topic finder organizes each entry into the following broad topics: scientific disciplines, theories and ideologies, new vistas, tools of science, institutions and projects, natural phenomena, scientific discoveries, science and society, studying science, and people. According to the preface individual scientists were chosen for inclusion based on their discoveries and/or to increase the breadth of the coverage of scientific disciplines. Articles vary in length, determined by the amount of change that occurred after 1950. The shortest is just under a page, while the longest, the article covering space exploration and space science, is about four pages. Some articles are accompanied by black-and-white photographs, illustrations, or maps.

Each article entry is followed with a list of references related to the article entry and a *see also* section listing related articles within the encyclopedia. The comprehensive index is augmented with a chronology from 1950 to 2004, and a selected bibliography with approximately 158 entries. *Science in the Contemporary World* is recommended for high school, college, and public libraries.—**Danielle Andrea Kane**

S

445.   **The World Book Student Discovery Science Encyclopedia.** Chicago, World Book, 2006. 13v. illus. maps. index. $369.00/set. ISBN 0-7166-7500-5.

The World Book Student Discovery Science Encyclopedia is a multivolume set compiled by the World Book staff and that draws its information from World Book. The subject matter includes a mixture of human, animal, and marine biology; geology; astronomy; chemistry; and prominent people in the field of science. There are also entries on computer science, botany, ecology, entomology, dinosaurs, mechanics, and concepts, such as emotions and dreams. The volumes also contain special feature articles and suggested experiments; these sections are clearly distinguished from the entries. The entries are generally brief and informative.

The major glaring error of the set is that volume 6 is bound upside down and backwards; aside from that this was a good science resource. Volumes 1-12 contain the entries with volume 13 providing the index and additional science resources, such as facts and theories and useful Websites. Entries are generally a half a page with the longest being about four pages. The language is simple and clear. All entries generally have an accompanying photograph or graphic and include related article lists and cross-references where applicable. The volumes themselves are slim with sturdy binding. Each one runs from slightly over 100 pages with the thicker volumes at a little over 200 pages. The pages are glossy and thick. Since the set is geared toward children in elementary school the individual books are built to take a bit of abuse. Aside from the binding mishap this is a good resource for elementary school media centers. —**Melissa M. Johnson**

HANDBOOKS AND YEARBOOKS

C, P

446.   Edis, Taner. **Science and Nonbelief.** Westport, Conn., Greenwood Press, 2006. 285p. illus. index. (Greenwood Guides to Science and Religion). $65.00. ISBN 0-313-33078-6.

This book, written by a physicist, explores the connections between science and disbelief, and how it is that attempts by creationists, modern intelligent designers, and even physicists who see in the randomness of events a role for theology, should all be discounted. In charting the history of nonbelievers, those from antiquity to the present who have questioned the necessity for appeals to supernatural powers to account for natural phenomena, this book provides a clear and straightforward evaluation of both sides of the science-religion divide. Contrary to the approach taken by Galileo to the science-religion problem, that the two should be regarded as mutually exclusive realms, tolerating a "principle of respectful noninterference" in the words of Stephen Jay Gould, this book explores the extent to which this is impossible to do, and investigates the historical dimensions of the reasons why religion in particular is fundamentally interested in the connection between man and nature. This book considers these matters through comparisons between different historical periods and cultures, from primitive hunter-gatherer societies in Africa and Asia to modern industrial, technological societies east and west. On the subject of evolution, it concludes directly that recent interest in intelligent design (ID) is misguided, and in particular, that "ID simply has nothing to offer to science." There are few notes to guide the reader to specific references, but an appendix of primary sources reprints excerpts as examples of "various science-based arguments that are used to support skepticism about religion and the supernatural." These cover various topics discussed in the book, including physics, cosmology, evolution, materialist views of the mind, and criticisms of parapsychology. The book itself goes into all these matters in much greater detail, including sections that debunk UFOs, paranormal phenomena, mediums, psychics, astrology, and the like. It also considers more general issues of ethical behavior and morality, and how these can be understood in terms advanced by nonbelievers who advocate naturalism in understanding modern science. There is a substantial bibliography made more useful than most by the addition of insightful, critical annotations. For anyone interested in a well-written yet not overly technical account of naturalist arguments for understanding the world and universe we inhabit, this book is highly recommended.—**Joseph W. Dauben**

S

447.   Kipfer, Barbara Ann. **How It Happens: The Extraordinary Processes of Everyday Things.** New York, Random House, 2005. 322p. illus. $16.95pa. ISBN 0-375-72082-0.

Most people do not like a know-it-all, but it is hard to resist the charm of Barbara Ann Kipfer's knowledge level that she shares generously and without a trace of either arrogance or the egghead. Indeed, her alphabetically arranged compendium of things readers either simply take for granted or have never considered in the first place is truly amazing. If you want to know how pencils and baseball bats are made Kipfer give the salient details of both processes. The author not only lucidly explain procedures, she often provides diagrams as well. For example, in explaining how birds evolved from reptiles, the stages of how a tadpole becomes a frog, and the "secrets" of how to pull a rabbit out of a hat or put a ship inside a bottle, Kipfer's illustrations are first rate in terms of clarity.

It is hard to imagine any subject the author has left out, beginning as she does with the cause of "acne" and continuing through to an explanation of how a zipper works. Hopefully, readers will never need to know the details, but just in case, Kipfer explains how lie detector and breathalyzer tests are conducted. Along the way she also provides step-by-step and numbered details on the formation of snowflakes and soap bubbles, silver tarnishing, the weaving of a spider web, where thunder comes from, and how to change an automobile tire. She explains how ATM machines work and how one obtains a sore sunburn, along with explanation of how vacuum cleaners sweep and teeth decay. Some things readers might just as well avoid. Do men really wan to know how and why they become bald? Like it or not, the author tells them!

Kipfer has written more than 25 books, many of which carry such numerically impressive titles as *8,789 Words of Wisdom* (2001), *4,000 Questions for Getting to Know Anyone and Anything* (2004), and *14,000 Things to Be Happy About: The Happy Book* (1990). She has also been instrumental in editing many dictionaries and thesauri. With 500 entries, it is impossible for the author to go into great detail on any one subject, but her entries are so reader-friendly and fascinating, that many people will want to begin learning more about "Computerized Axial Tomography/CAT SCAN" once they have been introduced to the subject in such bright and coherent language. *How It Happens* is a gem that introduces readers to, well, just about everything.—**Jerry D. Flack**

S

448.   Walker, Pamela, and Elaine Wood. **Science Experiments on File. Volume 2.** New York, Facts on File, 2005. 1v. (various paging). illus. index. $185.00. ISBN 0-8160-5735-4.

Volume 2 of *Science Experiments on File* provides teachers with 60 "tried and true" science experiments that will service students in grades 6-12. The experiments have been chosen because they adhere to the national science standards and they utilize students' higher thinking skills (e.g., processing, assessing, estimating, relating, evaluating, analyzing). This work is one of a projected six-volume series; each volume in the series will include 60 new experiments and each will focus on the 5 core areas of science, plus one additional area. This volume's additional area of focus is marine sciences.

After an introduction and chapter on safety precautions, the volume is broken down into six areas: biology, chemistry, earth science, physics, astronomy, and marine science. Each section provides 10 experiments. The experiments are typically laid out on two to four pages and provide an introduction, estimated time, materials needed (most of which can be easily found), step-by-step instructions, tips for analysis, and a cross-reference to the appendix where students can find out more information about the experiment and its results. The work is supplemented with illustrations and charts as well as seven appendixes: experiments broken down by grade level, supervision recommended (e.g., adult supervision required, adult supervision recommended), appropriate setting for experiments (e.g., laboratory, home, outdoors), typical findings of experiments, a glossary, the periodic table, and recommended Internet resources. The volume concludes with an index for volume 2 and a cumulative index for volumes 1 and 2.

This work will be useful in middle and high school libraries. The pages are heavy stock paper and are looseleaf so they can easily be photocopied for classroom use. Homeschoolers and public libraries that cater to homeschoolers may also want to have this volume on hand.—**Shannon Graff Hysell**

30 Agricultural Sciences

FOOD SCIENCES AND TECHNOLOGY

Dictionaries and Encyclopedias

P

449.   Rolland, Jacques L. **The Cook's Essential Kitchen Dictionary: A Complete Culinary Resource.** New York, Firefly Books, 2004. 413p. $14.95pa. ISBN 0-7788-0098-9.

This book's collection of 4,000 terms covers not only food and beverages, but also processes, cooking ware, and utensils. The definition for each entry describes the item, how it is used, and often the history of the item. The book is arranged alphabetically with all the information in the entries. There are no appendixes. There are a few illustrations, which are mostly pencil drawings. When there are varieties of things, such as apples, the varieties are all listed under the main subject. Not every variety is mentioned, usually just the most common ones. The entries are easy to read and understand. The one thing lacking in the book is pronunciations for the words so if it is a foreign originating word one has no idea how it is pronounced. It would be a very good purchase for a beginning cook and at this price quite affordable. If a small public library needed a culinary dictionary this would be a good purchase due to its coverage and price.—**Betsy J. Kraus**

Handbooks and Yearbooks

C, P

450.   Berzok, Linda Murray. **American Indian Food.** Westport, Conn., Greenwood Press, 2005. 213p. illus. index. (Food in American History). $49.95. ISBN 0-313-32989-3.

Berzok, author of this excellent book, is a food writer and historian and has previously contributed articles and essays to *The Oxford Encyclopedia of Food and Drink in America* (see ARBA 2005, entry 1301) and the *Encyclopedia of Food and Culture* (see ARBA 2003, entry 1307). These contributions provide ample evidence of her interest and expertise in the history of food and culture. Her writing also demonstrates her understanding of and empathy for American Indian cultures, values, and issues. For example, the following excerpt honors the strength and tenacity of American Indian cultures: "In the case of the American Indians, these foodways have survived the unthinkable—the willful decimation of the native culture by a dominant force with more power, horses and guns and, most galling, a conviction of superiority. That there is anything left of Indian foodways is nothing short of a miracle and testament to the power of embedded culture memory and its transmission" (pp. xi-xii).

This reference includes a map of the locations of major tribes in 1500, before any significant European contact, an interesting preface, and a chronology. The book is organized into several chapters: "Food, History, and Culture"; "Food Preparation"; "Preservation and Storage"; "Food Customs"; "Food and Religion"; and "Concepts of Diet and Nutrition." Also included are a glossary, selected bibliography, and index.

As an aid in developing an understanding of the relationship between the natural resources found in varying environments and the many aspects of food, the author has denoted six cultural regions and corresponding six foodways. For each of the regions there is a brief explanation of the geography, environment, major tribes, and food culture (appropriate combinations of hunting, fishing, gathering, and farming).

Although this is a reference and not a recipe book, the author takes care to note that there are three types of recipes claiming to be American Indian that may be encountered: "Historical/Traditional"—recipes that cannot readily be duplicated today and that require many years of practiced skill; "Indian-inspired or originated recipes with modern accommodations"—recipes close to the original but adapted to modern foods or technology; and "Modern recipes loosely based on Indian ingredients"—recipes that are the least historically accurate and have been seriously Americanized. This reference provides engaging and informative reading and makes a genuine contribution to the understanding of Indian food.—**Karen D. Harvey**

C, P

451.   Long-Solís, Janet, and Luis Alberto Vargas. **Food Culture in Mexico.** Westport, Conn., Greenwood Press, 2005. illus. maps. index. (Food Culture Around the World). $49.95. ISBN 0-313-32431-X.

Food Culture in Mexico is a new title from the Food Culture Around the World series. The series editor believes that "understanding food traditions helps us to understand the people themselves." This book provides a panorama of how the Mexican people's food culture is intertwined with the 5,000-year history.

The traditional foods of the Mexican people are namely corn, beans, squash, tomatillos, and chili peppers. These food crops were easy to grow in the cool, arid soils of the countryside. Spanish conquerors influenced the native foods in the sixteenth century. They introduced meats and seafood and additional spices to the Mexican diet. The typical Mexican diets of the rural and urban populations, and the various social levels are discussed. The various restaurants, taquerias, torterias, fondas, cafes, and some of their recipes are provided. The Mexicans celebrate religious and national holidays with over 500 celebrations, called "fiestas," and the food and drink are prepared as a part of the celebration of these festivals. A timeline, a glossary, a resource guide, and an index accompany the text. I would recommend this book for food history and culture collections.—**Kay M. Stebbins**

C, P

452.   Oliver, Sandra L. **Food in Colonial and Federal America.** Westport, Conn., Greenwood Press, 2005. 230p. illus. index. (Food in American History). $49.95. ISBN 0-313-32988-5.

This is the second book in the Greenwood Press series, Food in American History. In this well-researched text Sandra Oliver, a culinary historian, provides insight into the eating customs, practices, and beliefs of colonial Americans. The author goes into great detail on the food of the time, its preparation, and the cooking utensils of the era. Foods we know, such as jams and preserves, as well as lesser-known items, like verjuice, are thoroughly described. The book contains a lengthy discussion on the different diets and nutritional philosophies of this historical period and includes interesting facts such as Benjamin Franklin's experimentation with vegetarianism, fast days, and the strong role of foods for medicinal purposes. In addition, the book provides an overview of the many ethnic and regional food-related issues of the Americas. The author highlights the differences in the growing seasons, storage capabilities, and immigration patterns that affected the food habits. Oliver acknowledges the vital contributions of the Native Americans who provided agricultural insights to the new settlers. The book includes a chronology (1567-1825) that covers food-related dates of early America. The resource also contains a limited glossary, a subject index, and a selected bibliography.

For the history and/or food connoisseur, this work will provide a mouth-watering and educational read. It is a wonderful addition to academic or public library reference collections and is an essential resource for culinary school libraries.—**Carol Anne Germain**

HORTICULTURE

Dictionaries and Encyclopedias

C, P

453.   Austin, Claire. **Irises: A Gardener's Encyclopedia.** Portland, Oreg., Timber Press, 2005. 339p. illus. index. $49.95. ISBN 0-88192-730-9.

Author Claire Austin, daughter of famed rose grower David Austin and co-owner of an English nursery specializing in hardy perennials (notably irises and peonies), is both an experienced nurserywoman and an excellent photographer. The more than 1,100 color photographs, most taken by her, in this book entice even readers with a casual interest in her subject. The foreword accurately describes this volume as "truly encyclopedic in its presentation of irises" and likely to inspire "iris lust" (p. 6). Austin, however, does caution readers that she has not tried to include all rare or hard-to-grow irises, and refers gardeners interested in these less-common irises to two other Timber Press titles, Brian Matthews *The Iris* (1981) and Fritz Köhlein's *Iris* (1987).

Part 1 includes almost 200 pages devoted to the very popular "bearded irises" and part 2 provides some 80 pages dealing with "beardless irises." Part 3 introduces the less-common "bulbous irises." All three sections open with descriptions of wild forms or species, then introduce hybrids. Individual iris descriptions appear alphabetically by scientific names (both here and in the index) and yield the original discoverer or hybridizer and year the name was published or registered, color, flower and stem shape, height, blooming time, and parentage. Part 4, "Cultivation," details how to plant and grow irises together with common pests and diseases affecting these diverse plants. "Sources" features nurseries in six countries. The glossary and bibliography will assist novice growers. Both public and academic libraries should acquire this stunning new guide to a beautiful perennial garden favorite.—**Julienne L. Wood**

Handbooks and Yearbooks

P

454.   Banks, David P. **Orchid Grower's Companion: Cultivation, Propagation, and Varieties.** Portland, Oreg., Timber Press, 2005. 224p. illus. index. $39.95. ISBN 0-88192-711-2.

Many people are discovering that orchids, those mysterious but very beautiful flowers, can be successfully raised in a home as well as a greenhouse. This is one of a number of books offering advice on how to grow them, as well as information and beautiful color photographs for an assortment of species and hybrids suitable for home growing. The author is a well-known Australian orchid expert and researcher, and editor of the *Australian Orchid Review*. This book would be helpful for a beginner because it has extensive advice on how to care for orchids in various situations, potting media, pests and diseases, and propagation. Descriptions of individual plants minimize technical terminology, and a glossary of botanical terms is included; however, a neophyte might still have some difficulty with the terminology. The photographs are clear and very beautiful.

Botanists would prefer more technical information, and those wanting descriptions and photographs of as many species as possible might prefer a book like the new Flora's Orchids, also from Timber Press, which includes many more species (see entry 464). Banks also wrote most of the text in that book. But as a less expensive, beautiful, and informative book for the novice, the *Orchid Grower's Companion* might be helpful and less intimidating. This guide is recommended for public libraries and those with collections on gardening and botany. —**Marit S. Taylor**

P

455.   Glattstein, Judy. **Bulbs for Garden Habitats.** Portland, Oreg., Timber Press, 2005. 296p. illus. index. $29.95. ISBN 0-88192-693-0.

     The publishers are correct when they say this is a groundbreaking book. The author here offers a new look at the growing of bulbs in the garden, matching bulbs to the garden environments and habitats where the bulbs will flourish and look wonderful. Unlike bulb books that discuss how to plant, colors, and varieties, Glattstein tells readers how to "adapt the planning scheme to the environment, not vice versa." Bulbs are defined here broadly to include corms and tubers. Based on climate and local ecology, the author talks of how to succeed with geophytes, the group word for bulbous plants. She says that with the proper consideration of environment, bulbs will thrive. Especially useful are the first chapter of definitions of geophytes and the second on geophyte care and cultivation. There are marvelous color illustrations which make one want to go out and garden immediately.

     The rest of the chapters are discussions of separate environmental regions of the United States from temperate woodland to Mediterranean, from Texas gardens to the South and Southeast. While most of the regions are in the United States, a few mentions are made of other locations in Europe, Africa, and Australia. The climate and environment of each region are well defined and then different appropriate geophytes are described with clear scientific nomenclature, placed within the context of the climate and ecology, and supported with planting and cultivation tips. There are short chapters on bulbs for the rock garden, for Autumn gardens, and for wild bulbs. There is a chatty tone to the writing. The author relies on personal experience, as well as that of friends and colleagues, to tell how she has succeeded with the bulbs in the various regions. It is a fun book to read—one would like to visit the gardens described.

     The sources section, listing sources for purchasing bulbs and geophytes-related societies, is adequate, but one imagines that this will become outdated soon. So many gardening books seem to have this "buying guide" and I question its value here and in other sources. The index is excellent; the book, like all Timber Press offerings, is well put together. One criticism, offered from a personal perspective, is that this book, like so many others, fails to mention the climate area and ecology of the arid west, the Rocky Mountains, or the Great Basin.

     Overall, the book is recommended for general library acquisition. It is a good read, a novel approach to the understanding of gardens and environments, and will be popular for library patrons, especially those who live in the analyzed geographic regions. It is too specialized for reference collections, but would be a nice addition to a general library collection, especially one with a gardening emphasis or focus.—**Paul A. Mogren**

VETERINARY SCIENCE

C

456.   Romich, Janet Amundson. **An Illustrated Guide to Veterinary Medical Terminology.** 2d ed. Clifton Park, N.Y., Delmar, 2006. 373p. illus. index. $57.95pa. (w/CD-ROM). ISBN 1-4018-7381-2.

     Becoming proficient in the pronunciation and cadence of veterinary medical terminology is less difficult than acquiring fluency in a foreign language. But proficiency does benefit from reading, listening, and speaking. The accompanying interactive CD-ROM is a gem. Hearing the word *trocar* or the word *agalactic* pronounced flawlessly, so as to mimic the same, is as important as knowing how to use the sharp instrument for withdrawing gasses and fluid or identifying the non-milk producing mare. An introduction to terms, especially the way they are constructed, including distinctions like those between noun and adjective endings that can vex students, leads off the text. For example, there is *mucus* the substance, but it is *mucous* lining when a noun is modified. Common species names are reviewed to remind students that *lapin* is a neutered male rabbit and a *cockerel* is an immature male chicken, and so on. System accounts, such as nervous, endocrine, and digestive, and specific guides to certain animals, such as dogs, cats, horses, swine, and ruminants are excellent. As are the guides to veterinary-related abbreviations of all sorts. More than veterinary students will welcome this book. Undergraduate pre-medical students and even early year medical students will also want a copy.—**Diane M. Calabrese**

31 Biological Sciences

BIOLOGY

Dictionaries and Encyclopedias

C

457.   **The Cambridge Dictionary of Human Biology and Evolution.** By Larry L. Mai, Marcus Young Owl, and M. Patricia Kersting. New York, Cambridge University Press, 2005. 648p. $60.00pa. ISBN 0-521-66486-1.

This dictionary covers many aspects of human biology: anatomy, growth, physiology, genetics, paleontology, physical anthropology, primatology, and zoology. It has 13,000 definitions, with cross-references and synonyms but no pronunciation. The entries are often much more than mere definitions, with some discussion. The 1,000 most common terms are marked. In addition to the terms there are boxes covering special subjects, such as an explanation of the dating of paleontological specimens, blood group factors, and nutritional deficiencies. A notable feature is the 10 appendixes. These cover taxonomy of extinct and living primates, a geological time scale, a chronology with the Pleistocene epoch (giving that epoch more detail), marine oxygen isotope chronology (a clue to climate variations), anatomy, and a timeline of the events in the history of human biology as a science. Also included are a hominid phylogeny and the Greek alphabet. There is a list of 1,000 word roots.

This is a scholarly work that is suitable for students and professionals. It covers a particular area that is not often covered, and contains some terms not found in medical or general biology dictionaries. Therefore, it fills a need. This work is strongly recommended for academic libraries.—**John Laurence Kelland**

C, P

458.   **McGraw-Hill Concise Encyclopedia of Bioscience.** New York, McGraw-Hill, 2004. 972p. index. $24.95pa. ISBN 0-07-143956-0.

The *McGraw-Hill Concise Encyclopedia of Bioscience* is part of a series of paperbacks that cover topics in the major science and engineering fields. The publisher's intent for this series is to offer shorter versions of articles distilled from those found in the 20 volume *McGraw-Hill Encyclopedia of Science & Technology* (9th ed.; see ARBA 2004, entry 1242). The articles are meant to provide essential information without too much detail.

This title in the discipline of bioscience contains more than 900 alphabetically arranged articles. The consulting editors as well as the authors are specialists in biological subject areas and connected to universities, museums, government, and research institutions from around the world. Each of the clearly written entries begins with a one- or two-sentence definition of the topic and is followed by a more in-depth explanation ranging from one paragraph to several pages in length. The majority of the entries are

cross-referenced to related information within the volume. Some of the articles contain black-and-white illustrations, diagrams, or tables to facilitate understanding. An appendix provides a bibliography for further reading arranged by major subject areas, tables of measurement units, a biological classification scheme, a biographical list of notable scientists, and a list of contributors. A comprehensive index allows easy access to information. This title will be of value in public libraries as well as college libraries.
—**Ignacio J. Ferrer-Vinent**

Handbooks and Yearbooks

S
459.   **The New Biology Series.** By Joseph Panno. New York, Facts on File, 2004. 6v. illus. index. $35.00/vol.; $210.00/set. ISBN 0-8160-4945-9.

The new biology encompasses the study of the structure and function of the cell and the use of other more advanced technologies. While some of these advanced technologies and therapies, such as gene therapy, cloning, and biotechnology, are being used to study and treat a wide variety of medical disorders some procedures remain controversial. The ability to produce genetically modified crops, plants, and animals, and the use of human stem cells have raised some ethical and environmental concerns.

This set of six volumes explores the subject areas encompassed by the "new biology"—The Cell, Animal Cloning, Stem Cell Research, Gene Therapy, Cancer, and Aging. The volumes are laid out in a specific order that reflects the natural progression of the discipline starting at the cellular level and going up the chain to the study of aging. The texts include in-depth background information on each topic, while controversial areas are explored with the use of case studies and an examination of the ethical and legal issues. Illustrations are scattered throughout and a further reading list and index are also included.

This set is recommended for purchase by all types of libraries that collect in this area. Note, however, that although the texts are geared toward middle and high school students, they may be too advanced for some of these readers. The information, however, is useful for anyone who wants to expand his or her knowledge of the contemporary and controversial nature of these topics. [R: SLJ, Feb 05, p. 84]—**Julia Perez**

ANATOMY

C, P, S
460.   **Gray's Anatomy for Students.** By Richard L. Drake, Wayne Vogl, and Adam W. M. Mitchell. St. Louis, Mo., Churchill Livingstone/Elsevier Science, 2005. 1058p. illus. index. $64.95pa. ISBN 0-443-06612-4.

This edition of the well-known, time-tested standard, *Gray's Anatomy*, is simply excellent. It is a re-organized, student-oriented version *Gray's Anatomy* with clinical focus, exceptional indexing, and system cross-referencing. The illustrations and clinical images are superb. It also features electronic integration. Full-text online access is extended to the purchaser, along with six months free access to *Gray's Anatomy* (39th edition).

The book consists of eight chapters: anatomy and imaging; back; thorax; abdomen; pelvis and perineum; lower limb; upper limb; head and neck. Each chapter consists of four sections: conceptual overview; regional anatomy; surface anatomy; clinical cases. The conceptual overview section can be utilized independently by anyone who wishes to acquire detailed basic level information. It also functions nicely as a summary review for medical students. Ease of use is enhanced first by thoughtful organization of material and second by subtle color coding. The cases presented with each chapter are integrated smoothly with the related material. Overall, this title should certainly be on every beginning medical student's gross anatomy resources must-have list. It is highly recommended for academic reference collections supporting any type of health-related curriculums and is also a useful supplement to *Gray's Anatomy*. Its user-friendly accessibility makes it a valuable general collection recommendation to public, school, and academic libraries. —**Barbara Delzell**

BOTANY

General Works

Dictionaries and Encyclopedias

C, P

461.   **Plant.** Janet Marinelli, ed. New York, DK Publishing, 2005. 512p. illus. index. $50.00. ISBN 0-7566-0589-X.

In a departure from other gardening reference works by Dorling Kindersley, which often focus more on plant systematics presented with trademark minimalist photographs on a stark white background, Plant, by contrast, places each of the mentioned plants in an environmentally attuned context with a combination of the minimalist features as well as bold, full-page illustrations. The work showcases some 2,000 rare and imperiled plant species and features efforts to protect plants by international organizations such as the World Conservation Union (IUCN), upon whose 1997 *Red List of Threatened Plants* and the annually updated IUCN *Red List of Threatened Species* this book is based. The goal of the book is to provide novice gardeners to professional horticulturalists with a resource that relates each plant to its original biome and assist them with making informed decisions about buying, propagating, and nurturing threatened plants. Divided into encyclopedic sections based on plant type, each section provides a general introduction to the plant type, followed by detailed entries for each plant within that group. Individual entries are marked with the status of the species based on the *Red Lists*, natural distribution, botanical family notes, habitat features, related invasive species (if any), and the main descriptive entry. The last section is devoted to a short treatise on invasive species, including an A-Z listing. As one might expect, the author includes this listing to help the gardening enthusiast avoid plants that would increase the impact on the threatened and endangered species listed before. Lastly, a "Useful Addresses" section, biodiversity hot spots, global ecoregions, glossary, and index round out the book and suggest additional related resources for the reader.

While the layout is visually enticing and novel, some of the maps that show the natural distribution are rather small and can be difficult to see. Other than the unfortunate choice of title, which does not suggest that the cited work has anything to do with threatened and endangered plants specifically, *Plant* is recommended for public libraries and academic libraries with botany, horticulture, or landscape architecture programs. [R: LJ, 1 May 05, pp. 116-118]—**Jim Latchney**

Handbooks and Yearbooks

P

462.   Pleasant, Barbara. **The Complete Houseplant Survival Manual: Essential Know-How for Keeping (Not Killing) More than 160 Indoor Plants.** North Adams, Mass., Storey, 2005. 365p. illus. index. $24.95pa. ISBN 1-58017-569-4.

An award-winning writer of gardening books, the author introduces this book as a truly comprehensive guide to 160 houseplants from the old tried-and-true to many new selections that have entered the retail market in the last 10 years.

Following the introduction, which includes a brief history of houseplants and a plant identification guide, the author provides a readable, highly illustrated discussion of background and general care under the categories blooming houseplants and foliage houseplants. Presented in alphabetic order, each variety is assured at least a full page (some fill several pages), which feature beautiful color photographs of the plant, specifications for light, temperature, fertilizer, water, and soil. Tips are offered on repotting, propagation, selections, and display. A troubleshooting guide accompanies each variety dealing with topics such as disease and insects.

Part 3 is an A-Z general guide to houseplant care, from choosing the right containers and soil to "interiorscaping." Following is a glossary of houseplant terms, a resource list of plants and supplies, a list of organizations of interest to houseplant enthusiasts, and an extremely helpful, 11-page botanical/common name cross-reference.

The book is very well organized and easy to use. Descriptions are clear and complete, allowing the user to take into account the many factors involved in houseplant selection and care. It is an invaluable source for the layperson.—**Rachael Green**

C, P

463.   van Wyk, Ben-Erik. **Food Plants of the World: An Illustrated Guide.** Portland, Oreg., Timber Press, 2005. 480p. illus. index. $39.95. ISBN 0-88192-743-0.

For those who have ever wondered what a loquat looks like, or which plant rooibos tea comes from, this is the book to consult. This photographic guide contains information on over 350 of the most common food plants from around the world, including herbs and spices, cereals, nuts, fruits, and vegetables. Each plant is covered in a standardized single-page entry of about 250 words, including description, origin and history, parts used, cultivation, nutritive value, and notes on medicinal and other nonfood uses. There are two or three photographs of each species, usually of the whole plant and a close-up of the edible parts. The plants are arranged by scientific name, with scientific synonyms and common names in several different languages also provided. The index includes both scientific and all common names listed in the entries, which is very helpful since users will usually know only common names. The book also includes introductory information on the different categories of food plants, such as legumes, fruits, or sugars, and lists the most important food plants in each category. An appendix explains the chemistry and physiology of plant-based nutrients, and there is a tabular quick guide to 900 commercial food plants including the 350 discussed in the book. The quick guide provides scientific and common name; region of origin; edible parts; and nutritive values for energy, protein, fat, minerals, and vitamins for each species.

The range of plants covered in the main text is impressive, including plants from all parts of the world. They range from well-known plants such as rice, maize, and cabbage to exotics such as stevia, durian, and jugo bean. Since each plant, no matter how widely used, has entries of the same length, the greatest value in the book lies in its provision of basic information on unfamiliar food plants. The guide will be useful in public libraries with an international clientele or as a ready-reference source at international grocery stores. It will also find use at academic libraries interested in cookery, agriculture, or ethnobotany.—**Diane Schmidt**

Flowering Plants

Dictionaries and Encyclopedias

P

464.   **Flora's Orchids.** Portland, Oreg., Timber Press, 2005. 368p. illus. index. $59.95. ISBN 0-88192-721-X.

A must-have for the public library's gardening section, this elegant survey of the orchid world bursts with color and meticulous photographic detail of orchids growing in the wild. The text introduces the beginner to the orchid family and to the traits that differentiate distinct types of blossoms, from lady slipper to foxtail orchid and wax-lip. Following essays on hybridizing, cultivating, propagating, and conserving orchids, an A-Z arrangement presents pictorial evidence of the flower's exotic beauty. Entries include size and spread, color, and common names of plants sold in hothouses. A three-page glossary summarizes essentials, such as binomial, deciduous, polyploid, and vandaceous. A detailed cultivation table summarizes species by their scientific names. More detailed information fills the 13-page index. Missing from coverage are names, addresses, and Websites of bonafide sources of plants and advice on raising them. The scope of *Flora's Orchids* suits the propagator, flower merchant, and purveyor of natural beauty. A suitably priced gift book and reference guide, this work suits the needs of a variety of readers. [R: BL, 1 & 15 Jan 06, pp. 150-151]—**Mary Ellen Snodgrass**

Trees and Shrubs

Dictionaries and Encyclopedias

C, P

465.   **Firefly Encyclopedia of Trees.** Steve Cafferty, ed. New York, Firefly Books, 2005. 288p. illus. maps. index. $49.95. ISBN 1-55407-051-1.

There are many splendid books on the market devoted to the description of trees, discussing all sorts of sizes, shapes, and contents. While a compilation of trees, worldwide in scope, would be physically impossible to rest in a book of manageable size, Steve Cafferty has succeeded in enumerating a list of the main species in the most significant genera in the world. When a tome like this runs the gamut from the plain-Jane Acer (maple) genus, through the genus Phellodendron (the Amur cork tree) and even includes the genus Spathodea (African tulip-tree) one is assured that the author understands trees.

The essential ingredients of the main section of Cafferty's encyclopedia include tables of the species in each family; fact boxes and distribution maps that summarize the ecology, cultivation, and economic uses of the main species. Further, the trees are grouped in evolutionary order, from primitive tree ferns, gingkoes, and cycads, to the conifers of the cold temperate regions. In the final section of the encyclopedia an extensive coverage of the native trees of the Americas, Asia, and Africa are followed by unusually detailed indexes. The color photography of the morphological aspects of the trees is stunning as well as those of the entire trees in their local landscapes.

A feature not usually found in "pure" tree books is a detailed section that is titled "What is a Tree?" It is accurately and expertly constructed to include the morphological characteristics of a tree and all essential elements related thereto. Testing the adequacy of the coverage it was a pleasure and a surprise to note that this section even included a discussion of wood anatomy and was supported by an accompanying photomicrograph of a magnified section of wood.

This book is a valuable, self-contained encyclopedia of an expertly selected set of species of trees designed to encompass a fairly representative family of trees throughout the world. The contents of these 288 pages exude professionalism of the editor and the value of his association at the Natural History Museum in London.—**James H. Flynn Jr.**

P

466.   More, David, and John White. **The Illustrated Encyclopedia of Trees.** 2d ed. Portland, Oreg., Timber Press, 2005. 832p. illus. index. $79.95. ISBN 0-88192-751-1.

This is an updated and expanded version of the 1st edition published in 2002 (see ARBA 2004, entry 1338). Changes include lengthened articles with greater detail, the addition of over 90 important trees from the Southern region of Europe and the Western part of the Mediterranean, and the inclusion of leaf shapes in the section on shoots and buds. Coverage is limited to over 1,800 trees that are found and cultivated in Britain, France, Germany, and the low countries. Most of these trees are also found in North America. The introduction includes information on selecting and planting trees, plus a list of suggested trees for problem sites or special needs with the tree's scientific and common names provided. The book is arranged by tree family using the common name followed by the scientific name. The textual information is given on the right-hand page with colored illustrations of the tree and its leaves or needles, bark, blossoms, fruit, cones, or nuts on the left page and below the text. The drawings are very realistic including imperfections in the trees. Within the text the author provides information beyond describing the physical features of the tree. He includes facts, such as when it was discovered and if the timber is used and how. At the end of each article rating scales are used to give the growth rate of the species at 10 years, 20 years, and its eventual height; the hardiness or tolerance of the tree to frost; the suitability of the tree for a garden; and rating the wood for cabinetry or other uses. The main body is followed by a section on the Southern trees; a glossary; a section with illustrations of shoots, buds, and leaves; an index of scientific names; and an index of English names. This book is written for the tree enthusiast and is not overly technical or scientific. The illustrations are outstanding. This would be an excellent edition for public or academic libraries. Students involved in leaf or tree identification projects will also find the book very helpful.—**Elaine Ezell**

GENETICS

C, P

467.   **The Gale Encyclopedia of Genetic Disorders.** 2d ed. Brigham Narins, ed. Farmington Hills, Mich., Gale, 2005. 2v. illus. index. $340.00/set. ISBN 1-4144-0365-8.

The 2d edition of *The Gale Encyclopedia of Genetic Disorders* is a well-organized, well-researched medical resource for readers seeking solid coverage of genetically based health conditions in an easy-to-comprehend format. Ease of use in this two-volume set is facilitated by the alphabetic arrangement of topics, table of contents, alphabetic list of entries, and subject index. Definitions to unfamiliar medical terms are included as a section in each entry, and also in the glossary available at the end of volume 2. Photographs and charts are included as necessary to illustrate the concepts presented. An appendix found in volume 2 includes a chromosome map and cumulative list of all the organizations cited throughout. Each of the 430 entries follows the same layout making it convenient for the reader to find all relevant information in one section. Entries include a thorough definition and description of the condition presented along with demographics, signs and symptoms, diagnosis, treatment, management, prognosis, key terms, and additional resources. The list of resources includes suggestions for further reading, support groups and organizations, Websites, and related conditions and terms. Several sections on genetic basics, such as DNA and genetic counseling, are included to provide the reader with additional background information. Entries were compiled and reviewed by medical professionals, including physicians and genetic experts, to ensure accuracy and currency of the information provided. A disclaimer in the front section of volume 1 notes that this resource is not meant to serve as a substitute for any diagnosis or treatment and correctly refers the reader to a health care professional for further information, diagnosis, treatment, and discussion. Written in nontechnical jargon for easy comprehension by the lay reader, the thoroughness of the entries will be of benefit to health care practitioners. The essays are easily comprehended by average readers at a high school level and above. Listed as a 2d edition, there is no information provided on any changes or updates made from the 1st edition (see ARBA 2003, entry 1367) edited by Stacey L. Blanchford. [R: LJ, Jan 06, p. 158]—**Susan E. Thomas**

ZOOLOGY

General Works

P, S

468.   **DK First Animal Encyclopedia.** New York, DK Publishing, 2004. 160p. illus. index. $15.99. ISBN 0-7566-0227-0.

This latest entry in the publisher's parade of juvenile nature titles proves the old adage that learning can be fun. Children, kindergarten through grade 3, will find fascinating facts about all types of animals while being subtly introduced to the organization of reference books.

Five sections cover the vertebrate groups: mammals, birds, reptiles, fish, and "creepy crawlies" (otherwise known as invertebrates). Each section opens with information about the common characteristics of the class and then introduces select families within the group. Entries present interesting facts about animals. For example, lemurs are only found in Madagascar and each zebra stripe is unique. "Weird or What?" buttons give unusual facts about animals. Interwoven is solid information that very young students can use for school assignments. The bird section has nicely illustrated lists of the types of bird feathers, feet, and bills. Each type is accompanied by a one-sentence annotation explaining how the feature is used by the bird. Insect metamorphosis is beautifully depicted in a two-page spread showing all the stages of the process. Students will also find pictures and descriptions of such things as the three types of fish, the eight varieties of bears, and how to identify an insect.

Each page is a visual delight of color photography for which the publisher is known. The photographs will draw children into the age-appropriate, two-sentence explanatory text. Questions related to the text appear at the bottom of each page reinforcing reading comprehension. "Become an Expert" buttons serve as *see also* references encouraging readers to recognize broad subject relationships. The well-organized, detailed table of contents and the index are easy to use and enable students to quickly find information.

Kids will find this a fun way to study animals or to simply pursue an interest. Reluctant readers or children with reading problems will find it an inviting, nonthreatening resource. Teachers, media specialists, and parents will appreciate the content and appearance of the book. It is a winner for all concerned. [R: SLJ, Feb 05, p. 81]—**Marlene M. Kuhl**

C, P, S

469.   **Encyclopedia of Animal Behavior.** Marc Bekoff, ed. Westport, Conn., Greenwood Press, 2004. 3v. illus. index. $349.95/set. ISBN 0-313-32745-9.

With over 300 entries written by nearly 300 contributors, this encyclopedia covers a wide range of areas in animal behavior. The topics are drawn from comparative psychology, ethology, behavioral ecology, sociobiology, and all of the other subdisciplines that study this fascinating subject in all its ramifications, both controversial and well-established. While the focus is not on animal welfare, there are several entries on this and related subjects. The *Encyclopedia* is arranged by broad subjects, such as cognition or reproductive behavior, with narrower entries clustered within these subjects. This clustering works in some cases but may not serve other users. There are cross-references within each article, a table of cross-references at the beginning of the first volume, and an index. Users may need to use all three resources to find all relevant articles on a topic. For instance, there is a valuable discussion of the domestication of foxes in an article on dog cognition that is not repeated in the domestication cluster, cannot be found in the index under domestication or foxes, and is only cross-referenced within one of the domestication entries.

The entries range from fairly brief, simple articles clearly aimed at high school or advanced grade school students to lengthier and more substantive entries. Many of the briefer articles deal with careers or are first-person descriptions of a project by individual researchers, so they are clearly aimed at piquing the interest of students. Some of them, especially the ones that mention personal encounters with animals, do this better than others. There is a great deal of variation among the more in-depth articles as well. They range from scientific articles discussing animal behavior in carefully non-anthropomorphic terms to an article by Rupert Sheldrake advocating for the existence of telepathy in animals. Besides articles on specific behaviors or animals, the *Encyclopedia* also includes biographies, historical articles, descriptions of methods used in studying animal behavior, and a very extensive list of animal behavior organizations and Websites. There are black-and-white photographs scattered throughout the text and a separate section of color plates in each volume. Overall, the quality of the entries is very high, striking that difficult balance between being easy to understand and being accurate and detailed, between being personal and being scientific. The *Encyclopedia* is recommended for academic and public libraries and large high schools. [R: LJ, 15 Mar 05, p. 110]—**Diane Schmidt**

S

470.   Warnau, Geneviève. **The Encyclopedia of Animals.** Chevy Chase, Md., Teora USA; distr., Ada, Mich., KSB Promotions, 2005. 301p. illus. index. $24.95. ISBN 1-59496-035-6.

This guidebook to animals is designed for elementary through middle school age children. Originally published in Belgium, this is the first U.S. edition of this volume. Unfortunately, there is no introduction or preface to explain the goal or the thought process behind the layout of the volume so users will have to fend for themselves to adjust to the unusual layout. The work is arranged into 13 geographical sections, with each providing additional information on 10 to 20 animals that live in that habitat. For example, one of the largest sections, "In Seas and on Seashores," provides information on whales, coral, dolphins, sea urchins, and pelicans, while "In the Savanna" provides information on lions, elephants, giraffes, ostriches, and porcupines, just to name a few. The guide also has sections on desert animals (e.g., rattlesnakes, scorpions), animals of the rainforest (e.g., chimpanzees, bats, tortoises), the mountains (e.g., eagles, yaks), the polar regions (e.g., reindeer, penguins), lake shores and rivers (e.g., beavers, toads, cranes), grassy plains (e.g., armadillos, rabbits), woods and forests (e.g., wolves, skunks), the countryside (e.g., horses, goats, chickens), gardens (e.g., ladybugs, moles), and at home (e.g., dogs, cats, flies). Each animal is featured on a one- or two-page spread and provides information on their physical features and how they help them adapt to their habitat, their food, and how they survive in their habitat. Many color and close-up photographs enhance the text and they will appeal to children in this age group.

This book is not a true encyclopedia—it is not alphabetically organized, nor is it comprehensive. It would be a useful addition to school and public libraries that need supplementary materials to other more inclusive resources on animals for this age group.—**Shannon Graff Hysell**

Birds

P

471.   **National Geographic Reference Atlas to the Birds of North America.** Washington, D.C., National Geographic Society, 2003. 480p. illus. maps. index. $35.00. ISBN 0-7922-3373-5.

The National Geographic Society has made a notable contribution to popular ornithology with this atlas/reference book. The main text reviews the birdlife of North America by groups of avian families, which summarize basic features of each taxonomic unit. There are standard accounts of structure and plumage, behavior (feeding, vocals, and breeding), and distribution (range, including migration). Of special interest are discussions of the conservation status for each family and updates on recent views of avian classification (family relationships). Throughout the text, large detailed maps illustrate many important geographic patterns (e.g., historic changes in range, unusual migration routes, or neotropical wintering areas). The volume concludes with a lengthy atlas section of 700 species range maps, with details of breeding and wintering areas. This reference will be a welcomed tool in the library of birders. [R: LJ, Jan 04, p. 92]—**Charles Leck**

Domestic Animals

P

472.   Coile, D. Caroline. **Encyclopedia of Dog Breeds.** 2d ed. Hauppauge, N.Y., Barron's Educational Series, 2005. 352p. illus. index. $29.95. ISBN 0-7641-5700-0.

Barron's Educational Series has managed to make a superb, low-price reference work as gorgeous as it is useful. In artistically designed facing pages, the text defines and characterizes each canine breed. Entries feature elegant portraiture and a black-and-white drawing of distinguishing skeletal and posture traits; for example, the aloof grace of the borzoi and the stamina of the herding class. Alongside are action shots of neatly coiffed dogs at play and at work. The only detail lacking from the layout are pictures of dogs in infancy and during training. Commentary is precise without being pedantic. Back matter offers the researcher and dog fancier specifics of constitutional malformation and disease, such as joint displasia. Indexing supplies common names as well as proper names. Coile's book combines the function of a reference book in the guise of a handsome coffee-table compendium. The 2d edition of the *Encyclopedia of Dog Breeds* is highly recommended for schools and public libraries. [R: BL, 1 &15 Jan 06, p. 132]—**Mary Ellen Snodgrass**

Fishes

P

473.   Alderton, David. **Encyclopedia of Aquarium & Pond Fish.** New York, DK Publishing, 2005. 400p. illus. index. $35.00. ISBN 0-7566-0941-0.

This attractive book is an introduction to fresh and saltwater aquariums and fish ponds for amateurs and enthusiasts. It is well illustrated with color photographs of aquariums, ponds, plants, and fish. After an introduction on fish biology, there are sections on freshwater and saltwater aquariums and on fish ponds, each with information on tank set-up and maintenance, health, and breeding, followed by descriptions of individual species of plants and fish, and in the saltwater section, some invertebrates. These directory sections offer, for each species, a photograph and information on origins, size, diet, water temperature and pH preferences, and temperament (e.g., "Aggressive and quarrelsome") . The text is clear and well written. The introductory section on fish taxonomy and biodiversity is very well done. This work will be a good choice for any public library. [R: LJ, 15 Feb 05, p. 156]—**Frederic F. Burchsted**

S

474.   **Grzimek's Student Animal Life Resource: Fishes.** By Catherine Judge Allen. Farmington Hills, Mich., U*X*L/Gale, 2005. 375p. illus. maps. index. $60.00. ISBN 0-7876-9242-5.

This reference is intended for young students seeking a simple natural history on fishes. The table of contents is easy to read and is visually appealing. The entries in this section are listed by popular name and arranged by the classification category of order. The "Getting to Know Fishes" section serves as a valuable overview on fishes. The main entries, titled chapters, consist of general information and highlight well-known species based on physical characteristics, geographic range, habitat, diet, behavior and reproduction, fishes and people, conservation status, and references. The index facilitates access to fishes by scientific names and to fishes by their common names, particularly to species not listed in the table of contents. There are additional sections that enhance this reference: a "Reader's Guide," "Pronunciation Guide for Scientific Names," "Words to Know," "Species List by Biome," and "Species List by Geographic Range." The professional illustrations, photographs, and distribution maps likewise add value to each entry.

Having stated the positive with regards to *Grzimek's Student Animal Life Resource: Fishes*, it is not without its shortcomings. The introduction omits a statement of purpose, authority, scope, audience, and format that leads to general confusion and ambiguity. The species accounts are structured by Order Chapters, although four chapters are titled Class Chapters. These Class Chapters omit order information. In comparison, the Order Chapters include class and order categories. The family classification information for each chapter is given as a total. At the species level, Coelacanths and Lungfishes are discussed by their class ranking—Sarcopterygii. This chapter highlights the coelacanth *Latimeria chalumnae* without any note for the other known species—*Latimeria menadoensis*. To an uninformed reader there appears to be only one species of coelacanth. Clearly, the scientific classification categories are incomplete and somewhat misleading throughout. As for the index, there is an explanatory note that states "Italic type indicates volume number" of which there is no evidence.

Given the aforementioned evaluation, this reference should stimulate the investigative interests of young children to explore more comprehensive references. The books and Websites recommended for each chapter will enable further research and materials acquisition. *Grzimek's Student Animal Life Resource: Fishes* is recommended for children library collections.—**Edward L. González**

Insects

S

475. **Grzimek's Student Animal Life Resource: Insects and Spiders.** By Arthur V. Evans. Farmington Hills, Mich., U*X*L/Gale, 2005. 2v. illus. maps. index. $110.00/set. ISBN 0-7876-9243-3.

The orchid mantid, which lives in Southeast Asia, demonstrates that even insects are pretty in pink. It is one of the insects introduced in a way that will engage some young readers, most likely primary grade students that are being guided by an adult through the text. Difficulty in discerning the age group the volumes target is a problem. If prospective readers are middle school students, there is not enough "oh my!" content or engrossing photographs to hook them. And they are likely to find the in-text nonphonetic pronunciation guides more disruptive than useful. Fifty pages of introductory text are identical in both volumes, which is puzzling because the books are sold as a set. Scientific information is accurate, but only half or so of the entries have listed resources for further reading. The index is easy to use. A species list by geographic range, which in some cases is a country and in others is a continent, rounds out the text.—**Diane M. Calabrese**

Mammals

C, P

476. **World Atlas of Great Apes and Their Conservation.** Julian Caldecott and Lera Miles, eds. Cambridge, United Kingdom, UNEP World Conservation Monitoring Centre, and Berkeley, Calif., University of California Press, 2005. 456p. illus. maps. index. $45.00. ISBN 0-520-24633-0.

There are six living great apes, all endangered, in three genera: *Pan*, chimpanzee and bonobo; *Gorilla*, eastern and western gorillas; and *Pongo*, Bornean and Sumatran orangutans. This work is a comprehensive summary, written by many of the world's best primatologists, of the current state of knowledge of humankind's closest relatives. The first section deals with great ape evolution (although the fossil record is frustratingly incomplete) and biology, and includes a brief summary of the lesser apes: the gibbons. The second section examines conservation issues; habitat loss to human development is the worst threat, but illegal hunting, trapping for the illicit pet trade, and infectious diseases (the Ebola virus poses a potentially serious threat in parts of Africa) are also factors. Great ape biology also works against them, as all six species have very low natural reproduction rates. The third section is the atlas proper: a series of country-by-country maps showing distribution in great detail and also including such relevant facts as national parks and wildlife reservations. There are numerous excellent color photographs, chapter bibliographies, and a good index. An "Annex" provides a directory of conservation organizations wholly or partially concerned with great apes and a list of relevant international conventions.

The level of treatment is scientifically rigorous, but accessible to nonspecialists with some background in zoology or wildlife conversation. This excellent reference will be well used in both academic and public libraries.—**Paul B. Cors**

Reptiles and Amphibians

P, S

477.   **World of Animals: Amphibians and Reptiles. Volumes 41-50.** Danbury, Conn., Grolier, 2005. 10v. illus. maps. index. (World of Animals, v.41-50). $499.00/set. ISBN 0-7172-5916-1.

The recent surge in both scientific and common interest in amphibians and reptiles are sure to make the final 10 volumes of the 50-volume *World of Animals* set a big hit with school and public libraries. Additionally, each volume is a feast for the eyes, drawing the browser into the text. The volumes cover Salamanders, Newts and Caecilians (v. 41); Frogs and Toads (vols. 42-43); Lizards (vols. 44-46); Turtles and Crocodilians (v. 47); and Snakes (vols. 48-50).

Besides the stunning photographs or drawings on every page, the layout and organization are particularly conducive to ease of use and pleasure. Each 128-page volume begins with a 2-page spread on "How to Use this Set" and "Find the Animal," and each volume ends with a glossary, IUCN categories, further reading, a lists of useful Websites, and a set index. "Find the Animal" has the scientific taxonomy of the groups (i.e., class, order, suborder, and family) making the set suitable for advanced students and adult learners. Initial chapters of 8-10 pages introduce the group (e.g., "What is a Reptile?") . This is followed with shorter chapters on subgroups (e.g., Lizards, Agamas, Chameleons) and on individual species (e.g., Thorny Devil, Plumed Basilisk, Tuataras). All are well written with clear, current scientific information. A "Data Panel" on the left page of each species layout is especially handy, including common name and full scientific taxa, key features, habits, breeding, diet, habitat, distribution, status, similar species, venom, and location on a world globe in red. Light green text boxes draw attention to topics of special interest. No other current multivolume set exists with the fine features and global coverage of this set of books on amphibians and reptiles.—**Georgia Briscoe**

32 Engineering

GENERAL WORKS

Dictionaries and Encyclopedias

C

478. **Encyclopedia of Nonlinear Science.** Alwyn Scott, ed. New York, Routledge/Taylor & Francis Group, 2005. 1053p. illus. index. $195.00. ISBN 1-57958-385-7.

Nonlinear science is remarkable among recent scientific advances for its interdisciplinary applications; many (if not most) scientific and technical fields have benefited from nonlinear concepts. This resource is a thorough guide to this wide-ranging and perplexing subject and should prove useful to users across a broad spectrum of disciplines and situations. The *Encyclopedia* addresses this breadth of audience through a "Thematic List of Entries," which organizes the articles by discipline and topic, as well as a more standard alphabetic listing supplemented with *see* and *see also* references. The entries tend to be of medium length; few are less than a page or greater than three. The majority of the longer articles are subdivided for clarity. The majority of the entries aim for a broad scope (one cause for the abundant *see* references), but some are particularly focused (e.g., Tacoma Narrows Bridge Collapse). Most articles include a brief further reading list; equations, graphs, and (less commonly) illustrations are included as needed. An index concludes the volume. A drawback of this largish reference tool is the binding, which does not inspire great confidence. Most institutions that benefit from its contents will likely pay for its rebinding sooner rather than later. Once that caveat is out of the way, however, this encyclopedia will likely prove useful to undergraduates, graduates, and faculty engaged in both multidisciplinary and more discipline-focused research. The general public will find less here, but the explanations are clear enough that a well-read layperson should have no trouble navigating this guide.—**Peter Larsen**

C, P, S

479. **McGraw-Hill Concise Encyclopedia of Engineering.** New York, McGraw-Hill, 2004. 912p. index. $24.95pa. ISBN 0-07-143952-8.

This encyclopedia is derived from the venerable *McGraw-Hill Encyclopedia of Science and Technology* (9th ed.; see ARBA 2004, entry 1242). The intent is to summarize current basic engineering information. The editor claims that the articles are designed to "include explanations, not definitions" and cover "every major engineering area." Each of the approximately 900 articles is a condensed version of the parent article. Some entries show the effects of too much condensing. For example, the word *eutectics* is defined as "microstructures that result when a solution of metal of eutectic composition solidifies." However, neither *eutectic composition* nor *eutectic* are specifically defined. Sadly, the entry on *Wikipedia* (http://en.wikipedia.org/wiki/Eutectic) has a more complete entry.

A more serious problem is the inclusion of words easily found in other sources, such as *aircraft, local area network*, or *virtual reality*. While this inclusion does add bulk, it does not add content. Some obviously missing content can be found, for example, under bridges. There is no entry in the index for cable-stayed bridges, nor is this modern bridge type covered in the text. This is a serious fault since the Sunshine Skyway bridge completed 1987 along with other modern bridges of this type have received a lot of attention. Also missing from the index is an entry for cavitation. Cavitation can be a serious engineering problem for engines; large machinery and various types of propellers are covered but without mention of cavitation.

The appendixes consist of a rather nice bibliography of references by section. There is an appendix that coverts the author's initials at the end of each article to their full name. Once the user has the full name they can check another listing for the author's work location. It is unclear why two separate listings are needed. There is also a biographical listing of important historical scientists

This is inexpensive and might be of interest to public and high school libraries. There is not enough depth to be more than a tertiary tool in engineering or technical libraries.—**Susan B. Ardis**

ASTRONAUTICAL ENGINEERING

C, P

480.   **The Cambridge Aerospace Dictionary.** By Bill Gunston. Edited by Jane's Information Group. New York, Cambridge University Press, 2004. 740. $75.00. ISBN 0-521-84140-2.

What really stands out in the 2d edition of this work is the amusing and interesting foreword by Gunston. In this foreword he defends the 1st edition from a reviewer criticism that there were too many words "which have no relevance to aerospace." Gunston decided in this edition to include as he says "any term or acronym that just might confuse an aerospace professional." In the same foreword Gunston discusses outlandish and "unpronounceable acronyms" as well as the excessive use of phrases that include the words *advanced*, *direct*, and *integrated*. He notes that in time these technologies are no longer as advanced or direct, and the term integrated probably has a different meaning.

As to the dictionary portion of this volume, all words, phrases, and acronyms are arranged in strictly alphabetic order; therefore, KTAS comes after krypton but before kuechemann carrot. Other types of terms included are names of aerospace materials, even if they are registered trade names. Probably the most limited but still interesting is the inclusion of some colloquial or slang terminology, such as prisoner nut, prime beef, or poopy suit. Who would have known that a poopy suit is a flight-crew-over water survival suit? Entries also include the country such as CAA or Sweden. Historical terms in use at a specific time are so marked. Cross-references are italicized and U.S. spellings predominate.

Included are a wealth of terms, phrases, and acronyms. Acronyms make up most of the 1,500 new entries and acronyms make up probably 25 percent of the text. Examples include FARRP (forward-area rearming and refueling point), not to be confused with FARP (forward arming), LRVD (lower rotating ventral door), PBDI (position bearing and distance indicator), and on and on. One minor complaint concerns prefixes. The definition of Pave states that this is a prefix, however, no examples are provided. It would have been easy to include examples of "pave-". There are 10 appendixes, including a list of Greek letters used as aerospace symbols.

This nice, well-done dictionary would be at home in any academic or public library. The compiler is an editor at Jane's Information Group.—**Susan B. Ardis**

ENVIRONMENTAL ENGINEERING

C

481.　Lee, C. C. **Environmental Engineering Dictionary.** 4th ed. Blue Ridge Summit, Pa., Government Institutes, 2005. 957p. $135.00. ISBN 0-86587-848-X.

This large volume defines at least 14,000 technical and regulatory engineering terms that apply to environmental engineering and technology, pollution control technologies, quality control, monitoring, risk assessment, sampling, and analysis. Many newly created terms are included in this 4th edition, and, to keep up with the constant changes in technology, the initial definitions in previous editions have been revised. Also new are three appendixes: one that defines terms related to fuel cell technology, one that includes special definitions on environmental management systems, and one on environmental calculations. This dictionary also covers the official EPA definition of terms and the origin of the definition. Appendix D provides environmental acronyms so the researcher can track down whether the acronym is from the Code of Federal Regulations (CFR), Clean Water Act (CWA), Department of Energy (DOE), Surface Mining Control and Reclamation Act (SMCRA), or elsewhere. Compiled by a research program manager who works at the U.S. Environmental Protection Agency, this updated resource will be valuable to select special libraries, most academic libraries, and large public libraries.—**Diane J. Turner**

33 Health Sciences

GENERAL WORKS

Directories

P

482. **America's Top Doctors.** 5th ed. New York, Castle Connolly Medical, 2005. 1278p. index. $24.95pa. ISBN 1-883769-90-6.

People tend to choose their physicians by recommendations from family or friends. Specialist recommendations tend to come from a referral from a primary care physician. This reference expands on that process by asking over 250,000 physicians, health care administrators, and representatives from professional organizations to name doctors who are "noted for excellence in a specialty area." The result is a listing of more than 4,000 physicians representing 42 medical and surgical specialties.

The directory section is organized alphabetically by medical specialty. Each section begins with a brief description of the specialty along with educational requirements. Selected physicians are then listed alphabetically with in one of seven U.S. geographic regions. Each doctor's listing provides the usual directory information along with board certification, medical school and residency, and fellowships and faculty appointments. The book begins with a number of explanatory chapters. Particularly helpful are sections on how to choose a specialist, which helps the layperson understand the language of medical training and education (e.g., what does it mean to be board certified?). The book concludes with several appendixes, most of which are further directory listings of hospitals, medical schools, medical specialty boards, and so on. Two indexes cross-reference the physician's listings alphabetically by specialty and last name only. Sponsored advertisements by major U.S. hospitals are interspersed. This book would be most helpful for people living in an area of high concentration of medical specialists. Within the reference, most specialties list at least one doctor in each region, but there is not a physician named for each specialty area in every state or major city. Because of health insurance restrictions, many citizens would not be able to consult a specialist out of their region unless they paid out of pocket. A person who is fortunate enough to have the resources to be able to travel outside of their geographic residence and/or to have portability of their health insurance will find this book to be most helpful. A cross listing by individual state enabling the reader to quickly check local specialist availability would have been helpful. Overall, however, this is a valuable resource for the best specialty medical care that the United States can offer. This information is also available online from the publisher at http://www.castleconnolly.com/. The online version will be the one that most libraries should choose; it is available for the very affordable price of $21.95 per year.—**Mary Ann Thompson**

C, P

483. **Health Professions Career and Education Directory, 2005-2006.** 33d ed. Chicago, American Medical Association, 2005. 666p. $165.00pa. ISBN 1-57947-675-9.

Fred Donini-Lenhoff of the American Medical Association Press served as the editor of the 666-page, 33d edition of this very informative directory. The volume consists of four sections and one appendix. Section 1 features descriptions of 64 different health-related professions and 6,745 program listings. Each description contains subsections. "The History" describes the profession from its inception, its evolution through current duties, responsibilities and accrediting institutions. "The Occupational Description" lists the general duties within the context of the health environment supported; for example, art therapy is "a human service profession that uses art media, images, the creative art process that . . . can help individuals access and express conflict not easily reached with words." "The Job Description" more fully explains the day-to-day activities of the profession. "Employment Characteristics" details lengths of typical shifts, salaries, and physical locations where the jobs are usually performed. "The Employment Outlook" section gives statistics and projections for demand, growth, and staffing needs. "Educational Programs" focuses on prerequisites, courses, and levels of educational attainment required to work in the field. "Licensure, Certification and Registration" specifies legal and professional requirements to practice a chosen profession. Section 2 lists 2,515 institutions sponsoring the 6,745 health professions' educational programs. Institutions are listed alphabetically by state. Section 3 provides detailed information on the education programs listed in section 1. These are the facts needed by prospective students and job seekers. Section 4 showcases "Health Professions Education Data"; for example, table 2 features the percentage of graduates finding employment within 6 months and/or seeking additional education (by occupation) for the academic year 2003-2004.

Because the data presented throughout this book were obtained by means of a survey administered in 2004, some of the information is out of date. For example, the new Director of the School of Information Resources and Library Science (SIRLS) at the University of Arizona is Jana Bradley, not Brooke Sheldon. Some errors notwithstanding, this directory provides valuable information for individuals doing research on the health professions in order to begin or enhance their careers. It is recommended for public, community college, and medical and academic libraries.—**Laura J. Bender**

Handbooks and Yearbooks

P

484.   **Health Care State Rankings 2005: Health Care in the 50 United States.** 13th ed. Kathleen O'Leary Morgan and Scott Morgan, eds. Lawrence, Kans., Morgan Quitno Press, 2005. 512p. index. $56.95pa. ISBN 0-7401-0941-3. ISSN 1065-1403.

Heath Care State Rankings 2005 provides one-page charts of state statistics divided into the following sections: birth and reproductive health, deaths, facilities, finance, incidence of disease, providers, and fitness. The information for these charts has been obtained from a variety of government and private sector sources. Each chart provides the national statistic, and then the rankings by state listed in two columns: the left-hand column lists the states alphabetically and the right-hand column places them from the highest ranking to the lowest. Information on the District of Columbia is included but not incorporated into the ranking. There is an extensive section of abortion statistics, as well as Medicare and Medicaid data, information about various cancers and sexually transmitted diseases, alcohol consumption, and the average wages of various health care providers. There is an appendix of population statistics to provide an additional basis of comparison. There is also a directory of sources giving the address, telephone number, and Web page of each entity providing statistics for the book. This book is useful from both a health care and a public policy perspective, and at the low price would be a good addition to the reference collection of most libraries. [R: LJ, 15 Oct 05, p. 82]—**Elaine Lasda Bergman**

P

485.   Ricotta, Mary C. **A Consumer's Guide to Laboratory Tests.** Amherst, N.Y., Prometheus Books, 2005. 301p. index. $21.00pa. ISBN 1-59102-247-9.

This book is simplistic in its approach to laboratory tests and not well organized. The headings for the chapters are better suited for a health care professional than the lay audience for which the book is written. Most health consumers will not know that clinical chemistry is the umbrella term for most of the tests for how well your body is functioning such as thyroid, liver, or diabetes. It would be better to be arranged by organ, by disease, or by body system than by how laboratory tests are organized. The index does not list terms for tests that would be listed on a laboratory slip such as TSH or fasting glucose. It could have been better cross-referenced with terms such as T3 instead of only triidothyronine or A1C in addition to glycosylated hemoglobin. The glossary is very complete and seems to have no logic as to the terms selected for inclusion. The appendixes are of minimal value in that many of the terms are beyond what a consumer is likely to know, such as integument for skin. The book is too simplistic to be in a medical library and not of sufficient detail or ease of use to be recommended for a consumer health or public library. —**Leslie M. Behm**

MEDICINE

General Works

Dictionaries and Encyclopedias

C, P, S
486.   **Merriam-Webster's Medical Desk Dictionary.** rev. ed. Springfield, Mass., Merriam-Webster, 2005. 918p. $21.95pa. ISBN 1-4180-0056-6.

This medical dictionary states that its purpose is to "serve as an interface between the language of the doctor and the patient . . .." As a result, the definitions consist more of common parlance than medical jargon, which is especially helpful to the health care consumer in understanding medical terminology. Entries in this volume tend to be more concise than, say, *Dorland's Illustrated Medical Dictionary* (30th ed.: W. B. Saunders Company, 2003). The volume does not include any illustrations, which is a detracting factor. The *Dictionary* does have several unique features, however. First, it provides a large number of biographical sketches of famous people in medicine; for example, if you look up Lennox-Gastaut Syndrome, there is a description of the disease as well as short biographies of both William Gordon Lennox and Henri Jean-Pascal Gastaut. In the back are a "Table of Signs and Symbols" and a medical writing "Style Guide," which looks like it would be more helpful for students than for advanced medical researchers. At the low price of this volume, it is recommended mainly for public and school libraries rather than medical or hospital libraries. [R: LJ, 1 Sept 05, pp. 180-182]—**Elaine Lasda Bergman**

P
487.   Rothfeld, Glenn S., and Deborah S. Romaine. **The Encyclopedia of Men's Health.** New York, Facts on File, 2005. 391p. index. (Facts on File Library of Health and Living). $75.00. ISBN 0-8160-5177-1.

American men are living longer than their ancestors, but they face a wide range of health issues. In 2004, more than 230,000 of them were diagnosed with prostate cancer. Cardiovascular disease, hypertension, insomnia, and sexual dysfunction are also problems, but they can be prevented with lifestyle modification. *The Encyclopedia of Men's Health*, written by a physician who practices integrative medicine and a medical writer, provides information that will help men stay healthy. More than 600 alphabetic entries discuss anatomy and physiology (e.g., gastrointestinal system, posterior cruciate ligament), diseases (e.g., cancer, diabetes), medications (e.g., antibiotic medications, saw palmetto), lifestyle issues (e.g., homosexuality, substance abuse), and medical procedures (e.g., bone scan, joint replacement). Drugs are listed by class or generic name with cross-references from brand names. Coverage of contemporary topics such as body piercing, anabolic steroid use, and tattoos as well as fitness, nutrition, and psychosocial issues (passive-aggressive behavior) as well as patient confidentiality regulations make this a comprehensive resource, although the entries are relatively brief. A series of appendixes offer lists of organizations and additional resources; health care specialties; preventative health care recommendations for men; and vitamins, minerals, and other nutrients based on current Recommended Dietary Allowances. A brief bibliography of current professional and lay books and articles completes the work. This addition to Facts on File's Library of Health and Living will be a welcome source in public and consumer health library reference collections.—**Barbara M. Bibel**

Handbooks and Yearbooks

P

488.   **American Medical Association Family Medical Guide.** 4th ed. Hoboken, N.J., John Wiley, 2004. 1184p. illus. index. $45.00. ISBN 0-471-26911-5.

The *American Medical Association Family Medical Guide* is intended as a medical reference source but is such a fascinating, well-written resource that it could easily be read cover-to-cover. The 4th edition has been thoroughly revised and updated with greater coverage of health issues and better organization. The book is divided into six main sections: "What You Should Know: Information to Keep You Healthy"; "Your Healthy Body"; "First Aid and Home Caregiving"; "What are Your Symptoms"; "Health Issues Throughout Life"; and "Diseases, Disorders, and Other Problems." Especially useful is the first section on maintaining health. Topics in this glossy-paged, well-illustrated section include healthy eating, exercise, weight, stress, aging well, cancer, genetics, the dangers of smoking, heart disease, and terrorism. Other useful sections include the "Visual Aids to Diagnosis" (with photographs illustrating visual signs of illness), the section on "Common Examinations and Tests" (which provides relevant descriptions of commonly ordered screening and diagnostic tests), and the "Self-Diagnosis Symptoms Charts" (which may be extremely helpful when describing health concerns to a doctor). The book is easy to use either by a quick scan of the table of contents or a check of the index. The information provided is succinct but informative with relevant illustrations scattered throughout the text. As appropriate, the book indicates that concerns about medical conditions and symptoms should be discussed with a doctor. The resource is written for an average adult reader, with a glossary of terms as well as a drug glossary of frequently prescribed drugs included. While most of the medical conditions presented would be heard in discussions with a health professional or found in mainstream literature sources, a pronunciation guide would have been helpful. [R: LJ, 1 Oct 04, p. 109]—**Susan E. Thomas**

P

489.   **The Menopause Bible: The Complete Practical Guide to Managing Your Menopause.** Robin N. Phillips, ed. New York, Firefly Books, 2005. 256p. illus. index. $27.95pa. ISBN 1-554007-067-.

The Menopause Bible capably and authoritatively provides answers to many of the questions that women will have about menopause. The guide is written by a team of medical experts, ranging from an assistant clinical professor of obstetrics, to a medical journalist, a nutritionist, a sex therapist, and an accredited herbalist. In 11 chapters this guide discusses all aspects of menopause, including what happens during menopause, self-help for symptoms and when one needs to consult their doctor, maintaining bone health, maintaining a healthy sex life, nutritional needs, exercise routines, the psychological effects of menopause, hormone therapy and its alternatives, and safeguarding one's health during this time. Within each chapter, specific topics are discussed in two- to three-page sections and many sidebars, charts, photographs, and advice (under the title "Wise Woman") are included.

This guide will help women make informed choices when entering menopause and learn what to expect of their physical, psychological, and emotional health. It would be welcome in any public library or consumer health collection.—**Shannon Graff Hysell**

Pediatrics

P
490.   **The Gale Encyclopedia of Children's Health.** Kristine Krapp and Jeffrey Wilson, eds. Farmington Hills, Mich., Gale, 2005. 4v. illus. index. $550.00/set. ISBN 0-7876-9241-7.

The Gale Encyclopedia of Children's Health is a four-volume reference source that covers over 600 pediatric wellness issues, including specific diseases and medical conditions as well as behavioral and developmental issues. Examples of specific topics covered include allergies, birthmarks, dyslexia, orthodontics, personality development, puberty, tantrums, and vitamins. The target audience for this source would include parents, students, and general readers interested in children's health issues.

Each volume begins with a comprehensive table of contents and an alphabetic list of all entries. At the end of the fourth volume there is a glossary, followed by a growth charts appendix, a common childhood medications appendix, and complete topic index to all volumes. Main entries are arranged alphabetically and have been written by medical experts. Entries fall into one of four broad categories: Diseases and Disorders, Development, Immunizations/Drugs, and Procedures. Entry lengths vary from 500 to 4,000 words. Some entries have accompanying color images, including photographs, charts, or tables. Within each entry the information presented is broken down into categories such as definition, description, causes and symptoms, treatment, prognosis, and parental concerns. Bolded terms within entries indicate they have their own main entry listing. Specific key vocabulary terms are defined within individual entries. Brief bibliographies and cross-references to related topics follow most entries. All entries are signed.

The Gale Encyclopedia of Children's Health offers students, parents, and teachers a general introduction to children's health and wellness topics. This set is appropriate for school and public libraries. [R: LJ, 1 Nov 05, p. 114; BL, 1 & 15 Jan 06, p. 154]—**Caroline L. Gilson**

Specific Diseases and Conditions

AIDS

C, P
491.   Marlink, Richard G., and Alison G. Kotin. **Global AIDS Crisis: A Reference Handbook.** Santa Barbara, Calif., ABC-CLIO, 2004. 283p. index. (Contemporary World Issues). $50.00; $55.00 (e-book). ISBN 1-85109-655-8.

In this volume in ABC-CLIO's Contemporary World Issues series, Marlink and Kotin present an overview of the global HIV/AIDS crisis. The authors examine common themes of the epidemic that exist despite diverse regional and national experiences, such as access to care, scientific progress and the development of new treatments, and health and human rights issues, making this volume unique.

Adhering to the standard arrangement of this series, *Global AIDS Crisis* begins with a comprehensive introduction that includes the biology, epidemiology, and developmental history of the disease. Other chapters include a discussion of the social, political, environmental, and economic issues surrounding the disease; a chronology of important events, policies, and other responses to the crisis; data and statistics presented in easy-to-read tables, charts, figures, and graphs; biographical sketches of over 15 key figures at the forefront of the fight against the epidemic; a survey of international organizations that seek to create true partnerships between individuals and governments; and a bibliography of selected print and nonprint resources for further readings and research. The volume also contains a comprehensive glossary and index.

Rather than focusing on one particular area or nation, this concise volume explores common issues and themes across geographic boundaries. Accessible to researchers at all levels, this volume is appropriate and highly recommended for all academic and public libraries. It is also available for purchase as an e-book. [R: SLJ, Aug 05, p. 76]—**Leanne M. VandeCreek**

Asthma

P, S

492.   **Asthma Information for Teens: Health Tips About Managing Asthma and Related Concerns.** Karen Bellenir, ed. Detroit, Omnigraphics, 2005. 386p. index. (Teen Health Series). $58.00. ISBN 0-7808-0770-7.

This book is specifically written for teenagers and is divided into six parts. Each part covers a particular aspect of asthma, such as general facts, diagnosis and treatment, medical issues, lifestyle issues, research, and information resources. Each chapter covers a very specific subject related to that part. Within the diagnosis part, one chapter is on pulmonary function tests. There are a small number of gray scale illustrations in the text. Each chapter has a box detailing where the information was taken from and if it is available online or from a printed source and if more current information is available from a Website. The chapters in the information resources part list the organization, address, telephone number, fax number, and Website and e-mail address if available. A bibliography of books and Web-based documents lists additional sources of information for further reading. An index with cross-references is also included. The book is clear, concise, and very readable and would be a good source of asthma information for anyone —not just teenagers. This work is highly recommended for medical libraries, public school libraries, and public libraries.—**Betsy J. Kraus**

Cancer

C, P

493.   **Breast Cancer Sourcebook.** 2d ed. Sandra J. Judd, ed. Detroit, Omnigraphics, 2004. 569p. index. (Health Reference Series). $78.00. ISBN 0-7808-0668-9.

Sandra Judd has edited a 595-page follow-up to the 1st, very readable, edition of the *Breast Cancer Sourcebook*. The latter is one of 97 titles in the comprehensive Health Reference Series published by Omnigraphics, and a listing of which can be seen at http://www.healthreferenceseries.com. Judd's 2d edition contains 6 more chapters than the 1st edition (see ARBA 2002, entry 1498), for a total of 71 chapters.

The new edition presents basic consumer health information about breast cancer. The chapters are divided into eight major sections: "Breast Health and Breast Cancer Fundamentals," "Breast Cancer Statistics and Special Cases," "Breast Cancer Risk Factors," "Prevention of Breast Cancer," "Breast Cancer Screening," "Diagnosis and Treatment Options," "Post-Treatment Concerns," and "Additional Help and Information." Authoritative information is provided by U.S. government agencies such as the Centers for Disease Control and Prevention (CDC), the National Cancer Institute (NCI), and the U.S. Food and Drug Administration (FDA). Several major organizations provided copyrighted documents to the work, including the American College of Physicians, the Cleveland Clinic Foundation, and the Susan G. Komen Breast Cancer Foundation.

There are complete lists of citations at the end of each chapter, including Websites that complement the printed documents. The format of the chapters contributes to the book's richness and readability. The motif is interview-like, with anticipated questions from readers presented in bold type, followed by answers in a narrative, conversational tone that encourages more study and questioning. Answers are factual and to the point, with suggestions for next steps. There is a 19-page index followed by a complete anno-tated catalog of the Health Reference Series (also featuring a list of the Teen Health Reference Series). This book will be an excellent addition to public, community college, medical, and academic libraries. —**Laura J. Bender**

C, P

494.　Turkington, Carol, and William LiPera. **The Encyclopedia of Cancer.** New York, Facts on File, 2005. 448p. index. (Facts on File Library of Health and Living). $65.00. ISBN 0-8160-5029-5.

　　Like other books in the Facts on File Health and Living series, this volume is comprehensive, acces-sible, and well organized. In the introduction her co-author, William LiPera, emphasizes the importance of education for people who may be forced to deal with this disease. This book is certainly a valuable tool in that work.

　　The book is arranged alphabetically and covers a broad scope of terms having to do with cancer. It covers not only the different types of cancer, but also both conventional and alternative treatments, possi-ble carcinogens, statistical information, and a variety of other terms of interest to anyone seeking informa-tion about this devastating disease. The entries range in length from a single paragraph to several pages. The longer entries are devoted to specific cancers, such as liver, prostate, and breast cancer. They cover the types of the particular cancer, risk factors, diagnosis, symptoms, prevention, and treatment.

　　Abundant cross-references enhance the usability of this book. One appendix organizes an outstand-ing list of cancer-related associations by topic. Another appendix provides a geographical directory of can-cer treatment centers. Other appendixes provide a list of known and suspected carcinogens and a glossary. The bibliography is very thorough and the book is well indexed. This book is strongly recommended. [R: LJ, 1 May 05, p. 120]—**Jeanne D. Galvin**

Heart Disease

P

495.　**Cardiovascular Diseases and Disorders Sourcebook.** 3d ed. Sandra J. Judd, ed. Detroit, Omnigraphics, 2005. 687p. index. (Health Reference Series). $78.00. ISBN 0-7808-0739-1.

　　This updated sourcebook is still the best first stop for comprehensive introductory information on cardiovascular diseases. The monograph starts with the workings of the cardiovascular system and goes on to discuss the various aliments that befall this system. Broken down into nine parts, each part contains sev-eral chapters on a particular topic. Topics covered include understanding risks, maintaining health, facts about diseases and disorders, diagnosing different disorders, medications, and procedures. The text in-cludes a special section for women. There is also a section on cardiovascular research. The book concludes with a short but helpful glossary, a longer section of heart healthy cookbooks, and a directory of resources for cardiovascular patients with contact information including current Web addresses for most entries.

　　The chapters range from a couple of pages to several pages. Where applicable chapters end with ref-erences; the references are a mixture of older (early to mid 1990s) to newer sources. The language is easily understood with manageable medical jargon. The most practical and useful aspects of the book are the en-tries on diseases and disorders and medications and procedures. These types of entries provide valuable in-formation in an easy-to-follow format. The typical entry under diseases and disorders include a definition, its causes, its symptoms, and its treatments. Entries under medications and procedures include information such as what it was, when it was used, and side effects and interactions. The latest addition to Omnigraphics' Health Reference Series upholds the series' reputation as a solid resource for all reference collections.—**Melissa M. Johnson**

NURSING

C, P

496.   **Nursing Programs 2006.** 11th ed. Lawrenceville, N.J., Peterson's Guides, 2005. 662p. index. $26.95pa. ISBN 0-7689-1748-4. ISSN 1073-7820.

Peterson's Guides' resources for educational programs are inevitably well reviewed. In addition, ARBA's review of the 7th edition (see ARBA 2002, entry 1509) points out that this volume was more accurately titled when it had a defining subtitle of "Baccalaureate and Graduate Nursing Education in the U.S. and Canada." Other than these minor points, it should be noted that the guide remains a valuable resource for any career collection in high school, community college, university, or public libraries.

The 11th edition format follows of previous editions, including the key fact that the American Association of Colleges of Nursing again collaborates with Peterson's in the production of the "only comprehensive and concise guide" to nursing careers (p. v). The introduction includes "an overview of the various components of the book" (p. 1), such as organization, descriptions of key data (e.g., nursing school profiles, general nursing college information), and basic information about the nursing field.

The bulk of the guide consists of profiles of individual programs arranged alphabetically, as in earlier editions, by state or province. The last main section is titled "In-depth Descriptions of Nursing Programs," which has two-page descriptions prepared by nursing schools or departments as they choose to do so; this means that not every program profiled earlier is described. The book concludes with eight indexes: "Baccalaureate Programs Offering Special Tracks," "Master's Degree Programs," "Concentrations Within Master's Degree Programs," "Doctoral Programs," "Postdoctoral Programs," "Distance Learning Programs," "Continuing Education Programs," and an "Institution Index." Taking all into consideration, the 11th edition of *Nursing Programs* continues its long tradition as a unique and valuable reference source.—**Laurel Grotzinger**

PHARMACY AND PHARMACEUTICAL SCIENCES

Directories

P

497.   Rybacki, James J. **The Essential Guide to Prescription Drugs.** 2006 ed. New York, HarperCollins, 2006. 1392p. illus. index. $21.95pa. ISBN 0-06-082051-9. ISSN 0894-7048.

With an aging population and an overworked health care system, the need for accurate, accessible information about prescription drugs is greater than ever. Rybacki, a clinical pharmacist who teaches at the University of Maryland, has written a guidebook that fills this need. This is the latest edition of a work published annually since 1996. The book provides information about more than 400 drugs encompassing over 2,000 brands. They are listed alphabetically by generic name with the brand names listed at the beginning of the entry. The entries include both American and Canadian brand names, the risks and benefits of taking the drug, indications for use, dosage information, contraindications, adverse effects, and precautions for use. A 16-page color insert has pictures of medications for identification.

While the material included above is similar to that in other books on prescription medications, Rybacki's work is far more comprehensive. He goes above and beyond the basics to empower and inform both patients and health care providers about the safe and effective use of drugs. He begins with advice on how to become a "powerful patient," which includes tips for communicating with health care providers, using the Internet safely for finding information and ordering drugs, preventing adverse drug reactions, and considerations for people over 65 years of age. He also has advice for physicians and pharmacists about safe prescribing and dispensing of medications. In addition, this book has a chapter about promising new drugs and treatment techniques in development, a list of drugs by class, a brief medical glossary, and a series of tables that list drugs that may cause adverse effects in specific age groups or organ systems. A list of assistance programs for patients who cannot afford their medications, a form for creating a personal drug profile, and an extensive bibliography complete the work. *The Essential Guide to Prescription Drugs* is more comprehensive than *The Pill Book* (11th ed.; see ARBA 2005, entry 1478) and more accessible and less expensive than the *Physicians' Desk Reference* (see ARBA 2006, entry 1462). It is an outstanding addition to public and consumer health libraries and a good choice for the home.—**Barbara M. Bibel**

34 High Technology

GENERAL WORKS

Dictionaries and Encyclopedias

C

498.   **Encyclopedia of Knowledge Management.** David G. Schwartz, ed. Hershey, Pa., Idea Group Publishing, 2006. 897p. index. $275.00. ISBN 1-59140-573-4; 1-59140-574-2 (e-book).

This encyclopedia is a valuable resource for individuals involved in the management of knowledge. The editor has successfully compiled contributions from individuals who are subject matter experts in their respective fields to create an encyclopedia that is rich with information.

The encyclopedia begins with a list of contributors. This allows the reader to look up contributors and easily locate them in the book by page number. Next are the content section and the contents by category section, both of which include page numbers. The preface provides an overview regarding the significance of the text, how it is structured, and how the book can be used as a reference. The end of the book includes an index of key terms that is easy to use.

The actual "knowledge management" content of this book spans more than 800 pages. Within these pages are contributions by authors who provide useful, relevant, and timely content regarding knowledge management as it applies in today's world. While the list of specialties is extensive, examples include technology, healthcare, and general business. The tables and graphics, illustrated in black and white, are easy to read and interpret. In general, this encyclopedia is contemporary, user-friendly, and allows for information to be located quickly.

The *Encyclopedia of Knowledge Management* is likely to be useful to professionals, executives, and students who are interested in knowledge management as it applies to the twenty-first century. It will complement any personal or professional library and may become an extremely useful reference tool for many individuals on a personal and professional level.—**Paul M. Murphy III**

COMPUTING

Dictionaries and Encyclopedias

C, P

499.   **Concise Encyclopedia of Computer Science.** Edwin D. Reilly, ed. Hoboken, N.J., John Wiley, 2004. 875p. illus. index. $55.00pa. ISBN 0-470-09095-2.

This title is based on the 4th edition of the *Encyclopedia of Computer Science*, issued in 2000 and edited by Anthony Ralston, Edwin D. Reilly, and David Hemmendinger (see ARBA 2001, entry 1497).

Reilly's goal is to provide a more portable, less-expensive version of the original encyclopedia. This adaptation contains 60 percent of the articles in the original, with the main exclusions being highly mathematical entries. The target audience is high school and college students or professionals in noncomputer fields. This reviewer questions that any but the most gifted high school student could understand the concepts presented here as the writing is quite technical and advanced; the shortened articles retain the authors' sentences except for editorial changes that reflect recent developments.

The *Concise Encyclopedia* contains 382 articles grouped into 9 classifications to assist the readers in ascertaining the interrelationships between the articles. For example, a researcher wishing to consider computer systems could, by using this feature, access all the articles dealing with this subject in the entire volume. The articles themselves are alphabetically arranged by title. At the beginning of each is a list of cross-references to related articles as an aid to the reader. Also, the editor has made use of frequent (q.v.) and *see* references sprinkled throughout the articles as needed. The volume contains three appendixes: Abbreviations and Acronyms, Notation and Units, and a Timeline of Significant Milestones in Computing. Finally, an index assists users in finding terms and individuals that may not warrant an entire article in the encyclopedia.

This is an excellent, scholarly work that thoroughly covers the field of computing. It will be a valuable asset in reference collections serving academic libraries and public libraries where there is an interest in computing beyond the very basic entry level. This volume is recommended for purchase.—**Nancy P. Reed**

INTERNET

C, P, S

500.   **Find it Online: The Complete Guide to Online Research.** 4th ed. Tempe, Ariz., Facts on Demand Press, 2004. 600p. index. $21.95pa. ISBN 1-88195-045-2.

From the basics of Internet terminology and concepts, to the details of international research, *Find it Online: The Complete Guide to Online Research* is an all-purpose, single-source reference to finding information on the Internet. This work provides the tools and techniques Internet users need to master online research. Its useful information will assist those looking for the latest and most useful information on everything, and the resource is for the advanced researcher as well as the novice. Individual chapters introduce online researching by addressing the basics of the Internet, framing one's search strategy, introducing the best tools and search engines available, evaluating the accuracy and credibility of information found on the Internet, and managing information overload.

The resource is not just an overview for the beginner, however. The work explains how to narrow and sharpen information searches, find specific background information about people and businesses, access the most useful news and business resources online, and points out the difference between government resources and public records (with "best" sites for both noted). Fee versus free sites are referenced throughout, and each of the 14 chapters includes an "additional web sites" section. One of the most helpful chapters includes sample searches, which includes scenarios and step-by-step thinking processes and suggested action steps. *Find it Online* is a highly recommended addition to any personal, professional, school, or public library Internet information resources reference collection.—**Jill Rooker**

C, P, S

501.   Hillstrom, Kevin. **The Internet Revolution.** Detroit, Omnigraphics, 2005. 203p. illus. index. (Defining Moments). $38.00. ISBN 0-7808-0767-7.

The blending of the Internet into every aspect of our society has been an astonishing journey over the last two decades. The fact that this occurred in such a short period defies belief, and has rightfully been labeled the "Internet Revolution." What does the user of the Internet know of the pioneers of the Internet and the technology itself? What has been the impact of this technology on our society? These are the issues explored in the book *The Internet Revolution*, which is the latest in Omnigraphics' Defining Moments series. From the early theories of the 1960s that laid the groundwork for computer networking, through the effects of the Internet on commerce and the dot.com crisis, the major touchstones of the Revolution are identified and explored.

The Defining Moments series, which examines historical events that shaped the American experience is intended for grades 8-12 and has explored the subjects women's suffrage (see ARBA 2006, entry 862), the Korean War, prohibition (see ARBA 2005, entry 447), Watergate (see ARBA 2005, entry 450), and *Brown v. Board of Education* (see entry 189). *The Internet Revolution* is unique to the series in that the focus is not a legal or political issue.

The book is divided in three major sections. "Narrative Overview" provides essays concerning the history of the Internet. "Biographies" provides information on the main players in the development of today's Internet. "Primary Sources" includes both bridged and unabridged documents that shaped the Internet and the public's perception of the technology. Also included are a glossary, chronology, and a bibliography

My only complaint with *The Internet Revolution* is the fact that the other titles in the series cover a distant historical event that is very much in the past. *The Internet Revolution* is still an event in progress. The book stands better alone than with the rest of the series. However, since it is part of the Defining Moments Series, I hope the Industrial Revolution will be considered as a future title to act as a comparison to our present day Revolution.

Libraries with limited budgets that are reluctant to start a standing order for a new series, will find that *The Internet Revolution* is a title that is worth purchasing as a single monograph. Due to the straightforward approach to this fascinating subject, I would highly recommend this title for public and high school libraries. The tool will also be useful to lower undergraduates to get an overview of the history and people behind the Internet.—**Rob Laurich**

C, P

502. **The Internet: A Historical Encyclopedia.** Hilary W. Poole, ed. Santa Barbara, Calif., ABC-CLIO, 2005. 3v. illus. index. $285.00/set; $310.00 (e-book). ISBN 1-85109-659-0; 1-59109-664-7 (e-book).

This encyclopedia consists of three volumes. Volume 1, by Laura Lambert, features 31 biographies of Internet pioneers. Volume 2, by Chris Woodford, discusses 35 issues surrounding the phenomenon that is the Internet. And volume 3, edited by Hilary W. Poole and Christos J. P. Moschovitis, details the many strands of the Internet in eight chapters of a chronology that turns out to be the 2d edition of a work first published in 1999, *History of the Internet*. The authors take researchers and general readers on a journey beginning in 1843, with the work of mathematician Charles Babbage, whose Difference Engine expedited the calculation of astronomical tables.

In volume 1, Laura Lambert introduces us to the names behind the Internet. She includes biographies of well-known people, such as Bill Gates, Marshall McLuhan, and Lawrence Lessig, but also provides fascinating information about lesser-known or more obscure contributors such as Aliza Sherman and Ann Winblad. The former is the founder of Cybergrrl, Webgrrls, and Femina.com. The latter is one of the few women venture capitalists dedicated solely to software businesses, especially those of the Internet.

In volume 2, full-time science and technology writer, Chris Woodford, provides us food for thought in 35 comprehensive essays about the controversies and psychological and social conundrums surrounding the Internet. Some of the titles include "Activism and the Internet," "Content Filtering," "Cyberterrorism," "Education and the Internet," "Hackers," "Games and the Internet," "Online Communities," and "Open Source." Problems that plague the Internet, such as spam, computer viruses, and threats to privacy, require a broad perspective far beyond simple technical fixes. These essays represent a balanced approach to how the Internet will affect individuals, business, and society in the twenty-first century.

Volume 3 recaps the main points of the 1999 chronology, but emphasizes the changes that have taken place since then. In 1999, AOL was just about to acquire Time Warner. Now, those two businesses have separated and the Internet is part of American life. Online and offline are fully integrated—friends meet in online and offline communities, e-commerce is increasing at an incredible rate, and bloggers add a new dimension to journalism. The chronology ends in 2004. Readers will acknowledge that changes are still occurring and will continue to occur at warp speed—wireless is more and more a part of our cyber lives at the tail end of 2005, and we are no closer to definitive answers to copyright or file sharing issues than we were in 2004.

Problems with currency notwithstanding (and a few minor typographical errors), this encyclopedia provides valuable information for students and general readers doing research on the Internet and the impact it has had on our world. It is recommended for public, community college, and academic libraries.
—**Laura J. Bender**

TELECOMMUNICATIONS

C, P

503.   **Plunkett's Wireless, WI-FI, RFID, & Cellular Industry Almanac.** Jack W. Plunkett, ed. Houston, Tex., Plunkett Research, 2005. 441p. index. $249.99pa. (w/CD-ROM). ISBN 1-59392-029-6.

Plunkett's Wireless, WI-FI, RFID, & Cellular Industry Almanac is a worthy addition to the Plunkett almanac series, which includes 29 titles at this writing. The format is well developed and includes a 12-page glossary; an overview of 27 major industry trends; industry statistics; a section on important industry contacts; an index of firms noted as hot spots for advancement for women and minorities; and an index by subsidiaries, brand names, and selected affiliations.

In addition, there is a "Wireless 350" international list of key companies operating in all facets of the wireless industry and selected supporting areas. Each profile contains contacts, locations, financials, brands/divisions/affiliates, and commentary on growth plans and special features. This section is indexed thoroughly and includes industry list with codes; index of rankings within industry groups; an alphabetical index; geographic indexes by state, region, and country; and indexes by subsidiaries, brand names, and selected affiliations. This *Almanac* is highly recommended for libraries supporting marketing, business, and career-related collections.—**Barbara Delzell**

35 Physical Sciences and Mathematics

PHYSICAL SCIENCES

Chemistry

Dictionaries and Encyclopedias

C, P, S
504.   **The Facts on File Dictionary of Chemistry.** 4th ed. John Daintith, ed. New York, Facts on File, 2005. 310p. (Facts on File Science Library). $45.00. ISBN 0-8160-5649-8.

Now in its 4th edition, the *Facts on File Dictionary of Chemistry* has become something of a venerable resource. Since the 1st edition 25 years ago (see ARBA 82, entry 1436), it has remained broadly useful as a basic guide to chemical terms. This edition contains 3000-plus terms, about the same as the previous edition (see ARBA 2000, entry 1479). Each entry has a short definition, often including notes on common uses and stability. Equations, formulae, and illustrations are used sparingly. New to this edition are pronunciation keys for roughly half of the entries, although it would be nice to see them expanded to cover all terms, if only for consistency's sake (plus, it is unclear why "Babo's law" gets a pronunciation but "Barft process" does not). *See* references help users navigate some of the variations in chemical names. The volume ends with a series of appendixes showing chemical structures, element data, the Greek alphabet, useful Websites, and a bibliography. Most users will find a handbook such as *The CRC Handbook of Chemistry and Physics* more useful for this kind of data, but their inclusion is no great distraction. As with the earlier editions, this resource should be most useful for public and high school libraries, but undergraduates and even more advanced users in academic libraries may find it useful for quick reference.—**Peter Larsen**

C
505.   **Van Nostrand's Encyclopedia of Chemistry.** 5th ed. Glenn D. Considine, ed. Hoboken, N.J., John Wiley, 2005. 1831p. illus. index. $195.95. ISBN 0-471-61525-0.

First published in 1957 as *The Encyclopedia of Chemistry*, and most recently in 1984 as *Van Nostrand Reinhold Encyclopedia of Chemistry*, this work has earned a solid reputation. Alphabetically listed entries range from brief paragraphs to multipage articles with diagrams and references, including general topics (e.g., Corrosion), types of reactions (e.g., Esterification), classes of compounds, elements, and brief biographies of notable chemists. Coverage includes chemical engineering and biochemical topics. This edition includes new topics, such as fullerenes, and new articles on hot fields, such as "Molecular and Supermolecular Electronics" and "Nanotechnology (Molecular)." Entries are interspersed with *see* references; there is an adequate, although sometimes frustrating index; for example "Fullerenes" is not listed and "Buckminsterfullerene" leads to a brief paragraph chiefly giving "*see also* Carbon Compounds" where substantial information is found.

The only real competition in single-volume chemistry encyclopedias is from the *Concise Encyclopedia Chemistry* (Walter de Gruyter, 1994), which includes many entries on individual chemical compounds, absent in *Van Nostrand's*, and many gems of concision. *Van Nostrand's*, however, has many valuable discursive articles. Any good chemistry collection should have both. This work is strongly recommended. [R: LJ, 1 Nov 05, p. 116]—**Robert Michaelson**

Earth and Planetary Sciences

General Works

C, P, S
506.   **Encyclopedia of Earth and Physical Sciences.** 2d ed. Tarrytown, N.Y., Marshall Cavendish, 2006. 13v. illus. maps. index. $459.95/set. ISBN 0-7614-7583-4.

The 2d edition of the *Encyclopedia of Earth and Physical Sciences* intends to describe major earth and physical science topics presented in alphabetically arranged articles that can be of interest to anyone, with or without a science background. It strives to provide established and more recent scientific information about everyday phenomena.

Like the 1st edition (see ARBA 99, entry 1514), this 2d edition is beautifully illustrated, mostly in color, with photographs, diagrams, and charts embedded in easy-to-read, signed articles, which vary in length from 1-25 pages. The general format facilitates the transmission of information through a concise definition at the head of each article, core facts boxes, cross-references to other articles, and side boxes with supplementary material. The editorial board consists of authoritative people from museums, universities, and hospitals. The 2d edition has been expanded to 13 volumes. There are 74 more articles, including new topics and a new category of articles about significant scientists. For easy reference, all volumes now include an updated periodic table and a chart of physical constants and units. The well-written articles have obviously been reviewed and revised, the cross-references expanded, and the lists of further readings updated. In the index volume, the "Internet Resources" list has been enlarged and the geologic time scale has been updated.

This work is recommended for public libraries, school libraries, community college libraries, and even home libraries. It would be useful for specific research and users may also find it fascinating to browse through any of the volumes.—**Ignacio J. Ferrer-Vinent**

Astronomy and Space Sciences

Atlases

C, P, S
507.   **Firefly Atlas of the Universe.** 3d ed. By Patrick Moore. New York, Firefly Books, 2005. 288p. illus. maps. index. $49.95. ISBN 1-55407-071-6.

Color maps, charts, drawings, and photographs combine to provide detailed information about the universe in the 3d edition of the *Firefly Atlas of the Universe*, by Sir Patrick Moore. Sections on the history of astronomy, space exploration, and telescopes; details on the solar system and outer space objects such as meteors, asteroids, and comets; and particulars on our sun and other stars contain a myriad amount of detailed information in a compact format. The final section provides advice for amateur astronomers about selecting and using a home telescope. The photographs are big and beautiful, and the information is current and accurate. This resource will be useful for students, educators, and anyone interested in the night sky.—**Denise A. Garofalo**

Biography

C, S

508.   Todd, Deborah, and Joseph A. Angelo Jr. **A to Z of Scientists in Space and Astronomy.** New York, Facts on File, 2005. 322p. illus. index. (Notable Scientists). $45.00. ISBN 0-8160-4639-5.

Not only is astronomy fascinating, but astronomers hold a certain fascination to the public as well. Their stories and circumstances of their work and research are wonderfully varied throughout the last couple of millennia. In this collection of short biographies of space scientists and astronomers, the reader will get a sense of the contributions of these people.

The 130 articles range from between 500 and 1,000 words. The authors paint a rich tapestry of the lives and research of these people in terms that most readers will understand and appreciate. Many of the articles include illustrations of the person. The time coverage begins in about the third century B.C., but most of the people listed lived since the seventeenth century. Unfortunately, the youngest person listed was born in 1949, which begs the question whether any notable scientist is doing astronomy or space science under the age of 55. Only about 6 percent of the people listed are women. Approximately 60 percent of the total come from just three countries—Germany, Great Britain, and the United States. This disproportion can give the impression that the contributions of women and non-westerners in astronomy and space science was minor or nearly non-existent, which is not the case.

There are several appendixes providing various arrangements of people by field, country of birth, country of major scientific activity, by year of birth, and a chronology showing life spans. Although no references are appended to any article, a collection of references and Websites is supplied at the end of the book. Finally, an adequate index provides some subject and keyword access to the contents.

Astronomy is one of the few sciences that has an avid and substantial amateur base; consequently, these biographies will appeal to a wide audience. This book, typical of the Notable Scientists series, is appropriate for middle and high school libraries, public libraries, and general academic collections. [R: BL, June 05, p. 1845]—**Margaret F. Dominy**

Dictionaries and Encyclopedias

C, P, S

509.   **National Geographic Encyclopedia of Space.** By Linda K. Glover and others. Washington, D.C., National Geographic Society, 2005. 400p. illus. index. $40.00. ISBN 0-7922-7319-2.

This wonderful book meets all those expectations we have from a National Geographic Society publication: accessible text, well-crafted prose, scientific accuracy, and the best, most creative illustrations possible. This book is also appearing at a time of intense interest in space fueled by extraordinary missions and dramatic discoveries. Some children are going to find this book on a coffee table, page through it, and resolve to be scientists and explorers, just as their parents did with earlier volumes from the National Geographic Society. We are fortunate not only to live during a scientific revolution, but to also have such competent chroniclers of it.

The text of his encyclopedia is divided into six parts. The first is "Deep Spacem" covering nebulae, stars, galaxies, the universe, the Big Bang, and, curiously, the history of astronomy and the development of telescopes. "The Solar System" follows with colorfully illustrated sections on the Sun, the planets, their moons, asteroids, and comets. The next four chapters are on human activities in space, from the basics of rockets and spacecraft to satellites, manned flight history, and the military uses of space. An extended appendix follows with star maps (too small to easily read, but this reviewer was glad they were there), excellent maps of the Moon, Mars, the Solar System, and the Milky Way, and an innovative, three-dimensional rendering of the structure of the universe. Every section has high-quality photographs, explanatory diagrams, and tables of data. The effect is to not only make the subject attractive, but also to teach its principles from the first glance.

Almost two dozen essayists contributed to this encyclopedia, which may be why this is an "encyclopedia" and not simply a book about space. These contributors include key figures from the history of space exploration and astronomical understanding, including Moon-walking astronaut Buzz Aldrin, astronomer James Trefil, and astrophysicist Robert Wilson. They enliven the text with their own styles and perspectives. Some of the best reading comes from the side stories in the boxes scattered through the book.

This book is highly recommended for all libraries. Children will be intrigued by the illustrations, adults will find the text fascinating, and even scientists will learn much from it, especially new ways to teach difficult concepts about the universe. Everyone has a stake in learning more about our neighborhood in space and how we study it. [R: LJ, 15 Mar 05, p. 110]—**Mark A. Wilson**

Ecology

S

510. **Habitats of the World.** Tarrytown, N.Y., Marshall Cavendish, 2006. 11v. illus. maps. index. $471.35/set. ISBN 0-7614-7523-0.

This is a set of volumes on global habitats (and general ecology) for older elementary and middle school students. Each volume is thin (around 50 pages) and colorfully illustrated, making them very attractive to curious children.

The volumes are alphabetically arranged by topics, like an encyclopedia. The topics are broad and include land, water and human habitats, people ("great ecologists") , unique places (such as the Aral Sea and Kilimanjaro), and general ecological topics (including the atmosphere, food webs, global warming, and the like). The topic chapters all start with a few "key facts" in a box, followed a general description punctuated by superb color photographs and boxes containing interesting stories or observations. A small "find out more" box at the end refers the reader to related topics in the volumes. Each book ends with a glossary of important terms and a thorough index.

Clearly the editor has been very effective in this series. There are multiple authors, but the writing is smooth and consistent throughout. The text is probably best for ages 12-16, but the illustrations will draw in younger and older children. Placing the "key facts" section at the front of each chapter was a brilliant idea. They provide those all-important first points for children writing reports, and then draw readers into the rest of the topic. I found myself then reading the stories within other boxes, then looking at the photographs, and always ending by reading the text. These books have been designed from the beginning with young readers in mind, but they will also interest teachers and parents.

The science behind the beautiful text appears to be flawless. Too often pretty books have a poor science framework, but that is not the case here. Ecological descriptions like these are filled with facts and figures, and there must be a timeliness on topics like global warming and deforestation. Again, the editor and publishing staff have produced an accurate and up-to-date text. This set is highly recommended for elementary and middle school libraries.—**Mark A. Wilson**

Geology

C, P, S

511.   Bonewitz, Ronald Louis, with Margaret Carruthers and Richard Efthim. **Rock and Gem.** New York, DK Publishing, 2005. 360p. illus. index. $40.00. ISBN 0-7566-0962-3.

Illustrated with color photographs, sketches, charts, and tables, *Rock and Gem* is not only a practical scientific and historical experience but also a captivating visual journey through the world of rocks and gems. The accessible language makes it a pleasure for the layperson to read, without sacrificing too much of the technical vocabulary to provide a good look into the world of geology.

The book is divided into four main sections. "Origins" discusses the geologic history of the universe and earth, their role in the creation of rocks and gems, and geology—both from a professional point of view and as a hobby. "Rocks" addresses their formation and different types, with references to famous natural rock formations (like the Devil's Tower), caves, and even man-made rock creations (like Stonehenge). "Minerals" discusses their formation, identification, associations, crystals, gems, and various other types, with references to famous gems (like the Hope diamond) and the uses of minerals. "Fossils" addresses their formation, fossil records and how they are used, and different types of fossils (plant, invertebrates, and vertebrates). And of course, what discussion of fossils would be complete with talking about dinosaurs? A glossary at the end provides a little extra help with unfamiliar terminology, and the index is thorough and easy to use. This work is highly recommended for public, school, and academic libraries.
—**Megan W. Lowe**

Oceanography

C

512.   **Encyclopedia of Coastal Science.** Maurice L. Schwartz, ed. New York, Springer Publishing, 2005. 1211p. illus. maps. index. $440.00. ISBN 1-4020-1903-3.

This massive volume is the latest in the invaluable Encyclopedia of Earth Sciences Series. With almost 250 contributors, including many of the top marine scientists in the world, this is going to be the professional resource on coastal properties and processes for many years. The articles are comprehensive, well-illustrated, up-to-date essays on hundreds of topics within the coastal sciences.

At almost 10 pounds, with the margins of each page set as narrow as possible and the typeface just large enough to be comfortably read, this book is an extraordinary mother lode of information. The articles are arranged alphabetically. Most have simple subheadings delineating the text. Almost all end with a brief set of conclusions, an extensive bibliography, and cross-references to other topics covered in the volume. Most articles read as subject essays rather than "encyclopedic" entries, which is a credit to the editor for what must have been a Herculean reviewing task with the hundreds of manuscripts. The illustrations are of the highest quality, including line drawings, maps, and photographs (some in color). Much of the artwork was specially produced for this volume. The appendixes include conversion tables, a list of journals in the coastal sciences (most with Websites and e-mail addresses), a guide to organizations devoted to coastal issues (hundreds of them), a long list of relevant databases, and a fully illustrated glossary of coastal geomorphology.

The coastal sciences have become increasingly important to society over the past two decades. In many ways they are the fastest growing disciplines within the earth sciences. Global warming and the consequent rise in sea level has given us strong reasons to better understand what happens at the margin between land and water. The recent devastating tsunami in Southeast Asia shows us how much more we have to learn about the dynamics of the shoreline environment. This volume covers the many diverse topics necessary to address the interdisciplinary nature of the coastal sciences. From ancient pluvial lake shores to bioerosion on coral reefs, from salt marshes to sequence stratigraphy, the fields of geology, biology, and aquatic chemistry are used to show the state of our knowledge of coastal systems. The information is assembled by a team of scientists that cannot be equaled in any other source. Even the Internet will not have this kind of authority on coastal science for a very long time.

This book is written for professionals, but it will also serve as an introduction to the coastal literature for students in college and graduate school. It is highly recommended for any library used by earth science students and professionals. [R: LJ, 15 Sept 05, p. 90]—**Mark A. Wilson**

P, S

513.   Hutchinson, Stephen, and Lawrence E. Hawkins. **Oceans: A Visual Guide.** New York, Firefly Books, 2005. 303p. illus. maps. index. $29.95. ISBN 1-55407-069-4.

This work presents what the authors call a "visual reference" guide to the world's oceans. The work is divided into six sections: "The Blue Planet"; "Exploring the Oceans"; "Ocean Life"; "Into the Deep"; "The Fringes" (e.g., atolls, estuaries); and "The Human Impact." Each section is lavishly illustrated with stunning photographs and line drawings. Appendixes include a "Factfile", a glossary, and an index. The "Factfile" contains lists of topics such as marine nature preserves and ocean subdivisions by area. Useful chronologies, such as the "5000 Years of Oceanography" on page 82, "A History of Submersibles" on page 92, and "A History of Ocean Exploration" on page 68, are scattered throughout the book. Students of the marine sciences and biology will find this work a visual treat. *Oceans: A Visual Guide* is recommended for all reference collections because of the enticing photography as well as the useful basic information on the world's oceans that is provided.—**Ralph Lee Scott**

Physics

C, S

514.   Rosen, Joe. **Encyclopedia of Physics.** New York, Facts on File, 2004. 386p. illus. index. (Facts on File Science Library). $75.00. ISBN 0-8160-4974-2.

Facts on File publishes a number of quality encyclopedias and handbooks and this is certainly no exception. It is a high-quality list of facts, names, and definitions of the history of physics. Each entry is relatively short, but not at the expense of omitting necessary information. For example, the entry for Richard Feynman covers his academic life and career, including his role in the investigation of the *Challenger* explosion near the end of his life. There is a second entry with detailed information about his Feynman diagrams. This article is longer and very complete. The book also includes 11 essay-length entries that are interspersed throughout the book.

The index to the book is necessary for the best use of the book. It cross-references the articles in the book so that the user may find all the information on any given topic. There are three appendixes as well. The first has a bibliography of references and Websites. The second is a list of Nobel prizes in physics listed by year. The third is a periodic table and list of chemical elements. The author, Joe Rosen, is a retired professor who is a Visiting Professor of Physics at the Catholic University of Washington, D.C. This is a book that would be useful for all libraries from high school to academic. [R: SLJ, Dec 04, p. 87; Choice, Jan 05, p. 832]—**James W. Oliver**

MATHEMATICS

Dictionaries and Encyclopedias

C, S

515.   Tanton, James. **Encyclopedia of Mathematics.** New York, Facts on File, 2005. 568p. index. (Facts on File Science Library). $75.00. ISBN 0-8160-5124-0.

According to the author, many primary and secondary students miss out on the beauty of mathematics because of the way they are taught the subject. Mathematics is often taught as a series of facts that need to be memorized in order to solve a particular problem. Students do not question these facts, so they do not develop a deep understanding or appreciation of the subject. This book aims to make mathematics interesting to students by telling its history. The author, James Tanton of St. Mark's Institute of Mathematics in Massachusetts, believes that each mathematical concept has its place in history and when students learn mathematics in context they will understand it better.

The 800 entries in this encyclopedia are arranged alphabetically and cover the standard undergraduate-level definitions and rules. However, the encyclopedia adds context to these rules with six essays on the history of equations and algebra, calculus, functions, geometry, probability and statistics, and trigonometry. In addition, the author includes lengthy biographies of many mathematicians from all over the world. Overall, the treatment of undergraduate-level mathematical concepts is comprehensive. The text is complemented by numerous charts, graphs, and pictures. The encyclopedia contains a very helpful index and a timeline of the history of mathematics. Finally, a bibliography and webliography of additional resources is included.

This encyclopedia is similar in scope to the two-volume *World of Mathematics* (see ARBA 2002, entry 1584), edited by Brigham Narins and published by the Gale Group in 2001. The work under review is a bit more concise and is recommended for libraries that serve high school and undergraduate students. [R: SLJ, Dec 05, pp. 92-94]—**Holly A Flynn**

Handbooks and Yearbooks

P, S

516.   Barnes-Svarney, Patricia, and Thomas E. Svarney. **The Handy Math Answer Book.** Detroit, Omnigraphics, 2006. 506p. illus. index. $44.00. ISBN 0-7808-0962-9.

The Handy Math Answer Book, the "Ask Jeeves" of mathematics books, is divided into four sections: "The History," "The Basics," "Math in Science and Engineering," and "Math All Around Us." Chapter topics include mathematics throughout history, math in the physical sciences, math in engineering, math in computing, math in the humanities, recreational mathematics, and mathematical resources, showing the evolution, involvement, and significance of mathematics from ancient cultures to today.

With over 1,400 questions, the reader is given clear explanations of different principles of mathematics such as geometry, statistics, and algebra, and then shown how and why different professionals, such as scientists, architects, and artists, implement those principles. Clear explanations are given when showing the connection between mathematics and everyday math hurdles, such as balancing a checkbook, getting a basketball player's statistics, or predicting the weather. However, with more heady topics, such as calculus, differential equations, and logarithms, the explanations may elude the average reader. Overall, this is a fun and understandable read and this reviewer would recommend this book for a high school or public library reference area.—**Linda W. Hacker**

36 Resource Sciences

ENERGY

Handbooks and Yearbooks

C, P, S

517.   Yount, Lisa. **Energy Supply.** New York, Facts on File, 2005. 296p. index. (Library in a Book). $45.00. ISBN 0-8160-5577-7.

With fossil fuels dwindling due to the ever-increasing demand for energy throughout the world, energy supply issues are becoming paramount in the eyes of the world. Hybrid cars, hydrogen driven cars, electric cars, wind power, corn oil fuel, and other alternatives are being pursued by inventors around the world because finding new sources of energy has become a priority that has been overlooked for too long. This compact reference source provides a vast amount of information on almost every hotly debated aspect of the energy situation. Eight chapters provide different kinds of help to teachers, librarians, politicians, environmentalists, journalists, and members of the general public who want to research the massive issues that are related to energy supply. Chapter 6, "How to Research Energy Issues," will be of great value to students researching energy issues and also provides useful tips on how to do research in general. The chronology in chapter 3 provides many ways to approach research on a variety of energy-related topics. This small book illustrates the profound economic, social, environmental, and political issues that affect or are affected by energy. The readable and informative sources listed in this book will be valuable to all libraries.—**Diane J. Turner**

ENVIRONMENTAL SCIENCE

Atlases

C, P

518.   **The New Atlas of Planet Management.** 3d ed. Norman Myers and Jennifer Kent, eds. Berkeley, Calif., University of California Press, 2005. 304p. illus. maps. index. $39.95pa. ISBN 0-520-23879-6.

This unique atlas is a completely revised and updated edition of what has become an indispensable volume for environmental scientists, activists, and politicians. The superb artwork, innovative charts and graphs, and incisive text make some of the most complex observations of our world strikingly clear. It is as close to an owner's manual for the Earth as we are going to find.

Any book that begins with a foreword by Edward O. Wilson must be high quality. There are seven major chapters: "Land," "Oceans," "Elements," "Evolution," "Humankind," "Civilization," and "Management." Each has a brief introduction by a prominent environmentalist thinker. The text that follows in each chapter is simply but forcefully written, emphasizing first the structure of the particular system and then how people have operated within it. It is the graphics, however, that keep the reader turning pages. This reviewer has never seen more ways of visually conveying detailed information. Pie charts, histograms, and maps are just a start. Rich diagrams show energy flows, trade imbalances, immigration, forest cover, political disputes, habitat distribution, and dozens of other concepts, all in vibrant colors. The effect is almost overwhelming, especially since nearly every topic ends with graphic examples of how humanity has made an extraordinary mess of it. A long list of Websites and other references are at the end of the book, along with a moderately comprehensive index.

The perspective of the editors is clear from the beginning: we better make radical changes in our lifestyles, especially in the West, or all will come crashing down around us, from a collapse of genetic diversity, to sudden climate change, to global "resource wars." The original Gaia aspect of this atlas has been toned down, and the editors make it clear that all our answers will not be found in leftist politics, but it is still a little jarring to read quotations from Fidel Castro and an essay on evolution from Paul Ehrlich of the failed "Population Bomb." Earth systems and human history are still too complex for even the most clever of books, but the message that we face tremendous difficulties comes through very clearly. Everyone should read this book, especially educators and politicians. *The New Atlas of Planet Management* is highly recommended for all libraries. No reference collection should be without this atlas.—**Mark A. Wilson**

Handbooks and Yearbooks

C, P, S

519.   Omi, Philip N. **Forest Fires: A Reference Handbook.** Santa Barbara, Calif., ABC-CLIO, 2005. 347p. index. (Contemporary World Issues). $50.00; $55.00 (e-book). ISBN 1-85109-438-5; 1-85109-443-1 (e-book).

Forest Fires is part of the Contemporary World Issues series that addresses topics vital to modern society. Series authors are professional writers, scholars, and nonacademic experts. The series provides a good first point of reference for research on these issues by high school and college students, researchers, and general readers.

Although forest fires have burned in North America since before recorded history, they have particularly occupied our headlines since the Yellowstone fires of 1988. Recent drought years and increasing building at the wildland-urban interface have made wildfires more expensive and more deadly in the past two decades. This book supplies a single-source, first-stop reference on this important natural phenomenon.

The book begins with a general chapter that puts forest fires in their proper current context, followed by a second chapter dealing with problems, controversies, and solutions, and a third chapter that supplies a chronology of fire in America from pre-settlement to current times. These first three chapters provide readers with a good introduction to forest fires past and present from a distinctly American viewpoint. The remaining four chapters are arranged in a format more common to reference books, and deal with people and events, facts and data, agencies and organization, and print and nonprint resources.

The reader needs no special training in forestry or forest fire science to appreciate this book, and anyone interested in the forest fires will gain from referencing it. It should be contained in the reference section of all public and school libraries.—**Michael G. Messina**

37 Transportation

AIR

P

520. **AIM/FAR 2006: Aeronautical Information Manual/Federal Aviation Regulations.** Charles F. Spence, ed. New York, McGraw-Hill, 2006. 983p. illus. index. $19.95pa. ISBN 0-07-146253-8.

The Aeronautical Information Manual (AIM)/Federal Aviation Regulations (FAR) for 2006 is a fundamental resource for every pilot. This McGraw–Hill edition is packed with essential aviation flight information. It is 983 pages, divided into 3 main sections of AIM (350 pages), FAR (almost 450 pages), and a section on the National Transportation Safety Board. The two main sections are followed by many brief appendix-like supplements. These include "Selected Aviation Web Sites," "VOR Test Facilities," a "State Aeronautic Offices" listing, and other similarly helpful information. A final extensive index (almost 30 pages) serves as an excellent quick guide to the preceding material.

This well-illustrated volume provides current comprehensive information for the very focused aeronautical and regulatory areas of flight. It is imperative, yet difficult, for pilots to be aware of the many rapid changes taking place in aviation today, especially in areas such as security and technology. The aeronautical concerns addressed here are not daily matters (such as runways closing for maintenance) but are clarifications of terms ("resume normal speed") , restatements of procedures (helicopter instrument approach speeds), or other operational aspects of regulated flight (an entry in the AIM describes changes in the use of Radio Navigation [RNAV] routes).

As an annual publication in the respected Aviation Week book series, the *AIM/FAR* is well established as a reliable source of important information. This source is a clearly organized and thoughtfully arranged compilation of government data. An "Explanation of Changes," shaded text, and special bulleted table of contents entries all direct the pilot to recently mandated changes.

The *AIM/FAR 2004* contains many new rules that are being imposed on pilots who are already extensively regulated. It is the pilot's responsibility to know current regulations. This book (including access to updates through the engineering/update-zone Website) is a valuable resource for pilots, whether private students or airline captains. Every academic library that supports any aspect of aviation, large public libraries, or special libraries whose clients may be pilots must have this reference available. This McGraw-Hill edition is recognized as an industry standard and as an excellent source of vital information for pilots. It should be a standing order.—**Jim Agee**

GROUND

P

521. Grant, H. Roger. **The Railroad: The Life Story of a Technology.** Westport, Conn., Greenwood Press, 2005. 182p. illus. index. (Greenwood Technographies). $45.00. ISBN 0-313-33079-4.

Grant, a professor of history at Clemson University, has assembled, mainly from secondary sources, a concise and straightforward history of the evolution of railroad technology from its beginnings at the turn of the nineteenth century to the present. The emphasis is on the United States, where indeed a great deal of innovation has occurred, but of course important advances in Europe that impacted American railroads are included. Locomotives, rolling stock, infrastructure and communications are all covered. The treatment is chronological—Grant recognizes five major periods and gives each a chapter—with topical subarrangement. The writing is clear and very readable, and the coverage is thorough. No special knowledge of engineering terminology or techniques is required to understand the concepts presented. A few minor typographical errors occur but they will cause no problems.

Supplemental matter includes an outline of the Whyte system of steam locomotive classification (the standard in the English-speaking world) and a helpful glossary. The illustrations are not numerous but are generally useful and adequately reproduced. The indexing is good and will facilitate reference use. This book will probably be most useful in public libraries, as it is intended for the general reader, but academic and high school libraries may also with to consider it.—**Paul B. Cors**

WATER

C, P

522.   **The Oxford Companion to Ships and the Sea.** 2d ed. I. C. B. Dear and Peter Kemp, eds. New York, Oxford University Press, 2005. 677p. illus. index. $65.00. ISBN 0-19-860616-8.

Humans have been drawn to the sea from the beginning of civilization, for reason as varied as commerce, warfare, food, aesthetic pleasure, and sports. This work covers all these areas very thoroughly, including individual vessels and seafarers, in alphabetically arranged entries ranging in length from concise definitions to multipage essays. There has been extensive revision from the 1st edition of 1976, not only in updating the earlier work but also in the addition of significant new material dealing with oceanography, marine biology, and environmental issues. The illustrations, all black-and-white, are well chosen and clearly printed. Some entries include references to more comprehensive information sources on their topics, both print and electronic. Reference use is enhanced by extensive cross-references in the text and an index for locating topics that do not receive a separate entry but are treated under related topics.

The writing is clear and straightforward, and while some knowledge of the general subject areas is assumed, the work is accessible to general readers with an interest in maritime matters as well as to specialists. One odd error was noted: the Confederate ram *Albemarle* sank the Union vessel *Southfield* at Plymouth, North Carolina, not Plymouth, "New England" as stated (p. 9).

This will be a valuable tool in all public and academic libraries where there is an interest in the subject. Libraries holding the 1st edition will want to replace it with this one.—**Paul B. Cors**

Author/Title Index

Reference is to entry number.

Subject Index

Reference is to entry number.